# THE DHAMMAPADA

Tipitaka. Suttapitaka.

# THE DHAMMAPADA

A New English Translation with the Pali Text
and the First English Translation of the
Commentary's Explanation of the Verses
With Notes Translated from Sinhala Sources
and Critical Textual Comments

by
John Ross Carter
and
Mahinda Palihawadana



New York * Oxford
OXFORD UNIVERSITY PRESS
1987

Oxford University Press

Oxford New York Toronto
Delhi Bombay Calcutta Madras Karachi
Petaling Jaya Singapore Hong Kong Tokyo
Nairobi Dar es Salaam Cape Town
Melbourne Auckland

and associated companies in
Beirut Berlin Ibadan Nicosia



Published by Oxford University Press, Inc.,
200 Madison Avenue, New York, New York 10016



Library of Congress Cataloging-in-Publication Data
Tipitaka. Suttapitaka. Khuddakanikāya. Dhammapada.
English & Pali.
The Dhammapada.
Bibliography: p. 1. Tipitaka. Suttapitaka. Khuddakanikaya.
Dhammapada—Commentaries. I. Carter, John Ross.
II. Palihawadana, Mahinda. III. Title.
BQ1372.E54C37 1987 294.3′823 86-18075
ISBN 0-19-504162-3

1 3 5 7 9 8 6 4 2
Printed in the United States of America
on acid-free paper

To
Kusuma and Sandra
And for
Priyamvada, Ravindra, Nirmala, Ruchira,
Christopher John, Mary Elizabeth

# PREFACE

On June 6, 1977, John Ross Carter wrote in a letter to Mahinda Palihawadana: "I have a dream to translate the *Dhammapada* and the portion of the commentary that glosses the technical vocabulary. . . . It strikes me that such a composite translation would present an English-reading student with some of the central teachings of the Buddha and . . . the flavor of the [Buddhist] worldview." He continued, "I think this would be so much more useful than merely another . . . translation of the *Dhammapada* and . . . personal opinions about the meanings of the verses. . . ."

Carter was in Sri Lanka from August 1977 to January 1978, completing one book[1] and launching another,[2] and during the course of this stay we discussed in detail what ideally should go into such a project and what would be the best way to set about it.

One of the facts that confronted us was the hold that the *Dhammapada* has been exercising on the minds of Buddhists in Sri Lanka from the third century B.C. (when the Buddhist tradition was introduced to the island) up to the present day. Here was a text that appealed to the religious sentiments of a people for twenty-two centuries. Was there some way we could do justice to this position of the text, while presenting to modern students of the Buddhist tradition a more accurate translation than has hitherto been available? We decided that there could be no better way to do this than to combine the translation of the verses of the *Dhammapada* with the expository text that immediately follows them in the traditional commentary

1. John Ross Carter, *Dhamma: Western Academic and Sinhalese Buddhist Interpretations—a study of a religious concept* (Tokyo: Hokuseido Press, 1978). This book has appeared in a Sinhala translation, *Dhamma: aparadiga śāstrajña saha siṃhala bauddha artha kathana āgamika saṃkalpayak piḷibaňda adhyayanayak,* translated by W. S. Karunatillake in consultation with G. D. Wijayawardhana (Colombo; M. D. Gunasena, 1985).

2. John Ross Carter, ed., *Religiousness in Sri Lanka* (Colombo: Marga Institute, 1979). This work has appeared in a Sinhala translation by the translation committee of Marga Institute, *Śrī laṅkāvē āgamika bhāvaya* (Colombo: Marga Institute, 1985). A Tamil translation is forthcoming.

(which is now extant only in the Pali translation made of it some time after the fifth century A.D.),[3] and to supplement this with notes drawn from some of the major interpretive works on the *Dhammapada* written in Sri Lanka, of which the earliest available dates from the tenth century. (It is not possible to speak of the latest: the tradition of writing such works still continues.)

In the course of these discussions we agreed that this was a task of considerable magnitude—which was compounded when later we thought that we could not possibly ignore the problems regarding the meaning of individual words and the status of the extant text of the *Dhammapada* as well as of the commentary, which would be brought to light by the study of the relevant sources. Although this latter aspect of critical textual study was never meant to be the primary focus of our attention, we thought that the work would be of greater use if attention were paid to these problems as well. This, however, meant that we would have to consult not only the Sri Lankan sources, but also others within our reach and competence—namely, the versions of the *Dhammapada* composed in India. In other words, we would have to go into works written not only in Pali and Sinhala but also several written in the Sanskrit and Prakrit languages.

We then decided that the task was sufficiently complex to warrant being tackled by both of us. And we decided that initially the English translation of the *Dhammapada* verses would be handled by Carter, and the translation of the commentary by Palihawadana; exegetical and doctrinal notes based on the Sinhala sources by Carter, and notes on grammar, semantics, and textual criticism by Palihawadana, with Carter overseeing the final edited copy. The final product, however, was to be the result of criticism, revision, and supplementation of each one's contribution by the other, so that the work when completed would in every sense be one of joint authorship. On

3. The purported background stories of the verses of the *Dhammapada* that are found in the Pali Commentary have been translated into English by Eugene Watson Burlingame, *Buddhist Legends: Translated from the Original Pali Text of the Dhammapada Commentary*, Harvard Oriental Series, vols. 28–30 (Cambridge, Mass.: Harvard University Press, 1921; reprinted for the Pali Text Society, London: Luzac & Co., Ltd., 1969).

this basis we set out on the work in earnest from mid-September 1977.

As the work proceeded, each completed segment of it was dispatched by its contributor to his co-worker for his comments, criticisms, and revisions. And this long-distance correspondence between Hamilton, New York, and Maharagama, Sri Lanka, had to be carried on in the midst of our other academic responsibilities on the one hand and of momentous social and political rumblings in Sri Lanka on the other. Many indeed were the occasions when our expectations were challenged as we progressed in this work ever so slowly—so much so that in retrospect it seems a most unlikely feat that we managed to complete it at all, even after the lapse of nearly a decade from the date of commencement.

In developing a first draft of the translations of notes from Sinhala sources (which were composed in different periods and represent differing developmental stages of the language and which abound in archaic Sinhala word forms—a feature that is not uncommon even in works of present-day bhikkhu authors), we are indebted to G. D. Wijayawardhana, Professor of Sinhala at the University of Colombo, for his guidance enthusiastically given and his scholarly constructive criticisms cheerfully shared.

We acknowledge gratefully the assistance of Elizabeth H. Davey and Gloria McNamara, former secretaries to the director of the Fund for the Study of the Great Religions, Colgate University, for their work in preparing earlier typed versions of this work, and that of Maxine Campbell and Joan Kokoska, present secretaries to the director, who prepared the final typed version with their customary methodical care. Joan Kokoska has also patiently read the proofs at each stage leading to the final publication. We are grateful, too, for her assistsance in developing the index to this volume.

*Hamilton, New York* J.R.C.
*Maharagama, Sri Lanka* M.P.
*April 1987*

# CORRIGENDA

| Page & Line | Error | Correct Form | Page & Line | Error | Correct Form |
|---|---|---|---|---|---|
| 28/14 | This | Their | 318/6 | vā | va |
| 95/30 | varena | verena | 322/24 | savanti | sevanti |
| 96/7 | avarena | averena | 328/8 | durabhirama | durabhiramaṃ |
| 101/25 | peccaya | paccaya | 335/16 | pākika | pāpikā |
| 105/32 | punnaṃ | puññaṃ | 336/15 | dupparāmaṭṭaṃ | dupparāmaṭṭhaṃ |
| 108/20 | suvimutto citto | suvimuttacitto | 337/18 | kayirath' | kayirāth' |
| 108/28 | one's | as one's | 345/23 | eath | eat |
| 113/14 | dhammajīvno | dhammajīvino | 346/7 | punapunnaṃ | punappunaṃ |
| 113/28 | saññemena | saññamena | 347/2 | niggahesāmi | niggahessāmi |
| 116/10 | dīro | dhīro | 351/4 | yāya | yāva |
| 124/6 | -nipatinaṃ | -nipātinaṃ | 352/33 | patiṭṭitā | patiṭṭhitā |
| 124/28 | guha- | guhā- | 355/16 | palavati | plavati |
| 126/8 | anavāhata- | ananvāhata- | 367/10 | -padda- | -pada- |
| 128/16 | yodetha | yodhetha | 369/25 | -dukkaṃ | -dukkhaṃ |
| 128/17 | kiles- | kilesa- | 372/14 | tiṇ- | tiṇa- |
| 129/6 | kiles- | kilesa- | 379/3 | sudhājīviṃ | suddhājīviṃ |
| 134/29 | adhi- | abhi- | 383/23 | -guṇa | -guṇe |
| 142/6 | paṭivatam | paṭivātam | 391/10 | parakkama | parakkamma |
| 160/10 | viveka | vivekam | 392/26 | vitaddaraṃ | vītaddaraṃ |
| 162/23 | medhāvin | medhāviṃ | 399/10 | -kula- | -kūla- |
| 169/27 | -dhāvanti | -dhāvati | 401/27 | Assault:aduṭṭho | Unangered: aduṭṭho |
| 176/3 | gocare | gocaro | 404/18 | gahaṭṭehi | gahaṭṭhehi |
| 189/6 | assamāhito | asamāhito | 407/27 | nirāsaṃ | nirāsayaṃ |
| 199/4 | pacetti | pacceti | 410/25 | kāmā- | kāma- |
| 199/15 | dussali | dussati | 412/4 | nirupadhiṃ | nirūpadhiṃ |
| 199/17 | pacetti | pacceti | 412/26 | buddaṃ | buddhaṃ |
| 202/9 | haneyya | na haneyya | 413/4 | uppatiṃ | upapattiṃ |
| 216/23 | yan' | yān' | 415/2 | vijitavinaṃ | vijitāvinaṃ |
| 235/21 | sangho | saṅgo | 420/3 | brāhamaṇaṃ | brāhmaṇaṃ |
| 243/7 | uppado | uppādo | 420/5 | the ... read | for the ... to read |
| 250/7 | sukkham | sukham | 423/15 | Maṭṭhakundali | Maṭṭakuṇḍali |
| 253/2 | saṅkahātuṃ | saṅkhātuṃ | 426/34 | catur- | catu- |
| 259/32 | siya | siyā | 427/23 | asare | asāra |
| 264/9 | vijjati | vijjanti | 435/27 | PDhp., 231, and | and PDhp., 231, |
| 273/20 | socāre | socare | 437/28 | hṛdayarūpu | hṛdayarūpa |
| 275/19 | -bhāsiṇaṃ | -bhāṇinaṃ | 439/19 | saddhādīdhi | saddhādīhi |
| 282/19 | nidhame | niddhame | 439/21 | paṇṇā | paññā |
| 287/31 | paggabbhena | pagabbhena | 439/35 | On | on |
| 289/9 | paṇam | pāṇam | 452/16 | (is | is |
| 292/8 | rāgasama | rāgasamo | 455/20 | sensation | ideation |
| 293/3 | vijjāni | vajjāni | 459/31 | hās- | has- |
| 293/5 | suddassaṃ | sudassaṃ | 478/3 | prasadaṃ | prasadanaṃ |
| 293/9 | parasaṃ | paresaṃ | 478/6a | mūlagacchaṃ | mūlogghaccaṃ |
| 293/16 | saṭha | saṭho | 478/6b | mūlagacchaṃ | mūlaghaccaṃ |
| 294/5 | āsvakkhayā | āsavakkhayā | 486/2 | 362 | 363 |
| 297/18 | nicchiya | niccheyya | 487/10 | p. 367 | 367 |
| 297/28 | and crime | the crime | 489/24 | ADB | APB |
| 305/25 | khandas | khandhas | 491/11 | cāha | āha |
| 305/26 | kandhas | khandhas | 492/11 | -samādano | -samādāno |
| 307/10 | māpād | māpādi | 492/20 | pavaru | pavuru |
| 309/7 | maggan' | maggān' | 498/5 | sattvidhena | sattavidhena |
| 310/22 | tumehi | tumhehi | | | |
| 317/19 | doting on | inebriated by | | | |

# CONTENTS

# THE DHAMMAPADA

# INTRODUCTION

## *The Dhammapada and the Buddhist Literary Tradition in Sri Lanka*

The *Dhammapada* is the Pali version of one of the most popular texts of the Buddhist canon. Like all religious texts in Pali, it belongs to the Theravāda school of the Buddhist tradition whose participants are at present found primarily in Burma, Cambodia, Laos, Sri Lanka, and Thailand. Other Buddhist schools that originated in India also seem to have had their own versions of this text, of which only three are extant at the present time—the *Udānavarga* in Sanskrit, the *Gāndhārī Dharmapada* in Prakrit, and the recently published text known as the *Patna Dharmapada*, which is in a language close to Pali.

The title *Dhammapada* means "sayings of dhamma"—that is, religiously inspiring statements thought to have been made by the Buddha on various occasions. They are all in verse. A considerable number of them are also found in other works of the Buddhist canon, and equivalents of some are also found, with varying degrees of difference, among old Indian aphoristic verses in such works as the *Mahābhārata* and the *Manusmṛti*. The work thus has essentially the character of an anthology. Although most of the verses of the anthology bear the specific flavor of Buddhist teachings, a not inconsiderable number of them would fit into the general tone of Indian religiousness and indeed also of universal religiousness.

One of the most significant aspects of the evolution of the Buddhist tradition of the Theravāda school was the early development of a body of "comments" on each canonical text. Although these comments were basically meant to explain the meaning of various portions of the original text in terms of the conventional teachings of the school, in some cases they also served to provide the supposed narrative background of the sayings attributed to the Buddha. In the case of the *Dhammapada*, the commentarial material served both these purposes.

When the Buddhist tradition was introduced into Sri Lanka in the third century B.C., the monks who brought the tradition from India are reported to have brought with them a rote knowledge not only of the canonical texts, but also of the comments that were studied along with these works. These comments were in a language sufficiently close to the ancient Sinhala to allow them to be adapted into it without much difficulty. So adapted, the commentarial material came to be known as the Sinhala Commentary or *Sīhalaṭṭhakathā*.

In the fifth century A.D., there started a movement to translate this Sinhala commentative material—which had grown in size since its first adaptation from the original body of comments introduced with the canonical works in the third century B.C.—back into the Pali language. The prime mover in this historic undertaking was an Indian Buddhist monk named Buddhaghosa, who came to Sri Lanka and lived at its famed monastery, Mahāvihāra, which was then the heart of Theravāda orthodoxy in the Buddhist world. He is known to have translated into Pali a voluminous portion of the Sinhala commentaries, though not the entire body of this material. He left untranslated parts of the commentarial corpus dealing with some specific texts, and this work was later completed by his successors. One of the texts whose commentary Buddhaghosa did not translate was the *Dhammapada*. The identity of its translator remains a mystery.[1]

With the translation of the old commentaries into Pali, the original Sinhala works went into comparative disuse but were available in Sri Lankan temples for several centuries to come. Some ancient scholars did continue to read them. One such scholar was the author of *Dhampiyā-aṭuvā-gäṭapadaya*, a work written in archaic Sinhala of the tenth century. According to tradition he was a king of Sri Lanka, Kassapa V (914–923). This is in fact another glossary on terms and usages of the Pali translation of the *Dhammapada* commentary. That the author consulted the old Sinhala commentary in writing this work is evident from the fact that at several places he quotes an occasional phrase from it. (See, e.g., note 6 in chapter 4, below, on Dhp., 46.)

About two hundred years or so after this, a monk by the name of Dhammasena wrote a narrative work in Sinhala known as the *Saddharma Ratnāvaliya*, a rather free adaptation of the stories of the *Dhammapada* commentary. After recounting the purported background stories of the verses of the *Dhammapada*, Dhammasena gives the gist of the verse concerned—which represents the moral of the story—and in this process he occasionally sheds some light on the form or meaning of the words in the Pali text.

offers a narrow monastic meaning, addressed primarily to bhikkhus (Buddhist monks), or a sectarian meaning attuned exclusively to the teachings of the Theravāda school.

## *The Arrangement of the Text in this Volume*

In the section entitled "Translation," we have presented a new translation of the *Dhammapada*. In the section, "Translation, Transliteration, And Commentary," we have kept the pattern provided by the *Dhammapada* commentary (*Dhammapadaṭṭhakathā*) of treating some of the verses of the *Dhammapada* singly and of grouping others, a pattern determined by the interlinking of the verses with background stories presented in the commentary. We have decided to number the verses in consecutive order, keeping the arrangement of the verses provided by the commentary, and also to number the verses by chapter and verse within parentheses, which will allow quick reference to editions of the *Dhammapada* printed in the West and those published in Sinhala (and Thai) scripts.

We have structured this work for a general reading audience. The text has been arranged so that readers neither interested in nor prepared to undertake a study of Pali will, in the course of a few pages, train their eyes to bypass the Pali segments with a minimum of inconvenience. At the same time, our hope is that the structure will be of assistance to those beginning to study Pali and of interest to those more advanced in their study, as well as informative for all readers seriously interested in the way Theravāda Buddhists have understood the *Dhammapada*.

Throughout, we have made ample use of parentheses and brackets, which we trust will not be judged pedantic. Words in parentheses in the headlines are taken in every case from the Pali verses. These are words explained in the commentary gloss but not found in its "headline words." When parentheses occur within quotations, the word or phrase within the parentheses is from the original source. We have departed from this principle only in our decision to provide Pali word forms in some of the notes in place of some Sinhala spellings.

Brackets are employed to convey the meaning of the passage with a word or phrase not strictly found in the original source. It is likely that rather early on the use of brackets will become less noticeable to the reader. The use of brackets enables one to see clearly the style of the commentary without having to pay the price of laboring through passages, which are not infrequently diffuse.

Notes, numbered consecutively beginning with each chapter, are provided at the end of the book. We have tried to spot those passages in the commentary that are less than explicit, or that are elliptical in enumeration, and to draw upon the continuing tradition to complete, and on occasion to elaborate, their sense. We have decided not to isolate elements of doctrine and practice and "trace them back" to passages in the canonical strata. Our concern has been to draw attention to the way elements of doctrine and practice, for the laity and bhikkhus, form a connected whole and are given expression as a cumulative synthesis of the Theravāda tradition.

Some of the notes are of a technical nature, drawing attention to problems in the Pali text of the stanzas or commentary. These notes are of little interest to someone not acquainted with Pali. Such notes are given in consecutive order along with the other references, but within parentheses.

Translating the Pali commentary was a challenging task in view of the intrinsic nature of this literary genre. The general nature of a Pali commentary may be shown by the manner in which the commentator of the text explains a given verse. The commentator picks out a key word (phrase/clause) to indicate that it, as well as the important words associated with it, are going to be commented on. An explanation is given of the general idea without necessarily paraphrasing it with grammatical accuracy. The words explained as well as the explanatory notes merge with the words left unexplained to form a complex commentarial sentence in which the original sentence might or might not be embedded. Such a commentarial sentence can at times become a tangled skein, which would be quite a tricky task to unravel in translation. Generally the technique we employed was to treat the commentator's key word (phrase/clause) as a headline and the rest of the commentarial sentence as the body of the comment, put immediately below it. Where the resulting translation was unduly complex, we attempted to simplify it to some extent by punctuation, division into several lines, combination of several headlines into one, expansion of a headline with words taken from the verse (indicated in parentheses), and at times also by change in the order of the comments. But we have tried throughout to give as literal a translation as possible, one that would resemble the original to a very great extent. It would thus be quite consistent if the translation reflects much of the complexity of the original.[4]

It was our endeavor to make this work as much as possible a "stitching of the centuries." What this reveals is on the one hand the profoundly evocative power of the religious sentiments expressed in the text, and on the other the conservatism of the tradition that interprets the text as we see in these documents. We may have thrown some light on matters textual and opened up some vistas for further scholarly inquiry. But from the way we set about it, what is of singular importance is the arrangement of this book: presenting the text itself as a text and presenting the history of its study in the setting of a growing tradition of interpretation. We want our readers to see both the handling of word forms and the considerations given to the teachings, to communicate which words are there. Although it was our wish to see the arrow of textual criticism point backward into the past, we wanted to make the text, as something in human hands, to point forward from past through present into the future.[5]

We are only too well aware of the pitfalls in this endeavor. Mistake the grammar of a single word and a whole set of explanations will be on the wrong track. We tried to be alert to all of this as far as possible, but if we had not erred, we would not be human.

# TRANSLATION

## *Chapter I The Pairs*

1. Preceded by perception are mental states,
For them is perception supreme,
From perception have they sprung.
If, with perception polluted, one speaks or acts,
Thence suffering follows
As a wheel the draught ox's foot.

2. Preceded by perception are mental states,
For them is perception supreme.
From perception have they sprung.
If, with tranquil perception, one speaks or acts,
Thence ease follows
As a shadow that never departs.

3. "He reviled me! He struck me!
He defeated me! He robbed me!"
They who gird themselves up with this,
For them enmity is not quelled.

4. "He reviled me! He struck me!
He defeated me! He robbed me!"
They who do not gird themselves up with this,
For them is enmity quelled.

5. Not by enmity are enmities quelled,
Whatever the occasion here.
By the absence of enmity are they quelled.
This is an ancient truth.

6. Others do not realize
"We here are struggling."
Those who realize this—for them
Are quarrels therefore quelled.

7. Whoever dwells seeing the pleasurable, in senses unrestrained,
Immoderate in food, indolent, inferior of enterprise,
Over him, indeed, Māra prevails,
Like the wind over a weak tree.

8. Whoever dwells seeing the nonpleasurable, in senses well restrained,
And moderate in food, faithful, resolute in enterprise,
Over him, indeed, Māra prevails not,
Like the wind over a rocky crag.

9. One not free of defilements,
Who will don a yellow robe,
That one, devoid of control and truth,
Is not worthy of a yellow robe.

10. But one who, well placed in virtues,
Would be with defilements ejected,
Endowed with control and truth,
That one is worthy of a yellow robe.

11. Those who consider the nonessential as the essential,
And see the essential as the nonessential,
They do not attain the essential,
Being in the pastures of improper intentions.

12. Having known the essential as the essential,
And the superficial as the superficial,
They attain the essential
Who are in the pastures of proper intentions.

13. As rain penetrates
The poorly thatched dwelling,
So passion penetrates
The untended mind.

14. As rain does not penetrate
The well-thatched dwelling,
So passion does not penetrate
The well-tended mind.

15. Here he grieves; having passed away, he grieves;
In both places the wrongdoer grieves.
He grieves; he is afflicted,
Having seen the stain of his own action.

16. Here he rejoices; having passed away he rejoices.
In both places he who has done wholesome deeds rejoices.
He rejoices; he is delighted,
Having seen the purity of his own action.

17. Here he is tormented; having passed away he is tormented.
In both places, the wrongdoer is tormented.
He is tormented, thinking, "I have done wrong."
Gone to a state of woe, he is tormented all the more.

18. Here he rejoices; having passed away he rejoices.
In both places he who has done wholesome deeds rejoices.
He rejoices, thinking, "I have done wholesome deeds."
Gone to a state of weal, he rejoices all the more.

19. If one, though reciting much of texts,
Is not a doer thereof, a heedless man;
He, like a cowherd counting others' cows,
Is not a partaker in the religious quest.

20. If one, though reciting little of texts,
Lives a life in accord with dhamma,
Having discarded passion, ill will, and unawareness,
Knowing full well, the mind well freed,
He, not grasping here, neither hereafter,
Is a partaker of the religious quest.

## *Chapter II Awareness*

21. The path to the Deathless is awareness;
Unawareness, the path of death.
They who are aware do not die;
They who are unaware are as dead.

22. Having known this distinctly,
Those who are wise in awareness,
Rejoice in awareness,
Delighted in the pasture of the noble ones.

23. Those meditators, persevering,
Forever firm of enterprise,
Those steadfast ones touch Nibbāna,
Incomparable release from bonds.

25. By standing alert, by awareness,
By restraint and control too,
The intelligent one could make an island
That a flood does not overwhelm.

24. Fame increases for the one who stands alert,
Mindful, and of pure deeds;
Who with due consideration acts, restrained,
Who lives dhamma, being aware.

26. People deficient in wisdom, childish ones,
Engage in unawareness.
But the wise one guards awareness
Like the greatest treasure.

27. Engage not in unawareness,
Nor in intimacy with sensual delight.
Meditating, the one who is aware
Attains extensive ease.

28. When the wise one by awareness expels unawareness,
Having ascended the palace of wisdom,
He, free from sorrow, steadfast,
The sorrowing folk observes, the childish,
As one standing on a mountain
[Observes] those standing on the ground below.

29. Among those unaware, the one aware,
Among the sleepers, the wide-awake,
The one with great wisdom moves on,
As a racehorse who leaves behind a nag.

30. By awareness, Maghavan
To supremacy among the gods arose.
Awareness they praise;
Always censured is unawareness.

31. The bhikkhu who delights in awareness,
Who sees in unawareness the fearful,
Goes, burning, like a fire,
The fetter subtle and gross.

32. The bhikkhu who delights in awareness,
Who sees in unawareness the fearful—
He is not liable to suffer fall;
In Nibbāna's presence is such a one.

## *Chapter III The Mind*

33. The quivering, wavering mind,
Hard to guard, hard to check,
The sagacious one makes straight,
Like a fletcher, an arrow shaft.

34. Like a water creature
Plucked from its watery home and thrown on land,
This mind flaps;
[Fit] to discard [is] Māra's sway.

35. Commendable is the taming
Of mind, which is hard to hold down,
Nimble, alighting wherever it wants.
Mind subdued brings ease.

36. The sagacious one may tend the mind,
Hard to be seen, extremely subtle,
Alighting wherever it wants.
The tended mind brings ease.

37. They who will restrain the mind,
Far-ranging, roaming alone,
Incorporeal, lying ahiding—
They are released from Māra's bonds.

38. For one of unsteady mind,
Who knows not dhamma true,
Whose serenity is adrifting,
Wisdom becomes not full.

39. No fear is there for the wide-awake
Who has mind undamped
And thought unsmitten—
The wholesome and the detrimental left behind.

40. Knowing this body as a pot of clay,
Securing this mind as a citadel,
One may fight Māra with wisdom's weapon,
Guard what has been gained—and be unattached.

41. Soon indeed
This body on the earth will lie,
Pitched aside, without consciousness,
Like a useless chip of wood.

42. What a foe may do to a foe,[1]
Or a hater to a hater—
Far worse than that
The mind ill held may do to him.

43. Not mother, father, nor even other kinsmen,
May do that [good to him—]
Far better than that
The mind well held may do to him.

1. The commentary takes this line to mean: What a thief may do to a thief.

## *Chapter IV Flowers*

44. Who shall conquer this earth and the realm of Yama,[2]
This [human realm] together with [the realm of] gods?
Who shall pluck a well-taught dhamma word
Like an expert, a flower?

45. A learner shall conquer this earth and the realm of Yama,[3]
This [human realm] together with [the realm of] gods.
A learner shall pluck a well-taught dhamma word
Like an expert, a flower.

46. Knowing this body to be like foam,
Awakening to its mirage nature,
Cutting out Māra's flowers, one may go
Beyond the sight of the King of Death.

47. Death takes away
The man with attached mind,
Plucking only flowers,
Like a great flood, a sleeping village.

48. The End-Maker overpowers
The man with attached mind,
Insatiate in sensual pleasures,
Plucking only flowers.

49. Even as a bee, having taken up nectar
From a flower, flies away,
Not harming its color and fragrance,[4]
So may a sage wander through a village.

2. The commentary takes this line to mean: Who shall discern this earth and the realm of Yama?

3. The commentary takes this line to mean: A learner shall discern this earth and the realm of Yama.

4. The commentary takes lines 1–3 thus: As a bee, without harming the flower, its color and fragrance, flies away, taking up the nectar.

50. Let one regard
Neither the discrepancies of others,
Nor what is done or left undone by others,
But only the things one has done oneself or left undone.

51. Just as a brilliant flower,
Full of color, [but] scentless,
So is a well-spoken word fruitless
For one who does not do it.

52. Just as a brilliant flower,
Full of color and fragrance,
So is a well-spoken word fruitful
For one who does it.

53. Just as many garland strands
One could make from a mass of flowers,
So, much that is wholesome ought to be done
By a mortal born [into this world].

54. No flower's fragrance moves against the wind
Neither sandalwood, *tagara*, nor *mallikā*,
But the fragrance of the good ones moves against the wind;
All directions a good person pervades.

55. Among these kinds of perfume,
Such as sandalwood, *tagara*,
Also waterlily and *vassikī*,
The fragrance of virtue is incomparable.

56. Slight is this fragrance—
The *tagara* and sandalwood—
But the fragrance of one who is virtuous
Wafts among the gods, supreme.

57. Māra does not find the path
Of those who have virtue abounding,
Who are living with awareness,
Liberated through realization.

58. Just as in a heap of rubbish
Cast away on a roadside,
A lotus there could bloom,
Of sweet fragrance, pleasing the mind,

59. So amid the wretched, blinded ordinary folk,
Among them who have turned to rubbish,
The disciple of the Fully Awakened One
Shines surpassingly with wisdom.

## *Chapter V The Childish*

60. Long is the night for one awake,
Long is a league to one exhausted,
Long is *saṃsāra* to the childish ones
Who know not dhamma true.

61. If while moving [through life], one were not to meet
Someone better or like unto oneself,
Then one should move firmly by oneself;
There is no companionship in the childish.

62. A childish person becomes anxious,
Thinking, "Sons are mine! Wealth is mine!"
Not even a self is there [to call] one's own.
Whence sons? Whence wealth?

63. A childish one who knows his childishness
Is, for that reason, even like a wise person.
But a childish one who thinks himself wise
Is truly called a childish one.

64. Even though, throughout his life,
A childish one attends on a wise person,
He does not [thereby] perceive dhamma,
As a ladle, the flavor of the dish.

65. Even though, for a brief moment,
An intelligent one attends on a wise person,
He quickly perceives dhamma,
As the tongue, the flavor of the dish.

66. Childish ones, of little intelligence,
Go about with a self that is truly an enemy;
Performing the deed that is bad,
Which is of bitter fruit.

67. That deed done is not good,
Having done which, one regrets;
The consequence of which one receives,
Crying with tear-stained face.

68. But that deed done is good,
Having done which, one does not regret;
The consequence of which one receives,
With pleasure and with joy.

69. The childish one thinks it is like honey
While the bad [he has done] is not yet matured.
But when the bad [he has done] is matured,
Then the childish one comes by suffering.

70. Month by month a childish one
Might eat food with a *kusa* grass blade.
He is not worth a sixteenth part
Of those who have understood dhamma.

71. For a bad act done does not coagulate
Like freshly extracted milk.
Burning, it follows the childish one,
Like fire concealed in ashes.

72. Only for his detriment
Does knowledge arise for the childish one.
It ruins his good fortune,
Causing his [very] head to fall.

73. He would desire unreal glory
And preeminence among bhikkhus,
Authority, too, concerning dwellings,
And offerings in other families.

74. "Let both householders and those who have gone forth
Think that it is my work alone;
In whatever is to be done or not done,
Let them be dependent on me alone!"
Such is the thought of the childish one;
Desire and pride increase.

75. The means of acquisition is one,
And another the way leading to Nibbāna.
Having recognized this as so,
Let a bhikkhu who is a disciple of the Buddha
Not delight in [receiving] esteem;
Let him cherish disengagement.

## *Chapter VI The Sagacious*

76. The one who sees one's faults,
Who speaks reprovingly, wise,
Whom one would see as an indicator of treasures,
With such a sagacious person, one would associate.
To one associating with such a person,
The better it will be, not the worse.

77. He would counsel, instruct,
And restrain [one] from rude behavior.
To the good, he is pleasant;
To the bad is he unpleasant.

78. Let one not associate
With low persons, bad friends.
But let one associate
With noble persons, worthy friends.

79. One who drinks of dhamma sleeps at ease,
With mind calmly clear.
In dhamma made known by noble ones,
The wise one constantly delights.

80. Irrigators guide the water.
Fletchers bend the arrow shaft.
Wood the carpenters bend.
Themselves the wise ones tame.

81. Even as a solid rock
Does not move on account of the wind,
So are the wise not shaken
In the face of blame and praise.

82. Even as a deep lake
Is very clear and undisturbed,
So do the wise become calm,
Having heard the words of dhamma.

83. Everywhere, indeed, good persons "let go."
The good ones do not occasion talk, hankering for pleasure.
Touched now by ease and now by misery,
The wise manifest no high and low.

84. Neither for one's own sake nor for the sake of another,
A son would one wish, or wealth, or kingdom.
One would not wish one's own prosperity by undhammic means.
Such a one would be possessed of virtue, wisdom, dhamma.

85. Few are they among humans,
The people who reach the shore beyond.
But these other folk
Only run along the [hither] bank.

86. But those who live according to dhamma—
In dhamma well proclaimed—
Those people will reach the shore beyond.
The realm of death is hard to cross.

87. Having forsaken a shadowy dhamma,
The wise one would cultivate the bright,
Having come from familiar abode to no abode
In disengagement, hard to relish.

88. There he would wish for delight,
Having discarded sensual desires—he who has nothing.
The wise one would purify oneself
Of the defilements of the mind.

89. Whose mind is fully well cultivated in the factors of enlightenment,
Who, without clinging, delight in the rejection of grasping,
Lustrous ones, who have destroyed intoxicants,
They have, in [this] world, attained Nibbāna.

## *Chapter VII The Worthy*

90. To one who has gone the distance,
Who is free of sorrows, freed in every respect;
To one who has left behind all bonds,
Fever there exists not.

91. The mindful ones gird up [themselves].
In no abode do they delight.
Like swans having left behind a pond,
One shelter after another they leave.[5]

92. Those for whom there is no hoarding,
Who have fully understood [the nature] of food,
And whose pasture is freedom
That is empty, that has no sign,
This course is hard to trace
As that of birds in the sky.

93. In whom the influxes are fully extinct,
Who is not attached to sustenance,
And whose pasture is freedom
That is empty and signless,
His track is hard to trace,
As [that] of birds in the sky.

94. Whose senses have reached an even temper,
Like horses well trained by a charioteer,
Who has discarded self-estimation, who is free of influxes,
Even the gods cherish such a one.

95. Like the earth, he does not oppose.
A firm pillar is such a one, well cultured,
Like a lake rid of mud.
To such a one, travels in *saṃsāra* there are not.

5. This line may also mean: Home they abandon, the flood.

96. Of such a one, pacified,
Released by proper understanding,
Calm is the mind,
Calm his speech and act.

97. Who has no faith, the ungrateful one,
The man who is a burglar,
Who has destroyed opportunities, ejected wish,
Truly he is a person supreme.

98. Whether in village or in forest,
Whether in valley or on plateau,
Delightful is the ground
Where Arahants dwell.

99. Delightful are forests
Where people do not take delight.
[There] those without passions will delight;
They no sensual pleasures seek.

## *Chapter VIII The Thousands*

100. Though a thousand be the statements,
With words of no avail,
Better is a single word of welfare,
Having heard which, one is pacified.

101. Though a thousand be the verses,
With words of no avail,
Better is a single line of verse,
Having heard which, one is pacified.

102. And should one recite a hundred verses,
With words of no avail,
Better is one dhamma word,
Having heard which, one is pacified.

103. He, truly, is supreme in battle,
Who would conquer himself alone,
Rather than he who would conquer in battle
A thousand, thousand men.

104. Better, indeed, oneself conquered
[Rather than] these other folk.
Of a person who has won himself,
Who is constantly living in self-control.

105. Neither a god nor a *gandhabba*,
Nor Māra together with Brahmā,
Could turn the victory into defeat
Of a living being like that.

106. Month by month, with a thousand,
One might offer sacrifice a hundred times,
And another, to one self-composed,
Might offer worship for but a second;
Truly, that worship is better
Than what was offered a hundred years.

107. And were a living being for a hundred years
To tend a fire in a forest,
And were another, to one self-composed,
To offer worship for but a second;
Truly, that worship is better
Than what was offered a hundred years.

108. Whatever sacrifice or offering in the world
One seeking merit might sacrifice for a year;
Even all that does not "reach a quarter"—
Better the respectful greetings to the straight of gait.

109. For one in the habit of showing respect,
Of always honoring elder ones,
Four qualities increase:
Life, complexion, ease, and strength.

110. And should one live a hundred years
Devoid of virtue, uncomposed;
Better still is one day lived
Of one possessed of virtue, a meditator.

111. And should one live a hundred years
Devoid of insight, uncomposed;
Better still is one day lived
Of one possessed of insight, a meditator.

112. And should one live a hundred years
Indolent, of inferior enterprise;
Better still is one day lived
Of one initiating enterprise, firm.

113. And should one live a hundred years
Not seeing "the rise and demise";
Better still is one day lived
Of one seeing "the rise and demise."

114. And should one live a hundred years
Not seeing the immortal state;
Better still is one day lived
Of one who sees the immortal state.

115. And should one live a hundred years
Not seeing dhamma supreme;
Better still is one day lived
Of one seeing dhamma supreme.

## *Chapter IX The Wrong*

116. Be quick in goodness;
From wrong hold back your thought.
Indeed, of one performing the good tardily,
The mind delights in wrong.

117. Should a person do a wrong,
Let him not do it again and again.
Let him not form a desire toward it,
A suffering is the accumulation of wrong.

118. Should a person do some good,
Let him do it again and again.
Let him form a desire toward it.
A happiness is the accumulation of good.

119. Even a wrongdoer experiences what is good
As long as the detrimental has not matured.
But when the detrimental is matured,
The wrongdoer then experiences the detrimental.

120. Even the good one experiences the detrimental
As long as the good is not matured.
But when the good is matured,
Then the good one experiences the good.

121. Think not triflingly of wrong,
"It will not come to me!"
With falling drops of water,
Even a waterpot is filled.
A childish one is filled with wrong,
Acquiring bit by bit.

122. Think not triflingly of good,
"It will not come to me!"
With falling drops of water

Even a waterpot is filled.
A wise one is filled with good,
Acquiring bit by bit.

123. One would avoid wrongs,
Like the rich merchant with small caravan
The fearful road;
Like one who loves life, poison.

124. If on the hand a wound were not,
One could carry poison with [that] hand.
Poison does not follow one without a wound.
No wrong there is for one not doing it.

125. Whoever offends an inoffensive man,
A pure person without blemish,
The wrong recoils on just that childish one,
Like fine dust hurled against the wind.

126. Some are born in a womb,
Wrongdoers, in hell.
Those of good course go to heaven,
To Nibbāna those without influxes.

127. That spot in the world is not found,
Neither in the sky nor in the ocean's depths,
Nor having entered into a cleft in mountains,
Where abiding, one would be released from the bad deed.

128. That spot one does not find,
Neither in the sky nor in the ocean's depths,
Nor having entered into a cleft in mountains,
Where abiding, death would not overwhelm one.

## *Chapter X The Rod*

129. All are frightened of the rod.
Of death all are afraid.
Having made oneself the example,
One should neither slay nor cause to slay.

130. All are frightened of the rod.
For all, life is dear.
Having made oneself the example,
One should neither slay nor cause to slay.

131. Who with a rod does hurt
Beings who desire ease,
While himself looking for ease—
He, having departed, ease does not get.

132. Who with a rod does not hurt
Beings who desire ease,
While himself looking for ease—
Having departed, ease he will get.

133. To none speak harshly.
Those thus addressed would retort to you.
Miserable indeed is contentious talk.
Retaliatory rods would touch you.

134. If, like a flattened out metal pot,
You yourself do not move,
Why, Nibbāna you have attained!
No contention is found in you.

135. As with a rod a cowherd
To the pasture goads his cows,
So does old age and death
Goad the life of living beings.

136. The childish one knows it not,
Even while doing bad deeds.
The one deficient in wisdom, by his own deeds
Suffers like one burnt by fire.

137. Who with a rod harms the offenseless, the harmless,
To one of ten places quite quickly one goes down:

138. [1] harshly painful feelings, [2] destitution, and [3] fracturing of the body,
[4] grave illness too, [5] even disarrayed mind, one would attain,

139. [6] trouble from the king or [7] severe slander,
[8] even loss of relatives or [9] dissolution of possessions,

140. And also [10] fire, the purifier, burns his houses.
And upon the breaking of his body, the unwise one falls into hell.

141. Neither wandering about naked, nor matted hair, nor mud,
Neither fasting, nor sleeping on hard ground,
Nor dust and dirt, nor austere acts in the crouching posture,
Cleanses a mortal who has not transcended doubts.

142. Though well adorned, if one would move with tranquility,
At peace, restrained, assured, living the higher life,
Having put down the rod toward all beings,
He is a *brāhmaṇa*, he, a recluse, he, a bhikkhu.

143. [Rarely] in the world is found
A person restrained by shame,
Who awakens to insult
As a good horse to the whip.

144. Like a good horse struck by a whip,
Be ardent and deeply moved.
With faith and virtue and enterprise,
With concentration and dhamma-discernment,
With understanding and conduct endowed, mindful,
You will leave behind this weighty misery.

145. Irrigators guide the water,
Fletchers bend the arrow shaft,
Wood the carpenters bend;
Themselves the amenable ones tame.

## *Chapter XI Old Age*

146. Oh, what laughter and why joy,
When constantly aflame?
In darkness enveloped,
You do not seek the lamp.

147. Oh, see this beautified image;
A mass of sores erected.
Full of illness, highly fancied,
Permanence it has not—or constancy.

148. Quite wasted away is this form,
A nest for disease, perishable.
This putrid accumulation breaks up.
For life has its end in death.

149. Like these gourds
Discarded in autumn,
Are gray-hued bones.
Having seen them, what delight?

150. Of bones the city is made,
Plastered with flesh and blood,
Where decay and death are deposited,
And pride and ingratitude.

151. Even well-decked royal chariots wear away;
And the body too falls into decay.
But the dhamma of the good ones goes not to decay,
For the good speak [of it ] with the good.

152. This unlearned person
Grows up like an ox.
His bulk increases,
His wisdom increases not.

153. I ran through *saṃsāra*, with its many births,
Searching for, but not finding, the house-builder.
Misery is birth again and again.

154. House-builder, you are seen!
The house you shall not build again!
Broken are your rafters, all,
Your roof beam destroyed.
Freedom from the *saṃkhāra*s has the mind attained.
To the end of cravings has it come.[6]

155. Not having lived the higher life,
Nor having acquired wealth in youth,
They wither away like old herons
In a lake without fish.

156. Not having lived the higher life,
Nor having acquired wealth in youth,
Like [arrows] discharged from a bow they lie
Brooding over the things of yore.

6. The commentary takes this line to mean: To the end of cravings have I come.

## *Chapter XII The Self*

157. If one would regard oneself as dear,
One would guard oneself with diligence.
The wise one would look after [himself]
During any one of the [night's] three watches.

158. First, one would get oneself
Established in what is proper;
Then one would advise another.
[Thus] the wise one would not suffer.

159. One would oneself so do
As one advises another.
Then it is the restrained one who would restrain.
For, truly, it is the self that is hard to restrain.

160. Oneself indeed is patron of oneself.
Who else indeed could be one's patron?
With oneself well restrained,
One gets a patron hard to get.[7]

161. The wrong done by oneself
Is born of oneself, is produced in oneself.
It grinds one deficient in wisdom
As a diamond grinds a rock-gem.

162. Whose extreme unvirtue overspreads [him],
Like the *māluvā* creeper a *sāla* tree,
He does to himself,
Just as a foe wishes [to do] to him.

163. Easy to do are things not good
And those harmful for oneself.
But what is beneficial and good,
Is exceedingly difficult to do.

7. Commentary: One gets a support hard to get.

164. Who is deficient in wisdom,
Because of detrimental view,
Obstructs the instruction of the Arahants,
The Noble Ones who live dhamma;
For one's own destruction one ripens,
Like the fruits of a reed.

165. By oneself is wrong done,
By oneself is one defiled.
By oneself wrong is not done,
By oneself, surely, is one cleansed.
One cannot purify another;
Purity and impurity are in oneself [alone].

166. One would not abandon one's own purpose
Because of the purpose of another, even though great,
Having well understood one's own purpose,
One would be intent on the true purpose.

## *Chapter XIII The World*

167. To lowly quality one should not resort;
With heedlessness one should not live.
To an improper view one should not resort.
And one should not be a "world-augmenter."

168. One should stand up, not be neglectful,
Follow dhamma, which is good conduct.
One who lives dhamma, sleeps at ease
In this world and also in the next.

169. One should follow dhamma, which is good conduct,
Not that which is poor conduct.
One who lives dhamma, sleeps at ease
In this world and also in the next.

170. As upon a bubble one would look,
As one would look upon a mirage,
The one considering the world thus,
King Death does not see.

171. Come ye, look at this world—
Like an adorned royal chariot—
Wherein childish ones are immersed;
No clinging there is among those who really know.

172. And who having been heedless formerly
But later is heedless not,
He this world illumines
Like the moon set free from a cloud.

173. Whose bad deed done
Is covered by what is wholesome,
He this world illumines
Like the moon set free from a cloud.

174. This world has become blinded, as it were.
Few here see insightfully.
Like a bird set free from a net,
Few to heaven go.

175. Swans go along the path of the sun.
And in the air they go with psychic power.
The wise ones are led from the world,
Having conquered Māra and his cohorts.

176. Of person who has overstepped one dhamma,
Who speaks falsehood,
Who has turned the back on the world beyond—
There is no wrong that cannot be done.

177. Truly, no misers get to the world of gods.
Certainly, childish ones do not applaud giving.
The wise one gladly approves giving;
Hence indeed is he at ease in the hereafter.

178. Better than sole sovereignty over the earth,
Or the journey to heaven,
Than lordship over all the worlds,
Is the Fruit of Stream Attainment.

## *Chapter XIV The Awakened One*

179. Whose victory is not turned into defeat,
Whose victory no one in this world reaches,[8]
That Awakened One whose range is limitless,
Him, the trackless, by what track will you lead?

180. For whom craving there is not, the netlike, the clinging,
To lead him wheresoever,
That Awakened One whose range is limitless,
Him, the trackless, by what track will you lead?

181. Those who are intent on meditating, the wise ones,
Delighting in the calm of going out,
Even gods long for them,
The Fully Enlightened Ones, the mindful.

182. Difficult is the attainment of the human state.
Difficult the life of mortals.
Difficult is the hearing of dhamma true.
Difficult the appearance of Awakened Ones.

183. Refraining from all that is detrimental,
The attainment of what is wholesome,
The purification of one's mind:
This is the instruction of Awakened Ones.

184. Forbearing patience is the highest austerity;
Nibbāna is supreme, the Awakened Ones say.
One who has gone forth is not one who hurts another,
No harasser of others is a recluse.

185. No faultfinding, no hurting, restraint in the *pātimokkha*,
Knowing the measure regarding food, solitary bed and chair,
Application, too, of higher perception:
This is the instruction of the Awakened Ones.

8. The commentary takes this line to mean: After whose victory no [defilement] remains.

186. Not even with a rain of golden coins
Is contentment found among sensual pleasures.
"Sensual pleasures are of little delight, are a misery."
Knowing so, the wise one

187. Takes no delight
Even for heavenly sensual pleasures.
One who delights in the ending of craving
Is a disciple of the Fully Enlightened One.

188. Many for refuge go
To mountains and to forests,
To shrines that are groves or trees—
Humans who are threatened by fear.

189. This is not a refuge secure,
This refuge is not the highest.
Having come to this refuge,
One is not released from all misery.

190. But who to the Buddha, Dhamma,
And Saṅgha as refuge has gone,
Sees with full insight
The four noble truths;

191. Misery, the arising of misery,
And the transcending of misery,
The noble Eightfold Path
Leading to the allaying of misery.

192. This, indeed, is a refuge secure.
This is the highest refuge.
Having come to this refuge,
One is released from all misery.

193. Hard to come by is a person of nobility;
Not everywhere is he born.
Wherever that wise one is born,
That family prospers in happiness.

194. Joyful is the arising of Awakened Ones.
Joyful, the teaching of Dhamma true.
Joyful, too, the concord of the Saṅgha.
Joyful, the austere practice of those in concord.

195. Of one worshiping those worthy of worship,
Whether Awakened Ones or disciples,
Who have transcended preoccupying tendencies,
Crossed over grief and lamentation,

196. Of one worshiping such as them,
Calmed ones who fear nothing,
The merit cannot be quantified
By anyone saying, "It is of this extent."

## *Chapter XV Happiness*

197. Ah, so pleasantly we live
Without enmity among those with enmity.
Among humans with enmity
Do we dwell without enmity.

198. Ah, so pleasantly we live
Without affliction among the afflicted.
Among humans with affliction
Do we dwell without affliction.

199. Ah, so pleasantly we live
Without restlessness among the restless.
Among humans who are restless
Do we dwell without restlessness.

200. Ah, so pleasantly we live,
For whom there is nothing at all our own.
We shall become partakers of joy,
Even as the Radiant Devas.

201. Winning, one engenders enmity;
Miserably sleeps the defeated.
The one at peace sleeps pleasantly,
Having abandoned victory and defeat.

202. There is no fire like passion,
No offense there is like ill-will,
There is no misery like the *khandha*s,
No ease there is higher than peace.

203. Hunger is the illness most severe,
The *saṃkhāra*s the greatest misery.
Knowing this as it is,
[One realizes] Nibbāna is ease supreme.

204. Health is the highest gain,
Contentment is the highest wealth,
Those inspiring trust are kinsmen supreme,
Nibbāna is ease supreme.

205. Having tasted the flavor of seclusion
And the flavor of calm,
One is without distress, free from the bad,
Drinking the flavor of the joys of dhamma.

206. Good is the sight of noble ones,
Their company is always pleasant.
Without the sight of childish ones,
One would constantly be at ease.

207. One moving with childish ones
Grieves for long time.
Misery is it to live with childish ones,
As it always is with a foe.
The wise one is one with whom to live is pleasant,
As is a gathering of relations.

Wherefore:

208. The wise one, the insightful, and the learned,
Having the virtue of enduring, dutiful, noble,
A person true, intelligent,
With such a one as this, one would associate,
As the moon the path of the stars.

## *Chapter XVI The Pleasant*

209. One who exerts oneself in what is not befitting
And in the befitting exerts not,
Having abandoned the beneficial, grasping for the dear,
Envies the one who applies himself.

210. Let one not be together with the dear,
Nor ever with those that are not dear;
Not to see the dear is misery,
So too is it to see the nondear.

211. Therefore, let one not make endearment,
For separation from the dear is bad.
For whom there is neither the dear nor nondear,
For them are bonds not found.

212. From the dear arises grief.
From the dear arises fear.
For one set free from endearment,
There is not grief. Whence fear?

213. From affection arises grief.
From affection arises fear.
For one set free from affection,
There is no grief. Whence fear?

214. From sensual attachment arises grief,
From sensual attachment arises fear.
For one set free from sensual attachment,
There is not grief. Whence fear?

215. From sensual desire arises grief.
From sensual desire arises fear.
For one set free from sensual desire,
There is no grief. Whence fear?

216. From craving arises grief.
From craving arises fear.
For one set free from craving,
There is no grief. Whence fear?

217. The one endowed with virtue and vision,
Established in dhamma, speaking truth,
That one, doing his own tasks,
The folk holds dear.

218. One in whom a wish for the Undefined is born,
Who would be clear in mind,
Whose heart is not bound in sensual pleasures,
Is called "one whose stream is upward bound."

219. As when a person long absent
Has come safely from afar,
Relatives, friends, and well-wishers
Greet with delight the one who has returned;

220. Just so, one who has done wholesome deeds
Has gone from this world to the beyond—
The wholesome deeds receive such a one,
Like relatives, a dear one who has returned.

## *Chapter XVII Wrath*

221. Wrath one would leave behind,
Measurement one would abandon, every fetter transcend.
Who clings not to name and form, and possesses no thing.
Upon that one miseries do not fall.

222. Who can hold back arisen wrath,
Like a swerving chariot,
That one I call "a charioteer,"
Any other one is merely a reins-holder.

223. With absence of wrath one would conquer the wrathful one;
With good, one would conquer the bad one;
With giving, one would conquer the stingy one;
With truth, the one speaking falsehood.

224. Let one tell the truth, let one not be angry.
Asked, let one give even when one has but little.
By these three factors,
One would go into the presence of the gods.

225. They who are gentle sages,
Constantly restrained in body,
Go to the Unshakeable Abode,
Whither having gone, they do not grieve.

226. Of those who always keep awake,
Learning day and night,
Upon Nibbāna intent,
"Intoxicants" come to an end.

227. Of old this is, Atula,
It is not just of today:
They find fault with one sitting silently;
They find fault with one speaking much,
And even with one speaking in moderation do they find fault.
In [this] world there is no one not faulted.

228. There was not and will not be,
And now there is not found,
A person absolutely faulted,
Or absolutely praised.

229. Whom the wise praise,
Having observed day after day,
That one of faultless conduct, intelligent,
Of wisdom and virtue well composed—

230. Who is fit to fault that one,
Who is like a coin of gold?
Even the gods praise that one;
One praised by Brahmā too.

231. Let one guard against physical intemperance;
In body, let one be restrained.
Having abandoned physical misconduct,
In proper conduct with the body let one live.

232. Let one guard against intemperance of speech;
In speech, let one be restrained.
Having abandoned verbal misconduct,
In proper conduct with speech let one live.

233. Let one guard against intemperance of mind;
In mind, let one be restrained.
Having abandoned mental misconduct,
In proper conduct with the mind let one live.

234. Those restrained in body, wise,
And also restrained in speech,
Restrained in mind, wise,
They indeed are perfectly restrained.

## *Chapter XVIII Stains*

235. Like a yellow leaf are you now;
And even Yama's men have appeared for you;
And at the threshold of depature you stand;
But even the journey's provisions you do not have.

236. Make a lamp for yourself.
Strive quickly! Become a wise one;
With stains blown out, free of blemish,
You shall go to the heavenly realm of the nobles.

237. And You are now well advanced in age;
You have started the journey to the presence of Yama.
And, in between, there is not even a resting place for you;
Even the journey's provisions you do not have.

238. Make a lamp for yourself;
Strive quickly! Become a wise one;
With stains blown out, free of blemish,
You shall not undergo birth and old age again.

239. Gradually, would the wise one,
Bit by bit, moment by moment,
Blow out the stain that is one's own,
Like a smith the stain of silver.

240. As rust sprung from iron,
Springing from that, eats that itself,
So one's own actions lead
One of unwise conduct to a state of woe.

241. For chants [memorized], nonrepetition is corrosive;
For houses, nonmaintenance is corrosive;
Corrosive is sloth for physical appearance;
For one who guards, heedlessness is corrosive.

242. The stain of a woman is misconduct;
To the giver, stinginess is the stain.
Bad qualities indeed are stains,
In this world and in that beyond.

243. More staining than that stain
Is ignorance, the worst of stains.
Having abandoned this stain,
Be you free of stains, O bhikkhus!

244. Life is easily lived
By a shameless one,
A disparager, crafty as a crow,
An obtruder, impudent and corrupt.

245. But life is lived with hardship
By one sensitive to shame, ever seeking purity,
Free from clinging, and not impudent,
Discerning, pure in the mode of life.

246. Whoever in [this] world destroys life,
And falsehood speaks,
Takes what is not given,
And goes to another's wife,

247. And the man who engages in
The drinking of intoxicants,
Right here in this world
He digs up his own root.

248. Know this, dear fellow,
Bad qualities are intemperate.
Let not greed and the undhammalike way
Oppress you into prolonged suffering.

249. People give according to their faith,
According as they are pleased.
There one who becomes sullen,
About the food and drink of others [gotten],

He does not gain integration,
Be it by day or by night.

250. But the one in whom this is extirpated,
Destroyed at its roots, abolished,
He does gain integration,
Be it by day or by night.

251. There is no fire like passion.
There is no grip like ill will.
There is no snare like delusion.
There is no river like craving.

252. Easily seen is the fault of others,
But one's own is hard to see.
The faults of others
He winnows like chaff;
But conceals his own,
As a shrewd gambler, the defeating throw.[9]

253. Of one who sees the faults of others,
Constantly holding ideas of disdain—
His intoxicants increase;
Far is he from the extinction of intoxicants.

254. In the sky there is no footstep;
The recluse is not in externals;
Enamored with mental proliferation are the generations;
Free of proliferations are Tathāgatas.

255. In the sky there is no footstep;
The recluse is not in externals;
No *saṅkhāra* is eternal;
There is no agitation among Buddhas.

9. The commentary takes this line to mean: As a hunter, his body, with a covering of sticks.

## *Chapter XIX The Firm in Dhamma*

256. Were one to settle a case capriciously,
One thereby does not become firm in dhamma.
But the one who would discriminate
Both what is and what is not the case— the sagacious one—

257. Who leads others impartially
With dhamma, not capriciously,
The intelligent one, guarded by dhamma,
Is called "one firm in dhamma."

258. One is not a learned one
Merely because one speaks much.
The one secure, without enmity, without fear,
Is called a "learned one."

259. One is not a dhamma-bearer
Merely because one speaks much,
But who, having heard even a little,
Sees dhamma for himself,
And dhamma does not neglect,
He, indeed, is a dhamma-bearer.

260. One does not become an Elder
Because one's head is gray-haired;
Ripened his age,
"Grown old in vain" is he called.

261. In whom there is truth and dhamma,
Harmlessness, restraint, control,
Who has the stains ejected, and is wise,
He indeed is called "Elder."

262. Not because of speech-making
Or by attractiveness of appearance
Does one, envious, avaricious, deceitful,
Become a commendable man.

263. But in whom this is extirpated,
Destroyed at its roots, abolished,
He, having ill will ejected, wise,
Is called "commendable."

264. Not by a shaven head is one a recluse,
If one lacks due observance, speaks untruth.
How can one possessed of longing and greed
Become a recluse?

265. But he who calms away the wrongs,
Great and small, in every way;
For having [so] calmed away the wrongs,
"A recluse" he is called.

266. Not for this is one a bhikkhu,
Merely that one begs of others;
Having taken up a foul dhamma,
One is not thereby a bhikkhu.

267. Setting aside both merit and wrong
Who lives here the higher life,
Courses in the world discriminately,
He, indeed, is called "bhikkhu."

268. One does not become a sage by silence,
If confused and ignorant.
But a wise one, as if holding a set of scales,
Takes up the best,

269. And shuns wrongs, he is a sage;
For that reason he is a sage.
Who knows both in this world,
Is, for that, called a sage.

270. By harmlessness toward living beings
Is one called a Noble One.
One who is harmless toward all living beings
Is called "noble one."

271. Not by precepts and rites,
Nor again by much learning,
Nor by acquisition of concentration,
Nor by secluded lodging,

272. Thinking "I touched the ease of renunciation
Not resorted to by ordinary people,"
O bhikkhu, get not into contentedness,
Not having attained extinction of intoxicants.

## *Chapter XX The Path*

273. Of paths, the eightfold is the best.
Of truths, the four statements.
Detachment is the best of dhammas.
And of two-footed ones, the one endowed with eyes.

274. Just this path, there is no other
For purity of vision.
Do ye go along this [path];
This is what will bewilder Māra.

275. Entered upon this,
An end of misery you will make.
Proclaimed indeed is the path by me,
Having known the extrication of the arrows.

276. By you is the task strenuously to be done;
Tathāgatas are proclaimers.
Entered upon this path, the meditators
Are released from the bond of Māra.

277. When through wisdom one perceives,
"All *saṅkhāra*s are transient,"
Then one is detached as to misery.
This is the path of purity.

278. When through wisdom one perceives
"All *saṅkhāra*s are suffering,"
Then one is detached as to misery.
This is the path of purity.

279. When through wisdom one perceives,
"All dhammas are without self,"
Then one is detached as to misery.
This is the path of purity.

280. Who is not exerting at the time for exertion,
Young, strong, possessed of laziness,
With mind filled with confused notions, indolent, lethargic—
Does not find the way to wisdom.

281. Watchful of speech, well restrained in mind,
One would not do what is unwholesome by body too.
These three modes of action one would purify.
Let one fulfill the path made known by the sages.

282. From meditativeness arises the great;
From its absence, there is destruction of the great.
Having known this twofold path for gain and loss
Let one conduct oneself so that the great increases.

283. Cut down the forest! Not a tree.
From the forest, fear arises.
Having cut down both forest and underbrush,
O bhikkhus, be ye without forests.

284. Insofar as the underbrush is not cut away,
Even to the smallest bit, of a man for women,
Insofar is he one having [his] mind tethered,
Like a suckling calf to its mother.

285. Cut down affection for yourself,
As with the hand, an autumn lily.
Foster just the path to peace, Nibbāṇa,
Taught by the One Who Has Traveled Well.

286. "Here I shall dwell during the rains,
Here in winter and summer, too."
So the childish one thinks.
He does not know of the danger.

287. That man of entangled mind,
Inebriated by sons and cattle,
Death carries away
Like a great flood, a sleeping village.

288. No sons there are for protection,
Neither father nor even relations,
For one seized by the End-Maker;
Among relations there is no protection.

289. Knowing this fact,
The wise one, restrained by virtue,
Would make clear, right quickly,
The path leading to Nibbāna.

## *Chapter XXI Miscellaneous*

290. If by sacrificing a limited pleasure
An extensive pleasure one would see,
Let the wise one beholding extensive pleasure,
A limited pleasure forsake.

291. Who wishes his own pleasure,
By imposing misery on others,
Who is contaminated by the contact of hate,
He is not released from hate.

292. What is to be done, that is rejected.
And what is not to be done, is done.
Of those who are vain, heedless,
The intoxicants increase.

293. But those who have well undertaken,
Constantly, mindfulness with regard to body,
Persevering in what is to be done,
They do not resort to what is not to be done.
Of those mindful, attentive ones,
The intoxicants come to an end.

294. Having slain mother and father
And two *khattiya* kings,
Having slain a kingdom together with the subordinate,
Without trembling, the *brāhmaṇa* goes.

295. Having slain mother and father
And two learned kings,
Having slain the tiger's domain, as fifth,
Without trembling, the *brāhmaṇa* goes.

296. Well awake they arise, at all times,
The disciples of Gotama,
In whom, both day and night,
Constantly there is mindfulness on the Buddha.

297. Well awake they arise, at all times,
The disciples of Gotama,
In whom both day and night,
Constantly there is mindfulness on Dhamma.

298. Well awake they arise, at all times,
The disciples of Gotama,
In whom, both day and night,
Constantly there is mindfulness on the Saṅgha.

299. Well awake they arise, at all times,
The disciples of Gotama,
In whom, both day and night,
Constantly there is mindfulness on the body.

300. Well awake they arise, at all times,
The disciples of Gotama,
In whom, both day and night,
The mind delights in harmlessness.

301. Well awake they arise, at all times,
The disciples of Gotama,
In whom, both day and night,
The mind delights in meditation.

302. Difficult it is to go forth, difficult to delight therein;
Difficult to live in are households—a suffering.
Suffering it is to live with uneven ones;
And travelers are trapped in suffering.
So, be not a traveler,
And be not trapped in suffering.

303. The faithful one, endowed with virtue,
Possessed of fame and wealth,
To whatever region he resorts,
There, indeed, he is worshiped.

304. From afar the good ones are visible,
Like the snowy mountain.

The bad ones here are not seen,
Like arrows shot in the night.

305. Sitting alone, resting alone,
Walking alone, unwearied,
The one alone, who controls oneself,
Would be delighted in the forest.

## *Chapter XXII Hell*

306. The one who speaks lies, goes to hell,
And the one who having done says, "I don't do this."
Both of these, people of base deeds,
Having passed away, become equal in the beyond.

307. Many having the yellow robe about their necks
Are of bad qualities, uncontrolled.
They, the bad ones,
By bad deeds are led to hell.

308. Better that an iron ball be eaten,
Glowing, like a flame of fire,
Than that one should eat a country's alms food,
Being poor in virtue, lacking control.

309. Four conditions the heedless man comes by,
Who resorts to the wives of others;
Acquisition of demerit,
Lack of agreeable sleep,
Disgrace is third; hell is the fourth.

310. Acquisition of demerit
And a lowly [future] course.
And brief the delight of a frightened man with a frightened woman,
The king too gives a heavy punishment—
So let a man not resort to the wife of another.

311. Just as *kusa* grass, wrongly grasped,
Cuts the hand itself,
So, recluseness wrongly handled,
Drags one down to hell.

312. Whatever is a loose act,
And what is a defiled observance—
A "higher life" filled with suspicion—
That is not of great fruit.

313. If it is a thing to be done, let one do it,
Let one advance decisively to it;
For religious conduct that is slack
Throws up dirt all the more.

314. A misdeed is better not done;
The misdeed torments hereafter.
But a good deed is better done,
Having done which, one does not regret.

315. Like a border city
Guarded both within and without,
So, guard yourself.
Let not the moment slip you by.
Those for whom the moment is past
Do indeed grieve, consigned to hell.

316. They are ashamed of what is not shameful,
They are not ashamed of what is shameful.
Ones who endorse wrong views,
Such beings go to a state of woe.

317. Those who see what is not fear as fear,
And see no fear in fear,
Ones who endorse wrong views,
Such beings go to a state of woe.

318. Those who regard what is not error as error,
And see no error in error,
Ones who endorse wrong views,
Such beings go to a state of woe.

319. But having known error as error,
And nonerror as nonerror,
Ones who endorse proper views,
Such beings go to a state of weal.

## *Chapter XXIII The Elephant*

320. Like an elephant in battle,
The arrow shot from a bow,
I shall endure the unwarranted word;
The majority, indeed, are of poor virtue.

321. They take a tamed one to a crowd;
On a tamed one a king mounts.
Among humans a tamed one is best,
One who endures the unwarranted word.

322. Excellent are tamed mules,
Thoroughbreds and horses of Sindh,
Also tuskers, great elephants.
But better than them is one who has subdued oneself.

323. Truly, not by these vehicles
Could one go to a region unreached,
As a tamed one goes
By a well-subdued, disciplined self.

324. The tusker named Dhanapālaka,
Deep in rut, is hard to control.
Bound, the tusker does not eat a morsel,
But remembers the elephant forest.

325. When one is torpid and a big eater,
A sleeper, who lies rolling about
Like a great boar, nourished on grains—
Being dull one enters the womb again and again.

326. Formerly this mind set out awandering
As it wished, where it liked, according to its pleasure.
Today I will hold it back methodically
Like one seizing a goad, an elephant in rut.

327. Be delighters in awareness;
Keep watch over your mind.
Lift yourself up from the difficult road,
Like a tusker, sunk in mire.

328. Should one get a mature companion,
Who will move about with one, a wise one who leads a good life,
Let one move with him,
All dangers overcoming, mindful and happy.

329. Should one not get a mature companion,
Who will move about with one, a wise one who leads a good life,
Let one wander alone,
Like a king who has left behind a conquered land,
Like the elephant in the Mātaṅga forest.

330. A life of solitude is better;
There is no companionship with the childish one.
With little exertion, like the elephant in the Mātaṅga forest,
Let one wander alone, and do no wrongs.

331. When a need has arisen, friends are a blessing,
A blessing is contentment with whatever [there be],
A blessing is the wholesome deed at the end of life,
A blessing it is to relinquish all sorrow.

332. A blessing in the world is reverence for mother,
A blessing, too, is reverence for father,
A blessing in the world is reverence for the recluse,
A blessing too reverence for the *brāhmaṇa*.

333. A blessing is virtue into old age,
A blessing is faith established,
A blessing is the attainment of insight-wisdom,
A blessing it is to refrain from doing wrongs.

# *Chapter XXIV Craving*

334. The craving of a person who lives heedlessly
Grows like a *māluvā* creeper.
He moves from beyond to beyond,
Like a monkey, in a forest, wishing for fruit.

335. Whomsoever in the world
This childish entangled craving overcomes,
His sorrows grow,
Like *bīraṇa* grass, well rained upon.

336. But whosoever in the world
Overcomes this childish craving, hard to get beyond,
From him, sorrows fall away,
Like drops of water from a lotus leaf.

337. This I say to you. Good fortune to you [all],
As many as are here assembled.
Dig out the root of craving,
As one searching for *usīra* digs out *bīraṇa* grass.
Let not Māra break you again and again,
As a river, a reed.

338. As long as the roots are unharmed, firm,
A tree, though topped, grows yet again.
Just so, when the latent craving is not rooted out,
This suffering arises again and again.

339. For whom the thirty-six streams,
Flowing to what is pleasing, are mighty,
That one, whose view is debased,
The currents, which are thoughts settled on passion, carry away.

340. Streams flow everywhere;
A creeper, having burst upward, remains.
Having seen the creeper that has arisen,
Cut out with insight-wisdom its root.

341. Moved along and soaked by craving,
Delights arise in a being.
Those men who are bound to the agreeable, looking for pleasure,
Do indeed go on to birth and old age.

342. Accompanied by craving,
Folk crawl around like a trapped hare,
Being held by fetters and bonds.
They come by suffering again and again, for long.

343. Surrounded by craving,
Folk crawl around like a trapped hare.
Therefore, let a bhikkhu dispel craving,
Wishing for his own detachment.

344. Who is free of the underbrush, but attached to the forest,
Who, set free from the forest, runs back to the forest;
Come, see that person,
Who, released, runs back to bondage itself.

345. That is not a strong bond, say the wise,
Which is made of iron, of wood, or of [platted] grass.
Those excessively attached to jewels and ornaments [their attachment],
And affection for sons and wives,

346. This is a strong bond, say the wise,
Dragging down, lax [and yet] hard to loosen.
Having cut off even this, they set out,
Free of expectation, relinquishing sensual pleasures.

347. Those who are attached to passions fall back into the "stream,"
Like a spider, on a self-spun web.
Having cut off even this, the wise proceed
Free of expectation, relinquishing all suffering.

348. Let go in front, let go behind, let go in between!
Gone to the further shore of existence,
With mind released as to "everything,"
You shall not again come upon birth and old age.

349. For a person having thoughts disturbed,
Acute of passion, looking for the pleasurable,
Craving increases all the more.
That one, indeed, makes the bondage firm.

350. But one who delights in allaying thoughts,
Who, ever-mindful, develops meditation on the unpleasant,
That one, indeed will make an end,
That one will cut off Māra's bond.

351. The one who has arrived at the destination,
Free from fright, craving, and blemish,
Has broken the knives of existence.
This is the final bodily form.

352. Without craving, free from grasping,
Skilled in terms of expression,
Who would know the combination of letters, what precedes and what follows,
He, indeed, is called one having the last physical form,
Great person of great wisdom.

353. Conqueror of all, knower of all am I;
Untainted with regard to all dhammas.
Abandoning everything, released at the dissolution of craving,
Having comprehended by myself, whom shall I point out?

354. The gift of dhamma prevails over every gift,
The flavor of dhamma prevails over every flavor,
The delight in dhamma prevails over every delight,
The dissolution of craving subdues all suffering.

355. Possessions strike down one deficient in wisdom,
But not those seeking the beyond.
Through craving for possessions, one deficient in wisdom
Strikes oneself down as one would the others.

356. For fields, grasses are the bane,
For humankind, sensual attraction is the bane.
Hence, to those free from sensual attraction
What is given yields much fruit.

357. For fields, grasses are the bane,
For humankind, ill will is the bane.
Hence, to those free from ill will
What is given yields much fruit.

358. For fields, grasses are the bane,
For humankind, confusion is the bane.
Hence, to those free from confusion
What is given yields much fruit.

359. For fields, grasses are the bane,
For humankind, longing is the bane.
Hence, to those free from longing
What is given yields much fruit.

## *Chapter XXV The Bhikkhu*

360. Restraint with the eye is commendable,
Commendable is restraint with the ear.
Restraint with the nose is commendable,
Commendable is restraint with the tongue.

361. Restraint with the body is commendable,
Commendable is restraint with speech.
Restraint with the mind is commendable,
Commendable is restraint in all [the senses].
The bhikkhu who is restrained in all [the senses],
Is freed from all suffering.

362. The one restrained in hand, restrained in foot,
Restrained in speech, the one of best restraint,
Having delight in introspection, composed, solitary,
contented—
That one they call a bhikkhu.

363. A bhikkhu, restrained in speech,
Who speaks in moderation, who is not haughty,[10]
Who illustrates the meaning and the message,
Sweet is his speech.

364. Abiding in dhamma, delighting in dhamma,
Reflecting on dhamma, remembering dhamma,
A bhikkhu, does not fall away
From dhamma true.

365. Let one not treat what one has received with scorn,
Let one not live envying others.
A bhikkhu who is envying others
Does not come to integration [of mind].

10. The commentary understands the first part of this line to mean: who speaks with insight.

366. If though a bhikkhu has received but little,
He does not treat his receipt with scorn,
Him, indeed, the gods praise,
Who is living purely, unwearied.

367. For whom there is no "sense of mine"
Toward what is name-and-form, in every way,
Who does not grieve because of what is not;
He, indeed, is called a bhikkhu.

368. A bhikkhu dwelling in loving-kindness,
Who is pleased in the Buddha's instruction,
Would attain the state that is peace,
The pacification of the *saṅkhāras*, bliss.

369. O bhikkhu, bail out this boat.
Bailed out, it shall go quickly for you.
Having cut away both lust and hate,
You shall then reach Nibbāna.

370. Let one cut away the five, relinquish the five,
And, especially, cultivate the five.
A bhikkhu who has gone beyond five attachments
Is called "One who has crossed the flood."

371. Meditate, O bhikkhu, and be not heedless.
Let not your mind whirl in the strand of sensuality.
Do not swallow a metal ball, being heedless,
While burning; do not lament, "This is woe."

372. There is no meditative absorption for one who lacks insight;
There is no insight for one who is not meditating.
In whom there is meditative absorption and insight,
Truly, he is in Nibbāna's presence.

373. For a bhikkhu who has entered an empty house,
Whose mind is at peace,
Who perceives dhamma fully,
There is delight unlike that of mortals.

374. Howsoever one thoroughly knows
The rise and demise of the *khandha*s,
One attains joy and delight
That is ambrosia for those who are discerning.

375. Here, this is the first thing for a bhikkhu of insight:
Guarding the sense faculties, contentment,
And restraint in the *pātimokkha.*
Associate with good friends
Who are living purely, unwearied.

376. Let one be in the habit of friendly relations,
Of competent conduct let one be.
Being of abundant joy thereby,
One shall make an end of suffering.

377. As the jasmine
Sheds its withered flowers,
So, O bhikkhu,
Shed sensual attachment and hatred.

378. A bhikkhu, with body pacified, speech pacified,
Who is possessed of peace, well composed,
Who has thrown out the world's material things,
Is called the "one at peace."

379. You yourself reprove yourself,
You yourself set yourself in order.[11]
As a bhikkhu who is self-guarded, aware,
You shall dwell at ease.

380. Oneself, indeed, is patron of oneself,
Oneself is one's own guide.
Therefore, restrain yourself,
As a merchant, a noble steed.

381. A bhikkhu, of abundant joy,
Pleased in the Buddha's instruction,
Would attain the state of peace,
The blissful allayment of the *saṅkhāra*s.

11. The commentary understands this line to mean: You, yourself, examine yourself.

382. Truly, a young bhikkhu
Who engages in the Buddha's instruction
This world illumines,
Like the moon set free from a cloud.

## *Chapter XXVI The Brāhmaṇa*

383. Having striven, cut off the stream!
Dispel sensualities, O *brāhmaṇa*,
Having known the dissolution of the *saṅkhāras*,
A knower of the Unmade are you, O *brāhmaṇa*.

384. When, with regard to two dhammas,
A *brāhmaṇa* has reached the further shore,
Then of that knowing one
All fetters come to an end.

385. For whom the farther shore or the nearer shore
Or both does not exist,
Who is free of distress, unyoked,
That one I call a *brāhmaṇa*.

386. The one meditating, free of dirt, quietly sitting,
Tasks done, free of intoxicants,
Who has obtained the goal supreme,
That one I call a *brāhmaṇa*.

387. By day glows the sun,
At night shines the moon,
In war-array the monarch glows.
Meditating, a *brāhmaṇa* glows.
But all day and night
The Buddha glows in splendor.

388. As "one who has banished wrong" is one a *brāhmaṇa;*
Because of "living in calm" is one called a *samaṇa*.
Dispelling one's own stain
—Therefore is one called "gone forth."

389. A *brāhmaṇa* would not attack a *brāhmaṇa,*
Or let loose [wrath] upon him.
Shame on one who strikes a *brāhmaṇa,*
And greater shame [on one] who lets loose [wrath] upon him.

390. When there is exclusion from what is pleasant to the mind;
That is no little good for the *brāhmaṇa*—
Whenever the intent to harm does cease,
Then indeed is sorrow calmed.

391. Of whom there is nothing ill done
With body, with speech, with mind,
Who is restrained in these three bases,
That one I call a *brāhmaṇa*.

392. From whom one would learn dhamma
Taught by the Fully Enlightened One,
Let one pay homage to that one
As a *brāhmaṇa* to the sacrificial fire.

393. Not by matted hair, or by clan,
Or by birth does one become a *brāhmaṇa*.
In whom is truth and dhamma,
He is the pure one, and he is the *brāhmaṇa*.

394. What's the use of your matted hair, O you of poor insight?
What's the use of your deerskin garment?
Within you is the jungle;
The exterior you groom.

395. One who wears rags from a dust heap,
Lean, having veins [visibly] spread over body,
Meditating alone in the forest,
That one I call a *brāhmaṇa*.

396. And I do not call one a *brāhmaṇa*
Merely by being born from a [*brāhmaṇa*] womb,
Sprung from a [*brāhmaṇa*] mother.
He is merely a "*bho*-sayer"
If he is a possessor of things.
One who has nothing and takes nothing,
That one I call a *brāhmaṇa*.

397. Who does not tremble,
Having cut off every fetter,
Who has gone beyond attachments, unbound,
That one I call a *brāhmaṇa.*

398. Having cut off the strap and thong,
Cord, together with the bridle,
Who has lifted the bar, awakened,
That one I call a *brāhmaṇa.*

399. Who unangered endures
Insult, assault, and binding,
Whose strength is forebearance, who has an army's strength,
That one I call a *brāhmaṇa.*

400. Who is free of anger, who observes the duties,
Who is virtuous, free of the flow [of craving],
Controlled, and in the final body,
That one I call a *brāhmaṇa.*

401. Like water on a lotus petal,
Like a mustard seed on the point of an awl,
Who is not smeared with sensualities,
That one I call a *brāhmaṇa.*

402. Who comes to understand, even here,
The destruction of sorrow,
Who has put aside the burden, who is free of the bonds,
That one I call a *brāhmaṇa.*

403. One having profound insight, wise,
Proficient as to path and nonpath,
Who has attained the highest goal,
That one I call a *brāhmaṇa.*

404. One who is not gregarious
With both householders and homeless ones,
Living without an abode, desiring but little,
That one I call a *brāhmaṇa.*

405. Having laid down the rod
With regard to beings, the frightful and the firm,
Who neither slays nor causes to slay—
That one I call a *brāhmaṇa*.

406. One who is not opposing among those opposing,
Who is calmed among those who have taken weapons,
Free of grasping among those who are grasping,
That one I call a *brāhmaṇa*.

407. From whom passion and ill will,
Conceit and ingratitude, have been shed,
Like a mustard seed from the tip of an awl,
That one I call a *brāhmaṇa*.

408. Who would speak speech that is true,
That is instructive and not harsh,
By which one would anger none—
That one I call a *brāhmaṇa*.

409. Who, here in this world, does not take what is not given,
Whether long or short, small or great,
Pleasant or unpleasant,
That one I call a *brāhmaṇa*.

410. In whom are not found longings
For this world and for the beyond,
Without longing, released,
That one I call a *brāhmaṇa*.

411. In whom are not found attachments,
Who is without doubts due to understanding,
Who has attained the plunge into the Deathless,
That one I call a *brāhmaṇa*.

412. Who, here, has moved beyond attachment,
Both the meritorious and the detrimental,
Who is free of sorrow, free of dust, pure,
That one I call a *brāhmaṇa*.

413. Who, like the moon, is spotless, pure,
Serene, unagitated,
In whom is extinct the desire for existence,
That one I call a *brāhmaṇa*.

414. Who has passed over this [muddy] path, this fortress,
Delusion, which is *saṃsāra*,
Who has crossed over it, gone beyond it, a meditator,
Passionless, without doubts,
Without grasping, pacified,
That one I call a *brāhmaṇa*.

415. Who, here, having renounced lusts,
Would go forth, a homeless one,
In whom is extinct sensual lust and existence,
That one I call a *brāhmaṇa*.

416. Who, here, having renounced craving,
Would go forth, a homeless one,
In whom is extinct craving and existence,
That one I call a *brāhmaṇa*.

417. Who, having abandoned the human bond,
Has transcended the heavenly bond,
Who is released from all bonds,
That one I call a *brāhmaṇa*.

418. Who, having abandoned attachment and aversion,
Who has become cool, free from substrates,
A hero overcoming the entire world—
That one I call a *brāhmaṇa*.

419. Who knows in every way
The passing away and rebirth of beings,
Unattached, well gone, awakened,
That one I call a *brāhmaṇa*.

420. Whose course
Gods, *gandhabbas*, and humans do not know,
Whose intoxicants are extinct, an Arahant,
That one I call a *brāhmaṇa*.

421. For whom there is nothing
In front, behind, and in between,
The one, without anything, ungrasping,
That one I call a *brāhmaṇa*.

422. A bull, splendid, heroic,
A great sage, a victor,
Passionless, who has bathed, awakened,
That one I call a *brāhmaṇa*.

423. One who knows [one's] former lives,
And sees the heavens and the states of woe,
And who has reached the extinction of births,
Who has perfected higher knowledge,
Sage, who has fulfilled the final perfection,
That one I call a *brāhmaṇa*.

# RECOMMENDED FOR CONSULTATION

## I
## General Background


Adikaram, E. W. *Early History of Buddhism in Ceylon.* Colombo: M. D. Gunasena, 1953 (first published, 1946).

Horner, I. B. *Buddhism: The Theravada* in the *Concise Encyclopaedia of Living Faiths*, edited by R. C. Zaehner. Boston: Beacon Press, 1967 (first published, 1959).

Ñyāṇamoli, Bhikkhu. *The Path of Purification.* Colombo: A. Semage, 2nd ed., 1964 (first published, 1956).

Nyanaponika Thera. *Satipaṭṭhāna, The Heart of Buddhist Meditation.* York Beach, Maine: Samuel Weiser, 1984 (first published, 1962).

Nyanatiloka. *Guide to the Abhidhamma Piṭaka: Being a Synopsis of the Philosophical Collection Belonging to the Buddhist Pali Cannon.* Kandy: Buddhist Publication Society, 3rd ed., 1971.

Nyanatiloka. *Buddhist Dictionary, Manual of Buddhist Terms and Doctrines.* Third revised and enlarged edition edited by Nyanaponika. Colombo: Frewin & Co., 1972 (first published, 1952).

Rahula, Walpola Sri. *What the Buddha Taught* (revised edition). New York: Grove Press, 1974 (first published, 1959).

Upasak, C. S. *Dictionary of Early Buddhist Monastic Terms* (Based on Pali Literature). Varanasi: Bharati Prakashan, 1975.

Vajirañāṇa Mahāthera, Paravahera. *Buddhist Meditation in Theory and Practice, a General Exposition According to the Pali Canon of the Theravada School*, Colombo: M. D. Gunasena & Co., 1962.


## II
## Dhammapada Translations


Fausbøll, V. *Dhammapadam: Ex tribus codicibus hauniensibus palice edidit, latine vertit, excerptis ex commentario palico nostique illustravit.* Copenhagen: 1855. Second edition (text and Latin translation only), London, 1900.

Max Müller, F. *The Dhammapada: A Collection of Verses, being one of the canonical books of the Buddhists*. Translated from Pali, Sacred Books of the East, vol. 10, part 1. Oxford: Clarendon Press, 1881.

Radhakrishnan, S. *The Dhammapada, with Introductory Essays, Pali Text, English Translation and Notes*. London: Oxford University Press, 2nd impression, 1954 (first published, 1950).

Rhys Davids, C. A. F. *The Minor Anthologies of the Pali Canon;* Part I, Dhammapada and Khuddhakapāṭha. London: Pali Text Society, 1931 (Sacred Books of the Buddhists, vol. 7).

# TRANSLATION, TRANSLITERATION, AND COMMENTARY

# PROLOGUE

*Salutation to the Blessed One, the Worthy One,*
*the Fully Enlightened One*

In this world wrapped in the darkness of its great ignorance,
The blessed Dhamma's bright lamp He lit,
Aglow with his *iddhi* powers, far into the ends of the worlds seeing;
Unto his feet I bend low, the wond'rous Enlightened One!
I worship too His blessed Dhamma,
And fold my hands in reverence to the Saṅgha.

Knowing what is Dhamma, and what is not,
And to the state of blessed Dhamma come,[1]
The auspicious Dhamma-word the Teacher taught
As each occasion called,
His heart impelled by power of love.

Of that word, augmenter of gladness and of joy
Of gods and of men,
The exposition of meaning, skillfully wrought
In the island speech of Tambapanni's Isle
From generation to generation brought—
Yields not to beings outside that Isle
The blessing of their weal.

"Would that it serve the cause of the world entire,"
So wishing, did the Elder of steadfast mind,
Kumara Kassapa, of even conduct and good restraint,
Eager for the blessed Dhamma's stable stance
A seemly request make to me.
Leaving the island-speech
And its long-winded ways of expression,
I turn it into the winsome speech of holy texts
And amplify the expressed word of verse
Which there has not been amplified,

And the rest, just as it is,
In this other speech explain,
Bringing to the hearts of the wise gladness and joy,
That to their righteous weal is linked.

# CHAPTER I

## The Pairs
## *Yamaka-vaggo*

1. Preceded by perception are mental states,
For them is perception supreme,
From perception have they sprung.
If, with perception polluted, one speaks or acts,
Thence suffering follows
As a wheel the draught ox's foot. (1:1)

*manopubbaṅgamā dhammā manoseṭṭhā manomayā*(1)
*manasā ce paduṭṭhena bhāsati vā karoti vā*
*tato naṃ dukkham anveti cakkaṃ va vahato*(2) *padaṃ.*

### Perception: *mano*

"Perception" signifies consciousness in all the four levels [of manifestation]—that is, in its divisions, such as wholesome consciousness pertaining to the sensuous sphere of existence *(kāmāvacara-kusala* [*-citta*]*)*.[3] However, in this context, it is specified, defined, and limited, referring as it does to the thought that arose in the physician [who figured in the incidents that caused the Buddha to utter this stanza][4]—that is to say, perception here is [what would technically be called] consciousness linked with a hostile reaction having discontent as its concomitant *(domanassa-sahagata-paṭigha-sampayutta-citta)*.

### Preceded: *pubbaṅgamā*

This indicates that these [mental states: dhammas] are endowed with that [perceptive consciousness] as [their] precursor.

### Mental states: *dhammā*

Dhamma has four [main] usages as (1) virtue *(guṇa-dhammā)*, (2) religious discourse *(desanā-dhammā)*, (3) canonical text *(pariyatti-dhammā)*, and (4) that which is without a living substrate, without a living soul *(nissatta-nijjīva-*

*dhammā)*.(5) Of these [an example for] dhamma meaning "virtue" is: "Dhamma and *adhamma* [what is contradictory to dhamma] are indeed not of equal recompense: *adhamma* leads to the state of woe; dhamma leads to the state of weal."

[An example for] dhamma meaning "religious discourse" is: "O monks, I will declare to you the dhamma that is noble at the beginning . . . ."

[An example for] dhamma meaning "canonical text" is: "Here, O monks, some householders master the dhamma [in the form of] discourse *(sutta)* and chant *(geyya)*."

[An example for] dhamma meaning "that which is without a living substrate, without a living soul" is: "There are then the dhammas that are the *khandha*s."[6]

Of these, what dhamma means in the present context is "that which is without a living substrate, without a living soul"—that is, the [following] nonmaterial *khandha* processes: sensory-feeling *(vedanā)*, image *(saññā)*, and volitive-dynamic mental states *(saṅkhārā)*.

These [*khandha*s] are called "perception-preceded" *(manopubbaṅgamā)* because [in each] of them perceptive consciousness [occurs as] the preceding element.(7) It can be asked, "How is perception said to be 'preceding' these [dhammas],[8] for it and they have identical bases, identical objects, and arise together at one instant(9) without [the one] preceding or following [the other]?" [The answer is] in the sense that it is their generative condition *(uppādapaccaya)*. It is like the case of several persons getting together and committing such acts as doing violence to a village. If it is asked, "Who among them went as the first?," the one who was the cause, the one depending on whom they do that act, is pointed out as the first to go, be he Datta or Matta [by name]. So is the case to be understood in the present context: these [mental states] are "preceded by perception" in the sense that perception precedes them as [their] generative condition. Perception not arising, they cannot arise; but even where certain [of these] mental states *(cetasika*s*)* have not arisen, perception indeed does arise.

## (For them is) perception supreme: *manoseṭṭhā*

This means that perception as the predominant is supreme for them as the predominant [factor]; that just as among thieves, for example, their chiefs, such as their seniors, are the preeminent ones, so is perception to these [dhammas].

## From perception have they sprung: *manomayā*

Just as various goods made out of wood, for example, are known as wooden, so these [mental states] "spring from perception" inasmuch as they are produced out of perception.

## (With perception) polluted: *paduṭṭhena*

Polluted by intrusive faults such as covetous impulses, and so forth. Natural "mind" is the *bhavaṅga-citta.* It is unpolluted. Just as clear water is tainted by some color such as blue flowing into it and becomes distinguishable as "blue water," and so forth, but [other] fresh water is not so distinguished, nor [even] the [same] water [when it was] clear, prior [to the color flowing in]—in the same way, perception too becomes tainted by intrusive ills such as covetous impulses, and so forth. But neither is fresh "perception" [tainted by those impulses], nor is the prior *bhavaṅga-citta* [the initial point of the train of thoughts to which those ills intruded]. Hence has the Blessed One said, "Pure, O monks, is this mind. It is by intrusive pollutants that it is polluted."

## Speaks or acts: *bhāsati vā karoti vā*

Such a person [i.e., one with polluted perception] speaking commits the fourfold verbal misconduct *(vacīduccarita)*;[10] acting commits the threefold physical misconduct *(kāyaduccarita)*;[11] and [if he is] neither speaking nor acting, he still gives effect to the threefold mental misconduct *(manoduccarita)*.[12] Thus are the ten paths of unwholesome action *(akusalakamma)* trodden by him to the full.

## Thence suffering follows: *tato naṃ dukkham anveti*

From the threefold misconduct *(duccarita)*[13] suffering comes to that person. Due to the power of the misconduct, mental and physical suffering follow as a necessary result—suffering leading to the state of darkness,[14] physically based and otherwise, either in the four states of woe *(apāyas)* or among human beings.[15]

## As a wheel the draught ox's foot: *cakkaṃ va vahato padaṃ*

As a wheel [follows] the foot of the draught ox yoked to the carriage shaft and bearing that shaft. [The ox] may bear the yoke for a day, or five or ten days, a fortnight or a month—yet it cannot drive back the cartwheel or get away from it. If it tries to go beyond it from the front, the yoke arrests its neck; if it tries [to do so] from behind, the wheel cuts into the flesh of its back. Thus the wheel, which restricts [its movement] both ways, remains behind it from step to step. Similarly, physical and mental suffering follows the person who has committed the complement of the threefold misconduct due to a polluted mind—in the states of woe *(niraya)*, and so forth, whatsoever be the place to which he goes.

2. Preceded by perception are mental states,
For them is perception supreme.
From perception have they sprung.
If, with tranquil perception, one speaks or acts,
Thence ease follows
As a shadow that never departs. (1.2)

*manopubbaṅgamā dhammā manoseṭṭhā manomayā*
*manasā ce pasannena bhāsati vā karoti vā*
*tato naṃ sukham anveti chāyā va anapāyinī.*

## Perception: *mano*

Although the whole of consciousness in its four [possible] manifestations is meant by the term "perception," it is the eightfold wholesome consciousness pertaining to the sensuous sphere of existence *(kāmāvacara-kusala-citta)* that is applicable here, specified, defined, and limited [as it is in the present context]. Of that too, it is [more specifically] the consciousness linked with knowledge having mental ease as its concomitant *(somanassa-sahagata-ñāṇa-sampayutta-citta)* that is applicable here, that being what is brought to the fore by the context.[16]

## Preceded: *pubbaṅgamā*

Accompanied by that [perceptive-consciousness] as a prior constituent.

## Mental states: *dhammā*

The three *khandhas* beginning with *vedanā* [i.e., sensory-feeling, image, and volitive-dynamic mental states].

## Perception-preceded: *manopubbaṅgamā*

The consciousness linked with mental ease *(somanassa-sampayutta-citta)* is that which precedes in the sense [that it is] the generative condition for these [dhammas]. It is like the case of several persons getting together and doing such wholesome *(puñña)* acts as giving gifts of robes to the great community of monks *(mahābhikkhusaṅgha)*, making exalted offerings[17] or listening to dhamma or making lamps and garlands. If it is asked, "Who among them is foremost?" the one who was the [primary] cause, the one depending on whom they do these wholesome *(puñña)* acts is pointed out as the precursor.

So it should be understood here: These [dhammas] are "preceded by perception" in the sense that perception precedes them as [their] generative condition. Perception not arising, they cannot arise; but even where certain [of these] mental states *(cetasikas)* have not arisen, perception indeed does arise.

## Perception is supreme: *manoseṭṭhā*

Thus for them perception is supreme in that it is "supreme as the predominant factor." Just as the leading person of a group, and so forth, is called the chief of the group or the chief of the guild, so is perception to these [dhammas]—in that sense is supreme for them.

## Sprung from perception: *manomayā*

Just as, for example, various goods manufactured out of gold are said to be golden, so these [mental states] are said to be sprung from perception, owing to their being produced out of perception.

## With (mind) tranquil: *(manasā) pasannena*

Tranquil, due to such qualities as freedom from covetousness, and the like [i.e., malevolence and erroneous view].

## Speaks or acts: *bhāsati vā karoti vā*

With such perception, when one speaks one gives utterance to the fourfold verbal good conduct *(vacīsucarita)* only; when one acts, one performs the threefold physical good conduct *(kāyasucarita)* only; and [even] when one neither speaks nor acts, one still would fulfill the threefold mental good conduct *(manosucarita)* only—for one's perception is tranquil due to freedom from covetousness and the like. Thus are the ten paths of wholesome action *(kusalakamma)* trodden by one to the full.[18]

## Thence ease follows: *tato naṃ sukham anveti*

From that threefold good conduct *(sucarita)*, happiness comes to that person. Here what is wholesome *(kusala)* in all three levels of [saṃsāric] existence *(bhūmis)*[19] is meant [by "thence"]. Hence, and as a necessary sequel, mental and physical ease follows the person [as] born in a state of weal *(sugati)* or, if in a state of woe *(duggati)*, in a situation that allows him to enjoy ease—ease that is physically based or based otherwise, or free from any basis at all.[20] And such ease does not desert him. So the case must be understood.

And what would be an illustrative example? One is indicated by the words [that follow]:

## As a shadow that never departs: *chāyā va anapāyinī*

The shadow, being connected to the body, moves when one's body moves, stays when one's body stays, and sits when one's body sits. It is not possible to stop it by a command, howsoever softly or harshly spoken, nor [even] by physical assault. Why? Because it is connected to the body. Similarly, wheresoever one [with tranquil perception] goes, there follows mental and physical ease, such as the ease pertaining to the sphere of sensuality *(kāmāvacara-sukha)*, based on the constantly trodden ten paths of wholesome action *(kusalakamma)*—like a shadow that never departs.

3. "He reviled me! He struck me!
He defeated me! He robbed me!"
They who gird themselves up with this,
For them enmity is not quelled. (1.3)

4. "He reviled me! He struck me!
He defeated me! He robbed me!"
They who do not gird themselves up with this,
For them is enmity quelled. (1.4)

*akkocchi maṃ avadhi maṃ ajini maṃ ahāsi me*
*ye taṃ upanayhanti veraṃ tesaṃ na sammati.*

*akkocchi maṃ avadhi maṃ ajini maṃ ahāsi me*
*ye taṃ na upanayhanti veraṃ tesūpasammati.*

## He reviled: *akkocchi*

He reviled. [The commentary here glosses this word with another form of the same word in the aorist tense.]

## He struck: *avadhi*

He gave blows.

## He defeated: *ajini*

He got the better [of me] by bearing false witness, or by argumentation and cross talk, or by retaliatory acts.

### He robbed: *ahāsi*

He took away some possession of mine, vessels, or the like.

### They who . . . : *ye taṃ . . .*

Whoever, be they gods or humans, lay persons or monks, who "wrap up" anger—that is, wrap around [themselves] repeatedly the anger based on the thought "he reviled me," and so on, like wrapping up the pole of a cart with thongs, or putrid fish with straw—when enmity arises in such persons, it is not appeased, pacified.

### Not quelled: *na sammati*

When enmity once arises in them, it is not extinguished, appeased, pacified.

### They who do not gird themselves up: *ye taṃ na upanayhanti*

Those who do not wrap around themselves the anger based on [the experience of] being reviled, and the like.

### Is enmity quelled: *veraṃ . . . upasammati*

By not bearing it in awareness, by not reminding themselves of it, or by reflecting on [one's own] actions [thus]: "You too must have reviled some innocent person in a past life, beaten up and got the better of [someone] by bearing false witness, or must have deprived someone of something and so forth.(21) Therefore [now] have you too been undeservedly subjected to reviling and the like." In such persons even hate that arose due to carelessness is extinguished by this "not girding up," like fire whose supply of fuel has ceased.

5. Not by enmity are enmities quelled,
Whatever the occasion here.
By the absence of enmity are they quelled.
This is an ancient truth. (1.5)

*na hi verena verāni sammantīdha kudācanaṃ*
*averena ca sammanti esa dhammo sanantano.*

### Not by enmity: *na hi varena*

A spot smeared with impurities like spit and nasal mucous cannot be cleaned and freed of smells [by] washing it with the same impurities; on the contrary, [thereby] that spot will be all the more unclean and foul-smelling. In the same way, one who reviles the reviler, one who strikes back at the striker, is not able to pacify hatred with hatred. On the contrary, one [thereby] creates more hatred still. Thus, at no time whatever are enmities calmed through enmity—they only increase [thereby].

### By the absence of enmity are they quelled: *avarena ca sammanti*

Those impurities such as spit vanish when washed with clean water and that spot becomes clean and free of smells. In the same way, enmities are extinguished and pacified and they cease to be, by means of the absence of enmity, by the [clear] water of patience *(khanti)* and loving kindness *(mettā)*, and also by proper attentiveness.

### This is an ancient truth: *esa dhammo sanantano*

This time-honored truth—namely, that of pacifying enmity through the absence of enmity—is the path trodden by all Buddhas, Paccekabuddhas, and those in whom defilements are extinct [Arahants].[22]

6. Others do not realize
 "We here are struggling."
 Those who realize this—for them
 Are quarrels therefore quelled. (1.6)

(For line 2, the commentary gives another interpretation [which it takes up first for comment]:
"We here do cease to be.")

*pare ca na vijānanti 'mayam ettha yamāmase'*
*ye ca tattha vijānanti tato sammanti medhagā.*

### Others: *pare*

The makers of strife [i.e., all], those who are other than the wise, are known [in this context] as "others." They, creating strife in the midst of the Saṅgha, do not realize: "We cease to be, we perish; constantly and definitely we are [in the process of] going to the presence of Death."

### Those who realize: *ye . . . vijānanti*

There [in the Saṅgha] those that are wise realize that we are [in the process of] going to the presence of Death.

## Are quarrels quelled: *sammanti medhagā*

This means that they, realizing thus, generate proper attentiveness and reach the state where quarrels are pacified. Then, due to that conduct of theirs, those situations of strife are quelled.

Or else: "others" means "those who are not devoted to me" [the Buddha][23] due to their not accepting my advice, although they were earlier admonished: "Please, monks, let there be no quarrels!" They[24] do not realize: "Having taken to the wilderness of error due to desires and the like, we *here* (*ettha*), in the midst of the saṅgha, try to increase *strife* (*yamāmase*) and other such conditions." But now, the wise among you reflect with proper attentiveness and come to the realization: "In the past, striving under the influence of impulse and the like, we fell into nonattentiveness." And then, on account of such wise persons among them[25] these situations of strife (*medhagā*) are now quelled.

7. Whoever dwells seeing the pleasurable, in senses unrestrained,
Immoderate in food, indolent, inferior of enterprise,
Over him, indeed, Māra prevails,
Like the wind over a weak tree. (1.7)

8. Whoever dwells seeing the nonpleasurable, in senses well restrained,
And moderate in food, faithful, resolute in enterprise,
Over him, indeed, Māra prevails not,
Like the wind over a rocky crag. (1.8)

*subhānupassiṃ viharantaṃ indriyesu asaṃvutaṃ*
*bhojanamhi amattaññuṃ kusītaṃ hīnavīriyaṃ*
*taṃ ve pasahati māro vāto rukkhaṃ va dubbalaṃ.*

*asubhānupassiṃ viharantaṃ indriyesu susaṃvutaṃ*
*bhojanamhi ca mattaññuṃ saddhaṃ āraddhavīriyaṃ*
*taṃ ve nappasahati māro vāto selaṃ va pabbataṃ.*

[7.]

## Whoever dwells seeing the pleasurable: *subhānupassiṃ viharantaṃ*

This means the person who lives with his mind cast about for desired objects, who is [constantly] looking toward the pleasurable. The person who is in the habit of taking signs and characteristics as a theme for reflection regards as beautiful [such physical aspects as] nails and fingers, hands and feet, leg and thigh, hip and belly, breast and neck, lips and teeth, mouth and nose, brows and forehead, head-hair and body-hair, skin and complexion [as well as] structural features [of the body]. Such is the one who looks for the pleasurable. [When the text refers to] the one who dwells seeing the pleasurable [in the accusative case, it] means that [kind of person].

### In senses unrestrained: *indriyesu asaṃvutaṃ*

Not restrained with regard to the senses such as sight, [is] one who is not guarding the [sense] doors, such as the eye.[26]

### Immoderate in food: *bhojanamhi amattaññuṃ*

[One is referred to thus] due to not understanding the [appropriate] measure in regard to the quest [for food], the acceptance [of food], and the consumption [of food], and also due to not understanding the [appropriate] measure in regard to contemplation and disbursement [of food; such a person is one] who does not have the knowledge: "This food is agreeable with righteous living and this not."[27]

### Indolent: *kusītaṃ*

On account of being under the sway of thoughts tinged with lust, ill-will, and violence.

### Inferior of enterprise: *hīnavīriyaṃ*

Devoid of resoluteness, not of [purposeful] effort in regard to the four modes of deportment.[28]

### Prevails over: *pasahati*

Conquers, crushes.

### Like the wind over a weak tree: *vāto rukkhaṃ va dubbalaṃ*

As a powerful gale [overpowers] a weak tree that has grown on a tumbled-down declivity. Just as such a wind brings down the fruits and leaves, and so forth, of such a tree and destroys [them], breaks up its branches big and small, and leaves it after felling it so that its roots will be up and its branches down, in the same way Māra in the form of defilements *(kilesamāra)*[29] who is born [right] within him, prevails over such a person. Like the felling of a weak tree's flowers by a strong wind, [Māra] causes him to indulge in the commission of minor and trivial misdeeds [i.e., to defy minor *vinaya* rules] like the felling[30] of smaller branches, the commission of misdeeds such as *nissaggiya* offenses; like the felling of large branches, the commission of the thirteen *saṅghādisesa* offenses; and like uprooting [the tree] and turning the branches and roots upside down, the commission of *pārājikā* offenses.[31] [Māra] drives him away from the well-taught [monastic] instruction *(svākkhātasāsana)* and reverts him to lay status in a matter of a few days.

Thus the sense of the stanza is that Māra in the form of defilements holds such a person as this in his subjugation.

[8.]

### Seeing the nonpleasurable: *asubhānupassiṃ*

Someone who observes one or another of the ten disagreeable forms;[32] who is endowed with attentiveness to the loathesome, [e.g.,] looking on head-hair [of the human body] as disagreeable, [similarly] looking on body-hair, nails, teeth, skin, complexion, and physical structure as loathesome.

### In senses: *indriyesu*

This is with reference to the six senses.[33]

### Well restrained: *susaṃvutaṃ*

Not in the habit of taking signs, and the like, as a theme for reflection; whose [sense] doors are [carefully] "closed."[34]

### Moderate in food: *bhojanamhi mattaññuṃ*

Because of [his condition being] the [exact] opposite of the state of not knowing [the appropriate] measure [in regard to food].

### Faithful: *saddhaṃ*

Endowed with ordinary faithfulness, which is marked by faith in *kamma* and *phala,* as well as with transcendent faithfulness, which amounts to a firm sense of being pleased in the "three objects" [Buddha, Dhamma, and *Saṅgha*].[35]

### Resolute in enterprise: *āraddhavīriyaṃ*

With purposeful enterprise, with complete enterprise.[36]

### Over him, indeed: *taṃ ve*

Just as a weak wind slowly striking against a solid rock is not able to shake it up, so Māra in the form of defilements *(kilesamāra)*, even though appearing within such a person, does not prevail over him, [being] weak [in relation to him]—that is to say, [Māra] is not able to agitate [him and] cause him to swerve [from his path].

9. One not free of defilements,
Who will don a yellow robe,
That one, devoid of control and truth,
Is not worthy of a yellow robe. (1.9)

*anikkasāvo kāsāvaṃ yo vatthaṃ paridahessati*
*apeto damasaccena*(37) *na so kāsāvam arahati.*

## One not free of defilements: *anikkasāvo*

One who is defiled with defilements such as sensual passions.

## Will don: *paridahessati*

Will use as [an item of] clothing, wrapping, spreading.

## Devoid of control and truth: *apeto damasaccena*

The meaning [of this] is: destitute of, unendowed with, separated from restraint of senses and truthfulness of word that pertains to the sphere of [lit. "on the side of"] truth absolute.[38]

## That one is not (worthy to wear a yellow robe): *na so (kāsāvam arahati)*

That one, a person of that kind, does not deserve to wear a yellow robe.

10. But one who, well placed in virtues,
Would be with defilements ejected,
Endowed with control and truth,
That one is worthy of a yellow robe. (1.10)

*yo ca vantakasāv' assa sīlesu susamāhito*
*upeto damasaccena sa ve kāsāvam arahati.*

## Would be with defilements ejected: *vantakasāv' assa*

He who would have ejected, thrown out, who is freed of defilements by means of the Four Paths.[39]

## In virtues: *sīlesu*

In regard to the four kinds of virtue leading to purity *(catupārisuddhisīla)*.[40]

### Well placed: *susamāhito*

Well integrated, well established.

### Endowed: *upeto*

Endowed with sense-restraint and with truthfulness of the kind mentioned [in the comment on the previous verse].[41]

### That one: *sa ve*

That one, a person of that kind, does deserve *(arahati)* that fragrant yellow robe.

11. Those who consider the nonessential as the essential,
And see the essential as the nonessential,
They do not attain the essential,
Being in the pastures of improper intentions. (1.11)

12. Having known the essential as the essential,
And the superficial as the superficial,
They attain the essential
Who are in the pastures of proper intentions. (1.12)

*asāre sāramatino sāre cāsāradassino*
*te sāraṃ nādhigacchanti micchāsaṃkappagocara.*

*sāraṃ ca sārato ñatvā asāraṃ ca asārato*
*te sāram adhigacchanti sammāsaṃkappagocarā.*

[11.]

### Those who consider the nonessential as the essential: *asāre sāramatino*

The nonessential is the four requisites *(peccaya)* [i.e., mere physical necessities: robes, food, a dwelling place, and medicine], the wrong view of ten bases *(dasavatthukā micchādiṭṭhi)*[42] and of instruction in a doctrine (dhamma) that serves as a foundation to it [the wrong view mentioned above]. The meaning [of the words in question] is "those who see the essential in it" [i.e., in the nonessential].

### And see the essential as the nonessential: *sāre cāsāradassino*

The right view with ten bases *(dasavatthukā sammādiṭṭhi)* and the instruction in a doctrine that serves as a foundation to it: this is [what is] called the essential. The meaning is: those who see in it the nonessential, thinking, "this is not the essential" [of them is verified the following]:

### They (do not attain) the essential: *te sāraṃ (nādhigacchanti)*

They stay accepting that tangle of erroneous views and are in the pastures of improper intentions, under the sway of thought tinged with sensuality, and so forth; [hence] they do not attain to the essential of virtue *(sīla)*, integration *(samādhi)*, insight *(paññā)*, and liberation *(vimutti)*— the essential that is the experience of the gnosis of liberation, that is the supreme meaning—they do not attain to Nibbāna.

[12.]

### The essential: *sāraṃ ca*

Knowing the very essence that is virtue *(sīla)*, and so forth [i.e., *sāmadhi, paññā, vimutti*], as "the essential," and also recognizing the [previously] mentioned "nonessential" as such, [they attain] the essential. They, the wise, take the right view and come to range in the pastures of proper intentions, under the influence of thoughts of dispassionateness, and the like, and they attain to that [essential] as was mentioned [above].

13. As rain penetrates
The poorly thatched dwelling,
So passion penetrates
The untended mind. (1.13)

14. As rain does not penetrate
The well-thatched dwelling,
So passion does not penetrate
The well-tended mind. (1.14)

*yathā agāraṃ ducchannaṃ vuṭṭhī samativijjhati*
*evaṃ abhāvitaṃ cittaṃ rāgo samativijjhati.*

*yathā agāraṃ succhannaṃ vuṭṭhī na samativijjhati*
*evaṃ subhāvitaṃ cittaṃ rāgo na samativijjhati.*

[13.]

### Dwelling: *agāraṃ*

That is, any kind of house.

### Poorly thatched: *ducchannaṃ*

Sparsely thatched, marked all over by holes [in the roof].

### Penetrates: *samativijjhati*

A shower of rain pours through [such a roof].

### Untended: *abhāvitaṃ*

Just as rain [pours through] such [a roof of] a dwelling, so passion penetrates (*rāgo samativijjhati*). And not only passion, but all defilements, such as ill-will, unawareness, and self-estimation do indeed penetrate that kind of mind excessively.

[14.]

### Well-tended: *subhāvitaṃ*

Well-tended by means of tranquility *(samatha)* and insight-meditation *(vipassanā)*. Defilements such as passion, and so forth, cannot penetrate such a mind, just as rain [cannot penetrate] a house well thatched.

15. Here he grieves; having passed away he grieves,
In both places the wrongdoer grieves.
He grieves; he is afflicted,
Having seen the stain of his own action. (1.15)

*idha socati pecca socati pāpakārī ubhayattha socati*
*so socati so vihaññati disvā kammakiliṭṭham attano.*

### Wrongdoer: *pāpakārī*

A person who commits wrong deeds of various kinds.[43]

### Here he grieves: *idha socati*

"Good [action] has not been done by me; bad has been"—so thinking [he grieves here] definitely at the time of his death. This is grief over what has been done *(kamma)*.

### Having passed away, he grieves: *pecca socati*

That is, experiencing the fruit *(vipāka)* [of his *kamma*]. This is grief [that is] the fruit [of deeds done], [experienced] in the world beyond [i.e., life after death].[44] Thus, indeed:

### He grieves in both places: *ubhayattha socati*
### Having seen the stain of his own action: *disvā kammakiliṭṭham attano*

For that very reason [that he grieves at both places], Cunda Sūkarika[45] too grieves while yet alive, having seen his sullied action—that is, he is afflicted, bewailing in various ways.

16. Here he rejoices; having passed away he rejoices.
In both places he who has done wholesome deeds rejoices.
He rejoices; he is delighted,
Having seen the purity of his own action. (1.16)

*idha modati pecca modati katapuñño ubhayattha modati*
*so modati so pamodati disvā kammavisuddhim attano.*

### He who has done wholesome deeds: *katapuñño*

This designates the person who has done various wholesome *(kusala)* acts.[46]

### He rejoices: *modati*

Here he rejoices with the joy of deeds [done], thinking, "No evil was done by me, good indeed was done." And having passed away [he rejoices] with the joy of [experiencing] the fruit *(vipāka)* thereof.[47] Thus, indeed,

### He rejoices in both places . . . : *ubhayattha modati . . .*
### Purity of action: *kammavisuddhim*

[This is as in the case of] Dhammika Upāsaka.[48] Before his death, he rejoiced [lit. rejoices] in this world, having witnessed the purity of his deeds—that is, the splendor of wholesome acts; and now, having passed away, again:

### He rejoices: *modati*

In the world beyond, he is extremely delighted.

17. Here he is tormented; having passed away he is tormented.
In both places, the wrongdoer is tormented.
He is tormented, thinking, "I have done wrong."
Gone to a state of woe, he is tormented all the more. (1.17)

*idha tappati pecca tappati pāpakārī ubhayattha tappati*
*pāpaṃ me kataṃ ti tappati bhiyyo tappati duggatiṃ gato.*

### Here he is tormented: *idha tappati*

Here [the doer of unwholesome deeds] is tormented with the torment of deeds done—and this is merely a "feeling that is mentally painful" *(domanassa)*.

### Having passed away: *pecca*

In the world beyond, however, he is tormented by the torment of the fruit of deeds, which is the extremely painful misery of the state of woe *(apāya)*.

### Wrongdoer: *pāpakārī*

The perpetrator of all kinds of wrong acts.

### In both places: *ubhayattha*

He is tormented at both places with this torment as mentioned [above].

### "I have done wrong": *pāpaṃ me (kataṃ ti)*

Tormented with the torment of deeds [done], he suffers anguish, thinking, "Wrong was done by me;" that [after all] is [only] a slight anguish, but tormented with the torment of the fruit of deeds:

### Gone to a state of woe, he is tormented all the more: *bhiyyo tappati duggatiṃ gato*

[Which means that at that stage] he is tormented excessively by a very harsh torment.

18. Here he rejoices; having passed away he rejoices.
In both places he who has done wholesome deeds rejoices.
He rejoices, thinking, "I have done wholesome deeds."
Gone to a state of weal, he rejoices all the more. (1.18)

*idha nandati pecca nandati katapuñño ubhayattha nandati*
*puññaṃ me kataṃ ti nandati bhiyyo nandati sugatiṃ gato.*

### Here: *idha*

In this world, he rejoices with the joy of deeds [done];

### Having passed away: *pecca*

In the world to come, he rejoices with the joy of the fruits [thereof].

### He who has done wholesome deeds: *katapuñño*

A doer of various kinds of wholesome deeds.

### In both places: *ubhayattha*

Here he rejoices, thinking, "Wholesome acts have been done by me, unwholesome acts have not been done"; [and] in the world beyond, he rejoices experiencing the fruits [of action done here].

### Thinking, "I have done wholesome deeds": *puññaṃ me kataṃ ti*

He rejoices here, dependent on the joy of deeds [done], rejoicing with only a mere pleasant feeling based on deeds done, [reflecting], "I have done wholesome acts."

### All the more: *bhiyyo*

[But] having gone to a state of weal *(sugati)*, enjoying, with the delight of the fruits [of deeds done], divine glory for 576 million years, he experiences plenary happiness in Tusitapura.[49]

19. If one, though reciting much of texts,
Is not a doer thereof, a heedless man;
He, like a cowherd counting others' cows,
Is not a partaker in the religious quest. (1.19)

20. If one, though reciting little of texts,
Lives a life in accord with dhamma,
Having discarded passion, ill will, and unawareness,
Knowing full well, the mind well freed,
He, not grasping here, neither hereafter,
Is a partaker of the religious quest. (1.20)

*bahuṃ pi ce sahitaṃ bhāsamāno*
*na takkaro hoti naro pamatto*

*gopo va gāvo gaṇayaṃ paresaṃ*
*na bhāgavā sāmaññassa hoti.*

*appaṃ pi ce sahitaṃ bhāsamāno*
*dhammassa hoti anudhammacārī*
*rāgaṃ ca dosaṃ ca pahāya mohaṃ*
*sammappajāno suvimuttacitto*
*anupādiyāno idha vā huraṃ vā*
*sa bhāgavā sāmaññassa hoti.*

[19.]

## Text: *sahitaṃ*

This signifies the word of the Buddha [enshrined in] the three *piṭaka*s.[50] [A certain person] comes to a teacher and learns [a text] and recites it many times and causes others to repeat it, [but] is not a doer of what should be done by a person who hears dhamma and acts accordingly. Not even for [a moment as short as] the flapping of a cock's wings does he put into effect proper attentiveness [e.g.,] to impermanence *(anicca)*, and so forth [i.e., *anicca*, *dukkha*, and *anatta*]. As a cowherd who looks after cattle by day takes charge of them early in the morning, and in the evening counts them and turns them over to the owners and obtains only the day's wages, but does not get to enjoy at will the five flavorful milkfoods, in just the same way he becomes the recipient of routine attention from the presence of resident pupils, but not a partaker of the religious quest. Just as the owners alone enjoy the milkfoods obtained from the cows turned over to them by the cowherd, so, having heard dhamma uttered by this person,[(51)] [other] persons who put it into practice observe what was taught and some [of them] reach the first trance, and so forth, some develop insight-meditation *(vipassanā)* and reach the Paths and Fruits. These become partakers of the religious quest, as the owners of the cattle relish the milkfoods.

In this way the Teacher uttered the first stanza [1.19] in regard to the monk who was slack in proper attentiveness on impermanence, and so forth, who, though possessing virtue (*sīla*) and quite learned [in the texts], lived inattentively—and not in regard to the monk who was slack in virtue. The second stanza was uttered in regard to the person of action who, though of little learning, did the [necessary] deed in [the matter of] proper attentiveness.

[20.]

### Though (reciting) little: *appaṃ pi ce*

A small amount, such as a single chapter or a couple of chapters [of any canonical text].

### Lives a life in accord with dhamma: *dhammassa hoti anudhammacārī*

[This refers to] one who, having understood the meaning, having understood dhamma, is living in agreement with dhamma, by virtue of following what conforms to the ninefold world-transcending dhamma—that is, [by conduct] that consists of the first part of the practices, namely, the fourfold virtue (*sīla*) leading to purity, the constituents of ascetic practice (*dhutaṅga*), the topic for meditation that pertains to what is not pleasurable (*asubha kammaṭṭhāna*), and so forth.[52] He lives expecting realization [to occur] "[any time] today, today itself." By virtue of this right practice, he,

### Having discarded passion, ill will, and unawareness: *rāgaṃ ca dosaṃ ca pahāya mohaṃ*

Knowing the truths (dhamma) that ought to be known through proper reasoning and inference.[53]

### The mind well freed: *suvimutto citto*

By way of liberation, by developing the opposite *(tadaṅga)* of the defilements, by supression *(vikkhambhana)* of the defilements, by cutting off *(samuccheda)* the defilements, by calming down *(paṭippassaddhi)* the defilements, and by wholly transcending *(nissaraṇa)* the defilements.[54]

### Not grasping here, neither hereafter: *anupādiyāno idha vā huraṃ vā*

Not being led by the four modes of grasping[55] to grasp at [i.e., to cherish the illusion of regarding one's self] the *khandha* processes, the spheres of interaction of senses and sense objects *(āyatana)*, and the bases of interplay of consciousness, sense, and sense objects *(dhātu)*, whether included in this world or in the beyond, whether internal or external. Such a one, thus, as a great being in whom intoxicants have vanished, becomes a partaker of the religious quest [line 6]—that is, of the Paths and of the Fruits resulting therefrom, as well as of the "group of five qualities" of one who has passed beyond training *(pañca asekha-dhamma-kkhandha)*.[56]

# CHAPTER II

## Awareness
## *Appamāda-vaggo*

21. The path to the Deathless is awareness;
Unawareness, the path of death.
They who are aware do not die;
They who are unaware are as dead. (2.1)

22. Having known this distinctly,
Those who are wise in awareness,
Rejoice in awareness,
Delighted in the pasture of the noble ones. (2.2)

23. Those meditators, persevering,
Forever firm of enterprise,
Those steadfast ones touch Nibbāna,
Incomparable release from bonds. (2.3)

*appamādo amatapadaṃ pamādo maccuno padaṃ*
*appamattā na mīyanti ye pamattā yathā matā.*

*etaṃ visesato ñatvā appamādamhi paṇḍitā*
*appamāde pamodanti ariyānaṃ gocare ratā.*

*te jhāyino sātatikā niccaṃ daḷhaparakkamā*
*phusanti dhīrā nibbānaṃ yogakkhemaṃ anuttaraṃ.*

### Awareness: *appamādo*

"Awareness" illumines a massive meaning, spans a massive content; for the entire Word of the Buddha included in the three *piṭakas* taken up and given articulation, boils down to the word "awareness" only. Therefore has it been said: "It is, O Monks, like the case of the many kinds of footstep of moving creatures—all of them gain inclusion in the elephant's footstep: by its massiveness, the elephant's step occupies the foremost place among them. In the same way, O Monks, whatever wholesome mental states (dhammas)[1] there are, they are all awareness-based,[2] they all converge in awareness: awareness occupies the foremost place among those mental states."

Now this [awareness] is in essence "not being bereft of mindfulness"; it is [just another] name for constantly occurring mindfulness.[3]

## Path to the Deathless: *amatapadaṃ*

"Deathless" means Nibbāna. Nibbāna, because of being unborn [i.e., without beginning], is not subject to decay and death. Hence it is called the Deathless. "Path" is so called because by it they travel.(4) The meaning is [they] reach the Deathless [by this path]. "Path" and "Deathless" [compounded mean] the path to the Deathless—that is, it is said [that this path is] the means of attaining the Deathless.[5]

## Unawareness: *pamādo*

The state of being unaware. This is a term for the abandonment of mindfulness, which is the same as the state of having neglected mindfulness.

## Of death: *maccuno*

Of the process of dying.

## The path: *padaṃ*

The means, the way. The one who is unaware does not transcend birth; being born, such a one is subject to decay and death. Thus unawareness is called the path of death. [This means that] death approaches [the one who is unaware].

## They who are aware do not die: *appamattā na mīyanti*

Those who are aware—that is, beings who are endowed with mindfulness—do not die. It should not be considered that they become [literally] freed of decay and death. There is of course no being who is beyond death and decay. [What is meant is that] for the unaware the whirl [i.e., the round of births and deaths] is unbroken; for the one with awareness it is broken. Hence, because the unaware are not liberated from birth, and so forth, they are said to be dead, whether [factually] dead or alive.

Those who are aware, having developed the characteristic of awareness, in a short time realize the Paths and the Fruits, and do not take birth in a second or third life. Hence, they, whether living or dead, do not, indeed, die.

## They who are unaware are as dead: *ye pamattā yathā matā*

Because those who are unaware are [already] dead by the death that is unawareness, they are like those who have died by the interruption of the faculty of life—destitute of consciousness, like pieces of wood. [Where] such [persons are] householders, in them no consciousness ever arises to this effect: "We will give alms; we will observe the precepts; we will do the acts of the *uposatha* retreat." [Where they are] members of the religious order, no consciousness will ever arise in them to this effect: "We will perform the duties toward teachers and preceptors; we will enjoin on ourselves the constituents of ascetic practice *(dhutaṅga)*,[6] we will develop meditativeness." Thus they are not different(7) from the dead; whence it is said: "They who are heedless are as dead."

[22.]

## Having known this distinctly, those who are wise: *etaṃ visesato ñatvā appamādamhi paṇḍitā*

"To the unaware there is no way out of the whirl; to the one who is aware there is a way out"—knowing this distinction distinctly. Who [are they who] know this distinction? The wise, the sagacious, the insightful who, living by awareness, develop [that] awareness [evermore]—they understand this distinct point in this way.

## Rejoice in awareness: *appamāde pamodanti*

They, knowing so, rejoice in that awareness of theirs; with delighted appearance, they become satisfied and joyful.

## Delighted in the pasture of the noble ones: *ariyānaṃ gocare ratā*

Being so joyful in awareness, they develop it and become delighted, engaged in and attracted by the thirty-seven qualities contributing to enlightenment,[8] such as the fourfold establishment of mindfulness, and the ninefold dhamma that transcends the world[9]—which constitute the pastureland of the noble ones, Buddhas, Paccekabuddhas, and their disciples.[10] That is the meaning.

[23.]

## Those meditators: *te jhāyino*

They, the wise who have awareness, are meditators by virtue of the twofold meditation—namely, [1] the contemplation concerned with objects constituted by the eight attainments[11] and [2] the contemplation concerned with the [essential] characteristics [of existence], constituted by the Paths and the Fruits of insight.

## Persevering: *sātatikā*

Those who have maintained physical and mental enterprise constantly, from setting forth [in the religious quest] up to [the attainment of] the Path of Arahantship.

## Forever firm of enterprise: *niccaṃ daḷhaparakkamā*

"There will be no stabilization of enterprise until one arrives at that which can be reached by manly stamina, by manly enterprise, by manly endeavor," so it has been said; [what the phrase here means is] those endowed with such enterprise, with firm endeavor maintained constantly[(12)] without backing out midway.

## Touch: *phusanti*

[The] two kinds of contact [with Nibbāna are implied] in this context, [1] contact by understanding, [2] contact by way of result. The four Paths are known as "contact by way of understanding" and the four Fruits are known as "contact by way of result." Of these, "contact by way of result" is intended here.

## Those steadfast ones: *dhīrā*

The wise ones realizing Nibbāna by the noble Fruit, make contact with it,—that is, realize Nibbāna, through "contact by way of result."

## Incomparable release from bonds: *yogakkhemaṃ anuttaraṃ*

The state of release, of freedom from the fear [resulting] from the four bonds[13] that submerge the multitude of people in the whirl, is incomparable because it is the foremost of all dhammas, ordinary and transcendent.

24. Fame increases for the one who stands alert,
Mindful, and of pure deeds;
Who with due consideration acts, restrained,
Who lives dhamma, being aware. (2.4)

*uṭṭhānavato satīmato sucikammassa nisammakārino*
*saññatassa ca dhammajīvino appamattassa yaso 'bhivaḍḍhati.*

## For the one who stands alert: *uṭṭhānavato*

For one having steadfast enterprise.

## Mindful: *satīmato*

Possessing mindfulness.

## Of pure deeds: *sucikammassa*

Who is endowed with blameless and faultless physical actions, and so forth.

## Who with due consideration acts: *nisammakārino*

For one who performs all actions after giving attention and careful consideration,(14) like treating a disease after giving consideration to the causative factors, thinking: "If it happens in this way, I will act thus" or, "When this deed is done in this way, this is what will happen";

## Restrained: *saññatassa*

Restrained through body, and so forth [i.e., body, speech, and thought], having no faults;

## Who lives dhamma: *dhammajīvno*

Living, if a householder, by agriculture, cowherding, and the like, avoiding [such practices as] the use of false weights, and so forth; if not a householder, maintaining life by mendicancy, righteously and peaceably, avoiding such occupations as medical practice, an emissary's work, and the like;

## Aware: *appamattassa*

Not bereft of mindfulness;

## Fame increases: *yaso 'bhivaḍḍhati*

Fame, constituted by wealth, enjoyment, and honor as well as by praise and glory, increases.

25. By standing alert, by awareness,
By restraint and control too,
The intelligent one could make an island
That a flood does not overwhelm. (2.5)

*uṭṭhānen 'appamādena saññemena damena ca*
*dīpaṃ kayirātha medhāvī yaṃ ogho nābhikīrati.*(15)

## One could make an island: *dīpaṃ kayirātha*
## By standing alert: *uṭṭhānena*

That is, by enterprise, *by awareness (appamādena)*, by not being bereft of mindfulness, *by restraint, by control (saññamena damena)* of the senses.

## The intelligent one: *medhāvī*

Endowed with insight *(paññā)*, which is the sap of dhamma, on account of the four qualities that are its causative factors;

## Could make an island: *dīpaṃ kayirātha*

In this ocean of *saṃsāra*, very deep because a supporting ground [a bottom] is hard to find [in it], one could make [for oneself] the island that is the Fruit of Arahantship, which becomes one's supporting ground.

What kind of an island?

## That a flood does not overwhelm: *yaṃ ogho nābhikīrati*

[An island] that not even the fourfold flood[16] of defilements can disperse and destroy, for Arahantship cannot be dispersed by the "flood."

26. People deficient in wisdom, childish ones,
Engage in unawareness.
But the wise one guards awareness
Like the greatest treasure. (2.6)

27. Engage not in unawareness,
Nor in intimacy with sensual delight.
Meditating, the one who is aware
Attains extensive ease. (2.7)

*pamādam anuyuñjanti bālā dummedhino janā*
*appamādaṃ ca medhāvī dhanaṃ seṭṭhaṃ va rakkhati.*[17]

*mā pamādam anuyuñjetha mā kāmaratisanthavaṃ*
*appamatto hi jhāyanto pappoti vipulaṃ sukhaṃ.*

[26.]

### Childish ones: *bālā*

Those who are possessed of puerility, who do not know what is beneficial for this world and for the world beyond;

### Deficient in wisdom: *dummedhino*

Lacking in discernment; not seeing the ill effect of unawareness;

### Engage in unawareness: *pamādam anuyuñjanti*

They let [such conduct] prevail—that is, spend their time in unawareness.

### The wise one: *medhāvī*

The sagacious person, who is endowed with insight, the dhamma-sap;

### Guards awareness: *appamādaṃ . . . rakkhati*

*Like the greatest (seṭṭhaṃ)*, exalted, seven-treasure wealth, inherited in the family line.[18]

"With the aid of exalted wealth, we may attain the bliss of sensual pleasures, nourish son and wife, and clear the path leading to the world beyond"—as those who see the positive value of wealth, on such grounds look after it, so the sagacious person also [sees] positive value in awareness, thinking: "Being aware I will obtain(19) the first meditative-absorption, and so forth, attain the Paths and Fruits, provide the three forms of knowledge and the six forms of higher knowledge."[20] Seeing [so, the wise one] guards awareness *like the greatest treasure (dhanaṃ setthaṃ va)*. That is the meaning.

[27.]

### (Engage) not in unawareness: *mā pamādam (anuyuñjetha)*

This means: hence do you not engage [yourselves] in unawareness, do not spend [your] time with unawareness.

### (Nor in) intimacy with sensual delights: *kāmaratisanthavaṃ*

This means: do not engage in, do not think of, do not obtain [for yourself] intimacy with cravings too—that is, attachment to pleasures whether derived from things or from defilements.

### The one who is aware: *appamatto hi*

The one who, on account of [having] awareness [always] present, is not unaware, the *meditating (jhāyanto)* person, attains the *extensive (vipulaṃ)*, the lofty *ease (sukhaṃ)* of Nibbāna.

28. When the wise one by awareness expels unawareness,
Having ascended the palace of wisdom,
He, free from sorrow, steadfast,
The sorrowing folk observes, the childish,
As one standing on a mountain
[Observes] those standing on the ground below. (2.8)

*pamādaṃ appamādena yadā nudati paṇḍito*
*paññāpāsādam āruyha asoko sokiniṃ pajaṃ*
*pabbataṭṭho va bhummaṭṭhe dīro bāle avekkhati.*

## Expels: *nudati*

Just as fresh water that flows into a pond agitates the old water and, without giving it quarter, expels it and drives it away as it escapes from one end to another—when in the same way the sagacious person, fostering the characteristic of awareness, without making room for unawareness, *expels (nudati)* it, drives it away by means of awareness, then he, who [thus] has expelled unawareness, fulfilling the conduct that befits him and through the stairway of that conduct, *having*, as it were, *ascended (āruyha)*:

## The palace of wisdom: *paññāpāsādam*

Namely, the clear divine eye[21]—a palace because of its great loftiness—and being free from sorrow because one got rid of sorrow's arrow shaft;

## Observes: *avekkhati*

That is, sees with the divine eye;

## The sorrowing folk: *sokiniṃ pajaṃ*

The crowd of beings dying and being [re-]born, [sorrowing] because the arrow of suffering has not been got rid of [by them]; what [is that seeing ] like? [It is] *as one standing on a mountain (pabbataṭṭho va)* [seeing] *those standing on the ground below: bhummaṭṭhe.*

As one who stands atop a mountain [sees] without any effort those standing on the ground below, or as one standing on the top of a palace [sees] the buildings surrounding the palace, in the same way he the *steadfast (dhīro)*, sagacious person, the great being in whom intoxicants are extinct, sees *the childish (bāle)*—those in whom the seeds of the whirl are not eradicated—in the process of dying and being [re-]born.

29. Among those unaware, the one aware,
Among the sleepers, the wide-awake,
The one with great wisdom moves on,
As a racehorse who leaves behind a nag. (2.9)

*appamatto pamattesu suttesu bahujāgaro*
*abalassaṃ va sīghasso hitvā yāti sumedhaso.*

## The one aware: *appamatto*

The one who is endowed with awareness due to attainment of extensive mindfulness and in whom intoxicants are extinct.

## Among those unaware: *pamattesu*

Among beings who are in the state of having abandoned mindfulness.

## Among the sleepers: *suttesu*

Those who are "sleeping" in all the modes of deportment due to lack of the wakefulness [called] mindfulness.[22]

## Wide-awake: *bahujāgaro*

Abiding in great, extensive mindfulness, in wakefulness.

## As (a racehorse) a nag: *abalassam va (sīghasso)*

As a noble horse from Sindhu, swift of speed, [overtakes] a lame-legged, weak horse that has lost its swiftness of speed.

## The one with great wisdom: *sumedhaso*

The one who has supreme insight, *having left behind (hitvā)* such a person [as described earlier], *moves on (yati)* quickly in textual learning as well as in [religious] attainment. When the person of slow intelligence is attempting to memorize one discourse *(sutta)*, the one with great intelligence memorizes a whole chapter *(vagga)*: thus [the latter], having left [the former] behind, goes on in learning. Even as the person of slow wits is attempting to make the night lodgings and day lodgings, and so forth, and is repeating the topics of meditation *(kammaṭṭhānas)*[23] learned, the one with great wisdom enters, even [though] in the morning, the night lodgings and day lodgings made by another, contemplates the topics of meditation, and "brings under arm" the ninefold dhamma that transcends the world and puts an end to all defilements. Thus the one overtakes the other in attainment. [That is to say,] having discarded and relinquished the whirl's track, he indeed proceeds, moving beyond the whirl.

30. By awareness, Maghavan
To supremacy among the gods rose.
Awareness they praise;
Always censured is unawareness. (2.10)

*appamādena maghavā devānaṃ seṭṭhataṃ gato*
*appamādaṃ pasaṃsanti pamādo garahito sadā.*

## By awareness: *appamādena*

By means of awareness exercised, as in the case of [Maghavan's] clearing a section of the ground, and so forth, at Macalagāma.[24]

## Maghavan: *maghavā*

The young *brāhmaṇa* Magha, who is now known as Maghavan [Indra];

## To supremacy among the gods arose: *devanaṃ seṭṭhataṃ gato*

By virtue of kingship of the two *deva* worlds.

## They praise: *pasaṃsanti*

The wise, such as the Buddhas, and so forth, praise, extol awareness alone. Why? Because it is the cause for the attainment of every distinction, ordinary as well as transcendent.[25]

## Always censured is unawareness: *pamādo garahito sadā*

Unawareness is of course always censured, deprecated, by those noble ones. Why? Because it is the root condition for all calamities. Every [calamity], whether human adversity or birth in a state of woe, is indeed based on unawareness.

31. The bhikkhu who delights in awareness,
Who sees in unawareness the fearful,
Goes, burning, like a fire,
The fetter subtle and gross. (2.11)

*appamādarato bhikkhu pamāde bhayadassivā*(26)
*saṃyojanaṃ aṇuṃ thūlaṃ ḍahaṃ aggīva gacchati.*

### Who delights in awareness: *appamādarato*

Delighting in awareness, deeply taken up with awareness, spending time in awareness.

### Who sees in unawareness the fearful: *pamāde bhayadassivā*

Seeing in unawareness the fearful, such as birth in hell *(niraya)*, or the like; or, seeing unawareness as [something to] fear because it is the root cause of birth in such places.

### The fetter: *saṃyojanaṃ*

The tenfold fetter,[27] which can submerge [beings] in the whirl, which yokes or binds one to suffering in the whirl.

### Subtle and gross: *aṇuṃ thūlaṃ*

Big and small.

### Goes, burning, like a fire: *ḍahaṃ aggīva gacchati*

As a fire goes on burning the [fuel that is its] substratum, [be it] big or small, in the same way:

### The bhikkhu, who delights in awareness: *appamādarato bhikkhu*

Goes on burning this fetter with the fire of understanding obtained by mindfulness—that is, goes about making it incapable of arising.

32. The bhikkhu who delights in awareness,
Who sees in unawareness the fearful—
He is not liable to suffer fall;
In Nibbāna's presence is such a one. (2.12)

*appamādarato bhikkhu pamāde bhayadassivā*
*abhabbo parihānāya nibbānass' eva santike.*

### Not liable to suffer fall: *abhabbo parihānāya*

A bhikkhu who is so [mindful] is not liable to fall either from the contemplative processes of *samatha* and *vipassanā* or from the Paths and Fruits—that is, does not fall away from what has been reached, and will attain what has not [yet] been reached.

## In Nibbāna's presence: *nibbānass' eva santike*

He is indeed in the presence of Nibbāna, [the cessation] of defilements, as well as of perfect Nibbāna without substratum.[28]

# CHAPTER III

## The Mind
## *Citta-vaggo*

33. The quivering, wavering mind,
Hard to guard, hard to check,
The sagacious one makes straight,
Like a fletcher, an arrow shaft. (3.1)

34. Like a water creature
Plucked from its watery home and thrown on land,
This mind flaps;
[Fit] to discard [is] Māra's sway. (3.2)

*phandanaṃ capalaṃ cittaṃ dūrakkhaṃ dunnivārayaṃ*
*ujuṃ karoti medhāvī usukāro va tejanaṃ.*

*vārijo va thale khitto okamokata ubbhato*
*pariphandat' idaṃ cittaṃ māradheyyaṃ pahatave.*(1)

[33.]

### Quivering: *phandanaṃ*

Vacillating with regard to objects *(ārammaṇa)* such as form, and the like.

### Wavering: *capalaṃ*

Because [it is] unable to stay on one subject, like a village child not staying in any single mien, [the mind is called] "wavering."

### Mind: *cittaṃ*

Mind *(citta)* is consciousness *(viññāna)*; it is so called because it is varied(2) by way of plane, base, field [or object], [related] action, and so forth.[3]

### Hard to guard: *dūrakkhaṃ*

Because [it is] hard to keep fixed on a single wholesome object,[4] like a [rambling] bull that eats away the corn when the corn is thick.

### Hard to check: *dunnivārayaṃ*

Because [it is] hard to stop [when] moving on to "the dissimilar object."[5]

### Like a fletcher, an arrow shaft: *usukāro va tejanaṃ*

A fletcher brings a stick from the forest, strips it of bark, smears it with rice gruel, heats it in a vessel of charcoals, presses it on a wooden spike, and makes it unbent and straight and "fit to shoot a hair with." Having done so, [the fletcher] displays his skill before kings and ministers, and wins great favor and honor. In exactly the same way, a wise, sagacious, intelligent person [treats] the mind that has the nature of quivering, and so forth. He makes it "free of bark"—that is, free of coarse defilements by means of the *dhutaṅga* practice of forest-living, "wets" it with the "oil" of faith,[6] "heats" it with physical and mental enterprise, "presses" it on the spike of tranquility and insight-meditations, and:

### Makes straight: *ujuṃ karoti*

Unwarped, steady. And having done so, he contemplates the *saṅkhāras*,[7] breaks up the great mass of ignorance, "brings under [his] arm" [achieves] the distinction of the three forms of knowledge,[8] the six forms of "higher knowledge,"[9] and the nine dhammas that transcend the world; [he thus] achieves the state of being "eminently worthy to receive gifts."

[34.]

### Like a water creature . . . thrown on land: *vārijo va thale khitto*

Like a fish cast on dry ground by hand or net or any such [means].

### Plucked from its watery home: *okamokata ubbhato*

*Oka* means "water" in such a usage as "with robes filled by *oka*," and "home" in such a usage as "leaving *oka* and wandering without a home." Here both are applicable; [hence] the meaning is "plucked from its home, which is water."

### This mind flaps: *pariphandat' idaṃ cittaṃ*

So flutters this mind, attached to its "home" of the fivefold strand of sensuality,[10] being taken out of it and subjected to the ardor of mental and physical enterprise of insight and meditational exertion, for the purpose of discarding the whirl, which is the sway of Māra[11]—that is, it is not able to hold itself steady [in that condition]. Even though this is so, the sagacious one, without "quitting post," makes the mind straight, competent in the task, in the manner stated. That is the meaning.

There is also another way [to interpret this verse]. This mind, which is under the sway of Māra,—which stands without having quit the whirl of defilements[12]—flutters like that fish. Therefore "the sway of Māra" due to which it flutters—namely, the whirl of defilements—should be discarded.

35. Commendable is the taming
Of mind, which is hard to hold down,
Nimble, alighting wherever it wants,
Mind subdued brings ease. (3.3)

*dunniggahassa lahuno yatthakāmanipātino*
*cittassa damatho sādhu cittaṃ dantaṃ sukhāvahaṃ.*

## Hard to hold down: *dunniggahaṃ*

Mind is hard to hold down in the sense that it is restrained only with difficulty. It is "nimble" *(lahuṃ)* in the sense that it arises quickly, and quickly ceases to be. Of that [mind] which is hard to hold down, nimble, [taming is profitable].

## Alighting wherever it wants: *yatthakāmanipātino*

Having the nature of alighting at any place whatever. Because it does not know: "This is a thing possible to get; this is not a thing possible to get; this is a suitable thing; this is an unsuitable thing"; and also because it does not consider caste, clan, or age, but wherever it wishes, it settles—in that sense it is called "alighting wherever it wants." Of the mind *(cittassa)* that is such:

## The taming is profitable: *damatho sādhu*

The state of being controlled by the four noble Paths is good; having it so made that it becomes steady is good. For what reason? The mind controlled, made steady, brings the ease of Path and Fruit, and also the ease of Nibbāna—which is the most supreme truth.

36. The sagacious one may tend the mind,
Hard to be seen, extremely subtle,
Alighting wherever it wants.
The tended mind brings ease. (3.4)

*sududdasaṃ sunipuṇaṃ yatthakāmanipatinaṃ*
*cittaṃ rakkhetha medhāvī cittaṃ guttaṃ sukhāvahaṃ.*

### Hard to be seen: *sududdasaṃ*

Extremely imperceptible.

### Extremely subtle: *sunipuṇaṃ*

Very subtle, extremely fine.

### Alighting wherever it wants: *yatthakāmanipātinaṃ*

Having the nature of alighting, settling down, anywhere at all—that is, on things possible and impossible to get, proper and improper,[(13)] without taking into account [matters] such as caste, and so forth.

### The sagacious one may tend the mind: *cittaṃ rakkhetha medhāvī*

It is not the case that a foolish person who is "blind" and childish is able to guard his mind. Having become a slave of [the] mind one gets into error and distress. On the other hand only a wise, sagacious one is able to guard the mind. Hence you too guard the mind, for:

### Mind tended brings ease: *cittaṃ guttaṃ sukhāvahaṃ*

It brings about the ease of the Paths, of the Fruits, and of Nibbāna.

37. They who will restrain the mind,
Far-ranging, roaming alone,
Incorporeal, lying ahiding—
They are released from Māra's bonds. (3.5)

*dūraṅgamaṃ ekacaraṃ asarīraṃ guhasayaṃ*
*ye cittaṃ saññamessanti mokkhanti mārabandhanā.*

## Far-ranging: *dūraṅgamaṃ*

Of mind, there is no [spatial] movement, in the direction of the east, and so forth, not even so much as [the width of] a spider's thread. [And yet] it receives even the object that is far away—in the sense that it is called "far-ranging."

## Roaming alone: *ekacaraṃ*

It is not the case that more than one consciousness [lit. seven or eight consciousnesses] can arise at a single instant, [as if] bound together into a sheaf. When arising, consciousness arises singly; when it dies away, [a successor consciousness] singly arises again. Hence it [mind] roams alone.

## Incorporeal: *asarīraṃ*

Because there is no bodily structure for mind, and no distinction of form such as [that it is] blue, and so on, it is called incorporeal.

## Lying ahiding [lit. lying in a cave]: *guhāsayaṃ*

It is described thus because it occurs dependent on the "heart element" *(hadaya-rūpa)*. "Cave" here is the "cave" [of the body, which is made up] of the four great physical elements [earth, water, heat, and air].[14]

## They who: *ye*

The men or women, lay persons or those that have gone forth [into the religious order];

## Will restrain the mind: *cittaṃ saññamessanti*

Not allowing unborn defilements to be born and getting rid of defilements born by the neglect of mindfulness—that is, those who will make the mind restrained and undistracted:

## Are released from Māra's bonds: *mokkhanti mārabandhanā*

Due to their not having the bond of defilements, all of them will be freed of the "threefold whirl," which is known as the bond of Māra.[15]

38. For one of unsteady mind,
Who knows not dhamma true,
Whose serenity is adrifting,
Wisdom becomes not full. (3.6)

39. No fear is there for the wide-awake
Who has mind undamped
And thought unsmitten—
The wholesome and the detrimental left behind. (3.7)

*anavaṭṭhitacittassa saddhammaṃ avijānato*
*pariplavapasādassa paññā na paripūrati.*

*anavassutacittassa anavāhatacetaso*
*puññapāpapahīnassa natthi jāgarato bhayaṃ.*

[38.]

### For one of unsteady mind: *anavaṭṭhitacittassa*

Never steady or constant is the mind, whose ever [it is]. The person who [that is, whose mind] does not stay constant anywhere, like a gourd placed on a horse's back, like a stump erected on a heap of chaff, like a *kadamba* flower on a bald head, is "one of unsteady mind," whether a disciple of the Buddha,(16) whether a naked recluse *(acelaka)*, an *ājīvaka*, a *nigaṇṭha*, or [a member of] an ascetic [sect].[17] [The reference in the dative case means] "for that [person] with unsteady mind."

### Who knows not dhamma true: *saddhammaṃ avijānato*

[For] one who does not understand this true dhamma with its divisions into the thirty-seven qualities contributing to enlightenment;[18]

### Whose serenity is adrifting: *pariplavapasādassa*

Because of little faith, or of "drifting" faith, or of faith falling away;

### Wisdom becomes not full: *paññā na paripūrati*

That is, wisdom of the various kinds, such as that of the sensual sphere and of the fine material sphere. This illumines [the point] that when even [wisdom] of the sensual sphere does not become full, how will [wisdom] of the fine material sphere become complete, or that of the nonmaterial sphere, or that which transcends the worlds?

[39.]

### Who has mind undamped: *anavassutacittassa*

For one whose mind is not made wet with passion.

## And thought unsmitten: *ananvāhatacetaso*

In this reference, "One whose mind is smitten is the one in whom defilement [lit. the wasteland] has arisen,"(19) the fact is stated that mind is "attacked" by ill will. Here the meaning is "of the one whose mind is not attacked by ill will."

## The wholesome and detrimental left behind: *puññapāpapahīnassa*

For the [Arahant with] influxes extinct who has discarded by the fourth Path the wholesome *(puñña)* and the detrimental *(pāpa)*.[20]

## No fear is there for the wide-awake: *natthi jāgarato bhayaṃ*

What is mentioned is the lack of fear of the [Arahant with] influxes extinct just as of one who is wide-awake. He is said to be *awake* due to being endowed with the five qualities of wakefulness, such as faith, and so on.[21] Hence for him there is no fear from defilements, whether he is asleep or awake, due to the nonreturn of defilements. Defilements do not pursue him, due to the nonreturn of those [qualities] that have been dispelled by means of each of the [four] Paths. For this very reason, [in an authoritative text] it is said: "He does not return to those defilements that have been dispelled by the Path of Stream Entrance, he does not go back [to them]. Likewise he does not return, does not go back to, those defilements that have been dispelled by the Path of the Once Returner, the Path of the Non-Returner, the Path of Arahantship."

40. Knowing this body as a pot of clay,
Securing this mind as a citadel,
One may fight Māra with wisdom's weapon,
Guard what has been gained—and be unattached. (3.8)

*kumbhūpamaṃ kāyam imaṃ viditvā*
*nagarūpamaṃ cittam idaṃ ṭhapetvā*
*yodhetha māraṃ paññāvudhena*
*jitaṃ ca rakkhe anivesano siyā.*

## Knowing this body: *kāyam imaṃ viditvā*

Namely, the aggregate of [physical elements such as] hair, and so forth.

## As a pot of clay: *kumbhūpamaṃ*

Like a vessel [made] by a potter—in the sense that it is powerless and weak, [that it does] not [last] for [a long] time, [that it is] temporary.

## As a citadel: *nagarūpaṃ*

A city having a deep moat, encircled by a wall, containing gates and watchtowers, is firm from outside; inside, it is fitted out with well-apportioned streets, squares, crossroads, and shopping areas. Thieves come from without, saying "Let us loot it!" [But] being unable to enter, [they] remain(22) as if confronting, and being checked by, a [mighty] rock. As one standing in the city [attacks such] a horde of robbers with many kinds of weaponry—single-edged [weapons], and so on—in exactly the same way,

## Securing: *thapetvā*

Making firm his "insight-mind" (mind steeped in *vipassanā*), as if it were a citadel, the sagacious householder:

## May fight: *yodetha*

That is, strike, each Māra in the form of defilements *(kilesmāra)*,[23] warding off each such Māra which [only] the Paths can slay;

## With wisdom's weapon: *paññāvudhena*

Which consists of insight *(vipassanā)* and the noble Path *(magga)*.

## Guard what has been gained: *jitaṃ ca rakkhe*

[1] Resorting to the suitable lodgings, seasons, foods, associates, dhamma-hearing, and so forth, [2] attaining each successive [religious] attainment, and [3] rising(24) from such [attainment], contemplating the *saṅkhāra*s with clear mind—[thus the sagacious] should guard what has been gained—namely, the initial insight that has been engendered [in this process].

## And be unattached: *anivesano siyā*

He should be without clinging [to those very attainments]. Just as a warrior [king] erects a fortress at the head of the battleground and [issuing from it] fights his enemies; [then] being hungry or thirsty, he enters the fortress either when his armor has loosened or when his weapons have fallen; then he rests, takes food and drink, tightens his armor, takes up his weapons and returns [to the front]. [There,] fighting, he crushes the enemy ranks, wins new victories, and holds [the ground] that has [already] been gained. [But] if he were to stay within the fortress, resting and enjoying that [food and drink], he would [only] be allowing his kingdom to fall under [his] foe's control.

In exactly the same way a bhikkhu can guard the initial insight that has been gained, [by] contemplating the *saṅkhāras* with clear mind after obtaining the attainments and rising from them again and again [that is, contemplation following attainment repeatedly]. One then conquers Māra in the form of defilements *(kilesmāra)* by attaining the Path thereafter. On the other hand if one evinces delight in the attainment alone, but does not repeatedly contemplate the *saṅkhāras* with clear mind, then one cannot make the breakthrough to Path and Fruit. Hence, guarding what ought to be guarded, one should be free of "abiding," one should not make an "abode" of the attainments and dwell therein—should cherish no attachment thereto.

41. Soon indeed
This body on the earth will lie,
Pitched aside, without consciousness,
Like a useless chip of wood. (3.9)

*aciraṃ vat' ayaṃ kāyo paṭhaviṃ adhisessati*
*chuddho apetaviññāṇo*(25) *niratthaṃ va kaliṅgaraṃ.*

## Soon indeed: *aciraṃ vata*

Before long, O bhikkhu, this body will lie upon the earth; it will go to sleep upon the earth, which [too] is lying in its natural immobile condition [lit., sleeping in its natural sleep].

## Pitched aside: *chuddho*

Thrown away. [This] indicates that it will lie empty due to being without consciousness.

## Like a useless chip of wood: *niratthaṃ va kaliṅgaraṃ*

Like a piece of wood of no help [to anyone], useless. People who are in need of a stock of timber go into the forest, cut off [pieces of wood] and gather [them together], the straight in its straight shape and the crooked in its crooked. The rest, the hollow, the decayed, and the knotted [pieces], they cut off and leave there. Others who need timber come there, but there are none who take these [cut-off chips]; they look [at them] and take only what is of use [to them]. The rest remain on the ground. It would even be possible to turn that [wood] by various methods into a bed component, footstool, or bench. But, out of the thirty-two parts in this body of ours, there is not one part that may come into use as a bed component or in any other helpful guise. Within a few days it will lie on the earth bereft of consciousness entirely, like a useless chip of wood.

42. What a foe may do to a foe,
Or a hater to a hater—
Far worse than that
The mind ill held may do to him. (3.10)
(The commentary takes line 1 to read:
What a thief may do to a thief.)

*diso disaṃ yaṃ taṃ*(26) *kayirā verī vā pana verinaṃ*
*micchāpaṇihitaṃ cittaṃ pāpiyo naṃ tato kare.*

### A foe . . . to a foe/A thief . . . to a thief: *diso disaṃ*

The rest of the phrase is "having seen."

### What . . . may do: *yaṃ taṃ kayirā*

The distress, the harm, that [one robber] would do to the other [lit. to him]. The same procedure [should be followed] in the second line too [that is, it should be construed: "what a hater, having seen a hater, may do"]. What is meant is this: A certain robber, treacherous to friends, who wrongs [another person] with regard to family, landholdings, and livestock, sees that that other is also doing wrong to him in the same way [that is, as a robber].

### Or a hater: *verī vā pana*

Seeing a [certain other] hater who has formed an enmity [toward him] for some reason—whatever distress and harm [such a robber or hater] would inflict on that [other person concerned], due to the hardness of his [heart] and his fierceness: [e.g.,] he may oppress his family, destroy his lands, and so on or even deprive him of his life—

### Far worse than that the mind ill held may do to him: *micchāpaṇihitaṃ cittaṃ pāpiyo naṃ tato kare*

A mind ill held, because [it is] harmfully established in the ten paths of unwholesome deeds,[27] may inflict on that person an even greater harm [or make that person an even greater wretch]. An enemy or a hater would create misery, or bring about death, to another enemy or hater, in the ways stated above, only in [this] present life. But the mind harmfully established in the ten paths of unwholesome deeds [not only] brings distress and harm in this visible life, [but also] it throws one into the four states of woe and does not allow one to raise [one's] head in even a hundred thousand lives.[28]

43. Not mother, father, nor even other kinsmen,
May do that [good to him—]
Far better than that
The mind well held may do to him. (3.11)

*na taṃ mātā pitā kayirā*[(29)] *aññe vā pi ca ñātakā*
*sammāpaṇihitaṃ cittaṃ seyyaso naṃ tato kare.*

## Not . . . that: *na taṃ*

Neither could one's mother, nor [one's] father, nor other relations do that thing [which may bring the highest good to one's life].

## The (mind) well held: *sammāpaṇihitaṃ (cittaṃ)*

[The mind] well established in the ten paths of wholesome deeds.

## Far better than that . . . may do to him: *seyyaso naṃ tato kare*

Due to that reason [namely, that it is well held], [it] would make him—[indeed it] does make [him]—still better—that is, a better, nobler person: this is the meaning.

Parents, giving wealth to their children, can offer them riches that maintain their life in comfort, [even] without doing any work, in just this life [lit. in only one existence]. Even the parents of Visākhā,[30] who were so rich and wealthy, gave her [what sufficed for] livelihood with comfort in just one existence. There are no parents who can give their children the glory of universal kingship over the four continents, let alone the glory of heaven or that of the first meditative absorption, and so on. It is impossible even to speak of [parents] giving the bliss that transcends the world. But even all this bliss the well-held mind can grant. Hence it is said that it "may do far better to him."

# CHAPTER IV

## Flowers
## *Puppha-vaggo*

44. Who shall conquer this earth and the realm of Yama,
This [human realm] together with [the realm of] gods?
Who shall pluck a well-taught dhamma word
Like an expert, a flower? (4.1)

(The commentary takes line 1 to read:
Who shall discern this earth and the realm of Yama?)

45. A learner shall conquer this earth and the realm of Yama,
This [human realm] together with [the realm of] gods.
A learner shall pluck a well-taught dhamma word
Like an expert, a flower. (4.2)
(The commentary takes line 1 to read:
A learner shall discern this earth and the realm of Yama.)

*ko imaṃ paṭhaviṃ vijessati*(1)
*yamalokaṃ ca imaṃ sadevakaṃ*
*ko dhammapadaṃ sudesitaṃ*
*kusalo puppham iva pacessati.*

*sekho paṭhaviṃ vijessati*
*yamalokaṃ ca imaṃ sadevakaṃ*
*sekho dhammapadaṃ sudesitaṃ*
*kusalo puppham iva pacessati.*
(The commentary has *vicessati*,
"shall discern," for *vijessati.*)

[44.]

### Who shall discern this earth: *ko imaṃ paṭhaviṃ vicessati*

The meaning is: Who will understand, with personal knowledge, will penetratively see, realize, this "earth," that is one's existence?

### And the realm of Yama: *yamalokaṃ ca*

And also the fourfold world that constitutes the state of woe.[2]

### This [human realm] together with [the realm of] gods: *imaṃ sadevakaṃ*

And this human world together with the world of gods. Who will conquer, understand, penetratively see, realize [this world]?—That is the question asked [lit. thus he asks].

### Who shall pluck . . . like an expert, a flower: *kusalo puppham iva ko pacessati*

The meaning is: As an expert maker of garlands picking a flower, who will gather, understand, examine, penetratively see and realize:

### A well-taught dhamma word: *dhammapadaṃ sudesitaṃ*

The dhamma-word—namely, the dhamma of thirty-seven factors conducive to enlightenment,[3] [which is described as] "well-taught" because it has been explained in accordance with its true nature.

[45.]

### A learner: *sekho*

The seven kinds of person from the one in the Path of Stream Entrance to the Path of Arahantship[4] constitute the seven kinds of learner, because [they are in the process of] learning the threefold training—namely, the training in [1] higher virtue, [2] higher integration, and [3] higher insight.[5]

### Shall discern this earth: *paṭhaviṃ vicessati*

[The learner] shall win—that is, understand, penetratively see, and realize—this "earth" that is one's existence, removing desire and attachment from it by means of the path of Arahantship. And the selfsame [learner] will understand, penetratively see, and realize [the nature of] *this* world of humans *together with the gods (imaṃ sadevakaṃ) and* also *the realm of Yama (yamalokaṃ ca)*, which is of the kind mentioned [above, comment on st. 44].

## A learner: *sekho*

The selfsame seven kinds of persons-in-learning.

## (Like) an expert, (a flower): *kusalo (puppham iva)*

As an expert garland-maker enters a flower garden and gathers flowers that are beautiful and nicely grown, avoiding tender buds and flowers that are faded, warped, or attacked by insects:

## Shall pluck (a well-taught dhamma word): *(dhammapadaṃ sudesitaṃ) pacessati*

In just the same way they shall, with insight, pluck—that is, gather, examine, penetratively see, and realize—this well-explained and well-proclaimed dhamma word that is conducive to enlightenment.

46. Knowing this body to be like foam,
Awakening to its mirage nature,
Cutting out Māra's flowers, one may go
Beyond the sight of the King of Death. (4.3)

*pheṇūpamaṃ kāyam imaṃ viditvā*
*marīcidhammaṃ abhisambudhāno*
*chetvāna mārassa papupphakāni*[(6)]
*adassanaṃ maccurājassa gacche.*

## (Knowing) this (body to be like foam): *(pheṇūpamaṃ kāyam) imaṃ (viditvā)*

Knowing that this body—that is, the aggregate of [physical elements] such as hair—is like a ball of foam, in the sense that it is powerless and weak and does not last for a long time, that it is transient.

## Awakening to its mirage nature: *marīcidhammaṃ adhisambudhāno*

To those who stand far away, a mirage appears as having form, as tangible; but, as they come near [it], it is realized as empty, hollow, and intangible.

Awakening to, understanding, knowing that, similarly, this body too is of mirage nature in the sense of passing away and reappearing at every instant. The meaning here is "awakening to" *(abhisambudhāno)*, knowing, understanding, that [mirage-nature].

### (Cutting out Māra's) flowers: *(chetvāna mārassa) papupphakāni*

Having, by means of the noble Path, cut out the whirls of the three levels of existence, which are called the flowers of Māra;[7]

### One may go beyond the sight of the King of Death: *adassanaṃ maccurājassa gacche*

The monk in whom the influxes are extinct may go beyond Māra's sight, [beyond Māra's] range—that is, to the great, deathless Nibbāna.[8]

47. Death takes away
The man with attached mind,
Plucking only flowers,
Like a great flood, a sleeping village. (4.4)

*pupphāni heva pacinantaṃ byāsattamanasaṃ naraṃ*
*suttaṃ gāmaṃ mahoghova maccu ādāya gacchati.*

### The man with attached mind: *byāsattamanasaṃ naraṃ*

The one whose mind is attached to what has been obtained and what has been [desired but] not obtained.

### Plucking only flowers: *pupphāni heva pacinantaṃ*

This is what is said: A garland-maker goes into a garden of flowers and, thinking, "I will gather flowers," takes flowers from that [garden]. [Then] wishing for another [flower] plant and another, he turns his mind all over the garden, thinking: "I will gather flowers from here too." [But] without gathering flowers from there, he turns his mind(9) to [yet] another place and procrastinates, picking from that [other] plant [as well]. In just the same way someone gets down among the "five strands of sensuality" *(kāmaguṇa)*,[10] which are like a garden of flowers. When one has obtained a visible object that is pleasing, one wishes for a certain [other "object"] out of pleasant sounds, smells, tastes, and tangible things. Having obtained one of them, one desires for yet another. Or else having obtained a visible object, one keeps on relishing that very thing, not wanting [any] other;(11) or else [one accords the same treatment] to any one among [other sense objects such as] sounds, and so forth. [One follows] the same procedure in regard to cattle, servants, land, or [sovereignty over] villages and settlements, and the like. And even in the case of those who have gone forth [into the religious order, we may see the same conduct] in regard to monastic buildings, dwelling places, bowls, robes, and the like.

[The reference here is to] the person who in this way gathers solely the "flowers" that are the "strands of sensual pleasures," whose mind is attached to the strands of sensual pleasure, be it something obtained or something [desired but] not obtained.

## A sleeping village: *suttaṃ gāmaṃ*

In the case of walls of houses, and so forth, of a village, there is no "sleep" as such; [it] is said to be asleep on account of the sleep and unawareness of its inhabitants.

## Death takes away . . . like a great flood: *mahogho va maccu ādāya gacchati*

Death carries away such a sleeping village like a great flood that is two or three leagues wide and deep. Just as that great flood sweeps the whole village into the seas without leaving behind any trace whatever of its men and women, cattle and fowl, and so on, and makes it a prey to fishes and turtles, in just the same way Māra in the form of death takes away the person of the entangled mind and submerges him in the four seas that are the states of woe, having cut off his faculty of life.

48. The End-Maker overpowers
The man with attached mind,
Insatiate in sensual pleasures,
Plucking only flowers. (4.5)

*pupphāni heva pacinantaṃ byāsattamanasaṃ naraṃ*
*atittaṃ yeva kāmesu antako kurute vasaṃ.*

## Plucking only flowers: *pupphāni heva pacinantaṃ*

The person who, like the garland-maker [gathering] various kinds of flower in a flower garden, is gathering the flowers that are the "strands of sensual pleasure," be they connected with oneself, or with material objects;[12]

## The man with attached mind: *byāsattamanasaṃ naraṃ*

Who has the mind attached in various ways, by way of desiring what is not gotten and greedily clinging to what is gotten;

## Insatiate in sensual pleasures: *atittaṃ yeva kāmesu*

Being indeed insatiate in regard to pleasures in objects and pleasures that are the defilements, [insatiate] as to [their] attainment, consumption, and collection;

## The End-Maker overpowers: *antako kurute vasaṃ*

The End-Maker[13] that is death takes [him] away crying and lamenting, and leads him to his subjugation. That is the meaning.

49. Even as a bee, having taken up nectar
From a flower, flies away,
Not harming its color and fragrance,
So may a sage wander through a village. (4.6)
(The commentary takes lines 1–3 thus:
As a bee, without harming the flower,
its color and fragrance, flies away, taking up the
nectar.)

*yathāpi bhamaro pupphaṃ*(14) *vaṇṇagandhaṃ aheṭhayaṃ*
*paleti rasam ādāya evaṃ gāme munī care.*

## A bee: *bhamaro*

A certain honey-making kind [of insect].

## A flower: *pupphaṃ*

When [such a creature] moves about in a flower garden, it does so without harming, without destroying, the flower, [its] color and [its] fragrance. That is the meaning.

## Flies away: *paleti*

Having gone about in this way and drunk as much nectar as needed, [the bee] goes away, taking some more for the purpose of making honey. In this manner, plunging deep into the forest, it keeps that pollen-laden nectar in the recess of a tree and gradually turns it into honey, sweet of taste. On account of its having been in the flower garden, the flowers do not disappear, or their color and scent. On the contrary everything remains [in its] natural [condition].

### So may a sage wander through a village: *evaṃ gāme munī care*

The sage, who is not a home-dweller, being either a [1] "learner" or [2] "one beyond learning," goes, accepting alms in the village according to the order [in which the houses] of the families [are situated]; that is the meaning. On account of his having been in the village, there is neither loss of faith in those families, nor loss of riches. Both faith and riches remain as usual. The "learner" sage, having gone about [the village] thus, leaves it and lays his *sanghāṭi* robe in a place outside the village where water is easy [to get]; seated on it, he looks on the collected alms as if it were like the grease for an axle, the bandage on a wound, or the flesh of one's child. [The first two serve a purpose, the third is grievous. No sane person would "crave" for them.] Having partaken of it, he enters a befitting forest grove and contemplates the inward subjects of meditation[15] and realizes the four Paths and the four Fruits.

As for the sage who is "beyond learning," he engages in the immediate experiencing of the ease[16] [of Path and Fruit]. This is the comparability to be known [to exist] between his [conduct] and the honey-making of the bee. In this context [the Arahant] with influxes extinct is meant.

50. Let one regard
Neither the discrepancies of others,
Nor what is done or left undone by others,
But only the things one has done oneself or left undone. (4.7)

*na paresaṃ vilomāni na paresaṃ katākataṃ*
*attano va avekkheyya katāni akatāni ca.*

### Neither the discrepancies of others: *na paresaṃ vilomāni*

Others' discrepancies, harsh words deeply affecting one's sensibilities [lit. breaking vital spots], should not be paid attention to.

### Nor what is done or left undone by others: *na paresaṃ katākataṃ*

One should not regard what has been done or not done by others, thinking: "Such and such a devotee is lacking in faith, is not [of] pleased [mind]. In his house not even is food [for the visiting almsmen] served from the ladle [i.e., impromptu], nor alms given at regular intervals. Nor does he offer gifts of robes and such requisites." Or, likewise, "such a female devotee is lacking in faith and is not [of] pleased [mind]; in her house not even is food [for the visiting almsmen] served from the ladle, nor alms given at regular intervals, nor does she offer gifts of robes and such requisites." Or, likewise, "such and such a monk is lacking in faith and is not [of] pleased [mind]; he does not do the regular duties regarding preceptor, teacher, visitor, or one going out; or the regular duties regarding the *cetiya* yard, the house of the retreat *(uposatha)*, the lunchrooms or the bathing rooms. Nor does he follow any *dhutaṅga*[17] practice, nor even so much as an effort at devotion to meditation."

## Let one regard . . . only . . . oneself: *attano va avekkheyya*

"One who has gone forth into the religious order should constantly look back and consider, 'How do I spend the days and the nights?'"—remembering this admonition, let the householder who has gone forth with faith consider his own [actions] done and not done, thinking, "How now, have I been able to do the [necessary] deed in contemplative application, after reflecting on the three characteristics of impermanence, liability to suffering, and absence of self?"

51. Just as a brilliant flower,
Full of color, [but] scentless,
So is a well-spoken word fruitless
For one who does not do it. (4.8)

52. Just as a brilliant flower,
Full of color and fragrance,
So is a well-spoken word fruitful
For one who does it. (4.9)

*yathāpi ruciraṃ pupphaṃ vaṇṇavantaṃ agandhakaṃ*
*evaṃ subhāsitā vācā aphalā hoti akubbato.*

*yathāpi ruciraṃ pupphaṃ vaṇṇavantaṃ sagandhakaṃ*
*evaṃ subhāsitā vācā saphalā hoti sakubbato.*(18)

[51.]

## Brilliant: *ruciraṃ*

Beautiful.

## Full of color: *vaṇṇavantaṃ*

Possessing color and shape.

## Scentless: *agandhakaṃ*

Not having fragrance [i.e., a flower] of such kind as *pāribhaddaka,*(19) *girikaṇṇaka*, or *jayasumana.*

## So is a well-spoken word fruitless for one who does not do it: *evaṃ subhāsitā vācā aphalā hoti akubbato*

The "well-spoken word" means the Word of the Buddha (20) contained in the three *piṭaka*s. *Just as (yathāpi)* a scentless flower does not suffuse the body of him who wears it, in the same way this [well-spoken word] too does not spread the sweet smell of learning, charity, and [dhamma-]living for him who does not do what ought to be done in regard to it, who does not deal with it in the right manner—that is, the person who does not handle it properly by attentive listening, and so on. [For such person] it is fruitless. Hence it has been said: "So is a well-spoken word fruitless for one who does not do it."

[52.]

## Fragrance: *sagandhakaṃ*

A flower of such kind as the *campaka*, the blue lily, or the like.

## So is a well-spoken word fruitful for one who does it: *evaṃ subhāsitā vācā saphalā hoti sakubbato*

Just as a sweet smell suffuses the body of the person who wears that flower, similarly the well-spoken word—namely, the word of the Buddha contained in the three *piṭaka*s—is fruitful to that person who does what ought to be done in regard to it, by means of [attentive] listening, and so on. The meaning is that it is of great avail, great benefit, due to its spreading the sweet smell of [one's] learning, generosity, and [dhamma-]living.

53. Just as many garland strands
One could make from a mass of flowers,
So, much that is wholesome ought to be done
By a mortal born [into this world]. (4.10)

*yathāpi puppharāsimhā kayirā mālāguṇe bahū*
*evaṃ jātena maccena kattabbaṃ kusalaṃ bahuṃ.*

### One could make from a mass of flowers: *puppharāsimhā kayirā*

One could make from a mass of flowers of many kinds,

### Many garland strands: *mālāguṇe bahū*

Many different kinds of garlands(21) such as those with the stalks [of flowers] on one side, and so on.

### By a mortal born, much that is wholesome ought to be done: *maccena kattabbaṃ kusalaṃ bahuṃ*

By the living being called "the mortal one," because of the fact that one is liable to die, much wholesome work ought to be done.[22] Here the mention of a "mass of flowers" is to indicate a large quantity of flowers. If the flowers are not many, and the garland-maker is a skilled craftsman, he would [still] not be able to make many garlands [with them]. The one who is not a skilled craftsman does not [of course] succeed, whether the flowers be many or few. When the quantity of flowers is large, a skilful maker of garlands, clever and able, will turn out a large number of garlands. In the same way, if one's faith is meager and one's riches ample, one [still] is not able to do a great deal of wholesome *(kusala)* deeds. When faith is meager and riches are also meager, it is indeed not possible [to do much good]; [but] one is capable [of doing this] when faith is ample and riches are also ample. Such a person was Visākhā.[23] It is with reference to her that it is said: "Just as many garland strands. . . ."

54. No flower's fragrance moves against the wind,
Neither sandalwood, *tagara*, nor *mallikā*,
But the fragrance of the good ones moves against the wind;
All directions a good person pervades. (4.11)

55. Among these kinds of perfume,
Such as sandalwood, *tagara*,
Also waterlily and *vassikī*,
The fragrance of virtue is incomparable. (4.12.)

*na pupphagandho paṭivatam eti na candanaṃ tagaraṃ mallikā vā*
*sataṃ ca gandho paṭivātam eti sabbā disā sappuriso pavāti.*(24)

*candanaṃ tagaraṃ vāpi uppalaṃ atha vassikī*
*etesaṃ gandhajātānaṃ sīlagandho anuttaro.*

## No flower's fragrance moves against the wind: *na pupphagandho paṭivātam eti*

The *pāricchattaka* flower in the Tāvatiṃsa heaven is of a hundred leagues in length and breadth. The luster of its flowers spreads fifty leagues [in] distance and its sweet smell a hundred leagues, but that only along the wind; against the wind it cannot go even an inch. [Hence] the scent of flowers, even though of this nature, does not spread against the wind.

## Sandalwood: *candanaṃ*

The scent of the sandalwood.

## *Tagara* nor *mallikā: tagaraṃ mallikā vā*

Of these too the scent is intended. [The scent] of the red sandalwood, foremost among the noble scents, spreads along the wind, not against; so is it with *tagara* and *mallikā*.(25)

## But the fragrance of the good ones: *sataṃ ca gandho*

The sweet smell of the virtue of good persons—of Buddhas, Paccekabuddhas, and disciples—goes against the wind. Why?

## All directions a good person pervades: *sabbā disā sappuriso pavāti*

Because the good person covers all the directions with the scent of virtues—for that reason it is to be said that his scent goes against the wind. Hence it was said: "[The fragrance of a good person] moves against the wind."

[55.]

*Vassikī: vassikī*
[Great flowered] jasmine.

Among these kinds of perfume . . . the fragrance of virtue is incomparable: *etesaṃ gandhajātānaṃ sīlagandho anuttaro*
Incomparable with the scent of these various kinds of scent such as sandalwood is indeed the sweet smell of the virtue of good persons; it is unique, it is without counterpart.

56. Slight is this fragrance—
The *tagara* and sandalwood—
But the fragrance of one who is virtuous
Wafts among the gods, supreme. (4.13)

*appamatto ayaṃ gandho yā'yaṃ tagaracandanī*
*yo ca sīlavataṃ gandho vāti devesu uttamo.*

Slight: *appamatto*
Of slight extent.

But the fragrance of one who is virtuous:
*yo ca sīlavataṃ gandho*
Of virtuous ones, the sweet smell of virtue is not little, as [the scent is] in *tagara* and in sandalwood. It is quite plentiful and is liable to spread about. For that reason:

Wafts among the gods, supreme: *vāti devesu uttamo*
Being noble, supreme, it blows everywhere,(26) it goes spreading [itself] among gods and among human beings.

57. Māra does not find the path
Of those who have virtue abounding,
Who are living with awareness,
Liberated through realization. (4.14)

*tesaṃ sampannasīlānaṃ appamādavihārinaṃ*
*sammadaññāvimuttānaṃ māro maggaṃ na vindati.*

## Of those: *tesaṃ*

Just as Godhika,[27] the son of good family, passed away in complete Nibbāna, leaving no consciousness established [anywhere whatsoever]—so of those [others too] who pass away in complete Nibbāna,

## Who have virtue abounding: *sampannāsīlānaṃ*

Who are of perfect virtue,

## Who are living with awareness: *appamādavihārinaṃ*

Who are living with awareness, which is [the same as] not being bereft of mindfulness,

## Liberated through realization: *sammadaññāvimuttānaṃ*

Who, having understood [the nature of phenomena] by [perceiving] cause, by inference, by reason, have attained freedom through the fivefold release—that is, release through elimination *(vikkhambhana-vimutti)*, release through cultivating the opposite *(tadaṅga-vimutti)*, release through cutting off *(samuccheda-vimutti)*, release through subsidence *(paṭippassaddhi-vimutti)*, and release through moving away *(nissaraṇa-vimutti)*,[28]

## Māra does not find the path: *māro maggaṃ na vindati.*

58. Just as in a heap of rubbish
Cast away on a roadside,
A lotus there could bloom,
Of sweet fragrance, pleasing the mind, (4.15)

59. So amid the wretched, blinded ordinary folk,
Among them who have turned to rubbish,
The disciple of the Fully Awakened One
Shines surpassingly with wisdom. (4.16)

*yathāsaṃkāradhānasmiṃ ujjhitasmiṃ mahāpathe*
*padumaṃ tattha jāyetha sucigandhaṃ manoramaṃ.*

*evaṃ saṃkārabhūtesu andhabhūte puthujjane*(29)
*atirocati paññāya sammāsambuddhasāvako.*

[58.]

In a heap of rubbish: *saṃkāradhānasmiṃ*
The meaning is: In a place of garbage, in a heap of rubbish.

Cast away on a roadside: *ujjhitasmiṃ mahāpathe*
Thrown away on a high road.

Of sweet fragrance: *sucigandhaṃ*
Having sweet smell.

Pleasing the mind: *manoramaṃ*
Attractive *(mano-rama)* because the mind (mano) delights in it *(ramati)*.

[59.]

(So) amid the wretched . . . ordinary folk: *(evaṃ) saṃkārabhūtesu . . . puthujjane*
Among ordinary persons, who have acquired the name *puthujjana* because many (*puthu*) defilements are born ( $\sqrt{jan-}$) in them, who have become like a heap of rubbish.

This is what is said: Just as in a rubbish heap discarded on the high road, even though it is loathsome and repulsive, a sweet-smelling lotus could be born. Being attractive and pleasant, it would be worthy of being placed(30) on the heads of kings and ministers. In the same way:

The disciple of the Fully Awakened One: *sammāsambuddhasāvako*
The monk with influxes extinct, though born among ordinary persons who are [worthless like] rubbish, [i.e.,] born among the unwise, unperceptive multitude of people, sees by strength of his own insight the ill effects of sensual pleasures and the benefits of renunciation, leaves home and sets forth, and, over and above [that] mere setting forth, fulfills [the requirements of] virtue, concentration, insight, as well as the seeing of the gnosis of liberation—and shines surpassing(31) the ordinary folk who have "become blind."

# CHAPTER V

## The Childish
## *Bāla-vaggo*

60. Long is the night for one awake,
Long is a league to one exhausted,
Long is *saṃsāra* to the childish ones
Who know not dhamma true. (5.1)

*dīghā jāgarato ratti dīghaṃ santassa yojanaṃ*
*dīgho bālānaṃ saṃsāro saddhammaṃ avijānataṃ.*

### Long (is the night for one awake): *dīghā (jāgarato ratti)*

What is called "night" is only three watches *(yāma)*, [but] to one who stays awake it is long—that is, it seems [to be] three or four times [its actual length]. Neither the very lazy person who sleeps rolling about till sunrise, making himself food for the multitude of bedbugs, nor the sensualist who sleeps on a luxurious couch after consuming a rich meal, knows its length. [But] the one engaged in contemplation, exerting all through the night, knows its length, and the exponent of dhamma who "speaks the speech of dhamma," the one who listens to dhamma, seated close to [such a speaker's] seat, the one affected by ailments of the head, and so forth, the one afflicted by pain, having suffered mutilation of hands and feet, and so on, and the traveler who has set out on the road at night.

### Long is a league to one exhausted: *dīghaṃ santassa yojanaṃ*

A league is only four *gāvuta*s [in length]; but to one who is wearied, who is suffering, it is long, appearing as twice [its actual length]. Having walked the road the whole day and being weary, he sees a person coming(1) from the opposite direction and asks how far ahead is the village. Proceeding a little farther he asks another; when [the latter] says [it is] one league [away], he goes a little farther and asks another. He too says [it is] one league [away]. [Then] he thinks: "Everyone who is asked(2) says it is a league. This league is long! It seems to me like two or three leagues!"

## To the childish ones (not knowing dhamma true): *bālānaṃ (saddhammaṃ avijānataṃ)*

To the childish ones who do not know what is good for this world and the world beyond, who are not able to put an end to the whirl of *saṃsāra*, who do not know the noble dhamma—namely, the noble dhamma divided into the thirty-seven factors leading to enlightenment,[3] knowing which they put an end to *saṃsāra*—[to them] *saṃsāra* indeed is long. [To them] it is as a matter of fact *(dhammatā)* long. This has been [thus] stated: "This *saṃsāra*, O bhikkhus, is of unknown beginning, its prior end does not appear [to one's vision]."[4] For the childish ones who are unable to put an end to it, it is very long indeed!

61. If while moving [through life], one were not to meet
Someone better or like unto oneself,
Then one should move firmly by oneself;
There is no companionship in the childish. (5.2)

*caraṃ ce nādhigaccheyya seyyaṃ sadisam attano*
*ekacariyaṃ daḷhaṃ kayirā natthi bāle sahāyatā.*

## While moving: *caraṃ*

Here *caraṃ* [present participle from the root *car-*, "to move"] should not be taken to mean [physical] movement—namely, the four modes of deportment; it should be understood as "movement by mind." The meaning is: "Looking for" a noble friend.

## (If . . . one were not to meet) someone better or like unto oneself: *(ce nādhigaccheyya) seyyaṃ sadisam attano*

If one does not come across(5) someone better or equal to one in the qualities of virtue, integration, and insight.

## Then one should move firmly by oneself: *ekacariyaṃ daḷhaṃ kayirā*

Coming across one's better in these, one grows in virtue and the like; coming across an equal, one does not degenerate; but living and sharing [day-to-day amenities] with an inferior person, one degenerates in virtue and the like. Hence has it been said: "Such a person should not be associated with, or resorted to, or attended upon, except for [considerations of] mercy and caring." Hence, if it is possible to treat such a person helpfully without expecting anything from him in return, thinking, out of kindness, "He will grow in virtue, and so forth, because of me," [well then,] this is wholesome. But if not, one should be firmly set on being oneself and live alone in every mode of deportment. Why? [Because:]

## There is no companionship in the childish: *natthi bāle sahāyatā*

[1] The minor virtues, [2] the intermediate virtues, [3] the major virtues,[6] [4] the ten topics of discussion,[7] [5] the thirteen *dhutaṅga* practices, [6] the gnosis of insight,[8] [7] the four Paths, [8] the four Fruits,[9] [9] the three forms of knowledge, and [10] the six forms of higher knowledge[10]—[the possession of all] this [which constitutes] the quality of companionship is not [found] with the childish one.

62. A childish person becomes anxious,
Thinking, "Sons are mine! Wealth is mine!"
Not even a self is there [to call] one's own.
Whence sons? Whence wealth? (5.3)

*puttā m'atthi dhanaṃ m'atthi iti bālo vihaññati*
*attā hi attano natthi kuto puttā kuto dhanaṃ.*

## (A childish person) becomes anxious, thinking, "Sons are mine! Wealth is mine!": *puttā m'atthi dhanaṃ m'atthi iti (bālo) vihaññati*

The childish one is anxious, suffers pain, due to craving concerning sons and wealth. He is anxious, thinking [1] "My sons have died," [2] "They are dying," or [3] "They will die." [It is] the same case with regard to riches. Thus he is anxious in six ways,[11] day and night, on land, water and the highroads, and so forth, thinking: "Thus I will nourish my children." [Similarly] he indeed is anxious performing such [activities] as agriculture and trade, thinking: "Thus I will raise wealth." [But,] even for the one who is anxious:

## Not even a self is there [to call] one's own: *attā hi attano natthi*

For the one who is unable to make himself happy [when] pained by that anxiety, even a self is not there for his own [comfort], even during the continuance [of life]. And when [he is] lying on [his] deathbed, being consumed by mortal pains as if by flames of fire, [his] joints and ligaments torn asunder, [his] bones and skeletal frame cracking up, seeing this world when opening [his] eyes and the other world when closing them—then the self, though nourished all life long, bathed thrice a day and fed thrice a day and decked with scents and flowers, is [itself] not [available] to one, because it is unable to provide protection against suffering, being itself a party to it.

### Whence sons? Whence wealth?: *kuto puttā kuto dhanaṃ*

[Then] at that time what indeed will children or wealth do? To the rich merchant Ānanda who maintained wealth for the sake of children without giving anything to anyone—did sons or wealth take away [his] misery or did they bring about ease, as [he was] formerly lying in his deathbed or as [he is] now arrived at this misery?[12]

63. A childish one who knows his childishness
Is, for that reason even like a wise person.
But a childish one who thinks himself wise
Is truly called a childish one. (5.4)

*yo bālo maññati bālyaṃ paṇḍito vāpi tena so*
*bālo ca paṇḍitamānī sa ve bālo ti vuccati.*

### A childish one who knows his childishness; *yo bālo maññati bālyaṃ*

He who, being very childish[(13)] and unwise, knows his own childishness, thinking: "I am a childish person"—

### Is for that reason even like a wise person: *paṇḍito vāpi tena so*

He is, for that very reason, either a wise person or [very much] like one. For, he, knowing "I am a childish person," goes to another who is wise and, associating with him and being advised and instructed by him toward becoming a wise man, accepts that advice [and] turns out to be as wise [as that other person] or wiser [still].

### (But a childish one) who thinks himself wise is truly (called) a childish one: *(bālo ca) paṇḍitamānī sa ve bālo ti (vuccati)*

But he who, being childish, comes to regard himself wise, thinking: "Who else is there like me, learned, an exponent of dhamma, an expert in discipline, an advocate of the *dhuta*?"[14]—he, not going to any other wise man, not associating with such a person, neither learns the texts nor fulfills the practice. Like the thief who was picking purses,[15] he attains to decisive childishness.

64. Even though, throughout his life,
A childish one attends on a wise person,
He does not [thereby] perceive dhamma,
As a ladle, the flavor of the dish. (5.5)

*yāvajīvaṃ pi ce bālo paṇḍitaṃ payirupāsati*
*na so dhammaṃ vijānāti dabbī sūparasaṃ yathā.*

### Even though, throughout his life, a childish one attends on a wise person: *bālo yāvajīvaṃ pi paṇḍitaṃ payirupāsati*

One [who is] childish,(16) going to a wise person and associating with him for even a lifetime does not [come to] understand dhamma to be practiced *(paṭipatti)* nor dhamma to be penetratively realized *(paṭivedha)* [namely, he is incapable of discriminating thus]: "This is the Buddha-word; so much is the Buddha-word; this is dhamma as textual content *(pariyatti)*; this is [right] conduct(17) and [right] dwelling; this is propriety; this is pasture;[18] this is fault; this is faultless; this is worthy of practicing; this is not worthy of practicing; this is what has to be penetratively seen; this is what should be realized."[19] [What is this lack of discrimination like?]:

### As a ladle, the flavor of the dish: *dabbī sūparasaṃ yathā*

As the wooden ladle, though turned [this way and that] in all kinds of cooked food up to [the last moment of its] decay, does not become wise as to the taste of what is cooked [i.e., cannot discriminate thus]: "This is salty; this is not salty; [this is] bitter, alkaline, sharp, sour, not sour, astringent"—in just the same way the childish one does not know dhamma discriminatingly(20) as said before, even if he associates with the wise one for a [whole] lifetime.

65. Even though, for a brief moment,
An intelligent one attends on a wise person,

He quickly perceives dhamma,
As the tongue, the flavor of the dish. (5.6)

*muhuttam api ce viññū paṇḍitaṃ payirupāsati*
*khippaṃ dhammaṃ vijānāti jivhā sūparasaṃ yathā.*

### An intelligent one: *viññū*

The wise person

### Even though, for a brief moment . . . attends on a wise person: *muhuttam api ce paṇḍitaṃ payirupāsati*

If he associates with another wise person even for a very short time, [then] he, learning from the other and inquiring, comes to understand dhamma as textual content very soon indeed. Thereafter, getting [that other person] to say the topics of contemplation and engaging in the practice, striving, he understands dhamma that transcends the world soon indeed—just as one whose sensitivity of tongue is unimpaired understands taste, such as salty taste, and so forth, as soon as he places it on the tip of his tongue for the purpose of perceiving it.

66. Childish ones, of little intelligence,
Go about with a self that is truly an enemy;
Performing the deed that is bad,
Which is of bitter fruit. (5.7)

*caranti bālā dummedhā amitten' eva attanā*
*karontā pāpakaṃ kammaṃ yaṃ hoti kaṭukapphalaṃ.*

### Childish ones: *bālā*

Here "the childish" means: those who do not know what is good for this world as well as what is good for the other world.

### Of little intelligence: *dummedhā*

Deficient in wisdom.

### Go about: *caranti*

Go about doing only the unwholesome in [the] four modes of deportment.

(With a self) that is truly an enemy: *amittena eva (attanā)*
With [a self] become unfriendly, as it were, as though it has turned out to be like a foe.

Bitter fruit: *kaṭukapphalaṃ*
Of sharp [or "piercing"] effect, or painful effect.

67. That deed done is not good,
Having done which, one regrets;
The consequence of which one receives,
Crying with tear-stained face. (5.8)

*na taṃ kammaṃ kataṃ sādhu yaṃ katvā anutappati*
*yassa assumukho rodaṃ vipākaṃ paṭisevati.*

That deed (done) is not (good) having done which: *na taṃ kammaṃ (kataṃ sādhu) yaṃ katvā*
Having done a deed that can produce birth in states of woe, and so on, whose outcome is painful, remembering which one feels regret and grieves at the very instant of remembrance—that is a deed that is not good, not admirable, not gainful.

(The consequence) of which (one receives) with tear-stained face: *yassa assumukho (vipākaṃ paṭisevati)*
Whose result one experiences weeping, with face wet with tears.

68. But that deed done is good,
Having done which, one does not regret;
The consequence of which one receives,
With pleasure and with joy. (5.9)

*taṃ ca kammaṃ kataṃ sādhu yaṃ katvā nānutappati*
*yassa patīto sumano vipākaṃ paṭisevati.*

### Having done which (one does not regret): *yaṃ katvā (nānutappati)*

The deed that brings about ease, that can produce the glories of the [world] of gods and of [the world of] humans, and also the glory of Nibbāna, having done which, one does not have regrets—

### The consequence (of which) one receives with pleasure and with joy: *(yassa) patīto sumano vipākaṃ paṭisevati*

But [whose] outcome one experiences [1] pleased with the rush of delight and happy with the rush of happiness [that it brings] at every instance of remembrance in this very life, and [2] also in future [lives], as one in whom delight and happiness are engendered—

### That deed done is good: *tam kammaṃ kataṃ sādhu*

[That kind of deed is indeed] gainful.

69. The childish one thinks it is like honey
While the bad [he has done] is not yet matured.
But when the bad [he has done] is matured,
Then the childish one comes by suffering. (5.10)

*madhuvā*[21] *maññatī bālo yāva pāpaṃ na paccati*
*yadā ca paccatī pāpaṃ atha bālo dukkhaṃ nigacchati.*

### (The childish one thinks) it is like honey: *madhuvā (maññatī bālo)*

To the childish one who is doing a bad *(pāpa)*, unwholesome *(akusala)* deed, the deed appears desirable, attractive, and pleasant, like honey, like a sweet drink. Hence he regards it as if it were honey.

### (While) the bad [he has done] is not yet matured: *yāva pāpaṃ na paccati*

As long as that bad deed does not yield its fruit, either in this very life or in a future life, he regards it thus.

But when (the bad [he has done] is matured): *yadā ca (paccatī pāpaṃ)*

But when that bad deed matures [i.e., gives its effect] for him [as he is] being made to undergo various vicissitudes(22) in this very life, or, after this life, [as he is] living through great torment in hell, and so forth;

Then the childish one comes by suffering: *atha bālo dukkhaṃ nigacchati*

Then that childish person comes by suffering, experiences it, obtains it.

70. Month by month a childish one
Might eat food with a *kusa* grass blade.
He is not worth a sixteenth part
Of those who have understood dhamma. (5.11)

*māse māse kusaggena bālo bhuñjetha bhojanaṃ*
*na so saṃkhatadhammānaṃ*(23) *kalaṃ nāgghati soḷasiṃ.*

Month by month a childish one might eat food with a *kusa* grass blade: *māse māse kusaggena bālo bhuñjetha bhojanaṃ*

If a childish person, not fully conversant with dhamma and beyond the pale of qualities like virtue, and so forth,(24) having gone forth into an ascetic *(titthiya)* order with the thought, 'I will fulfill the ascetic way of life," were to eat food for a hundred years—eating out of a blade of *kusa* grass [i.e., in austerely minute quantities] once every month—[even then] that childish person does not measure up to a sixteenth part [of one] of the *saṃkhātadhammas*. [To explain:] *saṃkhātadhammas* are those who have understood dhamma, who have "measured" dhamma. Among them the Stream Entrant stands at the lower end, the "Intoxicants-Extinct" at the upper end. Thus is the discourse concerning [the relative merit of] individuals.(25)

The meaning of this is: [If one takes into account] [1] the intention of that person who is fulfilling the ascetic way of life for a hundred years and [2] the intention associated with the skipping of a single meal by one among the *saṃkhātadhammas* who refrains from eating,(26) being scrupulous as to the time and as to the food, that intention [of the ascetic], which was exercised for so long a time, does not equal a sixteenth part of the intention [of the *saṃkhātadhamma*]. In order words, [if one takes] the effect of that intention(27) of the *saṃkhātadhammas* and divides it into sixteen parts and divides each one [of those parts] into sixteen again and [measures] the effect of one such part, that would certainly be greater than the [effect of the entire hundred years of] ascetic conduct of that childish one.

71. For a bad act done does not coagulate
Like freshly extracted milk.(28)
Burning, it follows the childish one,
Like fire concealed in ashes. (5.12)

*na hi pāpaṃ kataṃ kammaṃ sajjukhīraṃ va muccati*
*ḍahan taṃ bālam anveti bhasmacchanno va pāvako.*

## Freshly extracted milk: *sajjukhīraṃ*

Warm milk that has issued immediately from the cow's udder.

## Coagulate: *muccati*

Undergoes change.

This is the meaning: Just as this fresh milk does not coagulate immediately, does not undergo [any] change, does not lose its natural form, and as long as they do not add some sour [stuff] like buttermilk to the vessel into which it was received after milking, as long as it does not go into a "souring vessel," such as a vessel of curds, so long as [it remains] without losing its natural form, but later loses it—in exactly the same way a harmful deed also does not mature [bring its effect] as soon as it is done. If it so matured, no one would dare to do a harmful deed. As long as the *khandha*s born by virtue of wholesome deeds last, so long do they protect him. But at their demise, [the harmful deed] gives its effect upon the [successor] *khandha*s that have appeared in the state of woe.

## Burning, it follows the childish one: *ḍahan taṃ bālam anveti*

And as it is giving its effect, it follows the childish one, burning [him].

Like what?

## Like fire concealed in ashes: *bhasmacchanno va pāvako*

Just as coals without flames, concealed in ashes, do not straightway burn one even if trod upon, because they are concealed in ashes; they make the ashes hot and then go on burning, burning the skin, and so forth, to begin with [and proceeding thereafter] as far up as the very head—in just the same way, the harmful deed too follows the childish one by whom it is done, burning him as he is born in hell, and so forth, in a second or a third existence [from that in which the deed was done].

72. Only for his detriment
Does knowledge arise for the childish one.
It ruins his good fortune,
Causing his [very] head to fall. (5.13)

*yāvad eva anatthāya ñattaṃ bālassa jāyati*
*hanti bālassa sukkaṃsaṃ*(29) *muddham assa vipātayaṃ.*

## Only: *yāvad eva*

[This is] a particle phrase indicating "for demarcating limit" [it means "as far as"].

## (For his detriment does) knowledge (arise for the childish one): *(anatthāya) ñattaṃ (bālassa jāyati)*

*Ñattaṃ* means "the quality of knowing." This refers to the craft of which one has knowledge, as also to the authority or fame or glory being established in which one becomes known by the people, becomes eminent and renowned.(30) Craftsmanship or authority or any other such state in the case of the childish one turns out to be only for his detriment: based on it he accomplishes only harm to himself.

## It ruins: *hanti*

It destroys.

## (The childish one's) good fortune: *(bālassa) sukkaṃsaṃ*

The part of wholesome [actions done by him]. In the case of the childish one, craftsmanship or authority arises only to destroy the portion of his wholesome [*kamma*] actions.

## Causing (his) [very] head to fall: *muddhaṃ (assa) vipātayaṃ*

The word "head" *(muddha)* is a synonym for "wisdom," and "causing to fall" *(vipātayaṃ)* means "ruining." That [craftsmanship, and so forth], of his(31) [i.e., the childish one's], when destroying his good fortune, destroys his [very] head, namely, his wisdom, bringing it down, ruining it.

73. He would desire unreal glory
And preeminence among bhikkhus,
Authority, too, concerning dwellings,
And offerings in other families. (5.14)

74. "Let both householders and those who have gone forth
Think that it is my work alone;
In whatever is to be done or not done,
Let them be dependent on me alone!"
Such is the thought of the childish one;
Desire and pride increase. (5.15)

*asataṃ bhāvanam iccheyya purekkhāraṃ ca bhikkhusu*
*āvāsesu ca issariyaṃ pūjā*[32] *parakulesu ca.*

*mam' eva kataṃ maññantu gihī pabbajitā ubho*
*mam' ev'ativasā assu kiccākiccesu*[33] *kismi ci*
*iti bālassa saṃkappo icchā māno ca vaḍḍhati.*[34]

[73.]

## He would desire unreal (glory): *asataṃ (bhāvanam) iccheyya*

The childish bhikkhu would desire a nonexistent [unrealistic] prestige. Being without faith, he wishes: "May the people regard me as one having faith!" As stated in the [comment on the word] *pāpicchatā* in the *Niddesa*[35] the childish one being without faith, deficient in virtue, of little learning, lacking in discernment, indolent, not constant in mindfulness, lacking concentration, deficient in wisdom, and being not with "intoxicants extinct," wishes for this unreal prestige, thinking: "Would that the people consider me thus: Here is a faithful person, virtuous, very learned, full of discernment, firm of enterprise, constant in mindfulness, concentrated [in mind], endowed with wisdom, and with intoxicants extinct."

## Preeminence: *purekkhāraṃ*

[This means] retinue. [The childish one] wishes to have a following among bhikkhus, establishing himself in such a process of desiring [as this]: "Would that the bhikkhus in the entire monastery surround me and go about with me asking me questions."

## (And authority) concerning dwellings: *āvāsesu (ca issariyaṃ)*

From among the dwelling places that belong [as common property] to the Saṅgha, assigning for bhikkhus who are his friends and companions the [more] comfortable lodging places at the center of the monastery, saying, "You stay here" and reserving [for] himself the best lodging place, and then assigning to other visiting bhikkhus the lodging places that are farthest away, which are soiled(36) and imperilled by nonhumans, saying [to them] "You stay here"—thus, he wishes for authoritative status in regard to monastic lodgings.

## And offerings in other families: *pūjā parakulesu ca*

He wishes for reverential gifts of the four kinds of requisites,[37] not indeed from his parents and relations but from the families of others, thinking: "Would that they give only to me and to no one else!"

[74.]

## Let them think that it is my work alone: *mam' eva kataṃ maññantu*

Whatever new work has been done in the monastery, such as the building of an *uposatha* hall, [in regard to that] this thought arises in the childish [bhikkhu]: "Let both lay persons and those who have gone forth regard that all that was done, was completed, solely on account of me, thinking, 'It has been done by our Elder.' "

## (In whatever is to be done or not done,) let them be dependent on me alone: *mam eva ativasā assu (kiccākiccesu kismi ci)*

"Let everyone be under my sway only, both lay persons and those who have gone forth! Let them be solely under my sway in regard to every single matter whatever among the things that have to be done, big or small—that is, such miscellaneous duties as what must be obtained(38) [for the monastery], like cart, ox, adze, axe, and so on, down to such slight things as the drinks [that are to be made] by cooking a little gruel. Let them do [them] after consulting only me!" This thought arises [in that childish one].

## Such (is the thought) of the childish one: *iti bālassa (saṃkappo)*

In the case of the childish one in whom such desire and such thought arise, insight, Path, and Fruit do not indeed develop. [On the other hand,] in his case, only the craving that rises at the six doors and also the ninefold self-estimation increase,[39] as do the ocean's waters at the rise of the moon [at high tide].

75. The means of acquisition is one,
And another the way leading to Nibbāna.
Having recognized this as so,
Let a bhikkhu who is a disciple of the Buddha
Not delight in [receiving] esteem;
Let him cherish disengagement. (5.16)

*aññā hi lābhūpanisā aññā nibbānagāminī*
*evam etaṃ abhiññāya bhikkhu buddhassa sāvako*
*sakkāraṃ nābhinandeyya vivekam anubrūhaye.*

## The means of acquisition is one, and another the way leading to Nibbāna: *aññā hi lābhūpanisā aññā nibbānagāminī*

What is known "as the means of [producing] gain" is one thing; the course leading to Nibbāna is another. A certain amount of unwholesome action has to be done by the bhikkhu who is bent on making profit; crookedness of action and the like has to be resorted to [by him]. It is when he does some crooked acts that profit arises. In the case of the person who dips the hand straight into the bowl of *pāyāsa* without making it crooked [without cupping it], the hand is merely smeared [with *pāyāsa*]; but of the one who dips the hand cupped and raises it out of the bowl, the hand comes out picking up a lump of *pāyāsa*. In this way profit arises only when resorting to crookedness of action, and so forth. This is an undhammalike "means of [producing] gain." [On the other hand] that gain is dhammalike which is produced by causes such as the good fortune of having the substrates [that make one what one is],(40) wearing robes [i.e., being a bhikkhu], learnedness, [having] a following and living in a forest retreat.

Crookedness of action and the like should be given up by the bhikkhu who is fulfilling the course leading to Nibbāna; he ought to be like one blind though indeed not blind, like one dumb though indeed not dumb, like one deaf though indeed not deaf. He ought not to be cunning and crafty.

## (Having recognized) this as so: *evam etaṃ (abhiññāya)*

Knowing in this way the course [of action that is] productive of [material] gain and the course leading to Nibbāna—

## A bhikkhu who is a disciple: *sāvako bhikkhu*

A disciple *(sāvaka)* is so called because he has become such after hearing dhamma or because he listens to[41] advice and instruction,[42]

## Of the Buddha: *buddhassa*

Of the Buddha [who is so called] because of his understanding[43] all compounded dhammas.[(44)]

## Let (him) not delight in receiving esteem: *sakkāraṃ nābhinandeyya*

Let [such a *bhikkhu*] not enjoy being served with the four kinds of requisites *(paccaya)* as are discordant with dhamma;[45] nor let him reject the [service] that is consonant with dhamma.

## Let him cherish disengagement: *viveka anubrūhaye*

Let him develop disengagement such as physical disengagement. Here physical disengagement is solitude physically; mental disengagement means the eight attainments; disengagements from the substrates is Nibbāna. Of these three, physical disengagement dispels [the harms accruing from] attachment to company; mental disengagement dispels attachment to the defilements; disengagement from substrates dispels the [state of] being attached to the *saṃkhāras*.

Physical disengagement is the condition [necessary] for mental disengagement, and mental disengagement is the condition [that is necessary] for disengagement from substrates. It has been said: "Physical disengagement is [a quality] of those who are physically withdrawn [from the crowds of humans], who delight in detachment. Mental disengagement is of those with pure thoughts, who have arrived at the highest purity [of mind]. Disengagements from substrates is of persons who are free of all attachments, who are liberated from the *saṃkharas*."

So let him develop and increase this threefold disengagement; let him arrive at that and live therein. That is the meaning.

# CHAPTER VI

## The Sagacious
## *Paṇḍita-vaggo*

76. The one who sees one's faults,
Who speaks reprovingly, wise,
Whom one would see as an indicator of treasures,
With such a sagacious person, one would associate.
To one associating with such a person,
The better it will be, not the worse. (6.1)

*nidhīnaṃ va pavattāraṃ*[1] *yaṃ passe vajjadassinaṃ*
*niggayhavādiṃ medhāviṃ tādisaṃ paṇḍitaṃ bhaje*
*tādisaṃ bhajamānassa seyyo hoti na pāpiyo.*

### Of treasures: *nidhīnaṃ*

Of pots of treasure filled with gold and the like, and kept at various places as deposits.

### (As) an indicator: *pavattāraṃ (va)*

Like a person who, having compassion on a poor man, takes him to a place of [such] deposited treasure and says, stretching his hand [toward it]: "Come, I will show you a means of living in ease. Take this and live in comfort."

### The one who sees one's faults: *vajjadassinaṃ*

There are two who point out one's errors: the seeker of faults who thinks, "I will insult him in the midst of the Saṅgha, by this impropriety or this lapse," and the person who is established in the tendency to pluck one away [from faults] by observing [one's] every error, in order to make one understand what has not been understood, with desire for the increase of one's virtues, and so forth.

Here [it is] the second one [that] is intended.

Just as the poor man does not become angry when someone shows him a treasure, even [though] after beating him and threatening him saying: "Take this!" but is only delighted—in the same way one should not become angry when a person of this kind sees one's impropriety or lapse, and tells one of it; [instead] one should only be delighted. One should indeed invite [him to continue doing this, saying] "Sir, what has been done by you, taking the position of a teacher and preceptor to me and admonishing me, is [indeed] a great deed; do speak [thus] to me again [and again]."

### Who speaks reprovingly: *niggayhavādiṃ*

Seeing the impropriety or the lapse of fellow bhikkhus and so on, a certain [bhikkhu is] unable to say [it to the person concerned, because he thinks]: "This man attends on me well with [helpful acts such as] serving water for rinsing the mouth, and so on. If I should tell him [of this impropriety], he will not attend on me, [and] this will be a loss to me." [Such a person] is not "one who speaks [the word of admonition] reprovingly"; he [is one who] "scatters garbage" in the order *(sāsana)*. But he who, seeing such error, causes [the wrongdoer] to learn, threatening him, as befits the error, turning him away, punishing him [or] expelling him from the monastery—such [a person] is "one who speaks [the word of admonition] reprovingly," as for instance, a Fully Awakened One. This has been mentioned [by the Buddha himself, thus]: "I, Ananda, will speak constantly reproving, constantly cleansing. That which is the pith will stand fast."[2]

### Wise: *medhāvin*

One who is endowed with insight, the sap of dhamma.

### With such a sagacious person one would associate: *tādisaṃ paṇḍitaṃ bhaje*

One would associate with, attend on, that kind of wise person.

### (To one associating with) such a person: *tādisaṃ (bhajamānassa)*

To him who associates with such a teacher, [as] an attendant.

### The better it will be, not the worse: *seyyo hoti na pāpiyo*

There will be growth, not decay [of wisdom].

77. He would counsel, instruct,
And restrain [one] from rude behavior.

To the good, he is pleasant;
To the bad is he unpleasant. (6.2)

*ovadeyyānusāseyya asabbhā ca nivāraye*
*sataṃ hi so piyo*(3) *hoti asataṃ hoti appiyo.*

### He would counsel, (instruct): *ovadeyya (anusāseyya)*

[It is when one is] speaking about a matter that has [actually] arisen [that] one "counsels" *(ovadati)*. One "instructs" when speaking with reference to the future, in regard to [any matter] that has not arisen, as for example [a matter which gives rise to the reflection]: "[By this offense] there might even be disrepute for us [in the monastery]." And also, one "counsels" when speaking [to the offender], face to face; one "instructs" when dispatching a message or a messenger [to the offender], without facing him. [Yet again] one "counsels," speaking [just] once; one "instructs," speaking again and again. Counseling, one indeed instructs,(4) thus "would one counsel and instruct."[5]

### And restrain one from rude behavior: *asabbhā ca nivāraye*

The meaning is: one would restrain [the wrongdoer] from that which is of unwholesome nature and [also] establish him in that which is of wholesome nature.

### To the good, he is pleasant: *sataṃ hi so piyo hoti*

A person of that kind is pleasant to worthy persons, such as the Buddhas.

### To the bad is he unpleasant: *asataṃ appiyo (hoti)*

Persons who have not seen dhamma, who have no concern for the world beyond, who have [only] an eye for material [gain], who have gone forth to earn a living—to [such] unwholesome persons, the counselor and instructor is not pleasant: [he is unplesant] to such persons who "pierce" him with the sharp weapon of their tongues saying, "You are not our preceptor or teacher. So why do you counsel us?"

78. Let one not associate
With low persons, bad friends.
But let one associate
With noble persons, worthy friends. (6.3)

*na bhaje pāpake mitte na bhaje purisādhame*
*bhajetha mitte kalyāṇe bhajetha purisuttame.*

## (Bad friends . . . low persons . . .): *(pāpake mitte . . . purisādhame . . .)*

The meaning of this is: Evil friends are those who are attached to unwholesome deeds, such as physical misconduct. And, low persons are those who set one in improper [conduct] such as housebreaking[6] or in the twenty-one kinds of wrongdoing.[7] They are both evil friends as well as low persons. Let one not associate with them, not attend upon them. Those with opposite qualities are good friends and worthy persons. Let one associate with them, attend upon them.

79. One who drinks of dhamma sleeps at ease,
With mind calmly clear.
In dhamma made known by noble ones,
The wise one constantly delights. (6.4)

*dhammapīti sukhaṃ seti vippasannena cetasā*
*ariyappavedite dhamme sadā ramati paṇḍito.*

## One who drinks of dhamma: *dhammapīti*

The meaning is: the one whose beverage is dhamma, who is drinking dhamma. That which is called dhamma is not possible to drink in a vessel, like gruel, or the like. Contacting with body[8] the ninefold dhamma that transcends the world, realizing as object, penetratively seeing the noble truths such as the noble truth of suffering, and so on, by means of comprehension, and so forth, through full knowledge:[9] [that is how] one "drinks of dhamma."

## Sleeps at ease: *sukhaṃ seti*

[Though] only this is [found in] the discourse, the (whole) meaning is: "one lives in ease in (all) the four modes of deportment."

## (With mind) calmly clear: *vippasannena (cetasā)*

Not befuddled, free of defilements.

## (The wise one) constantly delights: *sadā ramati (paṇḍito)*

A drinker of dhamma such as this, living with tranquil mind[(10)] and being endowed with sagaciousness, constantly delights, is pleased.

## In dhamma made known by the noble ones: *ariyappavedite (dhamme)*

In dhamma that is conducive to enlightenment in its [many] varieties, such as making awareness firm, and which has been proclaimed by noble ones, such as the Buddhas.

80. Irrigators guide the water.
    Fletchers bend the arrow shaft.
    Wood the carpenters bend.
    Themselves the wise ones tame. (6.5)

*udakaṃ hi nayanti nettikā usukārā namayanti tejanaṃ*
*dāruṃ namayanti tacchakā attānaṃ damayanti paṇḍitā.*

## Irrigators: *nettikā*

"Irrigators" [lit. those who lead] are so called because they cause water to flow into whatever place is desirable to them, digging up flat land or filling up low land or making conduits or fixing scooped-out tree trunks.

## (Fletchers bend) the arrow shaft: *(usukārā namayanti) tejanaṃ*

[*Tejanaṃ* means] the shaft [of an arrow].

What is stated is this: Irrigators lead the water as they please and arrow-makers also bend the arrow shaft after heating [the piece of wood used]—that is, they straighten it.

## Wood the carpenters bend: *dāruṃ namayanti tacchakā*

Carpenters square timber for the felly [of a cartwheel], and the like, and make it straight or bent as they wish.

## (Themselves the wise ones tame): *(attānaṃ damayanti paṇḍitā)*

In the same way the wise, making this much an object [of contemplation], develop the Paths such as Stream Entrance and [thus] tame themselves. When Arahantship is attained, then they become perfectly tamed.

81. Even as a solid rock
Does not move on account of the wind,
So are the wise not shaken
In the face of blame and praise. (6.6)

*selo yathā ekaghaṇo vātena na samīrati*
*evaṃ nindāpasaṃsāsu na samiñjanti paṇḍitā.*

### In the face of blame and praise: *nindāpasaṃsāsu*

Although(11) only two aspects of ordinary life are mentioned here, it should be understood that all eight [of them] are meant.

### (As a solid rock is not moved by wind): *(selo yathā ekaghano vātena na samīrati)*

As a rock, which is one solid mass devoid of crevices, does not shake in [any] wind, such as the east wind, and the others, does not tremble or move,

### (The wise ones are not shaken): *(na samiñjanti paṇḍitā)*

In the same way, when the eight aspects of ordinary life overwhelm [them], the wise neither are moved nor [do they] tremble—neither in repulsion nor in acquiescence.[12]

82. Even as a deep lake
Is very clear and undisturbed,
So do the wise become calm,
Having heard the words of dhamma. (6.7)

*yathā' pi rahado gambhīro vippasanno anāvilo*
*evaṃ dhammāni sutvāna*(13) *vippasīdanti paṇḍitā.*

### A deep lake: *rahado*

A reservoir of water, which is not agitated(14) [even] when a fourfold army plunges into it, is [called] a *rahada*: [or else] the great blue ocean, which is eightyfour thousand leagues deep all over, is [called] a *rahada*. In its lowest forty thousand leagues, the water is restless on account of the fish. In the part of similar extent at the top, the water is restless on account of the wind. But in between, in a part four thousand leagues in extent, the water remains motionless. This is [what is here called] the deep lake.

## So (the wise, having heard) the words of dhamma (become calm): *evam dhammāni (sutvāna vippasīdanti paṇḍitā)*

*Dhammāni* [words of dhamma] refer to dhamma that is taught. What is stated is this: Just as that lake is clear because it is free from impurities and undisturbed because it is motionless, in the same way, having heard my dhamma-teaching, attaining undefiled mind by way of the Path of Stream Entrance, and the rest, the wise become calmly clear. Having attained Arahantship they are perfectly calm.

83. Everywhere, indeed, good persons "let go",
The good ones do not occasion talk, hankering for pleasure.
Touched now by ease and now by misery,
The wise manifest no high and low. (6.8)

*sabbattha ve sappurisā cajanti* (15)
*na kāmakāmā lapayanti* (16) *santo*
*sukhena phuṭṭhā athavā dukhena*
*na uccāvacaṃ paṇḍitā dassayanti.*

## Everywhere: *sabbattha*

In regard to all phenomena such as the five *khandhas*, and so forth,(17)

## Good persons "let go": *sappurisā cajanti*

Good persons relinquish attachment and desire, removing [them] by the gnosis of the Path of Arahantship.

## The good ones do not occasion talk, hankering for pleasure: *na kāmakāmā lapayanti santo*

Good persons, such as Buddhas, do not prattle for their own part, nor do they get others to prattle, hankering for [various] sense pleasures—that is, for the sake of sensuality, for reasons of sensuality. Those who have entered the alms-round, entrenched in the practice of [furthering] desires, prattle [with householders] saying, "Devotees, is your family well? Is there no trouble to person and livestock from king and thieves, and so on?" And they get others to prattle, when, having said so, they get themselves invited [to what householders may offer, saying]: "Yes sir, everything is fine with us. There is no trouble. Now our home has plenty of food and drink. Do please stay here [and we will look after you]." Good persons do neither of these things.

## Touched now by ease and now by misery: *sukhena phuṭṭhā atha vā dukhena*

Only this is said in the discourse [but what is meant is]: affected by the eight occurrences of ordinary life.[18]

## The wise manifest no high and low: *uccāvacaṃ paṇḍitā na dassayanti*

The wise do not show high or low [elation or depression] either in the form of being satisfied or discontented or in the form of expressing the satisfactory or unsatisfactory [character of events].

84. Neither for one's own sake nor for the sake of another,
A son would one wish, or wealth, or kingdom.
One would not wish one's own prosperity by undhammic means.
Such a one would be possessed of virtue, wisdom, dhamma. (6.9)

*na attahetu na parassa hetu*
*na puttam icche na dhanaṃ na raṭṭhaṃ*
*na iccheyya adhammena samiddhim attano*
*sa sīlavā paññavā dhammiko siyā.*

## Neither for one's own sake (nor for the sake of another): *na attahetu (na parassa hetu)*

The wise one indeed does not do a detrimental act, neither for one's own sake nor the sake of others.

## Neither a son would one wish (or wealth, or kingdom): *na puttam icche (na dhanaṃ na raṭṭham)*

He would desire neither son nor wealth nor [the glories of] state through a detrimental act. The meaning is that he does not commit a detrimental act even desiring these things.

### One would not wish one's own prosperity by undhammic means: *na iccheyya adhammena samiddhim attano*

That which is one's own thriving, even that one would not desire [to secure] by undhammalike means. The meaning is that one indeed does not do a detrimental act even for the sake of prosperity. The meaning is: such a person indeed—and no other—*would be possessed of virtue, wisdom, dhamma (sa sīlavā paññavā dhammiko siyā)*.

85. Few are they among humans,
The people who reach the shore beyond.
But these other folk
Only run along the [hither] bank. (6.10)

86. But those who live according to dhamma—
In dhamma well-proclaimed—
Those people will reach the shore beyond.
The realm of death is hard to cross. (6.11)

*appakā te manussesu ye janā pāragāmino*
*athāyaṃ itarā pajā tīram evānudhāvati.*

*ye ca kho sammadakkhāte dhamme dhammānuvattino*
*te janā pāram essanti maccudheyyaṃ suduttaraṃ.*

[85.]

### Few: *appakā*

Few, not many.

### Who reach the shore beyond: *pāragāmino*

Those who reach the other shore—namely, Nibbāna.

### But these other folk only run along the [hither] bank: *athāyaṃ itarā pajā tīram evānudhāvanti*

The rest of the people run along the bank—that is, [cling to this] existing aggregate [of *khandhas*]. The meaning is: this is indeed the majority.

[86.]

### In dhamma well proclaimed: *sammadakkhāte dhamme*

In regard to dhamma that is the teaching, which is well proclaimed, well stated.

### Who live according to dhamma: *dhammānuvattino*

Those who live in accordance with [that] dhamma—that is, who having heard that dhamma, fulfill the observance that is consistent with it and live according to it by realization of Path and Fruit;

### Will reach the shore beyond: *pāram essanti*

They, people of this kind, will reach the further shore—namely, Nibbāna.

### The realm of death: *maccudheyyaṃ*

The threefold whirl which has become the dwelling place of Death—that is, the Māra of defilements—

### Hard to cross: *suduttaraṃ*

Those people who live in accordance with dhamma will cross, will go beyond this realm of Māra very hard to cross—and they will arrive at the other shore—namely, Nibbāna: that is the meaning.

87. Having forsaken a shadowy dhamma,
The wise one would cultivate the bright,
Having come from familiar abode to no abode
In disengagement, hard to relish. (6.12)

88. There he would wish for delight,
Having discarded sensual desires—he who has nothing.
The wise one would purify oneself
Of the defilements of the mind. (6.13)

89. Whose mind is fully well cultivated in the factors of enlightenment,
Who, without clinging, delight in the rejection of grasping,
Lustrous ones, who have destroyed intoxicants,
They have, in [this] world, attained Nibbāna. (6.14)

*kaṇhaṃ dhammaṃ vippahāya sukkaṃ bhāvetha paṇḍito*
*okā anokaṃ āgamma viveke yattha dūramaṃ.*(19)

*tatrābhiratim iccheyya hitvā kāme akiñcano*
*pariyodapeyya attānaṃ cittaklesehi paṇḍito.*

*yesam sambodhi-aṅgesu sammā cittaṃ subhāvitaṃ*
*ādānapaṭinissagge anupādāya ye ratā*
*khīnāsavā jutīmanto te loke parinibbutā.*

[87.]

## (Having forsaken) a shadowy dhamma: *kaṇhaṃ dhammaṃ (vippahāya)*

Having discarded the unwholesome dhamma classifiable as physical misconduct, and so forth,

## The wise one would cultivate the bright: *sukkhaṃ bhāvetha paṇḍito*

The bhikkhu would develop the bright dhamma, in its varieties such as physical good conduct, and so on, from the time of setting forth [into the religious life] up until [reaching] the Path of Arahantship. How [would such a one do that]?

## Having come from familiar abode to no abode: *okā anokam āgamma*

"Home" signifies attachment and "homelessness" nonattachment; having set out from "dwelling", [the wise one], would develop [the bright dhamma] for the sake of Nibbāna,[20] ardently wishing for it.

[88.]

## There he would wish for delight: *tatrābhiratim iccheyya*

He would desire the relishing of "non-dwelling"—that is, the disengagement that is Nibbāna, which is hard for these people to relish,

## Having discarded sensual desires: *hitvā kāme*

Having discarded the desire for objects and for defilements [that is, attachments to pleasures],

## He who has nothing: *akiñcano*

[And] having become one who has nothing,[21]

## There he would wish for delight: *tatrābhiratim iccheyya*

He would desire the relishing of disengagement; that is the meaning.

## (Would purify oneself) of the defilements of the mind: *(pariyodapeyya attānaṃ) cittaklesehi*

Would purify oneself, cleanse [oneself] of the five hindrances.[22]

[89.]

## (Whose mind is fully well cultivated) in the factors of enlightenment: *(sammā cittaṃ subhāvitaṃ) sambodhiaṅgesu*

The mind well developed, made to grow, in a rational and orderly way, in the factors conducive to enlightenment.[23]

## Who . . . delight in the rejection of grasping: *ādānapaṭinissagge ye ratā*

*Ādāna* means grasping. The meaning [of the phrase] is: those who are attracted to nongrasping—that is, to the rejection of that [grasping], not clinging to anything by the four kinds of gathering [or clinging].[24]

## Lustrous ones: *jutimanto*

Those who are endowed with "luster." The meaning is: those who stand illumining [to themselves] dhammas such as the *khandha*s by the radiance of the understanding accompanying the Path of Arahantship.

## They have, in [this] world, attained Nibbāna: *te loke parinibbutā*

In this world of *khandha*s, and so forth, they have entered into Nibbāna fully—that is, [1] "with substrata remaining" from the time of attaining Arahantship, on account of having exhausted the whirl of defilements; and [2] "without substrata remaining" at the cessation of the final [flicker of] thought [at the end of life], on account of having exhausted the whirl of the *khandha*s. Thus they have entered Nibbāna fully by both [aspects of] Nibbāna. The meaning is: [they are] gone to the state of undefinability[25] like [the flame of] a lamp, without fuel.

# CHAPTER VII

## The Worthy
## *Arahanta-vaggo*

90. To one who has gone the distance,
Who is free of sorrows, freed in every respect;
To one who has left behind all bonds
Fever there exists not. (7.1)

*gataddhino visokassa vippamuttassa sabbadhi*
*sabbaganthappahīnassa pariḷāho na vijjati.*

### To one who has gone the distance: *gataddhino*

To one who has finished [the] journey.

There are two "roads": the road through a difficult terrain and the road through the whirl. In regard to these, he who has set out on the road through a difficult terrain is a traveler only so long as he does not reach his desired goal; when he has reached it, he is "one who has gone the distance." Beings who are engulfed in the whirl too are travelers so long as they live in the whirl. Why? Because the whirl has not been exhausted. Stream Attainers, and others, too, are surely travelers. But the one with intoxicants extinct [Arahant], being one who has exhausted the whirl, is a person who has reached the journey's end. To such a person who has reached his journey's end,

### Who is free of sorrows: *visokassa*

Who is free of sorrows because sorrow, of which the whirl is the basis, has left him,

### Freed in every respect: *sabbadhi vippamuttassa*

Who is freed in regard to all phenomena (dhammas) such as the *khandha*s, and the like,

### To one who has left behind all bonds: *sabbaganthappahīnassa*

Because [all] four bonds have been discarded,[1]

## Fever there exists not: *parilāho va vijjati*

"Burning sensation" is of two kinds, physical and mental. Of these [two], the burning sensation that is physical, which arises in the form of cold and heat, is surely not extinguished to the influx-extinct [Arahant]. It is about that that Jīvaka [in the story] questions[the Buddha].[2] The Teacher, because he is the King of Dhamma due to his skill in the modes of discourse,[3] replies [to him], turning the discourse so as to refer to mental "burning:" "In the highest sense, Friend Jīvaka, there is no burning sensation to a person such as this, in whom the intoxicants are extinct."

91. The mindful ones gird up [themselves].
In no abode do they delight.
Like swans having left behind a pond,
One shelter after another they leave. (7.2)
(Line 4 may also mean: Home they abandon, the flood.)

*uyyuñjanti satīmanto na nikete ramanti te*
*haṃsā va pallalaṃ hitvā okamokaṃ jahanti te.*

## The mindful ones gird up [themselves]: *uyyuñjanti satīmanto*

Those in whom the intoxicants are extinct, who have attained to the plenitude of awareness, engage in, apply themselves to, the virtues they have penetratively realized, such as meditative-absorption and insight; [they engage in them] by way of recalling [them], attaining [them], arising [from them], resolving [thus: "for such and such a time I shall abide in them"] and reflecting [on them again and again].

## In no abode do they delight: *na nikete ramanti te*

In them there is surely no attachment to "dwelling."

## Like swans: *hamsā va*

This [phrase] constitutes the "crest" of the discourse. This is the meaning here: Just as birds at a waterhole with abundant food [such as fish] do not cherish an attachment to any object there when they leave after taking their food [i.e., they do not consider]: "[This is] my water, my lotus, my lily, my pericarp." Instead, they give up that location without [any further] expectation and fly away sporting in the [wide] firmament. In the same way those in whom the intoxicants are extinct, when living in any locality wheresoever, do not dwell attached to the families there; and, at the time of departure, they leave [that place] without attachment, without [any further] expectation [i.e., they do not consider]: "My monastery! My buildings! My attendants!"

### One shelter after another (they leave): *okamokaṃ (jahanti te)*

Every attachment.(4) The meaning is: They relinquish all attachments.(5)

92. Those for whom there is no hoarding,
Who have fully understood [the nature] of food,
And whose pasture is freedom
That is empty, that has no sign,
Their course is hard to trace
As that of birds in the sky. (7.3)

*yesaṃ sannicayo natthi ye pariññātabhojanā*
*suññato animitto ca vimokkho yassa gocaro*
*ākāse va sakuntānaṃ gati tesaṃ durannayā.*

### (Those for whom there is no) hoarding: *(yesaṃ) sannicayo (natthi)*

There are two forms of accumulation: accumulation of *kamma* and accumulation of requisites. One's wholesome and unwholesome deeds [amount to] accumulation of *kamma*. [One's] four requisites [constitute] accumulation of requisites. In this regard, a bhikkhu dwelling in a monastery, keeping one lump of sugar, four portions only of clarified butter, and one *nāḷi* [a measure of capacity] of uncooked rice is not accumulation of requisites, [but keeping] more than that is.

### Who have fully understood [the nature of] food: *(ye) pariññātabhojanā*

Those for whom there is no accumulation of these two kinds, [are they] who have fully understood food by means of the three forms of understanding.

To understand the gruel nature of gruel [for example] is [1] "understanding that is knowledge"; to understand food fully with the consciousness of [its ultimate] disagreeability is [2] "understanding-with-judgement"; the understanding that dispels desire and attachment toward material food is [3] "understanding leading to renunciation."

Those who have fully understood food by means of these three forms of understanding [are meant here].

### And (whose pasture is freedom) that is empty, that has no sign: *suññato animitto ca (vimokkho yassa gocare)*

Here in [the phrase] "[freedom] that is empty, that has no signs" [the third freedom, namely] "freedom that has no aspiring" is also indeed included. These three are names for Nibbāna itself. Nibbāna is "empty" because in it there is neither attachment, nor ill will, nor delusion: because it is free of these, it is [1] "freedom that is empty." It is devoid of signs because it has none of the three signs such as attachment, and the like [ill will and delusion]. Because it is free of these, it is [2] "freedom that has no signs." It is devoid of aspirations based on attachment, and so forth. Because it is free of these it is [3] "freedom that has no aspiring."

Those for whom this threefold freedom is "pasture," who live with that as [their] objective, by way of "attainment of Fruit,"

### Their course is hard to trace: *gati tesaṃ durannayā*

Just as the track of birds that fly through the sky is hard to trace, is impossible to know, because they leave no footsteps that one could see, similarly those in whom this twofold accumulation is not found, who understand food by these three forms of understanding, whose "pasture" is this freedom of the described kind, in their case too, the track by which they have departed is hard to trace; it cannot be indicated, due to lack of indications [as, e.g.,] gone by this [path] in these areas, namely the three states of existence, the four ways of birth, the five "courses," the seven states of consciousness, and the nine "abodes of beings."[6]

93. In whom the influxes are fully extinct,
Who is not attached to sustenance,
And whose pasture is freedom
That is empty and signless,
His track is hard to trace,
As [that] of birds in the sky. (7.4)

*yassāsavā parikkhīṇā āhāre ca anissito*
*suññato animitto ca vimokkho yassa gocaro*
*ākāse va sakuntānaṃ padaṃ tassa durannayam.*

### In whom the influxes (are fully extinct): *yassāsavā (parikkhīṇā)*

In whom the four influxes[7] are fully extinct.

### Who is not attached to sustenance: *āhāre ca anissito*

Who is free of the dependence on food through desire and views.

### His track is hard to trace: *padaṃ tassa durannayaṃ*

Just as, in the case of birds that fly through the sky, it is not possible to ascertain [their flight track thus]: "[They] set foot in this place, [they] touched this place with the breast, this with the wings, this with the head," in the same way it is not possible to indicate the "track" of a bhikkhu of this kind in such terms as the following: "He has gone by the path leading to the states of woe, by the path leading to birth among beasts, and so forth."

94. Whose senses have reached an even temper,
Like horses well trained by a charioteer,
Who has discarded self-estimation, who is free of influxes,
Even the gods cherish such a one. (7.5)

*yass' indriyāni samathaṃ gatāni assā yathā sārathinā sudantā*
*pahīnamānassa anāsavassa devā pi tassa pihayanti tādino.*

### (Whose senses) have reached an even temper (like) horses well trained by a charioteer: *(yass' indriyāni) samathaṃ gatāni assā (yathā) sārathinā sudantā*

Of the bhikkhu whose senses have reached a state of control, of steadiness, like horses well trained by a skillful charioteer,

### Who has discarded self-estimation, who is free of influxes: *pahīnamānassa anāsavassa tassa*

Who has "discarded self-estimation," owing to [his] having relinquished the ninefold self-estimation,[8] who is "free of influxes," owing to the absence of the four influxes in him,

### Even the gods cherish such a one: *devā pi . . . pihayanti tādino*

Even the gods and also human beings surely desire the sight and the arrival of that kind of person, who is steady in that [self-control and freedom].

95. Like the earth, he does not oppose.
A firm pillar is such a one, well cultured,
Like a lake rid of mud.
To such a one travels in *saṃsāra* there are not. (7.6)

*paṭhavīsamo no virujjhati indakhīlūpamo tādi subbato*
*rahado va apetakaddamo saṃsārā na bhavanti tādino.*

## Like the earth, he does not oppose. A firm pillar is such a one, well cultured: *pathavīsamo no virujjhati indakhīlūpamo tādi subbato*

Just as, O bhikkhus, [people] throw pure incense and flowers upon the earth and also foul urine and feces, similarly, although children and the like urinate and defecate upon the post of Inda *(indakhīla)*, which is set up by the city gate, others honor it with incense and flowers; but about that there arises neither approbation nor antagonism in the earth or in the post of Inda. In exactly the same way this bhikkhu in whom the influxes are extinct is steady because he is imperturbable in the face of the eight aspects of ordinary life. He is well cultured due to the excellence of his practices. He shows neither approbation toward those who treat him well nor antagonism toward those who treat him badly [for he does not think]: "These [persons] treat me well with the four requisites, but these [others] do not treat me so." Therefore he is "like the earth" and comparable to the post of Inda, indeed.(9)

## (Like a lake rid of mud): *(rahado va apetakaddamo)*

Just as a lake has clear water, in which the mud has disappeared, so, because the intoxicants have disappeared [in him] he is "free of mud"—that is, the mud that is desire. He indeed is calmly clear.

## To such a person: *tādino*

To the one who is such

## Travels in *saṃsāra* there are not: *saṃsāra na bhavanti*

There is no "moving round" by way of moving [from one existence to another] in the states of weal and woe.

96. Of such a one, pacified,
Released by proper understanding,

Calm is the mind,
Calm his speech and act. (7.7)

*santaṃ tassa manaṃ hoti santā vācā ca kamma ca*
*sammadaññāvimuttassa upasantassa tādino.*

## Calm (is the) mind, (calm his speech and act): *santaṃ (tassa) manaṃ (hoti santā vācā ca kamma ca)*

The mind of the bhikkhu in whom the intoxicants are extinct is indeed calmed, pacified, "extinguished" *(nibbutaṃ)*, due to the absence of greed, and the like. Similarly, due to there being no lying speech, and so forth, [in him], [his] speech [is calmed]. And, due to the absence of the taking of life, and so on, [his] physical action is also calmed indeed.

## Released by proper knowledge: *sammadaññā vimuttassa*

[In the case] of him who, after having understood [dhamma] in a rational and orderly way, is released by the five kinds of release,[10]

## Pacified: *upasantassa*

Who has become tranquil by the calming of desire, and the like, within him,

## Of such a person: *tādino*

Of that kind of person [the mind is calmed, the speech is calmed, and the deeds are calmed].

97. Who has no faith, the ungrateful one
The man who is a burglar,
Who has destroyed opportunities, ejected wish,
Truly he is a person supreme. (7.8)

*assaddho akataññū ca sandhicchedo ca yo naro*
*hatāvakāso vantāso sa ve uttamaporiso.*

## Who has no faith: *assaddho*

The quality that one has attained oneself, one does not take upon faith from the word of others: [one is] "not having faith" in that sense.[11]

## The ungrateful one: *akataññū*

[One is called] *akataññū* because one understands the uncreated *(akataṃ)*—that is, Nibbāna.[12] The meaning is: one who has realized Nibbāna.

## (The man who is) a burglar: *sandhicchedo*

[One is called] "a breaker of joints"[13] because one has cut off the "junction" of the whirl and the "junction" of *saṃsāra*.

## Who has destroyed opportunities: *hatāvakāso*

[One is said to have] "destroyed opportunities" because the seed for wholesome and unwholesome deeds has been eradicated and the opportunity for rebirth is destroyed.

## Ejected hope: *vantāso*

[One is said to have] "ejected hope" because the duty that has to be done has been done by means of the four paths and [all] wish is thereby discarded.

## A person supreme: *purisuttamo*

The person of this kind[(14)] is said to be noble because of having reached an exalted position among persons by virtue of having penetratively understood dhamma that transcends the world.

98. Whether in village or in forest,
Whether in valley or on plateau,
Delightful is the ground
Where Arahants dwell. (7.9)

*gāme vā yadi vā 'raññe ninne vā yadi vā thale*
*yatthārahanto viharanti taṃ bhūmiṃ rāmaṇeyyakaṃ.*

## Delightful is the ground where Arahants dwell: *yattha arahanto viharanti taṃ bhūmiṃ rāmaṇeyyakaṃ*

Even though Arahants do not obtain physical disengagement in a village, they do indeed obtain disengagement of mind. Not even objects that are comparable to the celestial can deflect their minds. Hence, be it a village, or one among such places as forests, *that place is lovely where Arahants dwell*: that territory is surely alluring. That is the meaning.

99. Delightful are forests,
Where people do not take delight.
[There] those without passions will delight;
They no sensual pleasures seek. (7.10)

*ramaṇīyāni araññāni yattha na ramatī jano*
*vītarāgā ramissanti na te kāmagavesino.*

### Delightful are forests: *ramaṇīyāni araññāni*

Forests decked with groves of blossoming trees and full of [streams and lakes with] clear water are alluring indeed.

### Where people do not take delight: *yattha na ranatī jano*

In which forests people who look for sensual pleasures do not take delight, as village flies [do not take delight] in clusters of blooming lotus plants.

### Those without passions (will delight): *vītarāgā (ramissanti)*

But those in whom intoxicants are extinct [Arahants] and from whom desires have disappeared will delight in forests of that kind, as honey-making bees [will delight] in clusters of lotus plants. For what reason?

### They no sensual pleasures seek: *na te kāmagavesino*

Because they are not in search of sensuality—that is the meaning.

# CHAPTER VIII

## The Thousands
## *Sahassa-vaggo*

100. Though a thousand be the statements,
With words of no avail,
Better is a single word of welfare,
Having heard which, one is pacified. (8.1)

*sahassam api ce*(1) *vācā anatthapadasaṃhitā*
*ekaṃ atthapadaṃ seyyo yaṃ sutvā upasammati.*

### A thousand (be the statements with words of no avail): *sahassam api (vācā anatthapadasaṃhitā)*

Here "thousand" is a word signifying a [numerical] specification. Suppose there are words that are [numerically] specified in thousands [as, e.g.,] one thousand or two thousand [words], and they are(2) composed of phrases that are of no avail, that do not illumine the way to transcendence, that serve [only] as descriptions of skies and mountains and forests, and so forth. [Then], as numerous as they be, so [are they] surely detrimental. This is the meaning.

### (Better) is a single word of welfare (having heard which, one is pacified): *ekaṃ atthapadaṃ (seyyo yaṃ sutvā upasamatti)*

On the other hand a single word of welfare such as this: "This is body; this is mindfulness pertaining to body; the three forms of knowledge[3] have been attained; the message of the Buddha has been fulfilled"—having heard which, one is pacified by the pacification of desires, and the like—that, even though [it is] one single word, is nobler, conducive [as it is] to welfare, linked with Nibbāna and serving to illuminate [such subjects as] the [five] aggregates,[4] the [eighteen] "bases,"[5] the [twelve] "spheres,"[6] the [twenty-two] "faculties,"[7] the [five] "powers,"[8] the [seven] "constituents of enlightenment,"[9] and the [four] "foundations of mindfulness."[10] That is the meaning.

101. Though a thousand be the verses,
With words of no avail,
Better is a single line of verse,
Having heard which, one is pacified. (8.2)

*sahassam api ce gāthā anatthapadasaṃhitā*
*ekaṃ gāthāpadaṃ seyyo yaṃ sutvā upasammati.*

## Better is a single line of verse: *ekaṃ gāthāpadaṃ seyyo*

A single verse such as [e.g.,] "Awareness is the path to the Deathless' [*Dhp.*, v. 21] is nobler; that is the meaning.

The rest should be understood as in the previous instance [st. 100].

102. And should one recite a hundred verses,
With words of no avail,
Better is one dhamma word,
Having heard which one is pacified. (8.3)

103. He, truly, is supreme in battle,
Who would conquer himself alone,
Rather than he who would conquer in battle
A thousand, thousand men. (8.4)

*yo ca gāthā sataṃ bhāse anatthapadasaṃhitā*
*ekaṃ dhammapadaṃ seyyo yaṃ sutvā upasammati.*

*yo sahassaṃ sahassena saṅgāme mānuse jine*
*ekaṃ ca jeyya-m-attānaṃ sa ve saṅgāma juttamo.*

[102.]

## (And should one recite) a hundred verses: *(yo ca) gāthā sataṃ (bhāse)*

The person who would recite many verses [i.e.,] hundreds by [numerical] specification,

## With words of no avail: *anatthapadasaṃhitā*

Which consist of words that are of no avail, such as descriptions of sky, and so forth—

## (Better is one) dhamma word: *(ekaṃ) dhammapadaṃ (seyyo)*

Better [than those] is a single word [or part] of dhamma, which affects one's welfare and which concerns [the understanding of the five] "aggregates" *(khandhas)*, and so on—that is, even a single part of dhamma out of the four parts of dhamma thus described:

> O wandering ascetics, there are these four parts of dhamma. What are they? Absence of covetousness . . . is a part of dhamma; absence of ill will . . . is a part of dhamma; proper mindfulness . . . is a part of dhamma; [and finally] proper integration of mind . . . is a part of dhamma.

[103.]

## Who (would conquer in battle) a thousand, thousand men: *yo sahassaṃ sahassena (saṅgāme mānuse jine)*

A single soldier in battle who in a single engagement would conquer men numbering a thousand multiplied by a thousand—that is, would conquer [an army of] one million and gain victory—even he is not said to be the best conqueror in battle.

## Would conquer himself alone: *ekañ ca jeyya-m-attānaṃ*

But he who contemplates on "internal topics of meditation" by day as well as by night and would conquer himself through the conquest of his defilements such as greed, and the like,

## He, truly, is supreme in battle: *sa ve saṃgāmajuttamo*

He is the best among conquerors in battle, he is the soldier at the head of battle, the noblest, the most excellent.

104. Better, indeed, oneself conquered
[Rather than] these other folk.
Of a person who has won himself,
Who is constantly living in self-control, (8.5)

105. Neither a god nor a *gandhabba,*
Nor Māra together with Brahmā,

Could turn the victory into defeat
Of a living being like that. (8.6)

*attā have jitaṃ seyyo yā cā'yaṃ itarā pajā*
*attadantassa posassa niccaṃ saññatacārino*

*n'eva devo na gandhabbo na māro saha brahmunā*
*jitaṃ apajitaṃ kayirā tathārūpassa jantuno.*

[104.]

### (Better) indeed (oneself) conquered: *(attā) have jitaṃ (seyyo)*

Here *ha ve* is merely a particle and *jitaṃ* [has taken this form by] change of gender.(11) The meaning is: Nobler is oneself conquered by triumphing over one's own defilements [rather than victory over others].

### [Rather than] these other folk: *yā cāyam itarā pajā*

If these other folk be defeated by gambling or extortion or by being conquered through strength in war, not noble is the [victory] that has been won by him who conquers them—that is the meaning.

Why is it that that victory [over oneself] alone is noble and not this [over others]?

[104–105.]

### Of a person who has won himself . . . of a living being like that: *attadantassa (posassa) . . . tathārūpassa jantuno*

What is stated is this: Inasmuch as this person is self-controlled due to freedom from defilements—in the case of that person who is self-controlled, who conducts himself with physical restraints, and so forth, neither a god, nor a *gandhabba,*[12] nor a Māra, rising [to put him down] even in the company of Brahmā, can ever turn into defeat [the victory] of that kind of person who is restrained by these physical restraints, and so forth, even [if such a god, or the others, were to be] striving [hard, thinking], "I will turn his victory into defeat. I will reproduce [in him] the defilements that have disappeared by development of the Paths." [He would not be able to turn the victory into defeat] as one who is defeated out of wealth, or the like, obtaining another [powerful] ally and winning back what was won by his opponent, turning [the latter's victory] into defeat.

106. Month by month, with a thousand,
One might offer sacrifice a hundred times,
And another, to one self-composed,
Might offer worship for but a second;
Truly, that worship is better
Than what was offered a hundred years. (8.7)

*māse māse sahassena yo yajetha sataṃ samaṃ*
*ekaṃ ca bhāvitattānaṃ muhuttam api pūjaye*
*sā yeva pūjanā seyyo yaṃ ce*(13) *vassasataṃ hutaṃ.*

## With a thousand: *sahassena*

This means: by giving thousands.

## One might offer sacrifice a hundred times: *yo yajetha sataṃ samaṃ*

[1] One who would give alms to ordinary people, making gifts of a thousand, month after month for a hundred years, and [2] one who would make an offering by giving a ladleful of alms or providing food just sufficient for physical maintenance or simply offering a coarse scarf to the one person who had come to the doorstep [and] whose mind is developed in [skilful] qualities—that is, a Stream-Attainer at the lowest level or an Influx-extinct [Arahant] at the highest—

## Truly, that worship is better: *sā yeva pūjanā seyyo*

That offering is surely better than what was sacrificed by the other person for a hundred years—it is noble, it is supreme. That is the meaning.

107. And were a living being for a hundred years
To tend a fire in a forest,
And were another, to one self-composed,
To offer worship for but a second;
Truly, that worship is better
Than what was offered a hundred years. (8.8)

*yo ca vassasataṃ jantu aggiṃ paricare vane*
*ekaṃ ca bhāvitattānaṃ muhuttam api pūjaye*
*sā yeva pūjanā seyyo yañ ce vassasataṃ hutaṃ.*

## A living being: *jantu*

This is a synonym for ["sentient] being."

## (Were to) tend a fire in a forest: *aggiṃ paricare vane*

[A living being] having gone into a forest(14) with the hope for freedom from entanglement [of mind], may tend the fire there [perform the fire sacrifice for a hundred years, and so forth]. The rest [of the stanza] is exactly like the previous instance [st. 106].

108. Whatever sacrifice or offering in the world
One seeking merit might sacrifice for a year;
Evan all that does not "reach a quarter"—
Better the respectful greetings to the straight of gait. (8.9)

*yam kiñci yiṭṭhaṃ va hutaṃ va loke saṃvaccharaṃ yajetha puññapekho sabbaṃ pi taṃ na catubhāgam eti abhivādanā ujjugatesu seyyo.*

## Whatever: *yaṃ kiñci*

This is to signify "total inclusion,"

## Sacrifice ([lit.] is sacrificed): *yiṭṭhaṃ*

[This] generally [means] offerings given in connection with festive activities.

## Offering ([lit.] offered): *hutaṃ*

[This means] both the prepared offerings given to invited guests,(15) as well as offerings given with faith in deeds and their effects.

## Might sacrifice for a year: *saṃ vaccharaṃ yajetha*

One may give, ceaselessly for a whole year, alms of the aforesaid kind, to ordinary people, even of the entire universe.

## One seeking merit: *puññapekho*

Hoping for merit.

## To the straight of gait: *ujjugatesu*

[This means respect] [1] at the lowest level, to Stream-Attainers, and [2] at the highest level, to Influx-extinct [Arahants]. This is what is stated:

Whatever is the effect of the wholesome intention of one who, with mind pleased, bends his body and shows obeisance to persons of this kind—all those [other] offerings do not have the value of even one quarter of that [effect]. Hence better surely is the respect shown to those who are "straight of gait."

109. For one in the habit of showing respect,
Of always honoring elder ones,
Four qualities increase:
Life, complexion, ease, and strength. (8.10)

*abhivādanasīlissa niccaṃ vaddhāpacāyino*
*cattāro dhammā vaḍḍhanti āyu vaṇṇo sukhaṃ balaṃ.*

## For one in the habit of: *abhivādanasīlissa*

For one who is in the habit of respectful greeting; for one who is engaged in the function of respectful greeting always: this is the meaning.

## (Always) honoring elder ones: *(niccaṃ) vaddhāpacāyino*

For a layman who honors even a young novice the very day of going forth or for a member of the order who honors one who is older in membership of the order, or in higher ordination, or is elderly on account of virtues.

The meaning is—for one who regularly venerates [such persons] with respectful greeting.

## Four qualities increase: (life, complexion, ease, and strength): *cattāro dhammā vaḍḍhanti (āyu vaṇṇo sukhaṃ balaṃ)*

When life span increases, [these] other qualities increase in proportion to the increase of life span. [Suppose there were a person] by whom wholesome deeds had been done conducive to a life of fifty years, and[(16)] suppose [some] danger were to threaten his life at the age of twenty-five years—that [danger] would abate due to [his cultivating] the habit of respectful greeting, and he would live to the end of his due lifespan. His complexion, and so forth, too will increase along with [the prolongation of] life. Beyond this too it is the same way [i.e., this is not restricted to a fifty-year life only].

[But suppose a person's life is not threatened by any premature dangers], there is no prolongation of [such] a life continuing without danger.

110. And should one live a hundred years
Devoid of virtue, uncomposed.
Better still is one day lived
Of one possessed of virtue, a meditator. (8.11)

*yo ca vassasataṃ jīve dussīlo assamāhito*
*ekāhaṃ jīvitaṃ seyyo sīlavantassa jhāyino.*

### Devoid of virtue: *dussīlo*

Not having virtue.

### (Better still is one day lived) of one possessed of virtue (a meditator): *(ekāhaṃ jīvitaṃ seyyo) sīlavantassa (jhāyino)*

Better is a single day's life, [or for that matter,] a single moment's, of a virtuous person, of one who is a meditator due to [following] the two meditations,[17] than a hundred years' of one who is devoid of virtue: that is the meaning.

111. And should one live a hundred years
Devoid of insight, uncomposed;
Better still is one day lived
Of one possessed of insight, a meditator. (8.12)

*yo ca vassasataṃ jīve duppañño asamāhito*
*ekāhaṃ jīvitaṃ seyyo paññāvantassa jhāyino.*

### Devoid of insight: *duppañño*

Not having insight.

### Of one possessed of insight: *paññāvantassa*

Of one who possesses insight. The rest is as in the previous instance [st. 110].

112. And should one live a hundred years
Indolent, of inferior enterprise;
Better still is one day lived
Of one initiating enterprise, firm. (8.13)

*yo ca vassasataṃ jīve kusīto hīnavīriyo*
*ekāhaṃ jīvitam̄ seyyo viriyaṃ ārabhato daḷhaṃ.*

### Indolent: *kusīto*

The person who spends time by [engaging in] thoughts such as thoughts directed to sensuality.[18]

### Of inferior enterprise: *hīnavīriyo*

Devoid of enterprise, energy.

### Of one initiating enterprise, firm: *viriyam ārabhato daḷhaṃ*

Of one who initiates enterprise capable of engendering the twofold meditation.[19]

113. And should one live a hundred years
Not seeing "the rise and demise";
Better still is one day lived
Of one seeing "the rise and demise." (8.14)

*yo ca vassasataṃ jīve apassaṃ udayavyayaṃ*
*ekāhaṃ jīvitaṃ seyyo passato udayavyayaṃ.*

### Not seeing "the rise and demise": *apassaṃ udayavyayaṃ*

Not seeing the rise and the demise of the five *khandha*s by means of [the] twenty-five characteristics.[20]

### (Better still is one day lived) of one seeing the "rise and demise": *(ekāham jivitaṃ seyyo) passato udayavyayaṃ*

Better is even a day's life of one who sees their rise and demise, than the [entire] life of the other.

114. And should one live a hundred years
Not seeing the immortal state;
Better still is one day lived
Of one who sees the immortal state. (8.15)

*yo ca vassasataṃ jīve apassaṃ amataṃ padaṃ*
*ekāhaṃ jīvitaṃ seyyo passato amataṃ padaṃ.*

## Immortal state: *amataṃ padaṃ*

The sphere that is without death. The meaning is: the great, immortal Nibbāna. The rest is exactly as in the previous instance [st. 114].

115. And should one live a hundred years
Not seeing dhamma supreme;
Better still is one day lived
Of one seeing dhamma supreme. (8.16)

*yo ca vassasataṃ jīve apassaṃ dhammam uttamaṃ*
*ekāhaṃ jīvitaṃ seyyo passato dhammam uttamaṃ.*

## Dhamma supreme: *dhammam uttamaṃ*

The ninefold dhamma that transcends the world. That is [what is] called the supreme dhamma. Better is even a single day's, even a single moment's, life of one who sees, who penetratively understands, that dhamma, than a hundred years' life of the one who does not see it.

# CHAPTER IX

## The Wrong
## *Pāpa-vaggo*

116. Be quick in goodness;
From wrong hold back your thought.
Indeed, of one performing the good tardily,
The mind delights in wrong. (9.1)

*abhittharetha kalyāṇe pāpā cittaṃ nivāraye*
*dandhaṃ hi karoto puññaṃ pāpasmiṃ ramatī mano.*

### Be quick (in goodness): *abhittharetha (kalyāṇe)*

Do [wholesome acts] very quickly, indeed, very promptly: that is the meaning here.

Wholesome deeds should be performed by the layperson when the thought arises. "Let me do some wholesome act such as offering *salāka* alms, and so forth; [they should be performed] promptly, very promptly, thinking: "Let me be ahead, let me!" so that no one else may get the chance. And also [wholesome deeds] should be performed promptly, very promptly indeed, by the bhikkhu who attends to duties relating to preceptor, and the like, without giving the chance to another, thinking: "Let me be ahead, let me!"

### From wrong (hold back your) thought: *pāpā cittaṃ (nivāraye)*

Hold back the mind with all might from detrimental acts like physical misconduct, and so on, or from allowing unwholesome thoughts to arise.

### Indeed, of one performing (the good) tardily: *dandhaṃ hi karoto (puññaṃ)*

One who does the wholesome [deed] tardily, like one treading a slippery road, thinking: "Shall I give? Shall I do? Will it give effect or not?"—to such a person a thousand unwholesome [thoughts of] miserliness gain access, as in the case of Ekasāṭaka.[1] Of such a person,

### The mind delights in wrong: *pāpasmiṃ ramate mano*

The mind takes [any] delight in the wholesome only at the time of performing wholesome deeds; when it has moved away from that [performance], it definitely becomes inclined toward the detrimental.

117. Should a person do a wrong,
Let him not do it again and again.
Let him not form a desire toward it.
A suffering is the accumulation of wrong. (9.2)

*pāpañ ce puriso kayirā na taṃ kayirā punappunaṃ*
*na tamhi chandaṃ kayirātha dukkho pāpassa uccayo.*

### Should a person (do a wrong): *(pāpam ce) puriso (kayirā)*

The meaning of this is: should a person do a detrimental act once, let him look back at that very instant [upon it, realizing] "this is improper and coarse."

### Let him not do it again and again: *na taṃ kayirā punappunaṃ*

Let him indeed not do it [again], having dispelled whatever desire or aptitude [may arise] in regard to it. Why?

### A suffering is the accumulation of wrong: *dukkho pāpassa uccayo*

For the growth, the increase, of the detrimental brings about only suffering, in this life and in the next.

118. Should a person do some good,
Let him do it again and again.
Let him form a desire toward it.
A happiness is the accumulation of good. (9.3)

*puññaṃ ce puriso kayirā kayirāth'enaṃ punappunaṃ*
*tamhi chandaṃ kayirātha sukho puññassa uccayo.*

(Should) a person (do) some good, (let him do it again and again): *puññaṃ (ce) puriso (kayirā kayirāth'enaṃ punappunaṃ)*

The meaning of this is: should a person do a wholesome deed [once], let him do it(2) again and again, without ceasing; [let him not think] "I have done a wholesome deed once; this is sufficient."

In that: *tamhi*

In regard to that wholesome deed,

(Let him form a) desire: *chandaṃ (kayirātha)*

Let him indeed form a desire, a pleasure, an effort, when it is not being done. Why?

A happiness is the accumulation of good: *sukho puññassa uccayo*

For the growth, the increase, of the wholesome is happiness, because it brings about happiness in this life and in the next.

119. Even a wrongdoer experiences what is good
As long as the detrimental has not matured.
But when the detrimental is matured,
The wrongdoer then experiences the detrimental. (9.4)

120. Even the good one experiences the detrimental
As long as the good is not matured
But when the good is matured,
Then the good one experiences the good. (9.5)

*pāpo pi passatī bhadraṃ yāva pāpaṃ na paccati*
*yadā ca paccatī pāpam atha pāpo pāpāni passati.*

*bhadro pi passatī pāpaṃ yāva bhadraṃ na paccati*
*yadā ca paccatī bhadraṃ atha bhadro bhadrāni passati.*

[119.]

Even the wrongdoer experiences what is good: *pāpo pi passati bhadraṃ*

The person who is involved with detrimental action such as physical misconduct, even he "experiences the pleasant" as he enjoys the happiness born of the power of former good conduct.

### As long as the detrimental has not matured: *yāva pāpaṃ na paccati*

[This he does] so long as that detrimental act of his does not produce effect, either in this very life, or in a future life.

### (But when the detrimental has matured, then) the wrongdoer experiences the detrimental: *(yadā ca paccati pāpam atha) pāpo pāpāni passati*

But when that [misdeed] of his gives effect, in this life or in a future life, then he *experiences the detrimental*—going through various vicissitudes in this life, and the misery of the states of woe in afterlife.

The second stanza [is] also [to be explained similarly]:

[120.]

### The good one: *bhadro*

The person who is involved with wholesome deeds such as physical good conduct, and so forth,

### Experiences the detrimental: *pāpaṃ passati*

He too "experiences the unpleasant" as he undergoes suffering born of the power of former bad conduct,

### As long as the good is not matured: *yāva bhadraṃ na paccati*

So long as that wholesome deed of his does not give effect, either in this very life or in a future life.

### The good one experiences the good: *bhadro bhadrāni passati*

But when it gives effect, then the good person *experiences the good* indeed, enjoying such bliss as gain and respect in this life or celestial bliss in afterlife.

121. Think not triflingly of wrong,
"It will not come to me!"
With falling drops of water,
Even a waterpot is filled.
A childish one is filled with wrong
Acquiring bit by bit. (9.6)

*māppamaññetha pāpassa na maṃ taṃ āgamissati*
*udabindunipātena udakumbho pi pūrati*
*pūrati bālo pāpassa thokathokam pi ācinaṃ.*

### Think not triflingly: *māppamaññetha*

Do not treat lightly,

### Of wrong: *pāpassa*

The detrimental act,

### "It will not come to me": *na maṃ taṃ āgamissati*

"The unwholesome act done by me is very minor. When will it mature? [i.e. never]." One should not treat the unwholesome deed lightly in this way. That is the meaning.

### (With falling drops of water) even a waterpot (is filled): *(udabindunipātena) udakumbho pi (pūrati)*

Any vessel made by a potter, kept [out] with its mouth open when it is raining. Just as such [a vessel] is filled gradually by the fall of each drop of rain,

### (Is filled . . . with wrong, acquiring), bit by bit: *(pūrati . . . pāpassa) thokaṃ thokaṃ pi (ācinaṃ)*

So a childish person, gathering the detrimental—that is, performing it and causing it to increase, is indeed filled with it bit by bit. That is the meaning.

122. Think not triflingly of good,
"It will not come to me!"
With falling drops of water
Even a waterpot is filled.

A wise one is filled with good,
Acquiring bit by bit. (9.7)

*māppamaññetha puññassa na maṃ taṃ āgamissati*
*udabindunipātena udakumbho pi pūrati*
*pūrati dhīro puññassa thokathokaṃ pi ācinaṃ.*

### Think not triflingly (of good), "It will not come to me!": *māppamaññetha (puññassa) na maṃ taṃ āgamissati*

The meaning of this is: Let wise persons, after doing a wholesome act, not think triflingly of it thus, "It is a slight wholesome act that was done by me. It will not come back to me in the form of an effect, or where will I see it? When will it[3] mature? [i.e., it will never]."

### With falling drops of water (even a waterpot is filled) (the wise) is filled with good (acquiring bit by bit): *udabindunipātena (udakumbho pi pūrati) pūrati (dhīro) puññassa (thokathokaṃ pi ācinaṃ)*

Just as a vessel made by a potter, left open [outside], is filled with the constantly falling drops of water, in the same way a steadfast wise person is filled with good even while acquiring it bit by bit.

123. One would avoid wrongs,
Like the rich merchant with small caravan
The fearful road;
Like one who loves life, poison. (9.8)

*vāṇijo va bhayaṃ maggaṃ appasattho mahaddhano*
*visaṃ jīvitukāmo va pāpāni parivajjaye.*

### The fearful (road): *bhayaṃ (maggaṃ)*

To be feared. This means: being a source of fear due to being infested with robbers.

(Like) the rich merchant with small caravan: *vāṇijo (va) appasattho mahaddhano*

This is what is stated: Just as the merchant Mahaddhana,[4] who had a scanty caravan, [avoided] the road that was a source of fear,

(Like) one who loves life, poison: *visaṃ jīvitukāmo (va)*

And just as one who is desirous of living avoids a deadly poison,

(One would avoid wrongs): *(pāpāni parivajjaye)*

So would the wise bhikkhu avoid even slight detrimental acts.

124. If on the hand a wound were not,
One could carry poison with [that] hand.
Poison does not follow one without a wound.
No wrong there is for one not doing it. (9.9)

*pāṇimhi ce vaṇo nāssa hareyya pāṇinā visaṃ*
*nābbaṇaṃ visam anveti natthi pāpaṃ akubbato.*

Were not: *nāssa*

Were there not . . .

One could carry: *hareyya*

One would be able to carry. . . . Why? Because,

Poison does not follow one without a wound: *nābbaṇaṃ visam anveti*

Poison cannot follow [i.e., penetrate] a hand that has no injury [on it].

In the same way, [in the case] of a person who is not [intentionally] committing a bad deed, even if handing out [weapons] such as bows, there is no unwholesome act—due to the absence of the unwholesome intention.[5] The unwholesome does not "follow" his mind, just as poison does not "follow" the hand without an injury.

125. Whoever offends an inoffensive man,
A pure person without blemish,
The wrong recoils on just that childish one,
Like fine dust hurled against the wind. (9.10)

*yo appaduṭṭhassa narassa dussati*
*suddhassa posassa anaṅganassa*
*tam eva bālaṃ pacetti pāpaṃ*
*sukhumo rajo paṭivātaṃ va khitto.*

### An inoffensive man: *appaduṭṭhassa narassa*

To a person who is inoffensive toward oneself as well as toward all [other] beings.

### Pure: *suddhassa*

One who is guiltless.

### Without blemish: *anaṅganassa*

Who is free of defilements.

### Person: *posassa*

This too is a word, [though] in another form, for [sentient] "being."

### Offends: *dussali*

Does harm.

### Recoils: *pacetti*

Comes back.

### Against the wind: *paṭivātaṃ*

Just as fine dust thrown by a person standing against the wind, intending [it] to hit [someone else], comes back on that same person, falls on him alone, in the same way does an individual do harm to a harmless person, striking blows with the hands, and so forth.

### On just that childish one: *tam eva bālaṃ*

That detrimental act turns back on just that childish one in the form of a painful consequence, maturing in this very life, or in states of woe, and so forth.

126. Some are born in a womb,
Wrongdoers, in hell.
Those of good course go to heaven,
To Nibbāna those without influxes. (9.11)

*gabbham eke uppajjanti nirayaṃ pāpakammino*
*saggaṃ sugatino yanti parinibbanti anāsavā.*

A womb: *gabbham*

Here the human itself is meant. The rest here is clear.

127. That spot in the world is not found
Neither in the sky nor in the ocean's depths
Nor having entered into a cleft in mountains,
Where abiding one would be released from the bad deed. (9.12)

*na antalikkhe na samuddamajjhe*
*na pabbatānaṃ vivaraṃ pavissa*
*na vijjati so jagatippadeso*
*yatthaṭṭhito muñceyya pāpakammā.*

The meaning is: If someone were to sit "*in the sky*" *(antalikkhe)* or plunge into the great ocean eighty-four thousand leagues deep, or sit inside a mountain, thinking: "By this means I will escape [the effect of] the detrimental act"—[even then] one will certainly not escape the detrimental act. In the regions of the world, such as the East, and so forth, in the [various] parts of the earth, there is not that space standing where one would be able to escape from the detrimental act—not even a space of the size of the tip of a hair. That is the meaning of this.

128. That spot one does not find,
Neither in the sky, nor in the ocean's depths,
Nor having entered into a cleft in mountains,
Where abiding, death would not overwhelm one. (9.13)

*na antalikkhe na samuddamajjhe*
*na pabbatānaṃ vivaraṃ pavissa*
*na vijjati so jagatippadeso*
*yatthaṭṭhitaṃ nappasahetha maccu.*

## Death would not overwhelm one: *nappasahetha maccu*

That place does not exist of the earth, even of the size of the tip of a hair, where if one stands, death would not challenge one, or defeat one.

The rest is as in the previous instance [st. 127].

# CHAPTER X

## The Rod
## *Daṇḍa-vaggo*

129. All are frightened of the rod.
Of death all are afraid.
Having made oneself the example,
One should neither slay nor cause to slay. (10.1)

*sabbe tasanti daṇḍassa sabbe bhāyanti maccuno*
*attānaṃ upamaṃ katvā haneyya na ghātaye.*

### All are frightened (of the rod): *sabbe tasanti (daṇḍassa)*

When a rod falls upon them, all beings are frightened of that rod;

### Of death: *maccuno*

And they are indeed frightened of death too. In this discourse the wording admits of no exception, but the sense does. When a king proclaims by drumbeat that all should assemble, all do assemble except the princes and ministers of the state. In the same way, even though it is said that all fear [the rod and death], it must be understood that all are frightened except the following four; the thoroughbred horse, the thoroughbred elephant, the thoroughbred bull, and the influx-extinct [Arahant]. Of these, the influx-extinct does not fear [death, and the like], not seeing a "being" that can die, due to the fact that the notion of a substantial being [or self] is extinct [in such a one]. The other three are not frightened, not seeing a being [that can] become an adversary to them, due to the fact that the notion of self is very strong [in them].

### (Having made oneself the example) one should neither slay nor cause to slay: *(attānaṃ upamaṃ katvā) na haneyya na ghātaye*

"As I am, so are other beings"—seeing thus, let one indeed not strike another, nor get another struck [by someone else]. That is the meaning.

130. All are frightened of the rod.
For all, life is dear.
Having made oneself the example,
One should neither slay nor cause to slay. (10.2)

*sabbe tasanti daṇḍassa sabbesaṃ jīvitaṃ piyaṃ*
*attānaṃ upamaṃ katvā na haneyya na ghātaye.*

## For all, life is dear: *sabbesaṃ jīvitaṃ piyaṃ*

Life is dear and sweet to all beings other than the one in whom intoxicants are extinct. The one in whom intoxicants are extinct, indeed, is detached both in regard to life and in regard to death. The rest is as in the previous [stanza].

131. Who with a rod does hurt
Beings who desire ease,
While himself looking for ease—
He, having departed, ease does not get. (10.3)

132. Who with a rod does not hurt
Beings who desire ease,
While himself looking for ease—
Having departed, ease he will get. (10.4)

*sukhakāmāni bhūtāni yo daṇḍena vihiṃsati*
*attano sukham esāno pecca so na labhate sukhaṃ.*

*sukhakāmāni bhūtāni yo daṇḍena na hiṃsati*
*attano sukham esāno pecca so labhate sukhaṃ.*

[13.]

## Who with a rod (hurts): *yo daṇḍena (vihiṃsati)*

The person who harasses [beings] with a rod, or with pebbles, and so forth,

### Having departed, ease does not get: *pecca so na labhate sukhaṃ*

That person does not obtain, in the world beyond, either the ease that a human being can get, or the ease that a god can get, or the ease of Nibbāna, which is ease absolute.

[132.]

### Having departed, ease he will get: *pecca so labhate sukhaṃ*

In the world beyond, that person gets the threefold ease of the kind stated [above]. That is the meaning.

133. To none speak harshly.
Those thus addressed would retort to you.
Miserable indeed is contentious talk.
Retaliatory rods would touch you. (10.5)

134. If, like a flattened out metal pot,(1)
You yourself do not move,
Why, Nibbāna you have attained!
No contention is found in you. (10.6)

*m' āvoca pharusaṃ kañci vuttā paṭivadeyyu taṃ*
*dukkhā hi sārambhakathā paṭidaṇḍā phuseyyu taṃ.*

*sace neresi attānaṃ kaṃso upahato yathā*
*esa patto'si nibbānaṃ sārambho te na vijjati.*

[133.]

### To none speak harshly: *m' āvoca pharusaṃ kaṃci*

Do not speak harshly to anyone, to any person whomsoever.

### Those thus addressed (would retort to you): *vuttā (paṭi-vadeyyu taṃ)*

Those others who are addressed by you as "ones without virtue" would retort to you in the same way.

(Miserable indeed) is contentious talk:
*(dukkhā hi) sārambhakathā*

This doing- and-retaliating, this [kind of] talk resorted to by two parties, is indeed misery.

Retaliatory rods (would touch you): *paṭidaṇḍā (phuseyyu taṃ)*

On you who harass(2) another with physical punitive acts, on your head would retaliatory punitive acts of the same kind alight.

[134.]

If you (yourself) do not move: *sace neresi (attānaṃ)*

If you are capable of making yourself tranquil [lit. immobile—that is, not reacting to violence],

Like a flattened out metal pot: *kaṃso upahato yathā*

Like a metal pot placed [on the ground], cut out at the rim, and flattened out—such [a pot] will not resound, even if struck with hands and feet or with a stick.

Why, (Nibbāna) you have attained: *esa patto' si (nibbānaṃ)*

If you are able to be such as this, you who are fulfilling this religious practice have "attained Nibbāna," even though (actually) not attained right now.

No contention is found in you: *sārambho te na vijjati*

When this is the case, there is no contention in you; [that is, conduct] that has the characteristic of retaliatory speech, such as "You are deficient in virtue; you all are deficient in virtue," and so forth. The meaning is: there indeed will not be.

135. As with a rod a cowherd
To the pasture goads his cows,
So does old age and death
Goad the life of living beings. (10.7)

*yathā daṇḍena gopālo gāvo pāceti(3) gocaraṃ*
*evaṃ jarā ca maccu ca āyuṃ pācenti pāṇinaṃ.*

### (As with a rod a cowherd) goads (his cows): *(yathā daṇḍena gopālo gāvo) pāceti*

A skilful cowherd checks cows with the rod, even as they move [from the proper area of pasturing] to another area, beats them with it and leads them to a pasture where grass and water is abundant [this is the simile].

### Goad the life: *ayuṃ pācenti*

They cut out the faculty of life, bring it to an end. Decay and mortality are like the cowherd. The faculty of life is like a bullock. Death is like a pasturing ground. Here, birth, right at the outset, directs the life faculty of beings to the proximity of decay, decay to that of disease, disease to that of death. Death deals "a blow with the axe," as it were, and breaks one up, and goes its way. This is the interpretation of the simile.

136. The childish one knows it not,
Even while doing bad deeds.
The one deficient in wisdom by his own deeds
Suffers like one burnt by fire. (10.8)

*atha pāpāni kammāni karaṃ bālo na bujjhati*
*sehi kammehi dummedho aggidaḍḍho va tappati.*

### (The childish one), even (while doing) bad (deeds): *atha pāpāni (kammāni karaṃ bālo)*

The meaning is not only is it that the childish one does detrimental acts under the sway of ill will, but also, even while doing [them], is not aware [of the consequences].

### Knows it not: *na bujjhati*

[Of course] it is not that, doing a detrimental act, a person is unaware [to the extent of not realizing], "Here I am doing a detrimental act." It is said that one is not aware in the sense that one does not know: "For this act, the consequence is such and such."

### The one deficient in wisdom by his own deeds (suffers like) one burnt by fire: *sehi kammehi dummedho aggidaḍḍho (va tappati)*

He, being a person deficient in wisdom, by these acts that are his own, is born in a state of woe and *suffers*(4) *like one burnt by fire:* that is the meaning.

137. Who with a rod harms the offenseless, the harmless
To one of ten places quite quickly one goes down: (10.9)

138. [1] harshly painful feelings, [2] destitution, and [3] fracturing of the body,
[4] grave illness too, [5] even disarrayed mind one would attain. (10.10)

139. [6] trouble from the king or [7] severe slander,
[8] even loss of relatives or [9] dissolution of possessions, (10.11)

140. And also [10] fire, the purifier, burns his houses.
And upon the breaking of his body, the unwise one falls into hell. (10.12)

*yo daṇḍena adaṇḍesu appaduṭṭhesu dussati*
*dasannam aññataraṃ ṭhānaṃ khippam eva nigacchati.*

*vedanaṃ pharusaṃ jāniṃ sarīrassa ca bhedanaṃ*
*garukaṃ vā pi ābādhaṃ cittakkhepaṃ va pāpuṇe.*

*rājato vā upassaggaṃ abbhakkhānaṃ va dāruṇaṃ*
*parikkhayaṃ va ñātīnaṃ bhogānaṃ va pabhaṅguraṃ.*

*athav' assa agārāni aggī ḍahati pāvako*
*kāyassa bhedā duppañño nirayaṃ so upapajjati.*

[137.]

## The offenseless: *adaṇḍesu*

On those who do not resort to punitive action, that is, on those in whom the influxes are extinct [Arahants], and the like.

## The harmless: *appaduṭṭhesu*

Who are without harm toward themselves or toward others.

To one of (ten) places: *(dasannam) aññataraṃ thānaṃ*
To one source among the ten sources of suffering.

[138.]

Feeling: *vedanaṃ*
Acute pain of various kinds such as pains of the head, and so forth.

Destitution: *jāniṃ*
Loss of [what] has been gained with difficulty.

Fracturing: *bhedanaṃ*
Physical mutilation, such as the cutting off of hands, and so forth.

Grave (illness too): *garukaṃ (vā pi ābādham)*
Or else grave ailments of various kinds, such as paralysis, blindness in one eye,(5) crippledness, deformity of arm, violent diseases of the skin, and so forth.

Disarrayed mind: *cittakkhepaṃ*
Lunacy.

[139.]

Trouble: *upassaggaṃ*
Loss of fame; or perils [from actions] of kings—for example, loss of such a position as that of army-chief, and the like.

Slander: *abbhakkhānaṃ*
Grave accusations such as these: "This burglary, and so on, this act against the interests of the monarch, was done by you"—which in reality was something that one neither saw, nor heard, nor thought about.

Even loss of relatives: *parikkhayaṃ ca ñātīnaṃ*
The demise of relations who are capable of being one's support.

Dissolution: *pabhaṅguraṃ*
Breakability [or] the state of rotting away. Grain that is in his house turns rotten, gold turns into charcoal, pearls become cottonseed, *kahāpaṇa* coins become potsherds, two-legged and four-legged creatures become blind and lame; that is the meaning.

[140.]

## Fire . . . burns: *aggī ḍahati*

Even if there is no other fire, at least lightning strikes two or three times a year and burns [ his property], or indeed a fire rises of its own accord and burns.

## Falls into hell: *nirayaṃ so upapajjati*

To show, after having come by one of these ten conditions in this very life, what is [left for such a person] to obtain for certainty in life hereafter, it is said, "He falls into the state of hell!"

141. Neither wandering about naked, nor matted hair, nor mud,
Neither fasting, nor sleeping on hard ground,
Nor dust and dirt, nor austere acts in the crouching posture
Cleanses a mortal who has not transcended doubts. (10.13)

*na naggacariyā na jaṭā na paṅkā nānāsakā thaṇḍilasāyikā vā*
*rajovajallaṃ*(6) *ukkuṭikappadhānaṃ sodhenti maccaṃ*
*avitiṇṇakaṅkhaṃ.*

## Neither fasting: *nānāsakā*

The word is to be broken up as *na+anāsakā*. It means: [austerities] involving the rejection of food.

## Sleeping on hard ground: *thaṇḍilasāyikā*

Sleeping on the ground.

## Dust and dirt: *rajovajallaṃ*

Dust gathered on one's body in the manner of an application of dirt.

## Austere acts in the crouching posture: *ukkuṭikappadhānaṃ*

Exertion made while being in the posture of squatting.

That is what is said; the mortal who would think, "Thus I will attain purity, which amounts to release from the world" and follows [a given course of] activity, after taking upon himself one or another of these [austerities] such as wandering about unclothed, that person would only strengthen his improper perception and become a partaker of [self-]exhaustion. Due to the fact that the eightfold doubt[7] has not been transcended, these, even if diligently followed, do not "*cleanse a mortal who has not transcended doubts.*"

142. Though well adorned, if one would move with tranquility,
At peace, restrained, assured, living the higher life,
Having put down the rod toward all beings,
He is a *brāhmaṇa*, he, a recluse, he, a bhikkhu. (10.14)

*alaṅkato ce pi samaṃ careyya santo danto niyato brahmacārī*
*sabbesu bhūtesu nidhāya daṇḍaṃ so brāhamaṇo so samaṇo sa bhikkhu.*

(Though) well adorned (one would move with tranquility): *alaṅkato (ce pi samaṃ careyya)*

Decked with [fine] clothing and ornaments. The meaning is: If a person though adorned with clothing and ornaments, *would move with tranquility* in physical conduct, and so forth;

At peace: *santo*

On account of the pacification of sensual passion, and so forth;

Restrained: *danto*

On account of control of the senses;

Assured: *niyato*

Assured [of release from the whirl, which is gained] by [attainment of the] four Paths;

Living the higher life: *brahmacārī*

On account of one's excellent way of living;

(Having put down the rod) toward all beings: *sabbesu bhūtesu (nidhāya daṇḍaṃ)*

On account of having laid down punitive acts, and so forth;

A *brahmaṇa*: *brāhmaṇo*

He, being such, should be called a *brāhmaṇa,* on account of having excluded detrimental acts;

## A recluse: *samaṇo*

A recluse on account of having pacified *(samita)* detrimental acts;

## A bhikkhu: *bhikkhu*

A bhikkhu on account of having cut off *(bhinna)* the defilements.

143. [Rarely] in the world is found
A person restrained by shame,
Who awakens to insult
As a good horse to the whip. (10.15)

144. Like a good horse struck by a whip,
Be ardent and deeply moved.
With faith and virtue and enterprise,
With concentration and dhamma-discernment,
With understanding and conduct endowed, mindful,
You will leave behind this weighty misery. (10.16)

*hirīnisedho puriso koci lokasmiṃ vijjati*
*yo nindaṃ appabodhati asso bhadro kasām iva.*

*asso yathā bhadro kasāniviṭṭho ātāpino saṃvegino bhavātha*
*saddhāya sīlena ca vīriyena ca samādhinā dhammavinicchayena ca*
*sampannavijjācaraṇā patissatā pahassatha dukkham idaṃ anappakaṃ.*

[143.]

## Restrained by shame: *hirīnisedho*

One is called "restrained by shame" when by means of [the sense of] shame one dispels the direction of mind toward the unwholesome that has arisen in oneself.

## [Rarely] in the world (is found): *koci lokasmiṃ (vijjati)*

Some such rare [person] is [occasionally] found in the world.

### Who (awakens to) insult: *yo nindaṃ (appabodhati)*

"Awakens" means understands, turning away [from mind] one's arisen sense of insult, performing the religious quester's functions with mindfulness.

### As (a good horse) the whip: *(asso bhadro) kasām iva*

Rare is he who awakens to insult [thus], like a good horse who turns away the whip that falls upon it, who does not allow it to fall on oneself; that is the meaning.

The meaning in brief of the second [stanza] is:

[144.]

### Like a good horse: *asso yathā bhadro*

Just as a good horse, struck by the whip [due to] having been neglectful, thereafter makes an earnest attempt [not to be so neglectful, thinking] "Even I was struck with the whip"—so you too, O bhikkhus,

### Be ardent and deeply moved: *ātāpino saṃvegino bhavātha*(8)

Having become such, and, being endowed

### With faith (and virtue and enterprise, with concentration): *saddhāya (sīlena ca viriyena samādhinā)*

With faith *(saddhā)*, which is twofold, namely, the customary faith and the faith that transcends the world,[9] and also [being endowed] with the fourfold virtue leading to purity,[10] with physical and mental enterprise, and with the integration by the eight attainments;[11]

### And dhamma-discernment: *dhammavinicchayena ca*

And with dhamma-discernment, which has the characteristic of understanding what is the cause and what is not the cause;

### With understanding and conduct endowed: *sampannavijjācaraṇā*

By the fulfillment of the three[12] or the eight forms of understanding,[13] and the fifteen forms of conduct,[14] and;

### Mindful: *patissatā*

On account of awareness that is [constantly] at hand—

(You will leave behind) this weighty (misery): *(pahassatha dukkham) idaṃ anappakaṃ*

Leave behind this misery of the whirl, which is by no means insignificant.

145. Irrigators guide the water.
Fletchers bend the arrow shaft.
Wood the carpenters bend.
Themselves the amenable ones tame. (10.17)

*udakaṃ hi nayanti nettikā usukārā namayanti tejanaṃ*
*dāruṃ namayanti tacchakā attānaṃ damayanti subbatā.*

The amenable ones: *subbatā*

Easy to speak to; easily amenable to advice and instruction; that is the meaning.

The rest is stated above [st. 80].

# CHAPTER XI

## Old Age
## *Jarā-vaggo*

146. Oh, what laughter and why joy,
When constantly aflame?
In darkness enveloped,
You do not seek the lamp. (11.1)

*ko nu hāso*[(1)] *kim ānando niccaṃ pajjalite sati*
*andhakārena onaddhā padīpaṃ na gavessatha.*

Joy: *ānando*

Contentment.

When constantly aflame: *niccaṃ pajjalite sati*

This is what is stated. When this life in the world is constantly aflame with the eleven fires such as sensual passion,[2]

Oh, what laughter: *ko nu hāso*

What laughter is there for you, or contentment? Is this [merriment] indeed not unworthy to be resorted to?

(In darkness) enveloped: *(andhakārena) onaddhā*

*Enveloped* by the *darkness* of the eightfold ignorance.[3]

You do not seek the lamp: *padīpaṃ na gavessatha*

Why *will you not seek* and why not make [for yourselves] *the lamp* of wisdom, for the banishment of that darkness?

147. Oh, see this beautified image;
A mass of sores erected.

Full of illness, highly fancied,
Permanence it has not—or constancy. (11.2)

*passa cittakataṃ bimbaṃ arukāyaṃ samussitaṃ*
*āturaṃ bahusaṃkappaṃ yassa natthi dhuvaṃ ṭhiti.*

### Beautified: *cittakataṃ*

Made beautiful—that is, beautiful on account of dress, ornaments, garlands, lac [a dye], and so forth. That is the meaning.

### Image: *bimbaṃ*

The [physical] personality, structured by limbs and features that are [well proportioned, as for example,] long where length is appropriate, and so forth.

### A mass of sores: *arukāyaṃ*

The body that is a "sore", on account of the nine orifices.

### Erected: *samussitaṃ*

Propped up by the three hundred kinds of bone.

### Full of illness: *āturaṃ*

Constantly [like] a patient because it has at all times to be helped along by [changing of] postures, and so forth.

### Highly fancied: *bahusaṃ kappaṃ*

Fancied in diverse ways by the mass of people.

### Permanence it has not—or constancy: *yassa natthi dhuvaṃ ṭhiti*

Of which there is neither permanency nor constancy. "Look at it! By nature it is definitely liable to break up, to get scattered and to perish." That is the meaning.

148. Quite wasted away is this form,
A nest for disease, perishable.
This putrid accumulation breaks up.
For life has its end in death. (11.3)

*parijiṇṇam idaṃ rūpaṃ roganiḍḍaṃ pabhaṅguraṃ*
*bhijjati*(4) *pūtisandeho maraṇantaṃ hi jīvitaṃ.*

### Quite wasted away (is this form): *parijiṇṇam (idaṃ rūpaṃ)*

The meaning is: "Sister, this form, this body of yours, is quite wasted away due to old age,[5] and [it is]:

### A nest for disease: *roga-niḍḍaṃ*

Because it is the abode of all illnesses."

### Perishable: *pabhaṅguraṃ*

Just as the jackal, even when it is young, is called *jarasigāla* [the ageing fox], and just as the *galoci* creeper, even when it is tender is called *pūtilatā* [the putrefying creeper], in the same way [the human body], even on the day of its birth, even when it is golden-hued, is [described as] perishable because it is [potentially] putrid(6) owing to [the fact that matter is] constantly emanating [from its nine orifices].

### Breaks up: *bhijjati*

This body of yours(7) breaks up, being putrid; it is well to recognize that it will break up in the not too distant future. Why so?

### For life has its end in death: *maraṇantaṃ hi jīvitaṃ*

It is said [to be such] because the life of all beings has death as its end.

149. Like these gourds
Discarded in autumn,
Are gray-hued bones.
Having seen them, what delight? (11.4)

*yan' imāni apatthāni alābūni va*(8) *sārade*
*kāpotakāni aṭṭhīni tāni disvāna kā rati.*

### (Like) gourds . . . in autumn: *sārade alābūni (va)*

Like gourds in the season of autumn, scattered here and there, attacked by wind and sun,

### Discarded: *apatthāni*

Thrown away,

### Gray-hued: *kāpotakāni*

Having the [gray] hue of pigeons—

### Having seen them: *tāni disvāna*

Having seen the bones that are such,[9]

### What delight: *kā rati*

What delight is there for you? Is it not the case that even a slight sensual delight is improper to be entertained? That is the meaning.

150. Of bones the city is made,
Plastered with flesh and blood,
Where decay and death are deposited,
And pride and ingratitude. (11.5)

*aṭṭhīnaṃ nagaraṃ kataṃ maṃsalohitalepanaṃ*
*yattha jarā ca maccu ca*(10) *māno makkho ca ohito.*

The meaning of this is [as follows]: Just as, to deposit [grains for] early and late food, and so forth,(11) they construct a shed called a "city" [i.e., a protected structure], making a scaffolding with timber, tying it up with creepers and plastering it over with mud—in the same way,

### The city is made: *nagaraṃ kataṃ*

Is this internal ["city", i.e., the body, made], raising [the scaffolding of] the three hundred bones, tied up with sinews, plastered over with flesh and blood, and covered with the skin—

### (Where decay and death) are deposited, and pride and ingratitude: *yattha jarā ca maccu ca) mano makkho ca ohito*

Which serves for the "depositing" of [1] decay that has the characteristic of withering away, [2] death that has the characteristic of perishing, [3] self-estimation that has the characteristic of self-consciousness based on [the pride of its] good health,(12) and so forth, and [4] ingratitude that has the characteristic of negating deeds well done.(13)

Such physical and mental disorder is indeed deposited here. Hence there is nothing worthy to be taken out of it.

151. Even well-decked royal chariots wear away;
And the body too falls into decay.
But the dhamma of the good ones goes not to decay,
For the good speak [of it] with the good.(14) (11.6)

*jīranti ve rājarathā sucittā atho sarīram pi jaraṃ upeti*
*sataṃ ca dhammo na jaraṃ upeti santo ha ve sabbhi pavedayanti.*

### Even: *ve*

This is a particle [of emphasis].

### Well-decked (royal chariots wear away): *(jīranti rājarathā) sucittā*

Even the chariots of kings, which are beautifully decked with the seven [kinds of] jewels and with other chariot ornaments—even they wear out.

### And the body too (falls into decay): *sarīram pi (jaraṃ upeti)*

Not only chariots, but indeed even this body, which is carefully maintained, wears out, reaching a state of decay, and so forth.

### But (the dhamma) of the good ones (goes not to decay): *sataṃ ca (dhammo na jaraṃ upeti)*

But the ninefold dhamma that transcends the world, of noble ones, such as the Buddhas, and the others, does not go to decay in the sense that it does not create any peril whatsoever [to someone who follows it].

### The good speak: *santo . . . pavedayanti*

The meaning is: In this manner, do the good ones, such as the Buddhas, and the others, speak with [other] good ones—that is, the wise.

152. This unlearned person
Grows up like an ox.
His bulk increases,
His wisdom increases not. (11.7)

*appassutāyaṃ puriso balivaddo va jīrati*
*maṃsāni tassa vaḍḍhanti paññā tassa na vaḍḍhati.*

### This unlearned (person): *appassutāyaṃ (puriso)*

This one[15] has learned little—due to not having [mastery of] one of the group of fifty discourses *(suttas)*, or of two such groups, or of several chapters *(vaggas)* or of even one [discourse] or two discourses, together with [their] final sections.

On the other hand one who has mastered the topics of meditation and is engaged [in their practice] is called "one who has learned much."

### Grows up like an ox: *balivaddo va jīrati*

Just as a bull, who is growing old and growing in size, does not grow for the benefit of its mother, or father, or for the others related to it, but just ages without purpose, in the same way this one too performs neither the duty regarding the preceptor, nor that regarding the teacher, nor the duties regarding visitors [to the monastery], and so forth, nor does he show a taste for meditativeness. He just ages without purpose.

### His bulk increases: *maṃsāni tassa vaḍḍhanti*

In the case of a bull discarded in the wilds because he is unable to bear the yoke or the plough, his bulk increases even as he lives there [in the forest]. In just the same way, in the case of this one, who has been given up by his preceptors, and so forth, his bulk increases as he looks after his body, obtaining the four requisites on account of [his membership in] the Saṅgha, and [as he attends to its medical care by] administering emetics, and so forth. He is [seen to be] moving about, having become opulent.

### (His) wisdom (increases not): *paññā (tassa na vaḍḍhati)*

But his wisdom, both the worldly and that which is beyond the world, does not grow so much as by an "inch." Like trees and creepers of the forest, only his greed and the ninefold self-estimation[16] increase—dependent on the six sense-doors.[17] That is the meaning.

153. I ran through *saṃsāra*, with its many births,
Searching for, but not finding, the house-builder.
Misery is birth again and again. (11.8)

154. House-builder, you are seen!
The house you shall not build again!
Broken are your rafters, all,
Your roof beam destroyed.
Freedom from the *saṃkhāras* has the mind attained.

To the end of cravings has it come. (11.9)
(The commentary takes line 6 to mean:
To the end of cravings have I come.)

*anekajātisaṃsāraṃ sandhāvissaṃ anibbisaṃ*
*gahakārakaṃ gavesanto dukkhā jāti punappunaṃ.*

*gahakāraka diṭṭho'si puna gehaṃ na kāhasi*
*sabbā te phāsukā bhaggā gahakūṭaṃ visaṃkhitaṃ*[18]
*visaṃkhāragataṃ cittaṃ taṇhānaṃ khayaṃ ajjhagā.*

[153.]

## I ran ... searching for the house-builder: *sandhāvissaṃ gahakārakaṃ gavesanto*

I did indeed travel along, did move from end to end, for so long over this whirl of *saṃsāra* consisting of many hundreds of thousands of births, searching for craving, the builder of this house of individuality, and with firm resolve, made at the feet of Dīpaṅkara, for the wisdom of enlightenment[19] wherewith it is possible to see him.

## But not finding: *anibbisaṃ*

[I traveled so long] not finding that wisdom.

## Misery is birth again and again: *dukkhā jāti punappunaṃ*

This statement [gives] the reason for the search for the house-builder: It is a torment to undergo this process of being born again and again, mixed up as it is[20] with decay, disease, and death. Nor does it cease as long as he [the builder] is not seen. Hence it is that I traveled along, looking for him; such is the meaning.

[154.]

## You are seen: *diṭṭho'si*

Now you are seen by me, as I penetrated through to the wisdom of complete enlightenment.

## The house you shall not build again: *puna gehaṃ no kāhasi*

No more will you build for me this house of individuality in this whirl of *saṃsāra*.

(Broken) are your rafters, all: *sabbā te phāsukā (bhaggā)*
All your remaining rafters of defilements have been shattered by me.

Your roof beam destroyed: *gahakūṭaṃ visaṃkhitaṃ*
And also destroyed by me is the pinnacle of this house of individuality that is built by you and is constituted by ignorance.

Freedom from the *saṃkhāras* has the mind attained: *visaṃkhāragataṃ cittaṃ*
Now my mind has entered the state of being free from the compounded—by way of making Nibbāna its objective.

To the end of cravings has it come: *taṇhānaṃ khayam ajjhagā*
And I have obtained(21) the worthy status that amounts to the extinction of (all) forms of greed.

155. Not having lived the higher life,
Nor having acquired wealth in youth,
They wither away like old herons
In a lake without fish. (11.10)

156. Not having lived the higher life,
Nor having acquired wealth in youth,
Like [arrows] discharged from a bow they lie
Brooding over the things of yore. (11.11)

*acaritvā brahmacariyaṃ aladdhā yobbane dhanaṃ*
*jiṇṇakoñcā va jhāyanti khīṇamacche va pallale.*

*acaritvā brahmacariyaṃ aladdhā yobbane dhanaṃ*
*senti cāpātikhīṇā*(22) *va purāṇāni anutthunaṃ*(23).

[155.]

Not having lived (the higher life): *acaritvā (brahmacariyam)*
Not having led the life of religiousness,

(Nor having acquired wealth) in youth: *(aladdhā) yobbane (dhanaṃ)*

And not having obtained wealth at the time when it is possible to earn unearned riches or to maintain riches earned,

(They wither away like old herons in a lake) without fish: *(jiṇṇakoñcā va jhāyanti) khīṇamacche (va pallale)*

Childish ones who are such wither away like old herons with fallen wings in a lake where the fish are dead. This is what is stated: the fact that these persons[24] did not have a place to live in is comparable with the absence of water in the lake. Their not having wealth is like there being no fish in the lake. Their inability to raise wealth now on land or water or highroad is like the fact that there is no flying up and getting away[(25)] for the herons whose wings have fallen. Hence, just like herons whose wings are fallen, they remain here and grieve.

[156.]

Like [arrows] discharged from a bow they lie: *senti cāpātikhīṇā va*

Discharged from a bow. The meaning is: released from a bow. This is what is said: Just as arrows released from a bow, having flown as far as the momentum allowed and having fallen [to the ground], become "food" for termites, there being no one to take them up [and use on the bow again], so these three persons too who have passed [their] span of life will [soon] meet death, being now unable to raise themselves up [and return to vigor]. Hence it is said, "Like [arrows] discharged from a bow they lie."

Brooding over the things of yore: *purāṇāni anutthunaṃ*

They lie, bewailing and grieving, and brooding, lamenting over what they had done and eaten and drunk and danced and sung and played, and so on, saying, "Thus had we eaten [in days past], thus had we drunk!"

# CHAPTER XII

## The Self
## *Atta-vaggo*

157. If one would regard oneself as dear,
One would guard oneself with diligence.
The wise one would look after [himself]
During any one of the [night's] three watches. (12.1)

*attānañ ce piyaṃ jaññā rakkheyya naṃ surakkhitaṃ*
*tiṇṇam aññataraṃ yāmaṃ paṭijaggeyya paṇḍito.*

In regard to the word "watch" (*yāma*) of this verse: By virtue of his being Master of Dhamma, by virtue of his skill in discourse,[1] the Teacher [here] indicates any one of the three stages [of life] as a "watch." Hence the meaning here must be understood as follows:

### If one would regard oneself as dear: *attānaṃ ce piyaṃ jaññā*

If one would regard oneself as dear,

### One would guard [oneself] with diligence: *rakkheyya naṃ surakkhitaṃ*

In such a way that one would be really well guarded.

In this respect one does not surely guard oneself even if one, being a layperson were living with defenses provided, having entered a well-enclosed inner room in the upper floor of a mansion, thinking, "I will guard myself"; nor, being a monk, if one were living in a rock cave with well-enclosed and covered doors and windows. On the other hand, one does guard oneself if, being a layperson, one were performing wholesome deeds such as the practices of giving and being virtuous, to the best of one's ability; or, being a monk, evincing eager interest in one's duties and services, study of texts and mindfulness. Even if one is unable [to do so] in [all] three stages [of life], the wise person does indeed look after oneself in one of them; if, as a layperson, one is not able to do wholesome deeds in the first stage [of life] because one is [then] engaged in playfulness, then one would become mindful and do wholesome deeds in the middle stage [of life]. And if in the middle stage [of life] one is unable to do wholesome deeds [because one is] looking after one's family, then one would do [them] in the final stage [of life]. By the one who does so, the self is really taken care of. To the one who does not do so, the self is indeed not dear, for such a one causes it to turn toward the states of woe.

And, being a monk, if one falls into heedlessness in the first stage [of life], because [then] one is engaged in the recitation of texts, committing them to memory and repeating them, [and also] attending to [prescribed] duties and services, then one would perform the [due] function of the monastic career with mindfulness in the middle stage [of life]. And if in the middle stage of life one lapses into heedlessness, [because then one is] engaged in determining the interpretation of texts learned in the first stage, [and also] inquiring into matters of propriety and impropriety, one would certainly perform with mindfulness the [due] function of the monastic career in the final stage [of one's life]. Thus indeed is the self well taken care of by the one who does so. To the one who does not do so, the self is indeed not dear. On the contrary such a one torments it with the torment of subsequent regret.

158. First, one would get oneself
Established in what is proper;
Then one would advise another.
[Thus] the wise one would not suffer. (12.2)

*attānam eva paṭhamaṃ patirūpe nivesaye*
*ath' aññam anusāseyya na kilisseyya paṇḍito.*

## One would get (oneself) established in what is proper: *patirūpe nivesaye*

One would cause [oneself] to be established in a befitting quality.

This is what is said: Who is desirous of instructing another, by [recommending] such qualities as wanting little or practicing the conduct of the "noble family,"[2]

## First . . . oneself: *attānam eva* . . .

He would, first of all, become established in that quality. Having [oneself] become so established,

## (Then) one would advise another: *(atha) aññam anusāseyya*

One would then instruct another by means of those qualities. He who is merely advising another, without causing himself to dwell in that [which he recommends], receives [only] insult from others and indeed is subjected to pain. [On the other hand] the one who advises [others] after having caused oneself to dwell in that [which one recommends] receives praise from others and hence is not subjected to pain. Acting in this way,

## The wise one would not suffer: *paṇḍito na kilisseyya*

The wise one would not be subjected to pain.

159. One would oneself so do
As one advises another.
Then it is the restrained one who would restrain.
For, truly, it is the self that is hard to restrain. (12.3).

*attānaṃ ce tathā kayirā yathaññam anusāsati*
*sudanto vata dammetha attā hi kira duddamo.*

## As one advises another: *yathaññam anusāsati*

The meaning of this is: In what manner a monk advises another—[for example,] that one should walk the cloister in the first watch [of the day], and so forth—one would on one's own part do just so, oneself performing the cloister walk, and so forth.

When such is the case,

## It is the restrained one who would restrain: *sudanto vata dammetha*

One would then be training the other, being oneself well controlled by that quality about which one advises another.

## For, truly, it is the self that is hard to restrain: *attā hi kira duddamo*

For this self is [what is ] hard to restrain. Hence, in what way it becomes well restrained, in that way it would be restrained.

160. Oneself indeed is patron of oneself.
Who else indeed could be one's patron?
With oneself well restrained,
One gets a patron hard to get. (12.4)

(Commentary: One gets a support hard to get.)

*attā hi attano nātho ko hi nātho paro siyā*
*attanā va sudantena nāthaṃ labhati dullabhaṃ.*

Here, *nātha* (patron) means "support." This is what is stated:

(Oneself indeed is patron of oneself): *(attā hi attano nātho)*
Inasmuch as it is possible for one who is self-accomplished and self-possessed to do wholesome deeds and attain a heavenly world or develop the Path or realize the Fruit, the self is the support of the self.

(Who else indeed could be one's patron): *(ko hi nātho paro siyā)*
Hence, what other peson could [indeed] be the support for anyone?

With oneself well restrained: *attanā va sudantena*
With steady self,

One gets a patron hard to get: *nāthaṃ labhati dullabhaṃ*
One obtains a rare support—namely, the Fruit of Arahantship. It is with reference to Arahantship that it is said here that one gets a support that is hard to get.

161. The wrong done by oneself
Is born of oneself, is produced in oneself.
It grinds one deficient in wisdom
As a diamond grinds a rock-gem. (12.5)

*attanā va kataṃ pāpaṃ attajaṃ attasambhavaṃ*
*abhimanthati dummedhaṃ vajiraṃ v'amhamayaṃ maṇiṃ.*

## (As) a diamond grinds a rock-gem: *vajiraṃ v'amhamayaṃ maṇiṃ*

Here the words are to be broken up as a *vajiraṃ va amhamayaṃ maniṃ.*

What is said is this: Just as a diamond, which is made of stone, a product of stone, "eats" into the rock-gem, which too is made of the selfsame [material, namely] stone, a product of stone—[i.e., it "eats" into] the very place out of which it originated, perforates it thoroughly, cuts it to bits, and makes it unsuitable for use—in the same way the unwholesome deed done by oneself, which originated in oneself, grinds into the person who is deficient in wisdom; it grinds him in the [four] states of woe and destroys him.

162. Whose extreme unvirtue overspreads [him]
Like the *māluvā* creeper a *sāla* tree,
He does to himself,
Just as a foe wishes [to do] to him.[3] (12.6)

*yassa accantadussīlyaṃ māluvā sālam iv' otataṃ*
*karoti so tath'attānaṃ yathā naṃ icchatī diso.*

## Extreme unvirtue: *accantadussīlyaṃ*

The condition of being definitely unvirtuous. A layperson who is from birth doing deeds that constitute the tenfold path of the unwholesome,[4] or a monk who falls into grave lapses in discipline from the day of his higher ordination, is said to be one who is definitely unvirtuous[(5)]. In this regard, he [may have been] unvirtuous in two or three lives: the [term] "condition of being unvirtuous" is used with reference to the unvirtuousness resulting from his behavior [as a perpetrator of the unwholesome in several lives]. In the present context, craving arisen in dependence upon the six [sense-]doors of an unvirtuous person should be understood as [that] condition of being unvirtuous.

In the case of the person[(6)] whose life the unvirtuousness that is craving has spread over and completely overshadowed

—just as a *māluvā* [creeper], spreading over[(7)] a *sāla* [tree], capturing water with its leaves, when it rains, completely overwhelms it by tearing it down—

[that person] does to himself as a foe wishing him ill wants [to do to him], as he is brought down to the states of woe, torn by craving that is unvirtuousness

—like that tree which is brought down to the ground torn by the *māluvā*.[8]

163. Easy to do are things not good
And those harmful for oneself.
But what is beneficial and good,
Is exceedingly difficult to do. (12.7)

*sukarāni asādhūni attano ahitāni ca*
*yaṃ ve hitaṃ ca sādhuṃ ca taṃ ve paramadukkaraṃ.*

### Things not good: *asādhūni*

The meaning is: Those deeds that are not good,

### And those harmful for oneself: *attano ahitāni ca*

That lead one to states of woe and are harmful simply because [they are] done.

### Easy to do: *sukarāni*

They are easy to do.

### But what is beneficial: *hitaṃ ca*

But that deed which, because it is done, is beneficial to oneself,

### And good: *sādhuṃ ca*

Which is commendable in the sense that it is faultless, and which leads one to states of weal and Nibbāna, that is extremely hard to do—like reversing the *Gaṅgā*, which is inclined toward the east, and turning it [so as to flow] to the west.

164. Who is deficient in wisdom,
Because of detrimental view,
Obstructs the instruction of the Arahants,
The Noble Ones who live dhamma;
For one's own destruction one ripens,
Like the fruits of a reed. (12.8)

*yo sāsanaṃ arahataṃ ariyānaṃ dhammajīvinaṃ*
*paṭikkosati dummedho diṭṭhiṃ nissāya pāpikaṃ*
*phalāni kaṭṭhakasseva*(9) *attaghaññāya phallati.*

## Deficient in wisdom: *dummedho*

The meaning is: The person who is deficient in wisdom and who, out of fear of losing the favors that he receives and [also] due to improper views, obstructs those who say, "We will hear dhamma, we will give alms."

## (Obstructs) the instruction of the Arahants, The Noble Ones, who live dhamma: *sāsanaṃ arahataṃ ariyānaṃ dhammajīvinaṃ (paṭikkosati)*

Such a one obstructs the instruction of worthy ones who live dhamma, the instruction of Buddhas.

## For one's own destruction one ripens (like the fruits of a reed): *(phalāni kaṭṭhakasseva) attaghaññāya phallati*

That obstruction of his and that improper view are like the *kaṭṭha(ka)*—that is, the bamboo [bearing] fruit. How so? Just as the *kaṭṭhaka* when bearing fruit does so for its own destruction, so does one "bear fruit" [i.e., do deeds which tend] toward one's own destruction. [Regarding the bamboo bearing fruit, and so forth] it has been said:

"Its fruit destroys the banana [plant], and the bamboo, and the reed; good treatment destroys the bad man, as pregnancy destroys the she-mule."(10)

165. By oneself is wrong done,
By oneself is one defiled.
By oneself wrong is not done,
By oneself, surely, is one cleansed.
One cannot purify another;
Purity and impurity are in oneself [alone]. (12.9)

*attanā va kataṃ pāpaṃ attanā saṃkilissati*
*attanā akataṃ pāpaṃ attanā va visujjhati*
*suddhi asuddhi paccattaṃ nāñño aññaṃ visodhaye.*

The meaning of this [verse] is:

## By oneself is one defiled: *attanā saṃkilissati*

He by whom the unwholesome deed has been done, he is defiled by his own [conduct], suffering misery in the four states of woe.[11]

### By oneself is wrong not done: *attanā akataṃ pāpaṃ*

[But] he by whom wrong has not been done,

### By oneself, surely, is one cleansed: *attanā va visujjhati*

He, proceeding to a state of weal, and to Nibbāna,(12) becomes purified by his own [conduct].

### (Purity and) impurity are in oneself: *(suddhi) asuddhi paccattaṃ*

Both purity, which amounts to wholesome deeds, and impurity, which amounts to unwholesome deeds, mature within the very self of the beings who are their doers.

### One cannot purify another: *nāñño aññaṃ visodhaye*

One person may not purify another.

What is said is [that] one neither purifies [another], nor defiles.

166. One would not abandon one's own purpose
Because of the purpose of another, even though great,
Having well understood one's own purpose,
One would be intent on the true purpose. (12.10)

*attadatthaṃ paratthena bahunā' pi na hāpaye*
*attadatthaṃ abhiññāya sadatthapasuto siyā.*

The meaning of this is: First of all [as for a layperson], one would not neglect one's own purpose, be it no more than a "pennyworth," for the sake of the purpose of another, be it worth even a thousand; for it is one's own purpose, be it a mere "pennyworth," that provides the wherewithal for one's sustenance, and not the purpose of another.

[In the text, however,] without putting it in this manner [the matter] has been stated as a "topic of meditation" [i.e., as advice for the meditating monk]. Hence, on account of the notion "I do not neglect my own purpose," the duty that has devolved on the Saṅgha, such as maintaining the shrine in good repair, would not be abandoned by a bhikkhu, nor the duty in respect of one's preceptor. For, only by fulfilling the conduct pertaining to [these] details, does one realize the noble Fruits, and so forth, [and] in that sense this too is "one's own purpose."

One who has embarked on insight to a pronounced degree and lives hoping for penetrative understanding [to occur] any moment in the present—would certainly perform one's own [meditative] task, fostering also [at the same time] the duties in respect of one's preceptor, and the like.(13)

## Having well understood one's own purpose:
*attadattham abhiññāya*

Having well understood one's own purpose, which is such, [i.e.,] having regarded [it as follows:] "This is [what constitutes] my own purpose,"

## One would be intent on the true purpose:
*sadatthapasuto siyā*

One would be diligently engaged in [the pursuit of ] one's own purpose.

# CHAPTER XIII

## The World
## *Loka-vaggo*

167. To lowly quality one should not resort;
With heedlessness one should not live.
To an improper view one should not resort.
And one should not be a "world-augmenter." (13.1)

*hīnaṃ dhammaṃ na seveyya pamādena na saṃvase*
*micchādiṭṭhiṃ na seveyya na siyā lokavaddhano.*

### To lowly quality (one should not resort): *hīnaṃ dhammaṃ (na seveyya)*

Here the "lowly quality" means the five strands of sensuality:[1] it is the lowly quality that is liable to be resorted to by[(2)] [beings unrefined such as] even camels and bullocks. It is called lowly because it causes one to be born in lowly stations [of existence] such as the states of woe. Let one not resort to it.

### With heedlessness one should not live: *pamādena na saṃvase*

And let one not live with heedlessness, which has the characteristic of slackening of awareness.

### (To an improper view one should not resort): *(micchādiṭṭhiṃ na seveyya)*

And let one not resort to an improper view.[3]

### (And) one should not be a "world-augmenter": *na siyā lokavaddhano*

He who does so [resorts to the lowly, etc.] is said to be "one who augments the world" [*saṃsāra*].[(4)] Hence, by not acting thus, be one who does not augment the world.

168. One should stand up, not be neglectful,
Follow dhamma, which is good conduct.
One who lives dhamma, sleeps at ease
In this world and also in the next. (13.2)

169. One should follow dhamma, which is good conduct,
Not that which is poor conduct.
One who lives dhamma, sleeps at ease
In this world and also in the next. (13.3)

*uttiṭṭhe*(5) *nappamajjeyya dhammaṃ sucaritaṃ care*
*dhammacārī sukhaṃ seti asmiṃ loke paramhi ca.*

*dhammaṃ care sucaritaṃ na taṃ duccaritaṃ care*
*dhammacārī sukhaṃ seti asmiṃ loke paramhi ca.*

The commentary follows another interpretation:

168. With regard to standing for alms, let one not be neglectful,
Let one follow the proper practice.
One following the [proper] practice sleeps at ease
In this world and also in the next. (13.2)

169. Let one follow the proper practice
Not that which is improper.
One following the [proper] practice sleeps at ease
In this world and also in the next. (13.3)

[168.]

### With regard to standing [for alms]: *uttiṭṭhe*

In regard to food that is to be accepted standing at the doorstep of others.

### Let one not be neglectful: *na pamajjeyya*

When one seeks fine food, [even though] not abandoning the practice of begging for alms, one is said to be neglectful of "standing [for alms]." [But] when one goes [for alms] in the order [of houses, not choosing the houses where fine foods may be available], one is said to be "not neglectful." Doing so, let one not be neglectful of standing [for alms].

## (Let one follow the [proper]) practice: *dhammaṃ (care sucaritaṃ)*

Proceeding in the order [of houses], casting aside impropriety, let one follow well that very practice of begging for alms.

## (One following the [proper] practice) sleeps at ease: *(dhammacārī) sukhaṃ seti*

This is only [the form of] discourse; [its] meaning is: the one who lives dhamma—that is, who is following this dhamma of going for alms in this manner, lives at ease in all the four modes of deportment[6] [not merely "sleeps" at ease], in this world and in the world beyond.

[169.]

## Not that which is improper: *na taṃ duccaritaṃ*

Going for alms at an unsuitable place such as [the house] of a prostitute, and so forth, one follows the practice badly. Without following the practice thus, let one follow it well, not badly. The rest [of the verse] has the same sense as that explained [above].

170. As upon a bubble one would look,
As one would look upon a mirage,
The one considering the world thus,
King Death does not see. (13.4)

*yathā bubbulakaṃ passe yathā passe marīcikaṃ*
*evaṃ lokaṃ avekkhantaṃ maccurājā na passati.*

## A mirage: *marīcikaṃ*

An illusion. An illusion appears in the form of a house, or the like, but is intangible, empty, and insubstantial to those who come close to it.

## The one considering (the world thus), King Death does not see: *(evaṃ lokaṃ) avekkhantaṃ maccurājā na passati*

The King of Death does not see the one who perceives the world of *khandha*s, and the like, as one would perceive a bubble, in the sense that it comes into being and breaks up, or as one would perceive an illusion—that is, as empty and insubstantial of nature.

171. Come ye, look at this world—
Like an adorned royal chariot—
Wherein childish ones are immersed;
No clinging there is among those who really know. (13.5)

*etha passath' imaṃ lokaṃ cittaṃ rājarathūpamaṃ*
*yattha bālā visīdanti natthi saṅgo vijānataṃ.*

### Come ye, look: *etha passatha*

[The Buddha] has said this with reference to the prince;[7]

### At this world: *imaṃ lokaṃ*

At this existence constituted by the world of *khandha*s, and so forth.

### Like an adorned royal chariot: *cittam rājarathūpamaṃ*

Bedecked with dress and ornament like a royal chariot beautified with the seven jewels, and the like.

### Wherein childish ones (are immersed): *yattha bālā (visīdanti)*

Which existence only the childish ones are immersed in.

### Among those who really know: *vijānataṃ*

To the wise ones who do understand—

### No clinging there is: *natthi sangho*

There is not a single attachment in regard to it, among attachments such as [sensual] desire, and so on.[8] That is the meaning.

172. And who having been heedless formerly
But later is heedless not,
He this world illumines
Like the moon set free from a cloud. (13.6)

*yo ca pubbe pamajjitvā pacchā so nappamajjati*
*so maṃ lokaṃ pabhāseti abbhā mutto va candimā.*

### (And who) having been heedless formerly but later is heedless not: *(yo) pubbe pamajjitvā pacchā nappamajjati*

The meaning of this is: the person who having been earlier neglectful, either in the performance of services and practices or in [textual] recitation, and so forth, is later not neglectful.

### He (this world illumines like the moon set free from a cloud): *so (maṃ lokaṃ pabhāseti abbhā mutto va candimā)*

He, spending his time in the ease of Path and Fruit, illumines this world of *khanda*s, and so forth, with understanding [obtained by] the Paths, as the moon, freed of clouds, [illumines] the world of space.

173. Whose bad deed done
Is covered by what is wholesome,
He this world illumines
Like the moon set free from a cloud. (13.7)

*yassa pāpaṃ kataṃ kammaṃ kusalena piṭhīyati*
*so maṃ lokaṃ pabhāseti abbhā mutto va candimā.*

Here "what is wholesome" is said with reference to the Path of Arahantship. The meaning of the rest is clear.

174. This world has become blinded, as it were.
Few here see insightfully.
Like a bird set free from a net,
Few to heaven go. (13:8)

*andhabhūto ayaṃ loko tanuk'ettha vipassati*
*sakunto jālamutto va appo saggāya gacchati.*

### This world: *ayaṃ loko*

This ordinary folk of the world.

### Has become blinded: *andhabhūto*

Blinded, due to not having the eye of insight.

### Few here (see) insightfully: *tanukettha (vipassati)*

A few here, not many, discern [life] in terms of impermanence, and so forth.

### Like (a bird) set free from a net: *(sakunto) jālamutto va*

Just as, among quails covered with a net and captured by a skilful hunter of birds, one escapes from the net, whereas the rest move [further] into that very net,

### (Few to heaven go): *(appo saggāya gacchati)*

In the same way, among beings who are overspread by the "net of Māra," many are they who move into the states of woe, and only an occasional person reaches a state of weal, or Nibbāna. That is the meaning.

175. Swans go along the path of the sun.
And in the air they go with psychic power.
The wise ones are led from the world,
Having conquered Māra and his cohorts. (13.9)

*haṃsādiccapathe yanti ākāse yanti iddhiyā*
*nīyanti dhīrā lokamhā jetvā māraṃ savāhiniṃ.*

### Swans (go) along the path of the sun: *haṃsā' diccapathe (yanti)*

These swans go through the sky.[9]

### And in the air they go with psychic power: *ākāse yanti iddhiyā*

They too go in the air whose "bases of psychic power" *(iddhipādā)* are well developed.[10]

### The wise ones (having conquered Māra and his cohorts): *dhīrā (savāhiniṃ māraṃ jetvā)*(11)

And the steadfast, wise ones too, having defeated Māra with his armies,[12]

### Are led (from the world): *nīyanti (lokamhā)*

Make [their] exit from this world, which is a whirl—they reach Nibbāna. That is the meaning.

176. Of person who has overstepped one dhamma,
Who speaks falsehood,
Who has turned the back on the world beyond—
There is no wrong that cannot be done. (13.10)

*ekaṃ dhammaṃ atītassa musāvādissa jantuno*
*vitiṇṇaparalokassa natthi pāpaṃ akāriyaṃ.*

## One dhamma: *ekaṃ dhammaṃ*

Here "one dhamma" means truthfulness.

## (Of a person) who speaks falsehood: *musāvādissa*

To that kind of liar in whose words truthfulness is not found, not even one word out of ten—

## Who has turned the back on the world beyond: *vitiṇṇaparalokassa*

Who has discarded the world beyond—such a person sees neither the bliss of [the world of] human beings, nor that of the worlds of the gods, nor finally that of Nibbāna. These three kinds of bliss he sees not.

## There is no wrong (that cannot be done): *natthi pāpaṃ (akāriyaṃ)*

To him who is such there is no [such thought]: "This detrimental act should not be done."

177. Truly, no misers get to the world of gods.
Certainly, childish ones do not applaud giving.
The wise one gladly approves giving;
Hence indeed is he at ease in the hereafter. (13.11)

*na ve kadariyā devalokaṃ vajanti bālā ha ve nappasaṃsanti dānaṃ*
*dhīro ca dānaṃ anumodamāno ten' eva so hoti sukhī parattha.*

## Misers: *kadariyā*

Here "misers" means those hardened in stinginess.

### Childish ones: *bālā*

Those who know neither this world nor the world beyond.

### The wise: *dhīro*

The wise person.

### (Hence indeed is he) at ease in the hereafter: *(ten' eva so hoti) sukhī parattha*

For that very reason [i.e., of being wise], he, due to the merit of gladly approving [another's] act of giving, is at ease, enjoying divine bliss in the world beyond.

178. Better than sole sovereignty over the earth,
Or the journey to heaven,
Than lordship over all the worlds,
Is the Fruit of Stream Attainment. (13.12)

*pathavyā ekarajjena saggassa gamanena vā*
*sabbalokādhipaccena sotāpattiphalaṃ varaṃ.*

### Than sole sovereignty over the earth: *pathavyā ekarajjena*

This means: than the regal status of a universal monarch.

### Or the journey to heaven: *saggassa gamanena vā*

Or than the attainment of the twenty-six kinds of heaven.[13]

### Than lordship over all the worlds: *sabbalokādhipaccena*

Than lordship in the entire world together with the *nāga*s, *supaṇṇa*s, and *vemānika-peta*s[14]—in the world that is of such extent—and not just in one[(15)] [sphere of it].

### Better . . . is the Fruit of Stream Attainment: *sotāpattiphalaṃ varaṃ*

Inasmuch as one is certainly not freed from [birth in] the states of woe, and so forth, even though one has exercised sovereignty in so much of the world, but one who has obtained Stream Attainment has the gates of those states closed and is not [liable to be] born in an eighth life [after the present one], even if one is the weakest among all [of the different kinds of noble person]—therefore the Fruit of Stream Attainment alone is better and nobler [than such sovereignty].

# CHAPTER XIV

## The Awakened One
## *Buddha-vaggo*

179. Whose victory is not turned into defeat,
Whose victory no one in this world reaches,
That Awakened One whose range is limitless,
Him, the trackless, by what track will you lead? (14.1)
(The commentary takes line 2 to mean:
After whose victory no [defilement] remains.)

180. For whom craving there is not, the netlike, the clinging,
To lead him wheresoever;
That Awakened One whose range is limitless,
Him, the trackless, by what track will you lead? (14.2)

*yassa jitaṃ nāvajīyati jitam assa noyāti koci loke*
*taṃ buddham anantagocaraṃ apadaṃ kena padena nessatha.*

*yassa jālinī visattikā taṇhā natthi kuhiṃci netave*
*taṃ buddham anantagocaraṃ apadaṃ kena padena nessatha.*

[179.]

Whose victory is not turned into defeat: *yassa jitaṃ nāvajīyati*
The victory of the Fully Awakened One is not turned to defeat, does not become a poor victory, due to the fact that the mass of defilements such as [sensual] attachments, and so forth, conquered [by him] by the various Paths, will not be reactivated.

## (Whose victory) no (one in this world) reaches: *(jitam assa) na yāti (koci loke)*

## (After whose victory) no [defilement] remains: *no yāti*

*No yāti* is [the equivalent of] *na uyyāti.*(1)

Of [sensual] attachments, and so forth, there is not [even] one defilement remaining behind the mass of defilements he has conquered; [the victory is complete; a defilement which] follows [it, there is] not.

## (That Awakened One) whose range is limitless: *(taṃ buddham) anantagocaraṃ*

[The Awakened One] whose range is limitless, who is of limitless range on account of his omniscient knowledge with its endless [field of potential] objectives.

## (Him, the trackless,) by what track (will you lead): *(apadaṃ) kena padena (nessatha)*

(Him, "the footless") by what "foot" [will you lead]? He in whom there is at least one of the three "tracks," such as sensual attachment [by which one walks into the whirl], him you will lead [into your trap] by that track; but not even one such track is there for the Buddha; by what track [then] will you lead that "trackless" Buddha [into your trap]?[2]

[180.]

## Netlike: *jālinī*

In the second line, craving is called "netlike" because it is sewn, sewn all around, enveloped,(3) in the sense that there is a net in it, that it makes a net, that it is comparable to a net.[4]

## The clinging: *visattikā*

[Craving is called "clinging"] because it is stuck *(visatta)* in sense-objects such as [visible] form, and the like; it is also called poisonous *(visattikā)* because of its being a poison food, a poison flower, and poison fruit, and also because its consumption poisons.(5)

## For whom (there is no) craving to lead him wheresoever: *taṇhā yassa kuhiṃci (natthi)*

For whom there is no craving. In whom such craving exists not, to lead [him] anywhere in [the realm of] existence.

### (Him, the trackless, by what track will you lead): *(apadaṃ buddhaṃ kena padena nessatha)*

*By what "track" will you lead* that "trackless" Buddha [to your trap]?

181. Those who are intent on meditating, the wise ones,
Delighting in the calm of going out,
Even gods long for them,
The Fully Enlightened Ones, the mindful. (14.3)

*ye jhānapasutā dhīrā nekkhammūpasame ratā*
*devā pi tesaṃ pihayanti sambuddhānaṃ satīmataṃ.*

### Those who are intent on meditating: *jhānapasutā*

Those who are engaged in and are devoted to these two kinds of meditative-absorption, by turning to, attaining, staying in, emerging from, and retrospection on them—namely, meditative-absorption that is concerned with [realizing] the characteristics [of phenomena] and meditative-absorption that is concerned with [concentrating on] objects.

### Who delight in the calm of going out: *nekkhammūpasame ratā*

Here "delighting in the calm of going out" is not to be taken as going forth [into the religious life]. It is said with reference to the delight in Nibbāna, which is the calming of defilements.

### Even gods: *devā pi*

Even gods, gods as well as human beings,

### Long for: *pihayanti*

Desire.

### (The Fully Enlightened Ones) the mindful: *(sambuddhānaṃ) satīmataṃ*

The meaning is: they long for the Fully Enlightened Ones who have such qualities, who are endowed with mindfulness, [themselves] desiring Buddhahood, thinking: "Oh, may we too become [such] enlightened ones."

182. Difficult is the attainment of the human state.
Difficult the life of mortals.
Difficult is the hearing of dhamma true.
Difficult the appearance of Awakened Ones. (14.4)

*kiccho manussapaṭilābho kicchaṃ maccāna jīvitaṃ*
*kicchaṃ saddhammasavaṇaṃ kiccho buddhānaṃ uppado.*

## Difficult is the attainment of the human state: *kiccho manussapaṭilābho*

The meaning is: the attainment of existence as a human being is hard to come by, due to the fact that it has to be obtained with great effort through plentiful moral wholesomeness.

## Difficult the life of mortals: *kicchaṃ maccāna jīvitaṃ*

The life of mortals is hard because it lasts only a short time, even though one's livelihood is [somehow] contrived, having engaged in constant [activity] such as agriculture, and so forth.

## Difficult is the hearing of dhamma true: *kicchaṃ saddhammasavaṇaṃ*

Hard too is it to hear the true dhamma because a person who proclaims dhamma is hard to come by, even over many aeons [of time].

## Difficult the appearance of Awakened Ones: *kiccho buddhānaṃ uppādo*

The birth [appearance] of a Buddha too is hard to come by, is extremely rare, because the resolve to become a Buddha succeeds only after enormous effort and because the birth of one having [such] successful resolve too is rare even through numerous thousands of aeons.

183. Refraining from all that is detrimental,
The attainment of what is wholesome,
The purification of one's mind:
This is the instruction of Awakened Ones. (14.5)

184. Forbearing patience is the highest austerity;
Nibbāna is supreme, the Awakened Ones say.
One who has gone forth is not one who hurts another,
No harasser of others is a recluse. (14.6)

185. No faultfinding, no hurting, restraint in the *pātimokkha,*
Knowing the measure regarding food, solitary bed and chair,
Application, too, of higher perception:
This is the instruction of the Awakened Ones. (14.7)

*sabbapāpassa akaraṇaṃ kusalassa upasampadā*
*sacittapariyodapanaṃ etaṃ buddhāna sāsanaṃ.*

*khantī paramaṃ tapo titikkhā nibbānaṃ paramaṃ vadanti buddhā*
*na hi pabbajito parūpaghātī samaṇo hoti paraṃ viheṭhayanto.*

*anūpavādo anūpaghāto pātimokkhe ca saṃvaro*
*mattaññutā ca bhattasmiṃ pantaṃ ca sayanāsanaṃ*
*adhicitte ca āyogo etaṃ buddhāna sāsanaṃ.*

[183.]

(Refraining) from all that is detrimental:
*sabbapāpassa (akaraṇaṃ)*

From every [kind of] unwholesome deed.

The attainment (of what is wholesome):
*(kusalassa) upasampadā*

The generation of the wholesome and the development of what is [so] generated—from the setting forth [into religious life] to the Path of Arahantship.

The purification of one's mind: *sacittapariyodapanaṃ*

Causing one's mind to be cleansed of the five hindrances.[6]

This is the instruction of Awakened Ones: *etaṃ buddhāna sāsanaṃ*

This is the teaching of all the Buddhas.

[184.]

Forbearing patience is the highest austerity: *khantī paramaṃ tapo titikkhā*

Patience that is called forbearance—this is the highest, the noblest austerity in this teaching *(sāsana)*.

Nibbāna is supreme, the Awakened Ones say: *nibbānaṃ paramaṃ vadanti buddhā*

Buddhas, Paccekabuddhas, and those enlightened beings who are almost like Buddhas[7]—these three kinds of Buddhas declare that Nibbāna is supreme.

One who has gone forth is not one who hurts another: *na hi pabbajito parūpaghātī*

One who is assaulting others with fists, and so on, who is wearying [others]—[such] a harasser of others is not "one who has gone forth."

A recluse: *samaṇo*

One who is wearying others as aforesaid is indeed no recluse either.

[185.]

No faultfinding: *anūpavādo*

Neither finding fault nor causing [others] to find fault;

No hurting: *anūpaghāto*

Neither hurting nor causing hurt [through others];

In the *pātimokkha*: *pātimokkhe*

In the seniormost virtue;

Restraint: *saṃvaro*

Shutting out [the detrimental];

Knowing the measure: *mattaññutā*

The fact of "knowing the measure," understanding [what is exactly] the needed amount;

Solitary: *pantaṃ*

[Having a] secluded [lodging];

Of higher perception: *adhicitte*

In the enhanced perception that consists in the eight attainments;

### Application: *āyogo*
Making endeavor;

### This: *etaṃ*
All of this [constitutes]:

### The instruction of the Awakened Ones: *buddhāna sāsanaṃ*
The teaching of the Buddhas.

Here, the virtue of [restrained] speech is referred to by "no faultfinding"; the virtue of [restrained] physical action by "no hurting"; the virtue of observing the *pātimokkha* and [the virtue of] sense control by "restraint in the *pātimokkha*"; the purity of livelihood and the virtue associated with [limiting one's] physical needs by "knowing the measure," propriety as regards dwelling place by "solitary bed and chair," and the eight [meditational] attainments by "higher perception." Thus all three kinds of training have been mentioned in this verse.

186. Not even with a rain of golden coins
Is contentment found among sensual pleasures.
"Sensual pleasures are of little delight, are a misery."
Knowing so, the wise one (14.8)

187. Takes no delight
Even for heavenly sensual pleasures.
One who delights in the ending of craving
Is a disciple of the Fully Enlightened One. (14.9)

*na kahāpaṇavassena titti kāmesu vijjati*
*appassādā dukhā kāmā iti viññāya paṇḍito.*

*api dibbesu kāmesu ratiṃ so nādhigacchati*
*taṇhakkhayarato hoti sammāsasambuddhasāvako.*

[186.]

### With a rain of golden coins: *kahāpaṇavassena*
What is referred to here as a rain of *kahāpaṇa*s is the shower of the seven kinds of jewels that he caused by clapping [hands].[8] Not even with it was there(9)

[for him] any contentment in regard to material things and the passions [related to them]. So hard to satisfy is this craving.

### Of little delight: *appassādā*

[Material possessions, and the like, are] of little satisfaction, for they are like dreams,

### A misery: *dukkhā*

Yielding much misery, as stated in the *Dukkhakkhanda Suttas*,(10) and so forth.

### Knowing so: *iti viññāya*

Having understood that these sensual pleasures are such,

[187.]

### Even for heavenly (sensual pleasures): *api dibbesu*

Even if one were to invite [the wise person to sensual enjoyment] with pleasures accruing to the gods, as Venerable Samiddhi [was invited][11]—even so he would indeed not find delight in those pleasures.

### Who delights in the ending of craving: *taṇhakkhayarato*

Is attracted to Arahantship and to Nibbāna and lives desiring it.

### A disciple of the Fully Enlightened One: *sammāsambuddhasāvako*

The monk devoted to [the life of] spiritual endeavor, "born" of hearing(12) dhamma proclaimed by the Fully Enlightened One.

188. Many for refuge go
To mountains and to forests,
To shrines that are groves or trees—
Humans who are threatened by fear. (14.10)

189. This is not a refuge secure,
This refuge is not the highest.
Having come to this refuge,
One is not released from all misery. (14.11)

190. But who to the Buddha, Dhamma,
And Saṅgha as refuge has gone,
Sees with full insight
The four noble truths; (14.12)

191. Misery, the arising of misery,
And the transcending of misery,
The noble Eightfold Path
Leading to the allaying of misery. (14.13)

192. This, indeed, is a refuge secure.
This is the highest refuge.
Having come to this refuge,
One is released from all misery. (14.14)

*bahuṃ*(13) *ve saraṇaṃ yanti pabbatāni*(14) *vanāni ca*
*ārāmarukkhacetyāni manussā bhayatajjitā.*

*n'etaṃ kho saraṇaṃ khemaṃ n'etaṃ saraṇaṃ uttamaṃ*
*n'etaṃ saraṇaṃ āgamma sabbadukkhā pamuccati.*

*yo ca buddhaṃ ca dhammaṃ ca saṅghaṃ ca saraṇaṃ gato*
*cattāri ariyasaccāni sammappaññāya passati.*

*dukkhaṃ dukkhasamuppādaṃ dukkhassa ca atikkamaṃ*
*ariyaṃ c'aṭṭhaṅgikaṃ maggaṃ dukkhūpasamagāminaṃ.*

*etaṃ kho saraṇaṃ khemaṃ etaṃ saraṇaṃ uttamaṃ*
*etaṃ saraṇaṃ āgamma sabbadukkhā pamuccati.*

[188.]

## Many: *bahuṃ*

In this context *bahuṃ* [accusative] stands for *bahū* [nominative].

## Mountains, forests: *pabbatāni vanāni*

Various persons, threatened by various kinds of fear and wishing to be free of fear or desiring to obtain sons, and so forth,[15] go for "refuge" to mountain [shrines] here and there, such as Isigili, Vepulla, Vebhāra, and the like; to garden [shrines] such as Mahāvana, the Gosiṅga *sāla* Grove, the Bamboo Grove, the Mango Grove of Jīvaka, and so forth; to tree [shrines] such as the Udena Shrine, the Gotama Shrine, and so on; that is the meaning.

[189.]

### This is not a refuge: *n'etaṃ saraṇaṃ*

All such "refuge" is insecure; it is not the highest [refuge]. And on account of it, not one among beings that are subject to birth, and so forth, is freed from [this] totality of suffering such as birth, and the like.

[190.]

### But who: *yo ca*

Having indicated this refuge, which is insecure and not supreme, [the next line] has begun, [with the words] "But who . . . " to indicate [what then is] the secure and supreme refuge. [This is] what it means: the one who, lay person or recluse,

### To the Buddha, Dhamma, and Saṅgha as refuge has gone: *buddhaṃ ca dhammaṃ ca saṅghaṃ ca saraṇaṃ gato*

Has gone to the Buddha, Dhamma, and Saṅgha as the best [refuge], resorting to the "topic of meditation" known as "calling to mind [the virtues of] Buddha, Dhamma, and Saṅgha" [in the formulas] beginning with "So is that Blessed One the Worthy Being, the Fully Enlightened One," and so forth,[16] even in this case, the "seeking of refuge" falls away and is [liable to be] disturbed by such [acts] as worshiping other *titthiyas*, and so on.[(17)] [The stanza] proclaiming solely the refuge that is derived from the Path, in order to show its undisturbability, declares:

### Sees with full insight the four noble truths: *cattāri ariyasaccāni sammappaññāya passati*

The one who has gone for refuge to these[18] [noble] truths by way of realizing them—this "going for refuge" is secure and supreme. That person is freed from the total misery of the whirl on account of this refuge. Hence it is said:

[192.]

### This, indeed, is a refuge secure: *etaṃ kho saraṇaṃ khemaṃ*

193. Hard to come by is a person of nobility;
Not everywhere is he born.
Wherever that wise one is born,
That family prospers in happiness. (14.15)

*dullabho purisājañño na so sabbattha jāyati*
*yattha so jāyatī dhīro taṃ kulaṃ sukkham edhati.*

## Hard to come by: *dullabho*

A noble person is hard to come by—not common, as are noble [animals such as] elephants, and so forth.

## Not everywhere is he: *na so sabbattha*

He is not born in a frontier area or in a lowly family. He is born in the middle country,[19] in a family that is wont to receive homage and respect, either among *khattiya* families or among *brāhmaṇa* families. And being born thus,

## Wherever that wise one is born: *yattha so jāyatī dhīro*

The Fully Awakened One, having wisdom supreme,

## That family prospers in happiness: *taṃ kulaṃ sukham edhati*

It indeed arrives at a state of bliss.[20]

194. Joyful is the arising of Awakened Ones.
Joyful, the teaching of Dhamma true.
Joyful, too, the concord of the Saṅgha.
Joyful, the austere practice of those in concord. (14.16)

*sukho buddhānaṃ uppādo sukhā saddhammadesanā*
*sukhā saṅghassa sāmaggī samaggānaṃ tapo sukho.*

## Joyful is the arising of Awakened Ones: *sukho buddhānaṃ uppādo*

The arising of Awakened Ones is joyful inasmuch as they, when they arise, "ferry" the people across the wastes of attachment, and so forth.

## Joyful, the teaching of Dhamma true: *sukhā saddhammadesanā*

The teaching of Dhamma true is joyful inasmuch as beings who are subject to aspects [of existence] such as birth, and the like, come by the teaching of Dhamma and are liberated from birth, and so forth.

## (Joyful) . . . the concord (of the Order): *(sukhā saṅghassa) sāmaggi*

Concord is the fact of being alike in thought; such unity of mind is also joyful.

## Joyful, the austere practice of those in concord: *samaggānaṃ tapo sukho*

Inasmuch as it is possible,(21) among those united, those of similar minds, to study the Buddha's teaching or to fulfill the *dhutaṅga* practices[22] or to accomplish the function of a recluse, so the austere endeavor of those in concord is [also] joyful. Hence has [the Buddha] said: "As long, O bhikkhus, unitedly the bhikkhus gather together, unitedly arise, and unitedly perform the functions of the Saṅgha, so long is progress of the bhikkhus to be expected and not their decline."[23]

195. Of one worshiping those worthy of worship,
Whether Awakened Ones or disciples,
Who have transcended preoccupying tendencies,
Crossed over grief and lamentation, (14.17)

196. Of one worshiping such as them,
Calmed ones who fear nothing,
The merit cannot be quantified
By anyone saying, "It is of this extent." (14.18)

*pūjārahe pūjayato buddhe yadi va sāvake*
*papañcasamatikkante tiṇṇasokapariddave.*

*te tādise pūjayato nibbute akutobhaye*
*na sakkā puññaṃ saṅkhātuṃ imettam iti kenaci.*

[195.]

## Of one worshiping those worthy of worship: *pūjārahe pūjayato*

*Pūjārahā* [is to be analyzed as] *pūjituṃ arahā*, [meaning] those whom it is fit to worship. [The words in the verse then mean:] For one who is worshiping [those worthy of worship], with salutation, and so forth, and also with the four requisites.[24]

## Awakened Ones: *buddhe*

With the words Awakened Ones, and so forth, [the text] indicates the ones who deserve worship. Awakened Ones are the Fully Enlightened Ones.

## Whether: *yadi*

*Yadi* stands for *yadi vā*, meaning: "and further." Therein is [the word] "Paccekabuddhas" [deemed to have been] mentioned.

## Disciples: *sāvake*

And the disciples of the Awakened Ones,

## Who have transcended preoccupying tendencies: *papañcasamatikkante*

Who have gone beyond preoccupying tendencies:(25) craving, [addiction to] views and self-estimation,

## Crossed over grief and lamentation: *tiṇṇasokapariddave*

The ones who have gone beyond these two—namely, grief and lamentation—that is the meaning.(26) By these [references] the nature of "deserving worship" has been shown.

[196.]

## Them: *te*

Buddhas, and the others.

## Such: *tādise*

"Such" by virtue of [their] holding of the said qualities,

## Calmed ones: *nibbute*

[Who are calmed] by the calming of attachment, and so forth,

## Who fear nothing: *akutobhaye*

There is no fear for these ones from anywhere whatsoever—from [continuity of] existence or from [any] object [of experience]; hence [they are] *akutobhayā* ["having fear from no source"],

## The merit cannot be quantified: *na sakkā puññaṃ saṅkahātuṃ*

It is not possible to calculate [the extent of their] merit. If [it be asked] how [is that?, the answer is]:

## By anyone saying, "it is of this extent": *imettam iti kenaci*

[Not possible to calculate] saying: "So much it is, so much." As regards *kena ci*, the word *api* should be combined [with it] here; [and the meaning then is: it is not possible to calculate their merit] by whatever person or measure.

By [whatever] person: by one such as that brahmā.[27]

By [whatever] measure: by the threefold measurement—namely, determining, weighing, filling. Determining: that is, determining by inference [that] it is "so much." Weighing: that is, holding in a pair of scales. Filling: filling out [vessels of measuring grain, and so forth], such as *addhapasata*, *pattha*, *nālikā*, and the like.

For no one is it possible, through these measurements, to calculate the merit accruing to a person who worships the Buddhas, and the like [i.e., that it yields so much] by way of effect—because of the absence of limit [in the case of that merit].

In [these] two instances, what is the difference—as regards the one who worships?

First, it is not possible to calculate the merit of one who worships Buddhas, and others, who are living. When they [Buddhas, and others, who are "gone to Nibbāna"] on account of the dispersal of defilements, are "gone to Nibbāna" again by the dispersal of the *khandha*s [at physical death] as well, it is not possible to calculate the worshiper's merit. Thus [only] are distinctions applicable[(28)] Wherefore it is said in the *Vimānavatthu*:[(29)]

Regarding [the Worthy One], alive or to Nibbāna gone,
The thought being same, the fruit is the same.
By serene faith of mind
Do beings attain to states of weal.

# CHAPTER XV

## Happiness
## *Sukha-vaggo*

197. Ah, so pleasantly we live
Without enmity among those with enmity.
Among humans with enmity
Do we dwell without enmity. (15.1)

198. Ah, so pleasantly we live
Without affliction among the afflicted.
Among humans with affliction
Do we dwell without affliction. (15.2)

199. Ah, so pleasantly we live
Without restlessness among the restless.
Among humans who are restless
Do we dwell without restlessness. (15.3)

*susukhaṃ vata jīvāma verinesu averino*
*verinesu manussesu viharāma averino.*

*susukhaṃ vata jīvāma āturesu anāturā.*
*āturesu manussesu viharāma anāturā.*

*susukhaṃ vata jīvāma ussukesu anussukā*
*ussukesu manussesu viharāma anussukā.*

[197.]

### Pleasantly: *susukhaṃ*

Very happily. This is what is meant. Lay persons making a living by robbery, and so forth, or recluses by medical practice, and so forth, say "We live at ease"—but it is we who live very much more at ease than they.

### Without enmity among those with enmity: *verinesu averino*

We who(1) are nonhaters among those who hate—[haters] on account of the five kinds of hate.[2]

[198.]

### Without affliction among those with affliction: *āturesu anāturā*

Who, due to being free of defilements, are without "sickness" among those who are sick with defilements.

[199.]

### Without restlessness among the restless: *ussukesu anussukā*

Who among those who are restless in the pursuit of the five strands of sensuality,[3] are "free from exertion," on account of the absence of that pursuit. The meaning of the rest is clear.

200. Ah, so pleasantly we live,
For whom there is nothing at all our own.
We shall become partakers of joy,
Even as the Radiant Devas. (15.4)

*susukhaṃ vata jīvāma yesam no natthi kiñcanaṃ*
*pītibhakkhā bhavissāma devā ābhassarā yathā.*

### For whom: *yesaṃ*

For us in whom there is not [found] a single "something" among the various "things" that function as obstructions, such as sensual attractions, and so forth.

### Partakers of joy: *pītibhakkhā*

The meaning is: just as the *Ābhassara* gods feed on joy and live out their days solely in joy, so too shall we become.[4]

201. Winning, one engenders enmity;
Miserably sleeps the defeated.
The one at peace sleeps pleasantly,
Having abandoned victory and defeat. (15.5)

*jayaṃ*[5] *veraṃ pasavati dukkhaṃ seti parājito*
*upasanto sukhaṃ seti hitvā jayaparājayaṃ.*

### Winning, one engenders enmity: *jayam veraṃ pasavati*

One conquering another gains the hatred [of the one vanquished].

### The defeated: *parājito*

The one who is defeated by another, lies in misery, thinking, "Oh, when shall I be able to see the adversary's back [succeed in making him flee]?" The meaning is: one lives in misery indeed, in all the modes of deportment [and not only while reclining].

### The one at peace: *upasanto*

The influx-extinct [arahant], within whom defilements such as sensual attachment, and so forth, are calmed.

### Sleeps pleasantly, having abandoned victory and defeat: *sukhaṃ seti hitvā jayaparājayaṃ*

202. There is no fire like passion,
No offense there is like ill will,
There is no misery like the *khandha*s,
No ease there is higher than peace. (15.6)

*natthi rāgasamo aggi natthi dosasamo kali*
*natthi khandhādisā dukkhā natthi santiparaṃ sukhaṃ.*

### There is no (fire) like passion: *natthi rāgasamo* (*aggi*)

There is no other fire like sensual attraction, which can turn one into a fistful of ashes, having burnt one from inside alone, without exhibiting smoke, flame, or charcoal.

### Offense: *kali*

Nor is there an offense comparable to ill will.

### Like the *khandha*s: *khandhādisā*

Like the *khandha*s: there is no other misery like the miseries [that are] the *khandha*s, which are being carried around.

### Higher than peace: *santiparaṃ*

There is no ease that is above Nibbāna. The meaning is: Nibbāna is the supreme ease.

203. Hunger is the illness most severe,
The *saṃkhāras* the greatest misery.
Knowing this as it is,
[One realizes] Nibbāna is ease supreme. (15.7)

*jighacchā paramā rogā saṃkhārā paramā dukhā*
*etaṃ ñatvā yathābhūtaṃ nibbānaṃ paramaṃ sukhaṃ.*

### Hunger is the illness most severe: *jigacchā paramā rogā*

Whereas [any] other disease is either routed out once medically treated or is eliminated(6) by diminution,(7) hunger has to be "treated" constantly [without a stop]; hence it is said to be more severe than all other diseases.

### The *saṃkhāras*: *saṃkhārā*

The five *khandhas*.[8]

### Knowing this as it is: *etaṃ ñatvā yathābhūtaṃ*

Having understood this fact as it is—namely, that there is no disease like hunger and no misery like having to bear the *khandhas*—the wise one attains to the realization of Nibbāna.

### Nibbāna is ease supreme: *nibbānaṃ paramaṃ sukhaṃ*

It is the highest and noblest ease.

204. Health is the highest gain,
Contentment is the highest wealth,
Those inspiring trust are kinsmen supreme,
Nibbāna is ease supreme. (15.8)

*ārogyaparamā lābhā santuṭṭhiparamaṃ dhanaṃ*
*vissāsaparamā ñāti nibbānaṃ paramaṃ sukhaṃ.*

Health is the highest gain: *ārogyaparamā lābhā*

[Lit. "health supreme" are gains]—that is, [gains are for those] who have healthiness as their supreme [form]. For a person who is sick, even available gains are indeed no gains. For the healthy person, all gains are indeed attained. Hence it is said: Health is the highest gain.

Contentment is the highest wealth: *santuṭṭhiparamaṃ dhanaṃ*

[Lit. "contentment supreme" is wealth]. For a layperson or a recluse to be satisfied with [what one has] obtained and with [what is one's] own possession is contentment. That is higher than other riches.

Those inspiring trust are kinsmen supreme: *vissāsaparamā ñāti*

[Lit. "trust supreme" are relatives.] The person in whom one has no confidence is a stranger indeed—be it even one's mother or one's father. Even a person who is unrelated but in whom one has confidence is the best kind of relative. Hence is it said: Those inspiring trust are kinsmen supreme.

Nibbāna is ease supreme: *nibbānaṃ paramaṃ sukhaṃ*

There is no ease comparable with Nibbāna. Hence says [the text:] Nibbāna is ease supreme.

205. Having tasted the flavor of seclusion
And the flavor of calm,
One is without distress, free from the bad,
Drinking the flavor of the joys of dhamma. (15.9)

*pavivekarasaṃ pītvā rasaṃ upasamassa ca*
*niddaro hoti nippāpo dhammapītirasaṃ pibaṃ.*

Flavor of seclusion: *pavivekarasaṃ*

The flavor born of seclusion. The meaning is: the ease [experienced] in aloneness.

Of calm: *upasamassa*

Having tasted the flavor of Nibbāna, the calming of defilements.

## Having tasted: *pītvā*

Effecting the understanding [of the noble truth] of suffering, and so forth, having tasted [Nibbāna] by making [it] the object and by realizing [it. Thereupon]:

## One is without distress: *niddaro hoti*

The bhikkhu in whom intoxicants are extinct by virtue of this twofold tasting of flavor [that is, of seclusion and of Nibbāna], is free of distress and of [all that is] bad due to there being no distress of sensual attraction, and so forth, within such a one.

## Drinking the flavor: *rasaṃ pibaṃ*

One is surely free of distress and of [all that is] bad even as one is tasting the flavor of joy born of [the attainment of] the ninefold dhamma that transcends the world[9]. That is the meaning.

206. Good is the sight of noble ones,
Their company is always pleasant.
Without the sight of childish ones,
One would constantly be at ease. (15.10)

207. One moving with childish ones
Grieves for long time.
Misery is it to live with childish ones,
As it always is with a foc.
The wise one is one with whom to live is pleasant,
As is a gathering of relations. (15.11)
Wherefore:

208. The wise one, the insightful, and the learned,
Having the virtue of enduring, dutiful, noble,
A person true, intelligent,
With such a one as this, one would associate,
As the moon the path of the stars. (15.12)

*sādhu dassanam ariyānaṃ sannivāso sadā sukho*
*adassanena bālānaṃ niccam eva sukhī siya.*

*bālasaṅgatacārī hi dīgham addhāna socati*
*dukkho bālehi saṃvāso amitteneva sabbadā.*
*dhīro ca sukhasaṃvāso*(10) *ñātīnaṃ va samāgamo.*
*tasmā hi:*

*dhīraṃ ca paññaṃ ca bahussutaṃ ca*(11) *dhorayhasīlaṃ*(12)
*vatavantam āriyaṃ*
*taṃ tādisaṃ sappurisaṃ sumedhaṃ bhajetha nakkhattapathaṃ va*
*candimā.*

[206.]

## Good: *sādhu*

Beautiful, wholesome,

## Company: *sannivāso*

Not only the sight of them, but also sitting at the same place with them and the opportunity(13)of attending on them are also wholesome indeed.

[207.]

## One moving with childish ones: *bālasaṅgatacārī*

He who is moving about in the company of the childish one,

## Grieves for a long time: *dīgham addhāna socati*

He, being urged [thus] by that childish companion, "Come let us burgle [houses], and so forth," becomes like-minded with him and, doing those [misdeeds], comes to [suffer punishments] such as having [one's] hands cut off and experiences misery for a long time.

## Always: *sabbadā*

The meaning is: just as living together with a foe armed with a sword, or with poisonous snakes, and so forth, is a constant misery, so is [living] with childish ones.

## The wise one is one with whom to live is pleasant: *dhīro ca sukhasaṃvāso*

Here [the compound is to be analysed thus:] one is *sukhasaṃvāsa* in the sense that living with that one *(saṃvāsa)* is pleasant *(sukha)*. The meaning is: living at the same place with the wise is pleasant. How?

As is a gathering of relations: *ñātīnaṃ va samāgamo*

Just as the coming together of relatives is pleasant, so pleasant [is living with the wise.]

Wherefore: *tasmā hi*

Because life with the childish one is miserable and that with the wise one is pleasant, therefore,

[208.]

The wise one: *dhīraṃ ca*

The one possessed of steadfastness,

The insightful: *paññaṃ ca*

Endowed with worldly and world-transcending insight,

And the learned: *bahussutaṃ ca*

Endowed with [textual] learning and [spiritual] attainments,[14]

Having the virtue of enduring: *dhorayhasīlaṃ*

Due to "being accustomed to bear the yoke"—that is, [the quality] leading on to the attainment of Arahantship,

Dutiful: *vatavantaṃ*

Possessed of [regular] practices—due to practicing virtues and the *dhutaṅga*s,

Noble: *ariyaṃ*

Who is a noble one *(ariya)*, distant *(āraka)* from defilements,

A person true: *sappurisaṃ*

Such a worthy person who has bright wisdom,

One would associate with: *bhajetha*

As the moon the path of the stars: *nakkhattapathaṃ va candimā*

As the moon associates with the spotless firmament that is the pathway of the stars.

# CHAPTER XVI

## The Pleasant
## *Piya-vaggo*

209. One who exerts oneself in what is not befitting
And in the befitting exerts not,
Having abandoned the beneficial, grasping for the dear,
Envies the one who applies himself. (16.1)

210. Let one not be together with the dear,
Nor ever with those that are not dear;
Not to see the dear is misery,
So too is it to see the nondear. (16.2)

211. Therefore, let one not make endearment,
For separation from the dear is bad.
For whom there is neither the dear nor nondear,
For them are bonds not found. (16.3)

*ayoge yuñjam attānaṃ yogasmiṃ ca ayojayaṃ*
*atthaṃ hitvā piyaggāhī pihet' attānuyoginaṃ.*(1)

*mā piyehi samāgañchi appiyehi kudācanaṃ*
*piyānaṃ adassanaṃ dukkhaṃ appiyānaṃ ca dassanaṃ.*

*tasmā piyaṃ na kayirātha piyāpāyo hi pāpako*
*ganthā tesaṃ na vijjanti yesaṃ natthi piyāppiyaṃ.*

[209.]

### (One who exerts oneself) in what is not befitting: *ayoge (yuñjaṃ)*

[Engaging] in thinking that is not well grounded, which ought not to be engaged in. Here, thinking that is not well grounded means resorting to the sixfold impropriety with [its] divisions such as "resorting to prostitutes,"(2) and so forth[3]. The meaning is: involving oneself in such "not-well-grounded thinking."

### (And) in the befitting (exerts not): *yogasmiṃ (ca ayojayaṃ)*

Not engaging in its opposite—that is, in well-grounded thinking,

### Having abandoned the beneficial: *atthaṃ hitvā*

The beneficial is the threefold learning such as [the training of] higher virtue, and so forth.[4] Having abandoned that, from the time of going forth,

### Grasping for the dear: *piyaggāhī*

Holding on to what is merely dear—namely, the five strands of sensuality,[5]

### Envies the one who applies himself: *piheta'ttānuyoginaṃ*

Separated from the monastic order *(sāsana)* on account of such conduct and having reached the lay status, one later envies those who obtain the respect of gods and humans, developing [higher] virtue, and so forth, involved in the engagement [that is beneficial] for oneself—that is, one wishes, "Oh, would that I too were such as this!" That is the meaning.

[210.]

### (Let) one not (be together) with the dear (nor ever with the nondear): *mā piyehi (samāgañchi appiyehi kudācanaṃ)*

Never, not even for a single instant, should one come together with those [that are] dear, [be they] living beings or [be they] things.(6) The same with those that are not dear. Why?

### (Not to see) the dear (is misery): *piyānaṃ (adassanaṃ dukkhaṃ)*

Not seeing those [that are] dear—that is, being separated [from them]—is a misery.

### So too is it to see the nondear: *appiyānañ ca dassanaṃ dukkhaṃ*

The seeing of those [that are] not dear, by way of coming close [to them], is also a misery.

[211.]

### Therefore: *tasmā*

Because both [of] this is misery, for that reason,

### (Let one) not (make) endearment: *piyaṃ na (kayirātha)*

Let one not make any being or thing dear [to oneself].

### For separation from the dear: *piyāpāyo hi*

The parting, the separation, from those that are dear,

### (Is) bad: *pāpako*

Is puerile [puts one in a state of childish weakness].

### (For whom there is neither the dear nor the nondear) for them are bonds not found: *ganthā tesaṃ na vijjati (yesaṃ natthi piyāppiyaṃ)*

They to whom there is nothing dear, in their case the physical bond of the mass of greed is discarded; they to whom there is nothing unpleasant, in their case the physical bond of the mass of ill will is discarded. These being discarded, other bonds are indeed as good as discarded. Hence no [thing and no one] should be made dear or not dear [to oneself]. That is the meaning.

212. From the dear arises grief.
From the dear arises fear.
For one set free from endearment,
There is not grief. Whence fear? (16.4)

*piyato jāyati soko piyato jāyatī bhayaṃ*
*piyato vippamuttassa natthi soko kuto bhayaṃ.*

### From the dear: *piyato*

Whatever suffering or fear based on the whirl is [seen to be] arising, it does arise on account of either a dear being or [a dear] thing. To the one who is liberated from that [feeling of endearment], neither of these exists. That is the meaning.

213. From affection arises grief.
From affection arises fear.
For one set free from affection,
There is no grief. Whence fear? (16.5)

*pemato jāyati soko pemato jāyatī bhayaṃ*
*pemato vippamuttassa natthi soko kuto bhayaṃ.*

### From affection: *pemato*

The meaning is: on account of the affection engendered in regard to sons and daughters, and so forth.

214. From sensual attachment arises grief,
From sensual attachment arises fear.
For one set free from sensual attachment,
There is no grief. Whence fear? (16.6)

*ratiyā jāyati soko ratiyā jāyatī bhayaṃ*
*ratiyā vippamuttassa natthi soko kuto bhayaṃ.*

### From sensual attachment: *ratiyā*

The meaning is: on account of attachment to the five strands of sensuality.

215. From sensual desire arises grief.
From sensual desire arises fear.
For one set free from sensual desire,
There is no grief. Whence fear? (16.7)

*kāmato jāyati soko kāmato jāyatī bhayaṃ*
*kāmato vippamuttassa natthi soko kuto bhayaṃ.*

### From sensual desire: *kāmato*

From desire for things *(vatthu)* and desire for passions *(kilesa)*. [Misery] arises on account of this twofold desire; that is the meaning.

216. From craving arises grief.
From craving arises fear.
For one set free from craving,
There is no grief. Whence fear? (16.8)

*taṇhāya jāyati soko taṇhāya jāyatī bhayaṃ*
*taṇhāya vippamuttassa natthi soko kuto bhayaṃ.*

## From craving: *taṇhāya*

From craving that ensues from the "doors" of the six [senses]. [Misery] arises on account of this craving; that is the meaning.

217. The one endowed with virtue and vision,
Established in dhamma, speaking truth,
That one, doing his own tasks,
The folk holds dear. (16.9)

*sīladassanasampannaṃ dhammaṭṭhaṃ saccavādinaṃ*(7)
*attano kamma kubbānaṃ taṃ jano kurute piyaṃ.*

## The one endowed with virtue and vision: *sīladassana-sampannaṃ*

The one who is endowed with the four virtues leading to purity[8] and also with right insight, which is conjoint with Path and Fruit,

## Established in dhamma: *dhammaṭṭhaṃ*

Who is established in the ninefold world-transcending dhamma; the meaning is: who has realized the world transcending dhamma—

## Speaking truth: *saccavādinaṃ*

Who speaks the truth by virtue of understanding truth [i.e.,] due to realization, in the sixteen ways, of the four [noble] truths—[9]

## Doing his own tasks: *attano kamma kubbānaṃ*

One's own tasks means the three kinds of training[10]—one who is in the process of fulfilling them,

## That one, the folk (holds dear); *taṃ jano (kurute piyaṃ)*

The worldly folk holds such a person dear, is desirous of seeing, worshiping, and of serving that one offerings of the requisites. That is the meaning.

218. One in whom a wish for the Undefined is born,
Who would be clear in mind,
Whose heart is not bound in sensual pleasures,
Is called "one whose stream is upward bound." (16.10)

*chandajāto anakkhāte*(11) *manasā ca phuṭo siyā*
*kāmesu ca appaṭibaddhacitto uddhaṃsoto ti vuccati.*

### One in whom a wish . . . is born: *chandajāto*

One in whom the wish [to transcend the wordly] is born as the inclination to do [the tasks needed for it]; one who has reached [the state of religious] endeavor—

### For the Undefined: *anakkhāte*

In regard to Nibbāna—it [Nibbāna] is called the undefined because of the impossibility to describe it as created by so-and-so; as having such attributes as blueness, and so forth—

### Who would be clear in mind: *manasā ca phuṭo siyā*

Who would be filled with the thoughts pertaining to the three prior Paths and Fruits,[12]

### Whose heart is not bound in sensual desire: *(kāmesu ca) appaṭibaddhacitto*

Unattached to sensual desires by virtue [of attainment] of the Path of Non-Returner,

### Is called one whose stream is upward bound: *uddhaṃsoto (ti vuccati)*

Such a bhikkhu is said to be "one whose stream is upward bound" because, having been born in the [heavenly] Aviha worlds, [he will be] going [upward] from there on to Akaniṭṭha by [the process of] rebirth.[13] Such a person was your preceptor.[14] This is the meaning.

219. As when a person long absent
Has come safely from afar,
Relatives, friends, and well-wishers
Greet with delight the one who has returned; (16.11)

220. Just so, one who has done wholesome deeds
Has gone from this world to the beyond—
The wholesome deeds receive such a one,
Like relatives, a dear one who has returned, (16.12)

*cirappavāsiṃ purisaṃ dūrato sotthim āgataṃ*
*ñātimittā suhajjā ca abhinandanti āgataṃ.*

*tath' eva katapuññam pi asmā lokā paraṃ gataṃ*
*puññāni paṭigaṇhanti piyam ñātī va āgataṃ.*

[219.]

A person long absent: *cirappavāsiṃ*
One who has lived away [from home] for a long time,

Has come safely from afar: *dūrato sotthim āgataṃ*
Who has returned safely from a far-off place, with profit obtained and achieved, having engaged in trade or service under a king;

Relatives, friends, and well-wishers: *ñātimittā suhajjā ca*
Those who are relations, because of connection to the clan, and friends, because of mutual association, and companions, because of [their] warmth of heart,

Greet with delight the one who has returned: *abhinandanti āgataṃ*
Welcome the one who has come home either simply with a word of welcome or simply with the folding of hands [in salutation] or by bringing all kinds of gift.

[220.]

Just so: *tath'eva*
In exactly the same way,

One who has done wholesome deeds: *katapuññam pi*
The person who has done wholesome deeds,

(Has gone from this world to the beyond): *(asmā lokaṃ paraṃ gataṃ)*

Who has gone from this world to the next,

(The wholesome deeds receive such a one):
*(puññāni paṭigaṇhanti)*

[The benefits of one's] wholesome deeds, occupying the position of [one's] parents, receive one delightedly, bringing[one] a tenfold gift, namely: a [long] span of life, [fair] complexion, pleasure, fame, and overlordship, as well as forms, sounds, smells, tastes, and tangibles that are celestial.

Like relatives, a dear one who has returned:
*piyaṃ ñātī va āgataṃ*

As in this world other relations [receive] a dear kinsman who has returned [from a far-off place].

# CHAPTER XVII

## Wrath
## *Kodha-vaggo*

221. Wrath one would leave behind,
Measurement one would abandon, every fetter transcend.
Who clings not to name and form, and possesses no thing,
Upon that one miseries do not fall. (17.1)

*kodhaṃ jahe vippajaheyya mānaṃ saṃyojanaṃ sabbam atikkameyya taṃ nāmarūpasmiṃ asajjamānaṃ akiñcanaṃ nānupatanti dukkhā.*

### Wrath: *kodhaṃ*

Wrath of every kind.

### Measurement (one would abandon): *mānaṃ (jahe)*

The ninefold measurement[1] one would abandon.

### (Every) fetter (one would transcend): *saṃyojanaṃ (sabbam atikkameyya)*

One would transcend every fetter, the tenfold [fetter] such as sensual attraction, and so forth.[2]

### Who clings not: *asajjamānaṃ*

[This] means one who is not getting stuck. He who grasps "name and form," considering, "[This is] my body, [these are] my sensations," and so forth, grieves and is afflicted when that [body] breaks up—one indeed clings to "name and form." [But] one who is not grasping, who is not being afflicted [in this way], does not indeed [so] cling.

### Possesses no thing . . . miseries do not fall: *akiñcanaṃ nānupatanti dukkhā*

On such a person, who is thus free from clinging, who is "not burdened with anything," due to absence of attachments, and so forth, miseries do not fall. That is the meaning.

222. Who can hold back arisen wrath,
Like a swerving chariot,
That one I call "a charioteer,"
Any other one is merely a reins-holder. (17.2)

*yo ve uppatitaṃ kodhaṃ rathaṃ bhantaṃ va dhāraye*
*tam ahaṃ sārathiṃ brūmi rasmiggāho itaro jano.*

Arisen: *uppatitaṃ*

Which has been produced.

Like a swerving chariot: *rathaṃ bhantaṃ va*

Just as an accomplished charioteer reins in a chariot that is rushing at excessive speed and directs it as desired, so the person who,

Can hold back arisen wrath: *uppatitaṃ . . . kodhaṃ . . . dhāraye*

Is able to rein in the arisen anger,

That one I call a charioteer: *tam ahaṃ brūmi sārathiṃ*

Any other one (is merely a reins-holder): *(rasmiggāho) itaro jano*

But any other person, [such as] a person who drives the chariot of a king or a prince, is said to be [merely] a holder of reins, not a great charioteer.

223. With absence of wrath one would conquer the wrathful one;
With good, one would conquer the bad one;
With giving, one would conquer the stingy one;
With truth, the one speaking falsehood. (17.3)

*akkodhena jine kodhaṃ asādhuṃ sādhunā jine*
*jine kadariyaṃ dānena saccenālikavādinaṃ.*

With absence of wrath (one would conquer the wrathful one): *akkodhena (jine kodhaṃ)*

The person who is given to anger would be won over, [by oneself] becoming free of anger.

(With good, one would conquer) the bad one:
*asādhum (sādhuna jine)*

The one who is not good would be won over, [by oneself] becoming good.

(With giving, one would conquer) the stingy one:
*(jine) kadariyaṃ (dānena)*

The excessively stingy person would be won over by a mind that is generous in regard to one's possessions.

(With truth, the one speaking falsehood):
*(saccena-alikavādinaṃ)*

The one who speaks falsehoods would be won over by means of the truthful word. Hence he [the Buddha] has said, "with absence of wrath let one conquer the wrathful one."

224. Let one tell the truth, let one not be angry.
Asked, let one give even when one has but little.
By these three factors,
One would go into the presence of the gods. (17.4)

*saccaṃ bhaṇe na kujjheyya dajjā 'ppasmiṃ pi*(3) *yācito*
*etehi tīhi ṭhānehi gacche devāna santike.*

Let one tell the truth: *saccaṃ bhaṇe*

Let one glorify the truth, deal in truth, be established in truth—that is the meaning.

Let one not be angry: *na kujjheyya*

Let one not bear anger toward another.

Asked, let one give even when one has but little: *dajjā'ppasmiṃ pi yācito*

"Those who beg" [in this context] are the virtuous ones who have gone forth [into the monastic life]. They stand at the doorstep [of householders], without requesting "Give something!" [but] in effect they do indeed beg. So requested by the virtuous, let one give even a little thing, if what is available to be given is little.

### By these three: *etehi tīhi*

One may go to the heavenly world by means of any one of these [three factors]. That is the meaning.

225. They who are gentle sages,
Constantly restrained in body,
Go to the Unshakeable Abode,
Whither having gone, they do not grieve. (17.5)

*ahiṃsakā ye munayo niccaṃ kāyena saṃvutā*
*te yanti accutaṃ ṭhānaṃ yattha gantvā na socare.*

### Sages: *munayo*

Here "sages" means the sages who are beyond training [Arahants], who have attained to Path and Fruit by following the way of the silent ones.[4]

### (Restrained) in body: *kāyena (saṃvutā)*

This is only the formal statement. The meaning is: restrained in the three "doors."[5]

### Unshakeable abode: *accutaṃ ṭhānaṃ*

Eternal, unshakeable place, the place that is firm,[6]

### Whither having gone, they do not grieve: *yattha gantvā na socare*

Having gone where [persons] do not grieve, are not afflicted—to that place do [sages] go. That is the meaning.

226. Of those who always keep awake,
Learning day and night,
Upon Nibbāna intent,
"Intoxicants" come to an end. (17.6)

*sadā jāgaramānānaṃ ahorattānusikkhinaṃ*
*nibbānaṃ adhimuttānaṃ atthaṃ gacchanti āsavā.*

### Learning day and night: *ahorattānusikkhinaṃ*

Of those who train themselves in the three trainings[7] day and night,

### Upon Nibbāna intent: *nibbānam adhimuttānaṃ*

Whose thoughts are concerned with Nibbāna,[8]

### Intoxicants come to an end: *atthaṃ gacchanti āsavā*

Of such persons all intoxicants come to rest, to the state of destruction or extinction. That is the meaning.

227. Of old this is, Atula,
It is not just of today:
They find fault with one sitting silently;
They find fault with one speaking much,
And even with one speaking in moderation do they find fault.
In [this] world there is no one not faulted. (17.7)

228. There was not and will not be,
And now there is not found,
A person absolutely faulted,
Or absolutely praised. (17.8)

229. Whom the wise praise,
Having observed day after day,
That one of faultless conduct, intelligent,
Of wisdom and virtue well composed— (17.9)

230. Who is fit to fault that one,
Who is like a coin of gold?
Even the gods praise that one;
One praised by Brahmā too. (17.10)

*porāṇam etaṃ atula n'etaṃ ajjatanām iva*
*nindanti tuṇhim āsīnaṃ nindanti bahubhāṇinaṃ*
*mitabhāṇinaṃ pi nindanti natthi loke anindito.*

*na cāhu na ca bhavissati na c'etarahi vijjati*
*ekantaṃ nindito poso ekantaṃ vā pasaṃsito.*

*yaṃ ca viññū pasaṃsanti anuvicca*(9) *suve suve*(10)
*acchiddavuttiṃ*(11) *medhāviṃ paññāsīlasamāhitaṃ.*

*nekkhaṃ jambonadass eva ko taṃ ninditum arahati*
*devā pi taṃ pasaṃsanti brahmuṇā pi pasaṃsito.*

[227.]

### Of old this is, Atula: *porāṇam etaṃ atula*

This is [something] ancient. By "Atula" he addresses the lay devotee of that name.[12]

### It is not just of today: *n'etaṃ ajjatanām iva*

This faultfinding or praising is not of this day; is not, as it were, something that has come to be at the present time.

### They find fault with one sitting silently: *nindanti tuṇhim āsīnaṃ*

"Why is this person silent, like one who is dumb, like one who is deaf, like one who does not know anything?"—thus they find fault with one [who sits silent].

### They find fault with one speaking much: *nindanti bahubhāsiṇaṃ*

"Why does this person clatter incessantly(13) like a palm leaf beaten by the wind? There is no end indeed to this talk!"(14)—thus they find fault with one [who talks much],

### And even with one speaking in moderation do they find fault: *mitabhāṇinaṃ pi nindanti*

"Why has he spoken a word or two and become silent, as if thinking that his speech is like precious gold?"—thus they find fault with [one who talks but little]. Thus, in every way, there is no one in this world who is not faulted. That is the meaning.

[228.]

### There was not (and will not be): *na cāhu (na ca bhavissati)*

There was not [a person not faulted in one way or another]—neither in the past, nor will there be [such a person] in the future.

[229.]

### Whom the wise: *yaṃ ca viññu*

The blame or the praise of childish ones is not a [true] measure. But having observed whom day after day the wise commend, knowing what is cause for blame and what is cause for praise,

### That one of faultless conduct: *acchiddavuttiṃ*

That one of faultless conduct [in the sense of] being on a blameless [religious] training, or due to being equipped with a blameless mode of life,

### Intelligent: *medhāviṃ*

Due to being endowed with wisdom that is the dhamma sap,

### Of wisdom and virtue well composed: *paññāsīlasamāhitaṃ*

Due to being endowed with worldly wisdom as well as [wisdom] that is beyond the world, and also with the fourfold virtue leading to [spiritual] purity,[15]

[230.]

### Who is fit to fault that one: *ko taṃ ninditum arahati*

That one who is like a coin of gold, free of the faults of gold [-ore], and fit to be beaten and polished [by artisans]. That is the meaning.

### Even the gods (praise that one): *devā pi (taṃ pasaṃsanti)*

Gods as well as wise men wait upon that bhikkhu and speak his praises.

### One praised by Brahmā too: *brahmuṇā pi pasaṃsito*

Such a one is praised not only by gods and humans, but indeed also by the great Brahmā [who has power] over ten thousand world-systems. That is the meaning.

231. Let one guard against physical intemperance;
In body, let one be restrained.
Having abandoned physical misconduct,
In proper conduct with the body let one live. (17.11)

232. Let one guard against intemperance of speech;[16]
In speech, let one be restrained.
Having abandoned verbal misconduct,
In proper conduct with speech let one live. (17.12)

233. Let one guard against intemperance of mind;[17]
In mind, let one be restrained.
Having abandoned mental misconduct,
In proper conduct with the mind let one live. (17.13)

234. Those restrained in body, wise,
And also restrained in speech,
Restrained in mind, wise,
They indeed are perfectly restrained. (17.14)

*kāyappakopaṃ rakkheyya kāyena saṃvuto siyā*
*kāyaduccaritaṃ hitvā kāyena sucaritaṃ care.*

*vacīpakopaṃ rakkheyya vācāya saṃvuto siyā*
*vacīduccaritaṃ hitvā vācāya sucaritaṃ care.*

*manopakopaṃ rakkheyya manasā saṃvuto siyā*
*manoduccaritaṃ hitvā manasā sucaritaṃ care.*

*kāyena saṃvutā dhīrā atho vācāya saṃvutā*
*manasā saṃvutā dhīrā te ve suparisaṃvutā.*

[231.]

## (Let one guard against) physical intemperance: *kāyappakopaṃ (rakkheyya)*

Let one guard against the threefold physical misconduct.[18]

## In body (let one be) restrained: *kāyena saṃvuto (siyā)*

Let one prevent the "entrance" of misconduct [into oneself] through the "door" of the body; let one be restrained, be "of closed doors."

### Having abandoned physical misconduct, in proper conduct with the body let one live: *kāyaduccaritaṃ hitvā kāyena sucaritaṃ care*

This is said in view of the fact that one who discards physical misconduct and observes proper conduct with the body achieves both of these [purposes].

In the two stanzas(19) that follow [17.12, 17.13], the same mode [of explanation applies].

[234.]

### Those restrained in body, wise . . . in speech . . . in mind: *kāyena saṃvutā dhīrā vācāya . . . manasā*

The wise ones who [are restrained] in body, not resorting to violation of life, and so forth [are restrained] in speech, not resorting to lying, and so forth, and are restrained in mind, not allowing covetousness, and so on, to arise.

### They . . . are perfectly restrained: *te . . . suparisaṃvutā*

In this world they indeed are well guarded, well controlled; they are those whose "doors" are well closed. That is the meaning.

# CHAPTER XVIII

## Stains
## *Mala-vaggo*

235. Like a yellow leaf are you now;
And even Yama's men have appeared for you;
And at the threshold of departure you stand;
But even the journey's provisions you do not have. (18.1)

236. Make a lamp for yourself.[1]
Strive quickly! Become a wise one;
With stains blown out, free of blemish,
You shall go to the heavenly realm of the nobles. (18.2)

*paṇḍupalāso va dāni 'si yamapurisā pi ca taṃ upaṭṭhitā*
*uyyogamukhe ca tiṭṭhasi pātheyyam pi ca te na vijjati.*

*so karohi dīpam attano khippaṃ vāyama paṇḍito bhava*
*niddhantamalo anaṅgaṇo dibbaṃ ariyabhūmim ehisi.*

[235.]

### Like a yellow leaf are you now: *paṇḍupalāso va dāni 'si*

"Devotee, you now have become like a yellow leaf sundered [from the parent plant] and falling onto the ground.

### Yama's men: *yamapurisā*

The messengers of Yama [god of death] are referred to thus. This has been said with reference to death [itself]. The meaning is: death has come close to you.

### Threshold of departure: *uyyogamukhe*

You are standing face to face with decay, deterioration; that is the meaning.

### Provisions: *pātheyyaṃ*

Just as rice, and so forth [are necessary as] provisions on the way for a traveler, so the provisions of wholesome deeds, [necessary] for one going to the world beyond, you do not have."

[236.]

### Make a lamp for yourself: *so karohi dīpam attano*

You who are such make for yourself a support of wholesome [*kamma*], like an island support for a ship wrecked on the sea.

### Strive quickly: *khippaṃ vāyama*

So doing, endeavor promptly; make a start quickly on earnest effort.

### Become a wise one: *paṇḍito bhava*

Be a wise person in making for yourself the support that is your own wholesome *kamma*. One who performs wholesome deeds at the time when one is able [to do so], without waiting for the approach of death, one who strives [to do this]—he is the wise one. Be such a one, not a childish one. That is the meaning.

### With stains blown out, free of blemish, you shall go to the heavenly realm of the nobles: *niddhantamalo anaṅgaṇo dibbaṃ ariyabhūmim ehisi*

Making earnest effort thus, being "one who has blown out the stains" due to the stains of sensual attraction, and so forth, having been removed, "unblemished" due to the absence of blemishes, [namely] being free of defilements, you will attain to the fivefold pure abode.[2] That is the meaning.

237. And you are now well advanced in age;
You have started the journey to the presence of Yama.
And, in between, there is not even a resting place for you;
Even the journey's provisions you do not have. (18.3)

238. Make a lamp for yourself;[3]
Strive quickly! Become a wise one;
With stains blown out, free of blemish,
You shall not undergo birth and old age again. (18.4)

*upanītavayo ca dāni 'si sampayāto' si yamassa santike*
*vāso pi ca te natthi antarā pātheyyam pi ca te na vijjati.*

*so karohi dīpam*(4) *attano khippaṃ vāyama paṇḍito bhava*
*niddhantamalo anaṅgaṇo na puna jātijaraṃ upehisi.*

[237.]

### You are now well advanced in age: *upanītavayo ca dāni 'si*

Here *upa-* is merely a particle [without any specific effect]. [So, the sentence means:] "You are now past [your due] span of life, far gone in age, advanced of age." It means, "You have passed the three ages [of life][5] and are standing at the brink of death."

### You have started the journey to the presence of Yama: *sampayāto'si yamassa santike*

You are standing ready to go to the presence of death. That is the meaning.

### And, in between, there is not even a resting place for you: *vāso pi ca te natthi antarā*

As those who travel on the road spend time doing various functions on the way—not so are those going to the world beyond. It is not possible for one going to the world beyond to say [to death], "Be patient for a few days until I give alms and hear dhamma," and so forth. As soon as one has departed from here, one is born in the world beyond. [It is] on account of this [that the above is] said.

### Provisions: *pātheyyaṃ*

Although this is exactly the same as what was said earlier [in st. 235], it has to be recited here too by the Teacher in order to emphasize [the idea] firmly to the devotee again and again.

[238.]

### Birth and old age: *jātijaraṃ*

Death and disease are also certainly included herein. The Path of Non-Returner was referred to with the earlier verses, here the Path of Arahantship.

239. Gradually, would the wise one,
Bit by bit, moment by moment,
Blow out the stain that is one's own,
Like a smith the stain of silver. (18.5)

*anupubbena medhāvī thokathokaṃ khaṇe khaṇe*
*kammāro rajatasseva niddhame malam attano.*

Gradually: *anupubbena*
In sequential order.

The wise one: *medhāvī*
The one who is endowed with wisdom that is the sap of dhamma.

Moment by moment: *khaṇe khaṇe*
At every opportunity, doing what is wholesome.

Like a smith [the stain] of silver: *kammāro rajatasseva*
Just as a goldsmith, by heating gold just once and beating it, is unable to remove impurity and make varieties of ornament; but, heating it and beating it again and again, he removes [impurity], and then makes many different kinds of ornament.

(Blow out the stain that is one's own): *(nidhame malam attano)*
In the same way, doing what is wholesome again and again, the wise one would "blow out" one's own "stain" such as sensual attractions, and so forth. The meaning is: thus does one become one whose stains are blown out, one free of defilement.

240. As rust sprung from iron,
Springing from that, eats that itself,
So one's own actions lead
One of unwise conduct to a state of woe. (18.6)

*ayasā va malaṃ samuṭṭhitaṃ taduṭṭhāya tam eva khādati*
*evaṃ atidhonacārinaṃ sakakammāni nayanti duggatiṃ.*

### From iron: *ayasā*

Sprung from iron,

### Springing from that: *taduṭṭhaya*

Having issued therefrom.

### One of unwise conduct: *atidhonacārinaṃ*

*Dhonā* means the wisdom of utilizing [the requisites] after reflection(6)—that they, the four requisites, are for this purpose [for such and such a purpose and no other].[7]

Someone conducting oneself in transgression of that [wisdom] is known as *atidhonacārī*: one who goes beyond [the limits set by] *dhonā*. What is stated is this: just as rust, having sprung from iron, eats into that very [iron] from which it sprang up, in the same way those deeds that(8) are one's own—because they are situated in oneself—lead into a state of woe the one who goes beyond *dhonā*, who utilizes the four requisites without having reflected [on their proper uses].

241. For chants [memorized], nonrepetition is corrosive;
For houses, nonmaintenance is corrosive;
Corrosive is sloth for physical appearance;
For one who guards, heedlessness is the corrosive. (18.7)

*asajjhāyamalā mantā anuṭṭhānamalā gharā*
*malaṃ vaṇṇassa kosajjaṃ pamādo rakkhato malaṃ.*

Because that textual learning or [mastery of] craft is either lost or is not recallable uninterruptedly to one who does not repeat it or does not engage in it, therefore it is said that—

### For chants [memorized], nonrepetition is corrosive: *asajjhāyamalā mantā*

Because the house gets destroyed of a person who lives the household life but does not diligently attend to repairs [needed] for decayed [masonry, woodwork, and so forth]; therefore it is said that—

### For houses nonmaintenance is corrosive: *anuṭṭhānamalā gharā*

Because the body turns ugly of anyone one who has gone forth, or of a lay person who, due to laziness, does not attend to the care of [the] body or the care for [its] requisites; therefore it is said that—

## Corrosive is sloth for physical appearance: *malaṃ vaṇṇassa kosajjaṃ*

Because, in the case of one who guards cows, who, due to heedlessness, sleeps or plays [without attending to the animals], those cows meet with destruction either by leaping [across] unfordable [waterways], or by any danger [arising] from wild animals and robbers, or by descending into others' paddy fields, and so on, and feeding thereon—or else [in such cases the herdsman] himself comes by punitive action or derision; [and because in the case of] one who has gone forth, who does not guard the six doors [of the senses], and so forth, defilements descend [on that person] on account of heedlessness and drive [that person] out of the monastic order; so it has been said that—

## For one who guards, heedlessness is the corrosive: *pamādo rakkhato malaṃ*

The meaning is: because it stands in the position of rust on account of bringing about destruction, heedlessness is a corrosive.

242. The stain of a woman is misconduct;
To the giver, stinginess is the stain.
Bad qualities indeed are stains,
In this world and in that beyond. (18.8)

243. More staining than that stain
Is ignorance, the worst of stains.
Having abandoned this stain,
Be you free of stains, O bhikkhus! (18.9)

*malitthiyā duccaritaṃ maccheraṃ dadato malaṃ*
*malā ve pāpakā dhammā asmiṃ loke paramhi ca.*

*tato malā malataraṃ avijjā paramaṃ malaṃ*
*etaṃ malaṃ pahatvāna nimmalā hotha bhikkhavo.*

[242.]

## (The stain of a woman is) misconduct: *(malitthiyā) duccaritaṃ*

In this context, misconduct means [moral] transgression. Even her husband expels from home a woman who is guilty of [such] transgression. Even when she has gone to [her own] parents, they expel her, (saying), "You have become the charcoal [the "burning," the cause of suffering][9] of the family. We do not wish even to see[(10)] you with [our] eyes." Wandering without [any] refuge, she comes by great misery. Hence it is said that misconduct is her stain.

### To the giver (stinginess is the stain): *(maccheraṃ) dadato (malaṃ)*

[The word *dadato* means] "to the giver."

In the case of one who thinks, at the time of plowing [his] field: "When [there is a] successful [harvest in] this field, I shall give *salāka* alms and so forth";[11] in whom stinginess arises and blocks that sentiment of generosity when the harvest has thrived—three fortunes he misses because the sentiment of generosity does not grow, due to stinginess, [namely] the fortune of the human state, the fortune of the divine state, and the fortune of Nibbāna. Hence it is said: To the giver, stinginess is the stain. The same holds good with reference to other similar [qualities] too.

### Bad qualities: *pāpakā dhammā*

Unwholesome dhammas are a stain in this world and in the world beyond.

### More staining: *malataraṃ*

The meaning is: I will tell you of a greater stain—

[243.]

### Than: *tato*

Than the stains mentioned earlier:

### Ignorance (the worst of stains): *avijjā (paramaṃ malaṃ)*

The eight-faceted[(12)] ignorance[13] is the greater stain, the worst stain.

### Having abandoned: *pahatvāna*

Having discarded this stain,

### Be you free of stains, (O bhikkhus): *nimmalā hotha (bhikkhavo)*

244. Life is easily lived
By a shameless one,
A disparager, crafty as a crow,
An obtruder, impudent and corrupt. (18.10)

245. But life is lived with hardship
By one sensitive to shame, ever seeking purity,
Free from clinging, and not impudent,
Discerning, pure in the mode of life. (18.11)

*sujīvaṃ ahirikena kākasūrena dhaṃsinā*(14)
*pakkhandinā pagabbhena saṃkiliṭṭhena jīvitaṃ.*

*hirīmatā ca dujjīvaṃ niccaṃ sucigavesinā*
*alīnen'appagabbhena suddhājīvena passatā.*

[244.]

## By a shameless one: *ahirikena*

By one in whom shame and fear have been annulled. It is possible for such a person to lead an easy life, saying "mother" to them who are not one's mother,(15) and saying "father" to them who are not one's father, and so forth, and having settled in impropriety of the twenty-one kinds.[16]

## Crafty as a crow: *kākasūrena*

By one who is like a crafty crow. Just as a crafty crow, wishing to snatch [foodstuffs] such as gruel, and so on, from households, sits upon walls, and so forth, aware of the fact that it is looking out [for an opportunity,[17] stays as if it is not looking out, as if it is attentive to something else, and as if it is dozing away; [then] notices a moment of heedlessness [on the part] of the people, alights on [the food], and flies away with a mouthful snatched from the vessel, even as they [shout to] shoo it away—in the same way, the shameless person, too, enters the village with bhikkhus [on the alms round] and makes [mental] note of [the households where] gruel and rice [are lavishly offered]. The bhikkhus having done the alms round there, take only as much as [is needed for their] maintenance and return to the sitting hall; they partake of the gruel, reflecting [upon the significance of what they do], then recite [appropriate texts] thinking of the topics of meditation and sweep the sitting room. This one does nothing; he stays just "turning to the village." Even though he is being watched by the [other] bhikkhus who say, "Look at this one!" he sits as if otherwise engaged, as if sleeping, as if "tying up the knot,"[18] as if arranging the robe, [and then] gets up from the seat, saying: "I have this work to do" and goes into the village, comes up to one of the houses [which he] noted in the morning; and, even as the people of the house are [engaged in] spinning [thread], sitting near at the door having half closed up the door panel, he opens out the door panel with one hand and enters within. Seeing him they invite him to sit, and, though unwillingly, offer him whatever is left of the [morning's] gruel, and so forth. He eats as much as needed and goes away taking the rest in [his] bowl. This is [the one who is] called "crafty as a crow." The meaning is: [life is] easily lived by such a shameless person.

## By a disparager: *dhaṃsinā*

When persons say, "Such and such an elder is modest in his wants," [there would be one who says] "are we too not modest in wants?" [What is meant here is] by [such] a disparager [lit. destroyer], [so called] because he disparages the virtues of others.(19) Hearing the talk of such a person, others regard him as worthy of receiving [alms, and the like], thinking, "This one is also endowed with qualities such as being modest in wants, and so forth." [But] thereafter, not being able to please the minds of the intelligent, he falls away from that gain too [which he thus secured]. In this way the disparaging person indeed destroys his own as well as another's gain.

## An obtruder: *pakkhandinā*

By one who moves about rushing,[20] showing off other's actions as his own.

When early in the morning the bhikkhus perform [their] regular duty regarding shrine, shrine yard, and so forth, sit for a while reflecting on the topics of meditation, get up and go into the village [for alms], [this one] washes his face and beautifies himself by putting on a pale yellow robe, applying collyrium on the eyes, oiling his head, and so forth, makes two or three strokes with the broom as if sweeping [the yard], and positions himself facing the entrance gate. The people who have arrived [there] early in the morning with the intention of worshiping at the shrine and making flower offerings, see him and think, "This temple gets [proper] maintenance on account of this young one. Do not neglect him." They consider him worthy of gifts. [Life is] easily lived by such an obtruder too.

## Impudent: *paggabbhena*

By one possessed of physical impudence,[21] and so forth.

## Lived . . . (by a) corrupt (one): *saṃkiliṭṭhena jīvitaṃ*

The person who has earned a livelihood in this way has indeed lived as one defiled. The meaning is: that is a bad life, an unwholesome life.

[245.]

### But . . . by one sensitive to shame: *hirīmatā ca*

[Life indeed is] lived with hardship by the person endowed with shame and fear. One does not say "mother" to them who are not ones mother, and so forth; despising like feces material things that do not accord with dhamma, [but] seeking [requisites] in accord with dhamma and with serene [mentality], one goes for alms [to all houses] in unbroken order [i.e., does not choose places so as to get what gratifies]. Obtaining [one's] livelihood [thus] one leads a hard life. That is the meaning.

### Ever seeking purity: *sucigavesinā*

By one who seeks [to have one's] physical deeds, and the like, [morally] clean,

### Free from clinging: *alīnena*

By one who is not attached(22) to the earning of a living,

### Discerning, pure in his mode of life: *suddhājīvena passatā*

Such a person as that is of a pure mode of life. By the one who is of such a pure mode of life, who sees(23) pure livelihood itself as what is of value, life is lived with hardship in [the sense] that it is a rough way of living. That is the meaning.

246. Whoever in [this] world destroys life,
And falsehood speaks,
Takes what is not given,
And goes to another's wife, (18.12)

247. And the man who engages in
The drinking of intoxicants,
Right here in this world
He digs up his own root. (18.13)

248. Know this, dear fellow,
Bad qualities are intemperate.
Let not greed and the undhammalike way
Oppress you into prolonged suffering. (18.14)

*yo pāṇaṃ atipāteti musāvādaṃ ca bhāsati*
*loke adinnaṃ ādiyati paradāraṃ ca gacchati.*

*surāmerayapānañ ca yo naro anuyuñjati*
*idh' eva-m-eso lokasmiṃ mūlaṃ khaṇati attano.*

*evaṃ bho purisa jānāhi pāpadhammā asaññatā*
*mā taṃ lobho adhammo ca ciraṃ dukkhāya randhayuṃ.*

[246.]

Whoever destroys life: *yo paṇam atipāteti*

Who makes the faculty of life of others extinct, by means of even one of the six means [of killing], such as "killing with one's own hands,"[24]

And falsehood speaks: *musāvādaṃ ca bhāsati*

[Who] speaks falsehood that is damaging to the welfare of others,

In this world . . . takes what is not given: loke adinnam ādiyati

[Who] takes what has been held as property by others, by even one of the means of appropriation in this world of beings, such as "appropriation by theft,"[25]

And goes to another's wife: *paradāraṃ ca gacchati*

[Who] treads the path of wrongdoing, offending with reference to "those to be maintained,"[(26)] [namely, wives] who are under guard and protection of another,

[247.]

And (the man who engages in) the drinking of intoxicants: *surāmerayapānañ ca (yo naro anuyuñjati)*

[Who] engages in, devotes himself to, frequently partakes of, the drinking of liquor and [intoxicating] spirits, of whatever kind,

He digs up (his own) root: *mūlaṃ khanati (attano)*

In this very world, let alone the next, that person digs at even that root by which one could establish oneself—namely, field, garden, and so forth—either without employing it for agriculture,[(27)] or spending it away drinking liquor. He lives on, having become helpless and destitute.

[248.]

Dear fellow: *evaṃ bho (purisa)*

Thus he [the Buddha] addresses the person who is prone to do the five kinds of unvirtuous deeds [mentioned above].

Bad qualities: *pāpadhammā*

"The childish-qualities,

Are intemperate: *asaññatā*

Are lacking in [restraint] such as physical restraint, and so forth." There is also the reading *acetasā*; the meaning [then] being "lacking in thoughtfulness."

Greed and the undhammalike way: *lobho adhammo*

Greed and ill will, for both of these constitute the root of what is unwholesome.(28)

Let (not) . . . oppress (you) into prolonged suffering: *(mā taṃ) ciraṃ dukkhāya randhayuṃ*

Let these dhammas not oppress you, agitate you, to bring about the sufferings of the states of woe, and so forth, for a long period of time. That is the meaning.

249. People give according to their faith,
According as they are pleased.
There one who becomes sullen,
About the food and drink of others [gotten],
He does not gain integration,
Be it by day or by night. (18.15)

250. But the one in whom this is extirpated,
Destroyed at its roots, abolished,
He does gain integration,
Be it by day or by night. (18.16)

*dadāti*(29) *ve yathāsaddhaṃ yathāpasādanaṃ jano*(30)
*tattha yo maṅku hoti paresaṃ pānabhojane*
*na so divā vā rattiṃ va samādhiṃ adhigacchati.*

*yassa c'etaṃ samucchinnaṃ mūlaghaccaṃ samūhataṃ*(31)
*sa ve divā vā rattiṃ vā samādhiṃ adhigacchati.*

[249.]

## (People) give according to their faith: *dadāti ve yathāsaddhaṃ*

Of [goods that are] coarse, fine, and so forth, the person those who gives anything whatever, does so in accordance with faith, as consistent with one's own faith indeed.

## According as they are pleased: *yathāpasādanaṃ*

One gives according as one is pleased, as one is taken up [with the recipient]—giving [only] to that one for whom one's admiration arises, among elders, novices, and others.

## So (one who becomes sullen): *tattha (maṅku yo hoti)*

In regard to that gift of another, [who] gets into a state of sullenness, thinking, "[What was] gotten by me is a little, a trifle,"

## He does not gain integration: *(na so) samādhim (adhigacchati)*

That person does not obtain integration of mind *(samādhi)* either as access *(upacāra)*, absorption *(appanā)*,[32] or as Path and Fruit,[33] either by day or by night.

[250.]

## But the one in whom this is extirpated: *yassa c'etaṃ samucchinnaṃ*

That person in whom this unwholesome [sentiment], namely, sullenness, is made extinct in relation to these factors,

## Destroyed at its roots, abolished: *mūlaghaccam samūhataṃ*

[In whom it is] fully destroyed by means of the wisdom of Arahantship,

## He does gain integration: *samādhiṃ adhigacchati*

Attains integration of the kinds stated. That is the meaning,

251. There is no firelike passion.
There is no grip like ill will.
There is no snare like delusion.
There is no river like craving. (18.17)

*natthi rāgasamo aggi natthi dosasamo gaho*
*natthi mohasamaṃ jālaṃ natthi taṇhāsamā nadī.*

### (There is no fire) like passion: *(natthi) rāgasama (aggi)*

There is no fire comparable with passion in that it arises only internally and burns [one] away without showing any [external signs] like smoke, and so forth.

### (There is no grip) like ill will: *(natthi) dosasamo (gaho)*

Seizure by a *yakkha*, a python, a crocodile, and so forth, can grip [a person] only in a single existence, [but] seizure by ill will grips once and for all. Hence there is no seizure comparable with ill will.

### (There is no) snare like delusion: *(natthi) mohasamaṃ jālaṃ*

There is no net comparable with delusion in that [it is] binding and entangling all round.

### (There is no river) like craving: *(natthi) taṇhāsamā (nadī)*

Of rivers such as the *Gangā* and so forth, there is found a season when they are full, a season when they are reduced, and also a season when they are dry. For craving there is no full season or dry season, but only the constant state of insufficiency.(34) In the sense that it is hard to be filled, there is no river like craving. That is the meaning.

252. Easily seen is the fault of others,
But one's own is hard to see.
The faults of others
He winnows like chaff;
But conceals his own,
As a shrewd gambler, the defeating throw.[35] (18.18)
(The commentary takes line 6 to mean:
"As a hunter, his body with a covering of sticks.")

*sudassaṃ vajjaṃ aññesaṃ attano pana duddasaṃ*
*paresaṃ hi so vijjāni opuṇāti*(36) *yathā bhusaṃ*
*attano pana chādeti kaliṃ va kitavā saṭho.*

## Easily seen is the fault of others: *suddassaṃ vajjaṃ aññesaṃ*

Another's fault, another's omission, is well perceptible, is possible to be seen easily, even though it be [as small] as an atom, but one's own is hard to perceive even though it be very large.

## (The faults) of others (he winnows like chaff): *parasaṃ hi (so vajjāni opuṇāti yathā bhusaṃ)*

For that very reason that person [who is prone to see the mistakes of others] "spreads out" in the midst of the Saṅgha, and so forth, the faults of others, as one raises [grains] to a high level [and pours them down in the wind, thus] winnowing the chaff away.

## As a shrewd gambler, the defeating throw: *kaliṃ va kitavā saṭha*(37)

Here *saṭha* means a hunter of birds; *kali* means the body, as the means of doing offense to the birds [that he hunts]; *kitavā* means a covering such as twigs of branches, and so forth.

[The line then means:] Just as a hunter of birds, wishing to capture birds and kill them, conceals his person with [a covering of] twigs of branches, so does one conceal one's own fault [who exposes that of another].

253. Of one who sees the faults of others,
Constantly holding ideas of disdain—
His intoxicants increase;
Far is he from the extinction of intoxicants. (18.19)

*paravajjānupassissa niccaṃ ujjhānasaññino*
*āsavā tassa vaḍḍhanti ārā so āsavakkhayā.*

## Holding ideas of disdain: *ujjhānasaññino*

Of the person in whom disdain(38) [of others] is abundant, due to looking for [their] mistakes [lit. holes], [by such talk] as, "One should dress thus, thus one should drape [the robe]", and so forth, [of such a person] not even a single dhamma develops from among the meditative-absorptions, and so forth.

## His intoxicants increase. Far is he from the extinction of intoxicants: *āsavā tassa vaḍḍhanti ārā so āsvakkhayā*

Then on account of the fact that intoxicants grow, he is gone far away from the extinction of intoxicants—namely, Arahantship.

254. In the sky there is no footstep;
The recluse is not in externals;
Enamored with mental proliferation are the generations;
Free of proliferations are Tathāgatas. (18.20)

255. In the sky there is no footstep;
The recluse is not in externals;
No *saṅkhāra* is eternal;
There is no agitation among Buddhas. (18.21)

*ākāse padaṃ natthi samaṇo natthi bāhire*(39)
*papañcābhiratā pajā nippapañcā tathāgatā.*

*ākase padaṃ natthi samaṇo natthi bāhire*
*saṅkhārā sassatā natthi natthi buddhānam iñjitaṃ.*

[254.]

## Footstep: *padaṃ*

In this [visible] sky there is no footstep of anyone, which may be specified to be such and such in terms of color and form.

## In externals: *bāhire*

Outside my dispensation *(sāsana)* there is no recluse who is established in the Paths and Fruits.

## Generations: *pajā*

This community constituting the world of beings is enamored of mental proliferations themselves, such as craving, and so forth.

## Free of proliferations: *nippapañcā*

The Tathāgatas are free of proliferations because, in their case, all proliferations have been cut off totally at the foot of the tree of enlightenment itself.

[255.]

## *Saṅkhāra: saṅkhārā*

The *saṅkhārā*s are the five *khandha*s. Of them is not even one that is eternal.

## Agitation: *iñjitaṃ*

In the case of Buddhas, not even a single agitation exists [for them] from among such agitations as craving, measurement, and views, due to which they would treat the *saṅkhārā*s as eternal. That is the meaning.

# CHAPTER XIX

## The Firm in Dhamma
## *Dhammaṭṭha-vaggo*

256. Were one to settle a case capriciously,
One thereby does not become firm in dhamma.
But the one who would discriminate
Both what is and what is not the case—the sagacious one— (19.1)

257. Who leads others impartially
With dhamma, not capriciously,
The intelligent one, guarded by dhamma,
Is called "one firm in dhamma." (19.2)

*na tena hoti dhammaṭṭho yen'atthaṃ sahasā naye*
*yo ca atthaṃ anatthaṃ ca ubho niccheyya paṇḍito.*

*asāhasena dhammena samena nayatī pare*
*dhammassa gutto medhāvī dhammaṭṭho ti pavuccati.*

[256.]

### Firm in dhamma: *dhammaṭṭho*

A king does not become "firm in dhamma" even though he stays on [the task of] adjudication incumbent upon him,(1)

### Thereby: *tena*

By that reason alone.

### A case: *attham*

A matter to which [he has] got down, that is to be adjudicated.

### Settle . . . capriciously: *sahasā naye*

"One settles a matter capriciously" means this: being established in favorable bias, and so forth, one may settle [a case] capriciously, wrongfully—that is, [1] established in "favorable bias," one falsely grants rights of ownership to a relation or friend who has no such rights;

[2] established in ill will, one falsely deprives an adversary of rights of ownership when he has such rights;

[3] established in delusion, having accepted a bribe, one [behaves] at the time of making a decision, as if one is attentive to some other matter, as if one is "looking this way and that" [not concentrating on the matter in hand] and deprives another [of rights] falsely, saying: "[The case is] won by him: the other is defeated";

[4] established in fear, one grants victory to some powerful person,(2) even though, lawfully, [that person] is facing defeat. The meaning is: he [who adjudicates thus] is not said to be firm in dhamma.

### (But the one who) would discriminate both what is and what is not the case: *attham̩ anattham̩ ca ubho nicchiya*

Who, being a learned person, adjudicates upon matters [of] both [kinds], that which is factual and that which is not, and states the judgment,

[257.]

### Leads others: *pare nayati*

Leads others(3) to victory and defeat,

### With dhamma, not capriciously: *asahāsena dhammena*

Impartially, not through "favorable bias," and so forth, [but] in conformity with the dhamma of adjudication,

### Impartially: *samena*

[And] strictly as befits and crime [committed],

### (The intelligent one) guarded by dhamma is called "one firm in dhamma": *dhammassa gutto (medhāvī) dhammaṭṭho ti pavuccati*

That one, who is protected, guarded, by dhamma, endowed with understanding that is the sap of dhamma, is said to be firm in dhamma, because of being established in the dhamma of adjudication.

258. One is not a learned one
Merely because one speaks much.
The one secure, without enmity, without fear,
Is called a "learned one." (19.3)

*na tena paṇḍito hoti yāvatā bahu bhāsati*
*khemī averī abhayo paṇḍito ti pavuccati.*

One is not a learned one merely because one speaks much: *na tena paṇḍito hoti yāvatā bahu bhāsati*

For the mere reason that one speaks much in the midst of the Saṅgha, and so forth, by that one is not said to be learned.

The one secure, without enmity, without fear: *khemī averī abhayo*

He who has security himself, who is not hostile, due to the absence of the five hostilities—or having come to whom, people have no fear,[4]

(He is called a "learned one"): *(paṇḍito ti pavuccati)*

He is said to be learned: that is the meaning.

259. One is not a dhamma-bearer
Merely because one speaks much,
But who, having heard even a little,
Sees dhamma for himself,
And dhamma does not neglect,
He, indeed, is a dhamma-bearer. (19.4)

*na tāvatā dhammadharo yāvatā bahu bhāsati*
*yo ca appaṃ pi sutvāna dhammaṃ kāyena passati*[(5)]
*sa ve dhammadharo hoti yo dhammaṃ nappamajjati.*

One is not a dhamma-bearer merely because one speaks much: *na tāvatā dhammadharo yāvatā bahu bhāsati*

For the mere reason that one speaks much, on account of study, remembrance, repetition, and so forth—by that one is not a dhamma-bearer. [By that] one [merely] becomes a "guardian of the family," a "protector of the lineage."

### But who, having heard even a little, sees dhamma for himself, He indeed, is a dhamma-bearer: *yo ca appaṃ pi sutvāna dhammaṃ kāyena passati sa ve dhammadharo hoti*

But he who having heard dhamma even a little bit, and understanding it, has become an observant of dhamma and [its] consequence, realizing fully [the truths] such as [the truth of] suffering, in his own mind sees the dhamma of the four truths—he is indeed the dhamma-bearer.

### (He, indeed, is a dhamma-bearer) who . . . dhamma does not neglect: *(sa ve dhammadharo hoti) yo dhammaṃ nappamajjati*

And one who having undertaken strenuous effort, is not neglectful of dhamma, and hopes for penetrative realization, thinking "[May it come] today, today itself!"—such a one too is indeed a dhamma-bearer. That is the meaning.

260. One does not become an Elder
Because one's head is gray-haired;
Ripened his age,
"Grown old in vain" is he called. (19.5)

261. In whom there is truth and dhamma,
Harmlessness, restraint, control,
Who has the stains ejected, and is wise,
He indeed is called "Elder." (19.6)

*na tena thero hoti yen' assa phalitaṃ siro*
*paripakko vayo tassa moghajiṇṇo ti vuccati.*

*yamhi saccañ ca dhammo ca ahimsā saññamo damo*
*sa ve vantamalo dhīro thero ti pavuccati.*

[260.]

### Ripened his age: *paripakko*

The meaning is: matured, come to old age.(6)

### Grown old in vain: *moghajiṇṇo*

One who is said to have grown in vain, on account of the absence within [him] of the qualities that [go to] make an Elder [in the true sense].

[261.]

### (In whom) there is truth (and dhamma): *(yamhi) saccañ (ca dhammo ca)*

The person in whom the fourfold truth exists, due to [its] being penetratively understood in the sixteen [specified] ways,[7] and [in whom] the ninefold world-transcending dhamma [exists] due to [its] being realized through understanding.

### (In whom) there is harmlessness: *(yamhi) ahimsā*

Due to the state of nonviolence:[(8)] this is only [the manner of] instruction. The [intended] meaning is: in whom there is the development of the fourfold "limitless" [feelings],[9]

### Restraint, control: *saññamo damo*

[In whom there is] virtue as well as the restraint of senses,

### Has the stains ejected: *vantamalo*

Whose stains have been removed by understanding of the Paths,

### Wise: *dhīro*

Who is endowed with steadfastness—

### Elder: *thero*

Such a one is called an Elder *(thera)* because he is endowed with those factors of the steadfast *(thira)* state. That is the meaning.

262. Not because of speech-making
Or by attractiveness of appearance
Does one, envious, avaricious, deceitful,
Become a commendable man. (19.7)

263. But in whom this is extirpated,
Destroyed at its roots, abolished,
He, having ill will ejected, wise,
Is called "commendable." (19.8)

*na vākkaraṇamattena vaṇṇapokkharatāya vā*
*sādhurūpo naro hoti issukī maccharī saṭho.*

*yassa c'etaṃ samucchinnaṃ mūlaghaccaṃ samūhataṃ*
*sa vantadoso medhāvī sādhurūpo ti vuccati.*

[262.]

### Because of speech-making: *vākkaraṇamattena*

By the mere making of speech—that is, merely by speech that is endowed with [pleasing] characteristics,

### Or by attractiveness of appearance: *vaṇṇapokkharatāya vā*

Or by the pleasantness of one's physical appearance,

### (He does not become a commendable) man: *(na sādhurūpo) naro (hoti)*

Just for this reason he does not become a good person [if at the same time he is one] who is envious(10) of others' gains, and so forth, is possessed of the five kinds of avarice,[11] and is crafty due to associating with the deceitful.

[263.]

### But in whom this is extirpated: *yassa c'etaṃ samucchinnaṃ*

The person in whom this multitude of evils such as enviousness, and so forth, is cut off at the root [that is] by bringing about the destruction of [its very] roots,

### (He) having ill will ejected (is called "commendable"): *(sa) vantadoso (sādhurūpo ti vuccati)*

Endowed with wisdom that is the dhamma-sap, is said to be the good person: that is the meaning.

264. Not by a shaven head is one a recluse,
If one lacks due observance, speaks untruth.
How can one possessed of longing and greed
Become a recluse? (19.9)

265. But he who calms away the wrongs
Great and small, in every way;
For having [so] calmed away the wrongs,
"A recluse" he is called. (19.10)

*na muṇḍakena samaṇo abbato alikaṃ bhaṇaṃ*
*icchālobhasamāpanno samaṇo kiṃ bhavissati.*

*yo ca sameti pāpāni aṇuṃ thūlāni sabbaso*
*samitattā hi pāpānaṃ samaṇo ti pavuccati.*

[264.]

[One who] lacks due observance: *abbato*
One who lacks observance of virtue and *dhutaṅga*[12] practice,

Speaks untruth: *alikam bhaṇaṃ*
Who is [given to] speaking falsehood,

(One possessed of longing and greed): *(icchālobhasamāpanno)*
Who is possessed of desire for objects unobtained and of greed for [objects] obtained,(13)

(How can one . . . become a recluse): *(samaṇo kiṃ bhavissati)*
Will such a person be a recluse,

By a shaven head: *muṇḍakena*
By the mere fact of having the head shaven?

[265.]

(But he who) calms away . . . (the wrongs): *(yo ca) sameti (pāpāni)*
But he who dissolves the unwholesome [impulses, be they] small or great,

(For having so calmed . . . away the wrongs, a "recluse" he is called): *(samitattā pāpānaṃ samaṇo ti pavuccati)*
He is called a recluse *(samaṇa)* because of the unwholesome having been dissolved *(samita)*. That is the meaning.

266. Not for this is one a bhikkhu,
Merely that one begs of others;
Having taken up a foul dhamma,
One is not thereby a bhikkhu. (19.11)

267. Setting aside both merit and wrong
Who lives here the higher life,
Courses in the world discriminately,
He, indeed, is called "bhikkhu." (19.12)

*na tena bhikkhu hoti yāvatā bhikkhate pare*
*vissaṃ dhammaṃ*(14) *samādāyā bhikkhu hoti na tāvatā.*

*yo 'dha puññaṃ ca pāpaṃ ca bāhetvā brahmacariyavā*
*saṃkhāya loke carati sa ve bhikkhū ti vuccati.*

[266.]

(Not for this is one a bhikkhu) merely that (one begs of others):
*(na tena bhikkhu hoti) yāvatā (bhikkhate pare)*

By the fact that one begs [for alms] of others—by that mere begging one is not a bhikkhu.

(Having taken up) a foul (dhamma one . . . is not a bhikkhu):
*vissaṃ (dhammam samādāya bhikkhu hoti . . . na)*

One who takes on a dhamma that is uneven or a dhamma that is foul, concerned with physical activities, and so forth, is not said to be a bhikkhu.

[267.]

Who . . . here: *yo'dha*

One who, in this monastic order,

Lives the higher life, setting aside both merit and wrong:
*puññaṃ pāpaṃ ca bāhitvā*(15) *brahmacariyavā*

Having set aside both the wholesome and the unwholesome by means of the higher life that is the Path—becomes a fulfiller of the religious life,

### Discriminately: *saṃkhāya*
With insight,

### Courses in the world: *loke carati*
Lives in the world—that is, the world of the *khandha*s, and so forth—understanding all dhammas thus: "These are the internal *khandha*s and these are the external *khandha*s,"

### (He, indeed, is called a "bhikkhu"): *(sa ve bhikkhu ti vuccati)*
He is said to be a bhikkhu, because of having broken [*bhid-*] the defilements through that understanding. That is the meaning.

268. One does not become a sage by silence,
If confused and ignorant.
But a wise one, as if holding a set of scales,
Takes up the best, (19.13)

269. And shuns wrongs, he is a sage;
For that reason he is a sage.
Who knows both in this world,
Is, for that, called a sage. (19.14)

*na monena munī hoti mūḷharūpo aviddasu*
*yo ca tulaṃ va paggayha varam ādāya paṇḍito.*

*pāpāni parivajjeti sa munī tena so munī*
*yo munāti ubho loke munī tena pavuccati.*

[268.]

### By silence: *monena*
Truly one is said to be a sage on account of the "sageliness" *(mona)* that is Path-understanding—which is known as "the way of sageliness—but here the word *mona* is used with reference to [mere] silence.

### Confused: *mūḷharūpo*
Having the character of worthlessness,

### Ignorant: *aviddasu*

Unwise—such a one is not said to be a sage *(muni)*, even though staying silent; on the other hand, [if] one is a sage by [mere] silence, [then] a person of worthless nature, lacking in wisdom, also becomes(16) [a sage]. That is the meaning.

### But . . . as if holding a set of scales: *yo ca tulaṃ va paggayha*

Just as one who holds a pair of scales takes away [from the pan] if there be more [than the due weight] and adds on [to the pan] if there be less [in it],

[268./269.]

### Takes up the best (and) shuns wrongs: *varam ādāya pāpāni parivajjeti*

Similarly, who discards the unwholesome—like removing what is overweight—and fulfills the wholesome—like adding on to what is underweight—one so doing takes on what is noble—namely, all that is constituted by virtue, concentration, wisdom, liberation, and the "vision of the understanding of liberation,"[17] and avoids unwholesome deeds,

### He is a sage: *sa muni*

He is said to be the sage. That is the meaning.

### For that reason he is a sage: *tena so muni*

Why(18) is he said to be a sage? It is on account of the reason given above that he is said to be a sage. That is the meaning.

### Who knows both in this world: *yo munāti ubho loke*

The person who "weighs" *(mināti)* both factors in this world constituted of *khanda*s, and so forth [reflecting] in such terms as, "These are the internal *khanda*s and these are the external ones"—like one who weighs out [things] putting [them] upon a pair of scales—

### Is, for that, called a sage: *muni tena pavuccati*

For that reason, is indeed called a sage. That is the meaning.

270. By harmlessness toward living beings
Is one called a Noble One.
One who is harmless toward all living beings
Is called "noble one." (19.15)

*na tena ariyo hoti yena pāṇāni hiṃsati*
*ahiṃsā sabbapāṇānaṃ ariyo ti pavuccati.*

## Harmlessness: *ahiṃsā*

Here the word *ahiṃsā* stands for *ahiṃsanena* [that is, has an instrumental-case meaning].(19)

What is said is this: by the fact that one harms beings—by that one is not a "noble one."

But one who, by refraining from harm toward all beings, such as harm done by hand, and so forth, stands away *(ārā)* from violence—on account of being established in the [meditational] development of loving-kindness, and so forth—is called a "noble one" *(ariya)*. That is the meaning.

271. Not by precepts and rites,
Nor again by much learning,
Nor by acquisition of concentration,
Nor by secluded lodging, (19.16)

272. Thinking "I touched the ease of renunciation
Not resorted to by ordinary people,"
O bhikkhu, get not into contentedness,
Not having attained extinction of intoxicants. (19.17)

*na sīlabbatamattena bāhusaccena vā puna*
*athavā samādhilābhena vivicca*(20) *sayanena vā.*

*phusāmi nekkhammasukhaṃ aputhujjanasevitaṃ*
*bhikkhu vissāsamāpādi*(21) *appatto āsavakkhayam.*

[271.]

## By precepts and rites: *sīlabbatamattena*

Either on account of just the four virtues that constitute purity, or on account of just the thirteen *dhutaṅga* virtues,

## Nor again by much learning: *bāhusaccena vā*

Or on account of mastering the three *piṭakas,*

## By acquisition of concentration: *samādhilābhena*

Or on account of obtaining the eight attainments,[22]

[272.]

## "I touched the ease of renunciation not resorted to by ordinary people": *phusāmi nekkhammasukhaṃ aputhujjanasevitaṃ*

Just on account of knowing, "I have attained the bliss of the state of Non-Returning," which is not experienced by ordinary persons, but is, indeed, experienced by noble ones,

## Get not into contentedness: *vissāsa māpād*

Let one not get into a state of contentedness,

## O bhikkhu: *bhikkhu*

Thus he spoke addressing one among them.[23]

What is said is this: O Monk, by just this condition of being endowed with moral virtues, and so forth—without having arrived at Arahantship, which is the state where intoxicants are extinct—let a bhikkhu not get into contentedness, thinking: "For me, existence is [now] but a little, trifling [thing] [that is, not a lengthy one]." Just as even a little bit of fecal matter smells bad, so is existence [a source of] suffering, howsoever short [it may be].

# CHAPTER XX

## The Path
## *Magga-vaggo*

273. Of paths, the eightfold is the best.
Of truths, the four statements.
Detachment is the best of dhammas.
And of two-footed ones, the one endowed with eyes. (20.1)

274. Just this path, there is no other
For purity of vision.
Go along this [path];
This is what will bewilder Māra. (20.2)

275. Entered upon this,
An end of misery you will make.
Proclaimed indeed is the path by me,
Having known the extrication of the arrows. (20.3)

276. By you is the task strenuously to be done;
Tathāgatas are proclaimers.
Entered upon this path, the meditators
Are released from the bond of Māra. (20.4)

*maggān' aṭṭhaṅgiko seṭṭho saccānaṃ caturo padā*
*virāgo seṭṭho dhammānaṃ dipadānaṃ ca cakkhumā.*

*eso va maggo natth' añño dassanassa visuddhiyā*
*etaṃ hi tumhe paṭipajjatha mārass' etaṃ pamohanaṃ.*

*etaṃ hi tumhe paṭipannā dukkhass' antaṃ karissatha*
*akkhāto ve mayā maggo aññāya sallasanthanaṃ.*(1)

*tumhehi kiccaṃ ātappaṃ akkhātāro tathāgatā*
*paṭipannā pamokkhanti jhāyino mārabandhanā.*

[273.]

## Of paths, the eightfold is the best: *maggan' aṭṭhaṅgiko seṭṭho*

Of the paths, be they such as footpaths, and so forth, or be they the paths traversed by the sixty-two [wrong] views[2]—of all such paths the eightfold is the noblest, which, with its eight constituent aspects such as right views, and so forth,[3] brings about the abandoning of [the contrary] eight, such as wrong views, and so forth, and which, having made cessation [of mental activities] its object, effects, in regard to all four truths, the function of complete understanding of suffering, and so on.[4]

## Of truths, the four statements: *saccānaṃ caturo padā*

Of truths—be it the truth of statement, as occurring in "I speak truth, do not be angry," [be it] conventional truth of such kinds [of usage] as "the true *brāhmaṇa*,"(5) "the true *kṣatriya*," and so forth, [be it] the truth [asserted] of views, as [in] "This alone is true, all else false," or be it the absolute truth, of such kinds as the noble truth of suffering—of all such truths, the four [truth-] statements such as the noble truth of suffering are the best in the sense that they [of all] are to be fully understood, realized,(6) cultivated, be uniquely penetrated into,[7] be penetrated into exactly as they are.

## Detachment is the best of dhammas: *virāgo seṭṭho dhammānaṃ*

By virtue of the statement, "However many dhammas [there be], O bhikkhus, conditioned or unconditioned, detachment is said to be the highest one of them," detachment—that is to say, Nibbāna—is the best of all dhammas.

## And of two-footed ones, the one endowed with eyes: *dipadānaṃ ca cakkhumā*

And of all two-footed beings of various categories, such as gods, humans, and the like, the Tathāgata who is endowed with the five [kinds of] "eyes" is the best.[8]

[274.]

Just this path, there is no other for purity of vision:
*eso va maggo natth' añño dassanassa visuddhiyā*

This path alone, which I [the Buddha] have called the best, is there for cleansing "the vision of Path and Fruit". Therefore,

Do ye go along this (path): *(etaṃ hi tumhe paṭipajjatha)*

This is what will bewilder Māra: *mārass' etaṃ pamohanaṃ*

This is the confounding of Māra; this indeed is the [way to] tricking Māra away.[9] That is what is stated.

[275.]

An end of misery you will make: *dukkhass' antaṃ karissatha*

Cut away the suffering of the entire whirl. That is the meaning.

Proclaimed indeed is the path by me, having known the extrication of the arrows: *akkhāto ve mayā maggo aññāya sallasanthanaṃ*

This path is the crushing, the "drawing out" of all "arrows," such as sensual attraction. This path has been declared by me, having understood [it] by way of self-realization, by means other than hearsay, and so forth.

[276.]

By you is the task strenuously to be done:
*tumehi kiccaṃ ātappaṃ*

Now the strenuous task of right exertion for attainment of this [path] should be done by you—which [task] has come to be known as "the burning," because of [its result, namely] the burning away of defilements.

Tathāgatas are proclaimers: *akkhātāro tathāgatā*

The Tathāgatas are indeed only they who proclaim [that path]. Hence, those who have stepped on [to the path], in accordance with what they [the Tathāgatas] have proclaimed, who meditate by the two [kinds of] meditation,[10] they are released from the bond of Māra known as "the whirl of the three planes [of existence]." That is the meaning.

277. When through wisdom one perceives,
"All *saṅkhāras* are transient,"

Then one is detached as to misery.
This is the path of purity. (20.5)

*sabbe saṃkhārā aniccā ti yadā paññāya passati*
*atha nibbindatī dukkhe*[11] *esa maggo visuddhiyā.*

(When through wisdom one perceives): *(yadā paññāya passati)*
When one, by insight-wisdom, sees:

All *saṅkhāra*s: *sabbe saṃkhārā*
The *khandha*s arisen in [various planes of existence] such as the world of sensual experience,

Are impermanent: *aniccā*
[Are] impermanent, ceasing to be [as they do][12] in [those] various places,

Then one is detached as to misery: *atha nibbindati dukkhe*
Then one becomes detached as to the suffering that is this maintenance of *khandha*s. Having become detached,[13] one penetrates into the truths by fully understanding [the nature of] suffering, and so forth.

This is the path of purity: *esa maggo visuddhiyā*
For purity, for the cleansing [of mind], this is the way. That is the meaning.

278. When through wisdom one perceives
"All *saṅkhāra*s are suffering,"
Then one is detached as to misery.
This is the path of purity. (20.6)

*sabbe saṃkhārā dukkhā ti yadā paññāya passati*
*atha nibbindatī dukkhe esa maggo visuddhiyā.*

Suffering: *dukkhā*
Here [the *saṃkhāra*s are said to be] "suffering" in the sense of oppression.[14] The rest is as in the previous [stanza].

279. When through wisdom one perceives,
"All dhammas are without self,"
Then one is detached as to misery.
This is the path of purity. (20.7)

*sabbe dhammā anattā ti yadā paññāya passati*
*atha nibbindatī dukkhe esa maggo visuddhiyā.*

### All dhammas: *sabbe dhammā*

Here, by "all dhammas" the five *khandha*s themselves are intended.

### Are without self: *anattā ti*

Because it is not possible to hold them in one's control, saying, "Let them not decay, let them not die away." In [that] sense of not being under control, [they are] "not self," "void";(15) there is no ownership or lordship [over them]. That is the meaning. The rest is as in the previous [stanza].

280. Who is not exerting at the time for exertion,
Young, strong, possessed of laziness,
With mind filled with confused notions, indolent, lethargic—
Does not find the way to wisdom. (20.8)

*uṭṭhānakālamhi anuṭṭhahāno yuvā balī ālasiyaṃ*(16) *upeto*
*saṃsannasaṃkappamano kusīto paññāya maggaṃ alaso na vindati.*

### Not exerting: *anuṭṭhahāno*

[One who], not rising up, not making effort,

### Young, strong, (possessed of laziness): *yuvā balī (ālasiyaṃ upeto)*

Even being in the prime of youth and having physical strength, is possessed of laziness and [only] eats and sleeps,

### With mind filled with confused notions: *saṃsanna-saṃkappa-mano*

And has one's mind thoroughly closed to right tnought on account of the three kinds of wrong thought,[17]

Indolent: *kusīto*
[And] is devoid of exertion,

Lethargic: *alaso*
Is lazy in the extreme,

Does not find the way to wisdom: *paññāya maggaṃ na vindati*
[Such a person], being not one who sees, does not obtain the noble path that can be seen [only] by insight-wisdom.

281. Watchful of speech, well restrained in mind,
One would not do what is unwholesome by body too.
These three modes of action one would purify.
Let one fulfill the path made known by the sages. (20.9)

*vācānurakkhī manasā susaṃvuto kāyena ca akusalaṃ na kayirā*
*ete tayo kammapathe visodhaye*(18) *ārādhaye maggaṃ isippaveditaṃ.*

Watchful of speech: *vācānurakkhī*
Being "watchful of speech" by avoiding the four forms of verbal misconduct,[19]

Well restrained in mind: *manasā susaṃvuto*
[And] being well restrained in mind by not causing thoughts of covetousness, and so forth, to arise,[20]

One would not do what is unwholesome by body too: *kāyena ca akusalaṃ na kayirā*
Avoiding the taking of life, and so forth,

These three modes of action one would purify: *ete tayo kammapathe visodhaye*
So cleansing [the modes of action], one would fulfill *(ārādhaye)* the eightfold path proclaimed by sages such as the Buddhas who are seekers of the mass of [factors that constitute] moral virtue, and so forth.[21]

282. From meditativeness arises the great;
From its absence, there is destruction of the great.
Having known this twofold path for gain and loss
Let one conduct oneself so that the great increases. (20.10)

*yogā ve jāyati bhūri ayogā bhūrisaṃkhayo*
*etaṃ dvedhāpathaṃ ñatvā bhavāya vibhavāya ca*
*tath' attānaṃ niveseyya yathā bhūri pavaḍḍhati.*

### From meditativeness: *yogā*

[By this is meant] well-grounded attention in regard to the thirty-eight objects.[22]

### The great: *bhūri*

This is a term for insight-wisdom, which is "as wide as the earth."

### Destruction: *saṅkhayo*

Destruction [of meditativeness].

### This twofold path: *etaṃ dvedhāpathaṃ*

This meditativeness and lack of meditativeness.

### For gain and loss: *bhavāya vibhavāya ca*

For growth and for lack of growth.

### Let one conduct oneself so that . . . : *tath' attānaṃ niveseyya*

Let one conduct oneself in such a way that wisdom that is called "growth" does increase.

283. Cut down the forest! Not a tree
From the forest, fear arises.
Having cut down both forest and underbrush,
O bhikkhus, be ye without forests. (20.11)

284. Insofar as the underbrush is not cut away,
Even to the smallest bit, of a man for women,
Insofar is he one having [his] mind tethered,
Like a suckling calf to its mother. (20.12)

*vanaṃ chindatha mā rukkhaṃ vanato jāyatī bhayaṃ*
*chetvā vanaṃ ca vanathaṃ ca nibbanā hotha bhikkhavo.*

*yāvaṃ hi vanatho na chijjati aṇumatto pi narassa nārisu*(23)
*paṭibaddhamano va tāva so vaccho khīrapako va mātari.*

[283.]

## (Cut down the forest!) Not a tree: *(vanaṃ chindatha) mā rukkhaṃ*

"Cut down the forest!"—when [this was] said by the Teacher, the wish arose in those bhikkhus who had [only] recently "gone forth," [literally] to cut down trees, [for they thought] "The Teacher is making us to take axes and cut down the forest." [And so] preventing [them from cutting down trees, he explained the matter further:] "I said this with reference to the 'forest' of defilements such as sensual passions, and so forth, not with reference to trees [literally]."[24]

## From the forest (fear arises): *vanato (jāyate bhayaṃ)*

Just as from a natural forest [there arise fears] such as fear of [beasts like] lions, and so forth, so from the forest of defilements there arise [fears] such as the fear of [continuing] birth, and so forth.(25) That is the meaning.

## Having cut down both forest and underbrush, O bhikkhus, be ye without forests: *chetvā vanaṃ ca vanathaṃ ca nibbanā hotha bhikkhavo*

Here the large trees are called *vana* ("forest") and the small ones are called *vanatha* ("underbrush"), because of [their] "standing in the forest," or, [alternately] trees that grew up first are called *vana,* those that grew up subsequently are called *vanatha.*

In the same way the bigger defilements are called *vana*—those that drag [one] into [future] existence; those that produce ill effects in [this] continuing [life itself] are called *vanatha*; or else, [defilements] that arose first are called *vana,* those that arose subsequently are called *vanatha.*

He said: "O bhikkhus, having cut down both forest and underbrush, be ye without forests" [i.e.] "be free of defilement"—because both of these [are] to be cut down by means of the gnosis of the Fourth Path.

[284.]

Insofar as the underbrush is not cut away:
*yāvaṃ hi vanatho na chijjati*

As long as this underbrush of defilement, or desire of a man toward women, remains without being cut down, even [in] minute [quantity], so long is he of mind attached, tied down, like a suckling calf to [its] mother. That is the meaning.

285. Cut down affection for yourself,
As with the hand, an autumn lily.
Foster just the path to peace, Nibbāna,
Taught by the One Who Has Traveled Well. (20.13)

*ucchinda sineham attano kumudaṃ sāradikaṃ va pāninā*
*santimaggam eva brūhaya nibbānaṃ sugatena desitaṃ.*

Cut down: *ucchinda*

Cut down, by means of the Path of Arahantship.

Autumn: *sāradikaṃ*

Arisen during autumn.

Path to peace: *santimaggaṃ*

The eightfold path leading to Nibbāna.

Foster: *brūhaya*

Make [it] grow.

Nibbāna taught by the One Who Has Traveled Well:
*nibbānaṃ hi sugatena desitaṃ*

For Nibbāna has been proclaimed by the One Who Has Traveled Well. Hence develop the path leading to it. That is the meaning.

286. "Here I shall dwell during the rains,
Here in winter and summer, too."
So the childish one thinks.
He does not know the danger. (20.14)

*idha vassaṃ vasissāmi*[26] *idha hemantagimhisu*
*iti bālo vicinteti antarāyaṃ na bujjhati.*

## Here (I shall dwell) during the rains: *idha vassaṃ (vasissāmi)*

"I will spend the four months of the winter and [the four months] of the summer here itself, doing such and such."

## So the childish one thinks: *iti balo vicinteti*

So thinks the childish one, who does not know what is good for this visible life and for the life hereafter.

## He does not know the danger: *antarāyaṃ na bujjhati*

One does not realize the danger to one's life [for one does not know], "At such and such a time or place or age I will die."

287. That man of entangled mind,
Inebriated by sons and cattle,
Death carries away
Like a great flood, a sleeping village. (20.15)

*taṃ puttapasusammattaṃ*[27] *byāsattamanasaṃ naraṃ*
*suttaṃ gāmaṃ mahogho va maccu ādāya gacchati.*

## That . . . doting on sons and cattle: *taṃ putta-pasu-sammattaṃ*

A man who, having obtained sons and [domestic] animals of good appearance, vigor, and so forth, and is inebriated[28] by [the possession of such] sons and animals, thinking: "My sons are handsome, strong, learned, and competent in all functions. My oxen are beautiful,[29] healthy and capable of driving heavy loads. My cows yield much milk,"

## Man of entangled mind: *byāsatta-manasaṃ naraṃ*

Or who, having obtained something—be it of gold and valuables or of bowl and robes, and so forth—has his mind entangled[30] in desiring for[31] [even] more than that [which he has], or whose mind is "entangled"[32] due to [its] clinging to whatever has been obtained—be it among [various] objects "knowable" by sight, and so forth, or among the [monastic] requisites [like those] mentioned that is, bowl, robes, and so forth.[33]

## A sleeping village: *suttaṃ gāmaṃ*

A multitude of beings who have fallen asleep.

## Like a great flood: *mahogho vā*

Just as a mighty flood, deep and broad, of great rivers, sweeps away such a multitude in entirety, without leaving out so much as a dog,

## Death carries away: *maccu ādāya gacchati*

So would death carry away a person of the kind mentioned above. That is the meaning.

288. No sons there are for protection,
Neither father nor even relations,
For one seized by the End-Maker;
Among relations there is no protection. (20.16)

289. Knowing this fact,
The wise one, restrained by virtue,
Would make clear, right quickly,
The path leading to Nibbāna. (20.17)

*na santi puttā tāṇāya na pitā nāpi bandhavā*
*antakenādhipannassa*(34) *natthi ñātīsu tāṇatā.*

*etaṃ atthavasaṃ ñatvā paṇḍito sīlasaṃvuto*
*nibbānagamanaṃ maggaṃ khippam eva visodhaye.*

[288.]

## For protection: *tāṇāya*

For protection; in order that there be support.

## Relations: *bandhavā*

Relations and friends other than son and father.(35)

### For one seized by the End-Maker: *antakenādhipannassa*

For one who is subject to death.

### Among relations there is no protection: *natthi ñātīsu tāṇatā*

By giving [one] food and drink, and so forth, and by helping through [any] need that has arisen, sons, and the like, become a protection [for one] during one's lifetime. But, at the time of death, because death cannot be banished by any means whatsoever, there indeed are none [to come to one's side] for protection or shelter. Hence it is said: "Among relations there is no protection."

[289.]

### Knowing this fact: *etaṃ atthavasaṃ ñatvā*

Knowing this fact about their [relations'] inability to be a protection to one another,

### The wise one, restrained by virtue: *paṇḍito sīla-saṃvuto*

The sagacious person, being restrained by the four virtues leading to purity,[36] and being guarded and protected [thereby],

### Would make clear, right quickly, the path leading to Nibbāna: *nibbānagamanaṃ maggaṃ khippam eva visodhaye*

Would clear the eightfold path leading to Nibbāna with all haste. That is the meaning.

# CHAPTER XXI

## Miscellaneous
## *Pakiṇṇaka-vaggo*

290. If by sacrificing a limited pleasure
An extensive pleasure one would see,
Let the wise one beholding extensive pleasure,
A limited pleasure forsake. (21.1)

*mattā*(1)*-sukhapariccāgā passe ce vipulaṃ sukhaṃ*
*caje mattāsukhaṃ dhīro sampassaṃ vipulaṃ sukhaṃ.*

### By sacrificing a limited pleasure: *mattāsukha-pariccāgā*

A limited amount of pleasure, a little pleasure. By sacrificing it,

### If . . . an extensive pleasure one would see: *passe ce vipulaṃ sukhaṃ*

The bliss of Nibbāna is what is called supreme pleasure. "If one were to see that." This is what is meant.

What is said is this: to one who prepares one bowl of food and enjoys it, there arises a limited amount of pleasure. To one who gives it up, and does the *uposatha* rites or gives alms,[2] there arises the extensive, supreme bliss of Nibbāna. Therefore, if in this way one sees great pleasure by the sacrifice of a little pleasure, then let the sagacious person, who clearly sees this great pleasure, abandon that limited pleasure. That is the meaning.

291. Who wishes his own pleasure,
By imposing misery on others,
Who is contaminated by the contact of hate,
He is not released from hate. (21.2)

*paradukkhūpadhānena attano sukham icchati*
*verasaṃsaggasaṃsaṭṭho verā so na parimuccati.*(3)

### Who is contaminated by the contact of hate: *vera-saṃsagga-saṃsaṭṭho*

The person who, by returning abuse for abuse, counter-assault for assault, is contaminated by the contact of hate exercised by one to the other,

### By imposing misery on others: *para-dukkhūpadhānena*

By imposing misery on another—by giving suffering to another; that is the meaning.

### He is not released from hate: *verā so na parimuccati*

He indeed, on account of [that] hate, constantly comes to grief. That is the meaning.

292. What is to be done, that is rejected.
And what is not to be done, is done.
Of those who are vain, heedless,
The intoxicants increase. (21.3)

293. But those who have well undertaken,
Constantly, mindfulness with regard to body,
Persevering in what is to be done,
They do not resort to what is not to be done.
Of those mindful, attentive ones,
The intoxicants come to an end. (21.4)

*yaṃ hi kiccaṃ tad apaviddhaṃ akiccaṃ pana kayirati*
*unnaḷānaṃ pamattānaṃ tesaṃ vaḍḍhanti āsāva.*

*yesaṃ ca susamāraddhā niccaṃ kāyagatā sati*
*akiccaṃ te na sevanti kicce sātaccakārino*
*satānaṃ sampajānānaṃ atthaṃ gacchanti āsavā.*

[292.]

### What is to be done: *yaṃ hi kiccaṃ*

The observance of an innumerable mass of moral precepts, living in the forest, maintenance of *dhutaṅga* practice,[4] attachment to meditation: this kind of task is [the proper function] of a bhikkhu from the time of "going forth."

### That is rejected: *tad apaviddhaṃ*

That which is their [proper] task has been abandoned by these [persons].

### Not to be done: *akiccaṃ*

Decorating umbrellas, shoes and sandals, bowls and beakers, water-pots, waistbands and shoulder straps is not the [proper] task of a bhikkhu.

### Of those who are vain: *unnaḷānaṃ*

Of those vain ones, by whom that [impropriety] is committed—["vain ones"] because of their conducting themselves with the "reed" of vanity upraised(5)—

### Heedless: *pamattānaṃ*

Who are heedless on account of [their] having slipped away from awareness,

### The intoxicants increase: *vaḍḍhanti āsavā*

[Of such persons] all four [kinds of] intoxicants[6] increase. That is the meaning.

[293.]

### Well undertaken: *susamāraddhā*

Well practiced.

### Mindfulness with regard to body: *kāya-gatā sati*

The meditation of "mindfulness of body."

### (They do not resort to) what is not to be done: *akiccaṃ (te na savanti)*

They do not do [what is] improper, such as decorating of umbrellas, and so forth. That is the meaning.

### Persevering in what is to be done: *kicce sātaccakārino*

Who are constant practicers, who unceasingly act with reference to the task to be done, from the time of "going forth," such as the observance of the innumerable mass of moral precepts, and so on.

### Of those mindful ones: *satānaṃ*

Of them, who are "mindful" on account of not being away from the life of [meditative] wakefulness,

### Attentive: *sampajānānaṃ*

Who are [called] attentive on account of the four [kinds of] "attentiveness" [i.e.,] in regard to purpose, suitability, the domain of meditation and undeluded [insight],

### The intoxicants come to an end: *atthaṃ gacchanti āsavā*

[Of such persons] all four [kinds of] intoxicants come to an end, attain nonexistence. That is the meaning.

294. Having slain mother and father
And two *khattiya*(7) kings,
Having slain a kingdom together with the subordinate,
Without trembling, the *brāhmaṇa* goes. (21.5)

*mātaraṃ pitaraṃ hantvā rājāno dve ca khattiye*
*raṭṭhaṃ sānucaraṃ hantvā anīgho yāti brāhmaṇo.*

### Together with a subordinate: *sānucaraṃ*

["Together with the subordinate"] here means "together with the officer who collects revenue."

### Mother: *mātaraṃ*

Here it is craving that is called "mother" because it produces beings in the three planes of existence, [as one can see] from the statement "craving gives birth to the person."

### Father: *pitaraṃ*

It is self-conceit that is called "father" because self-conceit arises depending on [the consciousness of the status of one's] father, [for we say,] "I am the son of such and such a king or royal officer."

### And two *khattiya* kings: *rājāno dve ca khattiye*

Just as the populace [resorts to] the king, so all [metaphysical] views [basically] resort to the two views of eternalism and annihilationism; therefore they are called the two "*khattiya* kings."

## A kingdom: *raṭṭham*

The twelve *āyatanas*[8] are called the "kingdom" because they are like a kingdom, owing to their pervasiveness.

## Together with the subordinate: *sānucaraṃ*

The passion for pleasure that is dependent on them [*the āyatanas*] is called "the subordinate," just as the revenue collecting officer [is called the king's subordinate].

## Without trembling: *anīgho*

Without suffering.

## The *brāhmana*: *brāhmaṇo*

The one in whom intoxicants are extinct [i.e., the Arahant].

The meaning here is that the one in whom the intoxicants *(āsava)* are extinct [the Arahant] goes without suffering, because craving, and so forth, have been destroyed by the sword *(asi)*[9] of the Path of Arahantship.

295. Having slain mother and father
And two learned kings,
Having slain the tiger's domain, as fifth,
Without trembling, the *brāhmaṇa* goes. (21.6)

*mātaraṃ pitaraṃ hantvā rājāno dve ca sotthiye*
*veyyagghapañcamaṃ hantvā anīgho yāti brāhmaṇo.*

## And two learned kings: *dve ca sotthiye*

Two *brāhmaṇas.*[10]

In this stanza the Teacher, by virtue of his mastery of dhamma and of his competence in the art of instruction, has characterized the eternalist and annihilationist views as "two *brāhmaṇa* kings."

## The tiger's domain, as fifth: *veyyaggha-pañcamaṃ*

Here a road that is traversed by tigers, is a source of fear, and is hard to travel on, is called the "tiger domain." The "hindrance" of skeptical doubt is also so called because of its similarity [to such a road]. Because the five "hindrances"[11] have that [i.e., skeptical doubt] as their fifth [member], they are called "[the group with the tiger domain as its fifth member]."

The *brāhmaṇa* [i.e., the Arahant] goes without suffering, having totally destroyed this "[group] with the tiger domain as its fifth [member]" too, by the sword of insight of the Path of Arahantship. This is the meaning here. The rest [is] as in the previous [stanza].

296. Well awake they arise, at all times,
The disciples of Gotama,
In whom, both day and night,
Constantly there is mindfulness on the Buddha. (21.7)

297. Well awake they arise, at all times,
The disciples of Gotama,
In whom both day and night,
Constantly there is mindfulness on Dhamma. (21.8)

298. Well awake they arise, at all times,
The disciples of Gotama,
In whom, both day and night,
Constantly there is mindfulness on the Saṅgha. (21.9)

299. Well awake they arise, at all times,
The disciples of Gotama,
In whom, both day and night,
Constantly there is mindfulness on the body. (21.10)

300. Well awake they arise, at all times,
The disciples of Gotama,
In whom, both day and night,
The mind delights in harmlessness. (21.11)

301. Well awake they arise, at all times,
The disciples of Gotama,
In whom, both day and night,
The mind delights in meditation. (21.12)

*suppabuddhaṃ pabujjhanti sadā gotamasāvakā*
*yesaṃ divā ca ratto ca niccaṃ buddhagatā sati.*

*suppabuddhaṃ pabujjhanti sadā gotamasāvakā*
*yesaṃ divā ca ratto ca niccaṃ dhammagatā sati.*

*suppabuddhaṃ pabujjhanti sadā gotamasāvakā*
*yesaṃ divā ca ratto ca niccaṃ saṅghagatā sati.*

*suppabuddhaṃ pabujjhanti sadā gotamasāvakā*
*yesaṃ divā ca ratto ca niccaṃ kāyagatā sati.*

*suppabuddhaṃ pabujjhanti sadā gotamasāvakā*
*yesaṃ divā ca ratto ca ahiṃsāya rato mano.*

*suppabuddhaṃ pabujjhanti sadā gotamasāvakā*
*yesaṃ divā ca ratto ca bhāvanāya rato mano.*

[296.]

## Well awake they arise: *suppabuddhaṃ pabujjhanti*

Those who [go to ] sleep with mindfulness directed toward the Buddha and who wake up the same way are said to "arise well awake."

## The disciples of Gotama: *gotama-sāvakā*

[Persons are called] disciples of Gotama because of [their discipleship] having come into being by listening to [lit. in the hearing of] the dhamma of the Buddha [ who was a member] of the Gotama family, [i.e.,] by virtue of their hearing the instruction of that Buddha.

## (Constantly) there is mindfulness on the Buddha: *(niccaṃ) buddhagatā sati*

[Those in whom] there is at all times mindfulness arising in regard to the virtues of the Buddha as [enumerated in the formula], "Thus is he the Blessed One," and so forth[12]—they "arise, well awake." That is the meaning. But those who are unable [to do] so, [they too] indeed "arise, well awake" [when they are] invoking the "mindfulness of the Buddha" thrice, or twice, or at least once every day.

[297.]

## Mindfulness on Dhamma: *dhammagatā sati*

The mindfulness of dhamma, arising with reference to the virtues of dhamma as [enumerated in the formula], "Well proclaimed by the Blessed One is dhamma,"[13] and so forth.

[298.]

## Mindfulness on the Saṅgha: *saṅghagatā sati*

The mindfulness of the Saṅgha arising with reference to the virtues of the Saṅgha as [enumerated in the formula], "Well has the Blessed One's community of disciples set out [upon the Path],"[14] and so forth.

[299.]

## Mindfulness on the body: *kāyagatā sati*

The mindfulness arising on account of "[the contemplation of] the thirty-two parts of the body,"[15] the nine "cemetery [contemplations],"[16] the "analysis of the four elements,"[17] or the "meditation of the fine material sphere," such as the "internal blue *kasina*,"[18] and so forth.

[300.]

## Delights in harmlessness: *ahiṃsāya rato*

One who is keenly delighted in the meditation on compassion, which is described as [follows]: "he radiates the feeling of compassion over one [whole] direction,"[19] and so forth.

[301.]

## Meditation: *bhāvanāya*

In the meditation on loving-kindness.

Although, because of the fact that in the previous [stanza], mention was made of the meditation on compassion,[20] all the other meditations [should have been mentioned] at this point, here the meditation on loving-kindness is in fact intended.[(21)]

The rest is to be understood as explained with reference to the first stanza [i.e., the commentary for the first two lines in each of the stanzas 297–301 is the same as for the first two lines of stanza 296].

302. Difficult it is to go forth, difficult to delight therein;
Difficult to live in are households—a suffering.
Suffering it is to live with uneven ones;
And travelers are trapped in suffering.
So, be not a traveler,
And be not trapped in suffering. (21.13)

*duppabbajjaṃ*[(22)] *durabhirama durāvāsā gharā dukhā*
*dukkho 'samānasaṃvāso dukkhānupatitaddhagū*
*tasmā na c'addhagu siyā na ca dukkhānupatito siyā.*

## Difficult it is to go forth: *duppabbajjaṃ*

It is a difficult thing to abandon the mass of one's wealth, [be it] small or large, and the circle or one's relations, and to go forth into this monastic order, giving one's heart to it.

## Difficult to delight therein: *durabhiramaṃ*

It is a difficult thing for one, even if [one has] gone forth thus and is finding sustenance of life by begging, to relish [the monastic life] by way of following innumerable moral precepts and fulfilling the observance that is consistent with dhamma.

## Difficult to live in are households—a suffering: *durāvāsā gharā dukhā*

Because official duty in relation to kings and loyal duty in relation to [one's] chiefs have to be performed by one living the household [life], and also [because] one's retinue and righteous recluses and *brāhmaṇas* have to be properly treated—this being the case, the [obligation of] household life too is hard to fulfill, as a pot with holes [is hard to fill with water] and as the great ocean [is hard to be "filled up" with water]. Therefore these households too are painful to live in; for that reason they are [sources of] suffering. That is the meaning.

## Suffering it is to live with uneven ones: *dukkho' samānasaṃvāso*

They are called "uneven" who are in the habit of disputing, saying: "Who are you and who am I?" even though they be even in moral conduct and learning, [in the case of ] those gone forth; in birth and lineage, family and wealth [in the case of] lay persons. To live together with them is a suffering; that is the meaning.

## Travelers are trapped in suffering: *dukkhānupatitaddhagū*

Those who are "travelers" on account of [their] having entered the road that is the whirl [of existence] are indeed trapped in suffering,

## So, be not a traveler: *tasmā na c'addhagu siyā*

Because the state of being trapped in suffering and the state of being a traveler [are] also [nothing but] suffering, therefore let one not be a traveler [set out] to traverse the road that is the whirl [of existence]. Let one not be trapped by suffering in the manner aforesaid. That is the meaning.

303. The faithful one, endowed with virtue,
Possessed of fame and wealth,
To whatever region he resorts,
There, indeed, he is worshiped. (21.14)

*saddho sīlena sampanno yasobhogasamappito*
*yaṃ yaṃ padesaṃ bhajati*(23) *tattha tatth' eva pūjito.*

## The faithful one: *saddho*

One who is endowed with faith, ordinary and transcendent.[24]

## (Endowed) with virtue: *sīlena (sampanno)*

Virtue is twofold: that of the household life and that of the homeless life. Of these, the virtue of lay life is intended here. "One who is endowed with that" is the meaning [here].

## Possessed of fame and wealth: *yaso-bhoga-samappito*

[a] [Endowed] with such fame as the "lay fame" of [householders] like Anāthapiṇḍika,(25) and so forth, which consisted of having a following of five hundred lay devotees; [b] wealth is twofold: [1] grains, and so forth, and [2] the sevenfold "noble wealth"[26]—endowed with each of these [a and b]; that is the meaning [of this line].

## To whatever region he resorts: *yaṃ yaṃ padesaṃ bhajati*

Whatever direction [i.e., region] such householder resorts to—among directions such as east, and so forth—in every such direction he is offered gain and respect of this kind. That is the meaning.

304. From afar the good ones are visible,
Like the snowy mountain.
The bad ones here are not seen,
Like arrows shot in the night. (21.15)

*dūre santo pakāsenti himavanto va pabbato*
*asant' ettha na dissanti rattikhittā yathā sarā.*

## The good ones: *santo*

Buddhas, and the like, are called "the pacified ones" *(santā)* due to the pacification of lusts, and so forth. But here, beings who have performed [their religious] functions under previous Buddhas, whose moral propensities are overflowing, and who are meditationally developed are meant by [the term] "the good ones" *(santo)*.

## Are visible: *pakāsenti*

Even though they are far away, they come within the range of knowledge of Buddhas and become clearly visible.

## Like the snowy (mountain): *himavanto va (pabbato)*

Just as the Himalaya mountain, [range], which is three thousand leagues broad and five hundred leagues high and is adorned by eighty-four thousand peaks, shines even to those who stand afar, as if it stood in their very presence, so do [the good ones] become visible [to the Buddhas].

## The bad ones here: *asant' ettha*

"The bad ones" are the childish persons, who care only for [this] visible life, who have abandoned the world beyond, whose eye is on the material, who have gone forth [only] to earn a living. They, even though they are seated close to the right knee of the Buddhas, are not seen [by them], do not become visible [to them].

## Like arrows shot in the night: *rattikkhittā sarā yathā*

Like arrows shot at night in the fourfold darkness,[27] such persons[(28)] do not become visible, owing to the absence of a previous cause that could be a basis for good fortune. That is the meaning.

305. Sitting alone, resting alone,
Walking alone, unwearied,

The one alone, who controls oneself,
Would be delighted in the forest. (21.16)

*ekāsanaṃ ekaseyyaṃ eko caram atandito*
*eko damayam*[29] *attānaṃ vanante ramito siyā.*

## Sitting alone, resting alone: *ekāsanaṃ eka-seyyaṃ*

The sitting posture of one who is seated even in the midst of a thousand bhikkhus, with [unflagging] attention, without letting off the basic meditational topic [adopted by him] is called "sitting alone." And "resting alone" is the resting posture of a bhikkhu who is lying down on his right side, even on a precious couch with beautiful cover and pillow set among a thousand bhikkhus in a mansion like the Brazen Palace,[30] with mindfulness awakened, with attention turned to the basic meditational topic. Resort to such "sitting alone" and "resting alone" is what is meant.

## Unwearied: *atandito*

Getting about alone, in the four postures,[31] being free of laziness on account of [finding the means for] maintaining life [solely] on the strength of [one's] feet [i.e., obtaining food by begging from house to house]. That is the meaning.

## The one alone, who controls (oneself): *eko damayam(attānaṃ)*

Disciplining oneself all by oneself, by means of attaining the Paths and Fruit, having [duly] engaged in [attention on] a meditational topic, at the places of [resting at] night, and so forth. That is the meaning.

## Would be delighted in the forest: *vanante ramito siya*

So disciplining oneself, one would take delight solely in the forest grove, which is secluded[32] from the sounds of men and women, and so forth, for it is not possible for the self to be so disciplined by one living [a] crowded [life]. That is the meaning.

# CHAPTER XXII

## Hell
## *Niraya-vaggo*

306. The one who speaks lies, goes to hell,
And the one who having done says, "I don't do this."
Both of these, people of base deeds,
Having passed away, become equal in the beyond. (22.1)

*abhūtavādī nirayaṃ upeti yo vāpi katvā na karomīti cāha*(1)
*ubho pi te pecca samā bhavanti nihīnakammā manujā parattha.*

[306.]

### The one who speaks lies: *abhūtavādī*

One who, without having seen [any] fault of another, lies and accuses another falsely,

### (And the one who) having done (says, "I don't do this"): *(yo vā pi) katvā (na karomī ti cāha)*

Or one who, having done a wrong deed, says, "I do not do this,"

### (Both of these,) people of base deeds, having passed away, become equal in the beyond: *(ubho pi te) pecca samā bhavanti nihīnakammā manujā parattha*

Both these persons, having gone to the world beyond, become equal so far as [their] destination is concerned, both going to the state of hell.

Only their exit [from this world] is qualified [by this "equality"]. Their life span [in the world beyond] is not qualified [by that]. For, having done much detrimental action, they are tormented long in hell; having done little, [they suffer] for only a short time. Because the action of both of them is indeed childish, it has been said:(2)"People of base deeds, in the beyond" [*Dhp.*, v. 306*d*]. The syntactical connection with the word *pecca* is before the word *parattha* [i.e., read *pecca parattha* to get the sense]. Those of base deeds, having passed away from here, become [one another's] equals in the beyond. That is the meaning.

307. Many having the yellow robe about their necks
Are of bad qualities, uncontrolled.
They, the bad ones,
By bad deeds are led to hell. (22.2)

*kāsāvakaṇṭhā bahavo pāpadhammā asaññatā*
*pāpā pāpehi kammehi nirayaṃ te upapajjare.*

### Having the yellow robe about their necks: *kāsāva-kaṇṭhā*

Having the yellow robe wrapped around the neck,

### Of bad qualities: *pāpadhammā*

Those of childish ways,

### Uncontrolled: *asaññatā*

Lacking in [restraints] such as physical restraint, and so forth,

### Bad ones . . . are led to hell: *pāpā . . . upapajjare*

Such persons of bad conduct are born in the state of hell owing to the unwholesome deeds done by them. Having suffered there, and having departed therefrom, they suffer similarly even among the *petas,*[3] on account of the remainder of the effect [of their unwholesome deeds]. That is the meaning.

308. Better that an iron ball be eaten,
Glowing, like a flame of fire,
Than that one should eat a country's alms food,
Being poor in virtue, lacking control. (22.3)

*seyyo ayoguḷo bhutto tatto aggisikhūpamo*
*yaṃ ce bhuñjeyya dussīlo raṭṭhapiṇḍaṃ asaññato.*

One . . . being poor in virtue, lacking control:
*yaṃ . . . dussīlo . . . asaññato*

That a person devoid of moral conduct, lacking [restraints] such as physical restraint,

Than that one should eat a country's alms food:
*ce bhuñjeyya . . . raṭṭhapiṇḍaṃ*

Should accept what is given with faith by citizens of the land and partake [of it], giving the impression, "I am a recluse,"

Better that an iron ball be eaten, glowing:
*seyyo ayoguḷo bhutto tatto*

Better than that (4) is it for one to have eaten a glowing, fire-hued ball of iron. Why? On account of that, just one existence [in *saṃsāra*] would be consumed by fire. Whereas, after eating [the food] given in faith [without deserving it], the immoral one would suffer for many hundreds of lives in the state of woe. That is the meaning.

309. Four conditions the heedless man comes by,
Who resorts to the wives of others;
Acquisition of demerit,
Lack of agreeable sleep,
Disgrace is third; hell is the fourth. (22.4)

310. Acquisition of demerit
And a lowly [future] course.
And brief the delight of a frightened man with a frightened woman,
The king too gives a heavy punishment—
So let a man not resort to the wife of another. (22.5)

*cattāri ṭhānāni naro pamatto āpajjati paradārūpasevī*
*apuññalābhaṃ na nikāmaseyyaṃ nindaṃ tatiyaṃ nirayaṃ catutthaṃ.*

*apuññalābho ca gatī ca pāpikā bhītassa bhītāya ratī ca thokikā*
*rājā ca daṇḍaṃ garukaṃ paṇeti tasmā naro paradāraṃ na seve.*

[309.]

Heedless: *pamatto*
One who is guilty [lit. possessed] of "relinquishing of mindfulness,"

Who resorts to the wives of others: *paradārū pasevī*
Who is resorting to the wife of another and is swerving from the path[5] [of good conduct],

Comes by: *āpajjati*
Attains,

Conditions: *ṭhāṇāni*
Causes for suffering,

Lack of agreeable sleep: *na nikāma-seyyaṃ*
Not obtaining sleep as desired—he gets [sleep] only for a short while.

[310.]

Acquisition of demerit and a lowly [future] course:
*apuññalābho ca gatī ca pākika apuñña-lābho . . . nirayaṃ*
Thus he gets this demerit. And on account of that demerit there is the detrimental course that constitutes the state of hell.

And brief the delight: *ratī ca thokikā*
[Because he is] frightened, his pleasure with the woman [who is herself] frightened, is slight.

(The king too gives) a heavy (punishment):
*(rājā ca daṇḍaṃ) garukaṃ (paṇeti)*
And the king too administers heavy punishment [to such a person], like cutting off [his] hands.

So (let a man not resort to the wife of another):
*tasmā (naro paradāraṃ na seve)*
Because one who is resorting to another's wife suffers these demerits, and so forth, therefore let one not resort to another's wife. That is the meaning.

311. Just as *kusa* grass, wrongly grasped,
Cuts the hand itself,
So, recluseness wrongly handled,
Drags one down to hell. (22.6)

312. Whatever is a loose act,
And what is a defiled observance—
A "higher life" filled with suspicion—
That is not of great fruit. (22.7)

313. If it is a thing to be done, let one do it,
Let one advance decisively to it;
For religious conduct that is slack
Throws up dirt all the more. (22.8)

*kuso yathā duggahito hattham evānukantati*
*sāmaññaṃ dupparāmaṭṭaṃ nirayāyūpakaḍḍhati.*

*yaṃ kiñci sithilaṃ kammaṃ saṃkiliṭṭhaṃ ca yaṃ vataṃ*
*saṃkassaraṃ brahmacariyaṃ na taṃ hoti mahapphalaṃ.*

*kayiraṃ*(6) *ce kayirāthenaṃ daḷham enaṃ parakkame*
*saṭhilo hi paribbājo bhiyyo ākirate rajaṃ.*

[311.]

## Kusa grass: *kuso*

By *kusa* here [is meant] any kind of grass with a sharp blade [or] even a talipot leaf.

Just as that *kusa* cuts, injures the hand by whom it is grasped in the wrong manner, so the monastic way [of life]—that is to say, the dhamma of the recluse—badly grasped due to broken moral precepts, and so forth, drags one to a state of woe, causes one to be born in a state of woe. That is the meaning.

[312.]

## Loose: *sithilaṃ*

Any action that is done with slackness, due to being done falteringly,

## Defiled: *saṃkiliṭṭhaṃ*

Which is defiled, due to resorting to the improper, such as [resorting to] the house of a prostitute,[7]

## Filled with suspicion: *saṅkassaraṃ*

Which has to be done with suspicions—whatever action is done with one's own suspicions, which is beset by repeated suspicion, by suspicion all around—such as, for example, [when one suspects] on seeing the Saṅgha assembled for any task such as one of the *uposatha* tasks, and so forth, "Undoubtedly these [bhikkhus] are assembled with the wish to expel me, having known my conduct,"

## This is not (of great fruit): *na taṃ hoti (mahapphalaṃ)*

This way of living the life of a recluse, of living the religious life, is of no great avail to that person. And because it is of no great avail to him, indeed [it is] of no great avail to those who give him alms. That is the meaning.

[313.]

## If it is a thing to be done, (let one do it): *kayiraṃ ce (kayirath' enaṃ)*

Therefore if one is to do any action, let one indeed do that,

## Let one advance decisively to it: *daḷham enaṃ parakkame*

Let one do that very firmly,(8) taking it on without turning back.(9)

## Religious conduct (that is slack): *(saṭhilo hi) paribbājo*

The way of recluseness that is performed with slackness, is beset with violations, and so forth,

## (Throws up dirt) all the more: *bhiyyo (ākirate rajaṃ)*

Such recluseness is not capable of removing the "dirt" of lusts, and so on, found within [oneself]—on the contrary, it scatters even more "dirt" of lusts, and so forth, thereon. That is the meaning.

314. A misdeed is better not done;
The misdeed torments hereafter.
But a good deed is better done,
Having done which, one does not regret. (22.9)

*akataṃ dukkataṃ seyyo pacchā tapati dukkataṃ*
*katam ca sukataṃ seyyo yaṃ katvā nānutappati.*

## A misdeed: *dukkataṃ*

Action that is blameworthy, that leads one to a state of woe,

## Better (not done): *(akataṃ) . . . seyyo*

It is indeed better, nobler (to leave) undone.

## Torments hereafter: *pacchā tapati*

It indeed gives torment whenever remembered.

## But a good deed (is better) done: *kataṃ ca sukataṃ (seyyo)*

But blameless action that gives happiness and indeed leads one to a good state is better [to be] done,

## Having done which, one does not regret: *yaṃ katvā nānutappati*

Which action having been done, one is not tormented later *(nānutappati)*, at the time of remembering [it]. Indeed [remembering it] one is made happy. Such [action] is better done.

315. Like a border city
Guarded both within and without,
So, guard yourself.
Let not the moment slip you by.
Those for whom the moment is past
Do indeed grieve, consigned to hell. (22.10)

*nagaraṃ yathā paccantaṃ guttaṃ santarabāhiraṃ*
*evaṃ gopetha attānaṃ khaṇo ve mā upaccagā*
*khaṇātītā hi socanti nirayamhi samappitā.*

## Within and without: *santarabāhiram*

"O bhikkhus, just as that frontier town was guarded by those people—with its inner parts when they fortified [its] doors and walls, with its outer parts when they fortified [its] gateways, watchtowers, ramparts, and moats[10]—in the same way you too protect yourselves, awakening mindfulness and closing the six inner doors [of the senses], without letting the Doorkeeper Mindfulness leave, making the six eternal bases firm by not grasping them in that way in which they conduce to the harm of the internal [sense-doors][11] and setting about [your tasks] without letting go the Doorkeeper Mindfulness, lest they [the external bases] gain access. That is the meaning.

## Let not the moment slip you by: *khaṇo ve mā upaccagā*

The one who does not guard oneself in this way, past that person does this "[fortunate] moment" slip in its entirety, namely:

[1] the moment when a Buddha is born [and is ministering],
[2] the moment of [that person's] birth in the Middle Country [of India],
[3] the moment of having obtained the right view,
[4] the moment of having the six bases unimpaired.[12]

## Those for whom the moment is past (do indeed grieve, consigned to hell): *khaṇātītā (hi socanti nirayamhi samappitā)*

Those who have slipped past that moment and those persons past whom that moment has slipped—they grieve, having been consigned to hell, having taken birth there. That is the meaning.

316. They are ashamed of what is not shameful,
They are not ashamed of what is shameful.
Ones who endorse wrong views,
Such beings go to a state of woe. (22.11)

317. Those who see what is not fear as fear,
And see no fear in fear,
Ones who endorse wrong views,
Such beings go to a state of woe. (22.12)

*alajjitāye lajjanti lajjitāye*[(13)] *na lajjare*
*micchādiṭṭhisamādānā sattā gacchanti duggatiṃ.*

*abhaye bhayadassino bhaye cābhayadassino*
*micchādiṭṭhisamādānā sattā gacchanti duggatiṃ.*

[316.]

### Those who . . . of what is not shameful: *alajjitā ye*

*Alajjitā* stands for *alajjitabbe*—that is, in regard to that of which one should not be ashamed. The begging bowl is a thing of which one should not be ashamed. They[14] get about covering that [the bowl]; they are said to be ashamed of it.

### They . . . of what is shameful: *lajjitāye*(15)

One should be ashamed of [having one's] private parts uncovered. But they who go about without covering them are said to be "not ashamed in regard to that of which one should be ashamed." Hence their being ashamed of that which one should not be ashamed, and being unashamed of that of which one should be ashamed, is a wrong view [held] on account of their acceptance of "the empty," [i.e.,] what is nonexistent, and of what is contrary to reality.[16]

They who have accepted that and who get about [their tasks in this way] are persons who have accepted an erroneous view, and they [will] go to the state of woe with its [various] divisions, such as hell, and so forth. That is the meaning.

[317.]

Because [sources of] fear such as sensual attraction, ill will, confusion, self-estimation, [speculative] opinion, defilement, and misconduct do not arise on account of the begging bowl, it is called "no-fear." Those who conceal it through fear are those who see fear in no-fear.

But, because sensual attraction, and so forth, arise on account of the private parts [of one's body], they are called "fear."

Those who "see no fear in fear" due to not covering that [part of the body] are beings "who endorse wrong views"—owing to their having accepted what is contrary to reality—and "such beings go to a state of woe." That is the meaning.

318. Those who regard what is not error as error,
And see no error in error,
Ones who endorse wrong views,
Such beings go to a state of woe. (22.13)

319. But having known error as error,
And nonerror as nonerror,

Ones who endorse proper views,
Such beings go to a state of weal. (22.14)

*avajje vajjamatino vajje cāvajjadassino*
*micchādiṭṭhisamādānā sattā gacchanti duggatiṃ.*

*vajjaṃ ca vajjato ñatvā avajjaṃ ca avajjato*
*sammādiṭṭhisamādānā sattā gacchanti suggatiṃ.*

[318.]

## What is not error: *avajje*

In regard to the tenfold right view and to the dhamma that has served as its foundation.[17]

## Those who regard as error: *vajjamatino*

Those in whom the notion has arisen, "this is error."

## And see no error in error: *vajje cāvajjadassinō*

Those who see no error in the [undoubted] error that is the tenfold wrong view and in the dhamma that has served as its foundation.[18]

[319.]

## But having known error as error and nonerror as nonerror: *vajjaṃ ca vajjato ñatvā avajjaṃ ca avajjato*

Those "who endorse wrong views" because they have endorsed this wrong view, which is the [great] entanglement—namely, the acceptance of error as nonerror and of nonerror as error—"such beings go to a state of woe."

The meaning of the second stanza should [also] be understood in the manner stated [above, i.e., as in st. 318].

# CHAPTER XXIII

## The Elephant
## *Nāga-vaggo*

320. Like an elephant in battle,
The arrow shot from a bow,
I shall endure the unwarranted word;
The majority, indeed, are of poor virtue. (23.1)

321. They take a tamed one to a crowd;
On a tamed one a king mounts.
Among humans a tamed one is best,
One who endures the unwarranted word. (23.2)

322. Excellent are tamed mules,
Thoroughbreds and horses of Sindh,
Also tuskers, great elephants.
But better than them is one who has subdued
oneself. (23.3)

*ahaṃ nāgo va saṃgāme cāpāto patitaṃ*(1) *saraṃ*
*ativākyaṃ titikkhissaṃ dussīlo hi bahujjano.*

*dantaṃ nayanti samitiṃ dantaṃ rājābhirūhati*
*danto seṭṭho manussesu yo 'tivākyaṃ titikkhati.*

*varaṃ assatarā dantā ājānīyā ca sindhavā*
*kuñjarā vā mahānāgā attadanto tato varaṃ.*

[320.]

### Like an elephant: *nāgo va*

Like an elephant *(hatthī)*.

## Shot from a bow: *cāpāto patitaṃ*

Released from a bow.

## The unwarranted word: *ativākyaṃ*

This is a term for transgression brought about by the eight [kinds of] ignoble behavior.[2]

## I shall endure: *titikkhissaṃ*

Just as a great, well disciplined elephant, capable of enduring attacks [made] with sharp weapons, which has descended on a battlefield, endures, without being tormented, the arrows released from a bow and fallen upon it—so shall I endure the unwarranted word such as this. That is the meaning.

## (The majority) indeed are of poor virtue: *dussīlo hi (bahujjano)*

This majority of worldly people, being of very poor virtue, speak out words according to individual inclination [i.e., without investigation] and go about creating conflict. There, my [proper] task(3) is to bc forbearing, to look on with patience.

[321.]

## A crowd: *samitiṃ*

Those going to the midst of an assembly of people, in sports arenas or parks, and the like, take only a tamcd kind of oxe or horse, yoked to a chariot.

## A king: *rājā*

A king going in that kind of vehicle also(4) mounts only a tamed [horse or elephant].

## Among humans: *manussesu*

Among human beings too the noblest is the one who is disciplined by the Four Noble Paths, who is free from the disturbance of defilement.(5)

## One who endures the unwarranted word: *yo'tivākyaṃ titikkhati*

Who does not strike back at this kind of unwarranted speech, even [if it is] uttered again and again, is not tormented [by it]. Such a disciplined person is the best [among humans]. That is the meaning.

[322.]

## Mules: *assatarā*

The offspring of a mare by a donkey.

## Thoroughbreds: *ājānīyā*

[Horses] that are able to understand swiftly what the trainer of tamable horses wants [them] to do.

## Horses of Sindh: *sindhavā*

Horses born in the land of Sindhu.

## Great elephants: *mahānāgā*

Great elephants that are also called tuskers *(kuñjaras)*.

## One who has subdued oneself: *attadanto*

These mules or horses of Sindhu or great elephants are good [when they have been] trained, not untrained. But one who is "self-tamed" on account of training oneself by the Four Noble Paths(6) and is free of the disturbance of defilements, is even better than that, is the noblest of them all. That is the meaning.

323. Truly, not by these vehicles
Could one go to a region unreached,
As a tamed one goes
By a well-subdued, disciplined self. (23.4)

*na hi etehi yānehi gaccheyya agataṃ disaṃ*
*yathā 'ttanā sudantena danto dantena gacchati.*

The meaning of the verse is: by these *vehicles (yānehi)*, such as vehicles of elephants, and so forth, no person *could go (gaccheyya)* toward the *region (disaṃ)* of Nibbāna—which is called the "*unreached*" *(agataṃ)* because of its not being reached even in the dream state—in the manner that a person goes toward that unreached region and comes to that "land of the disciplined," free of the disturbance of defilement, endowed with insight-wisdom, being disciplined [by a mind] that in the first part [of the religious life] is disciplined by the taming of the senses and that in the later part is further disciplined by development of the Noble paths. Therefore the taming of the self is the best among [all of] these. That is the meaning.

324. The tusker named Dhanapālaka,
Deep in rut, is hard to control.
Bound, the tusker does not eat a morsel,
But remembers the elephant forest. (23.5)

*dhanapālako nāma kuñjaro kaṭukappabhedano dunnivārayo baddho kabalaṃ na bhuñjati sumarati nāgavanassa kuñjaro.*

## Named Dhanapālaka: *dhanapālako nāma*[7]

This is the name of the elephant that was captured at the beautiful abode of elephants, the king of Kāsi having sent his master of elephant lore [for this purpose].

## Deep in rut, is hard to control: *kaṭuka-ppabhedano dunnivārayo*

Deep in rut.

At the time of rut, the root of the ear of elephants is ruptured. At that time elephants are by nature fierce and they either break the goads [used on them] or the spikes and lances.(8) But this [elephant] was indeed exceptionally fierce. So it is said, [it was] deep in rut and hard to control.

## Bound, (the tusker) does not eat a morsel: *baddho kabalaṃ na bhuñjati*

It, being bound and led to the stable and made to stand in a place with a beautiful awning fixed and on which fragrant flooring was applied, encircled with a fine curtain, did not wish to eath anything, even when different kinds of precious and delicious food were brought to it—[food] of the king, fit for a royal personage. It is in regard to this(9) that it has been said, "Bound, [the tusker] does not eat a morsel."

## Remembers the elephant forest: *sumarati nāgavanassa*

It remained reminiscing on the elephant forest,(10) thinking, "My [own] dwelling place is fine." And it thought only of the duty of looking after its mother, owing to its dhammalike nature, thinking: "My mother(11) was in grief in the forest on account of being separated from the son. [My] duty of looking after [my] mother is not being done. What is the use of this food?" Because that [duty] could be fulfilled only by one staying in the elephant forest, it has been said, "The tusker . . . remembers the elephant forest."(12)

325. When one is torpid and a big eater,
A sleeper, who lies rolling about
Like a great boar, nourished on grains—
Being dull one enters the womb again and again. (23.6)

*middhī yadā hoti mahagghaso ca niddāyitā samparivattasāyī mahāvarāho va nivāpapuṭṭho punapunnaṃ gabbham upeti mando.*

## Torpid: *middhī*

Overpowered by sloth and torper.

## A big eater: *mahagghaso*

Who eats profusely, like one of the [following]: [1] [one who cannot get up after eating and says] "Give [me your] hand!"(13) [2] [one who finds one's clothes too tight after the meal and says] "Enough of clothing!" [3] [one who cannot rise after the meal and remains] "lying down there"; [4] [one who takes such large mouthfuls that even] "crows [may] eat [of them";] [5] [one who would overeat and] "vomit what was eaten."

## Nourished on grains: *nivāpa-puṭṭho*

Fed on "hog food," such as rice bran. A domesticated pig, being fed from its young days, not being able to leave the house when its body is fat, just lies down under beds, and so forth, snorting in and out, rolling [left and right]. This is what is said: when a person is slothful, overfed, and like a great pig fed on hog food, lies down sleepily rolling [hither and thither], unable to stay in any other posture, then he is not able to reflect on the three characteristics [of existence, namely] impermanence, suffering, and absence of self. Due to not applying mind to these, he, being deficient in insight, "returns to the womb" [is subject to birth in *saṃsāra*] again and again, is not liberated from "dwelling in the womb."

326. Formerly this mind set out awandering
As it wished, where it liked, according to its pleasure.
Today I will hold it back methodically
Like one seizing a goad, an elephant in rut. (23.7)

*idaṃ pure cittam acāri cārikaṃ yen' icchakaṃ yatthakāmaṃ yathāsukhaṃ tad ajj'ahaṃ niggahesāmi yoniso hatthippabhinnaṃ viya aṅukusaggaho.*

### Formerly: *pure*
Prior to this,

### This: *idaṃ*
This mind,

### As it wished, where it liked: *yen' icchakaṃ yatthakāmaṃ*
Whenever desire arose in it in regard to objects [that are] unwholesome, and so forth, and for whatever cause—among causes [such as] lusts, and so on, under subjugation of that desire—

### According to its pleasure: *yathāsukhaṃ*
Behaving in that way in which it obtained pleasure,

### Set out awandering: *acāri cārikaṃ*
Roamed about for a long time.

### Today I will hold it back methodically, like one seizing a goad, an elephant in rut: *tad ajj'ahaṃ niggahessāmi yoniso hatthippabhinnaṃ viya aṅkusaggaho*
Today I will restrain [it] by well-grounded thinking as a skilful holder of the goad—namely, a master of [handling] elephants—[restrains] with the goad a furious elephant in rut. I will not let it transgress [the bounds].

327. Be delighters in awareness;
Keep watch over your mind.
Lift yourself up from the difficult road,
Like a tusker, sunk in mire. (23.8)

*appamādaratā hotha sacittaṃ anurakkhatha*
*duggā uddharath' attānaṃ paṅke sanno va kuñjaro.*

### Delighters in awareness: *appamāda ratā*
Be attached to remaining unseparated from mindfulness.

### Keep watch over your mind: *sacittam anurakkhatha*

Guard your mind in such a way that it does not do any transgression in regard to objects such as [visible] forms, and so forth.

### Lift yourself up from the difficult road, like a tusker, sunk in mire: *duggā uddharath' attānaṃ paṅke sanno va kuñjaro*

Just as that tusker, sunk in the mire, raised itself from the bog of that mire and stood on firm ground,[14] making effort with "hands and feet"—so you too raise yourselves from the mire of defilements and put yourselves on the firm land of Nibbāna. That is the meaning.

328. Should one get a mature companion,
Who will move about with one, a wise one who leads a good life,
Let one move with him,
All dangers overcoming, mindful and happy. (23.9)

329. Should one not get a mature companion,
Who will move about with one, a wise one who leads a good life,
Let one wander alone,
Like a king who has left behind a conquered land,
Like the elephant in the Mātaṅga forest.[(15)] (23.10)

330. A life of solitude is better;
There is no companionship with the childish one.
With little exertion, like the elephant in the Mātaṅga forest,
Let one wander alone, and do no wrongs. (23.11)

*sace labhetha nipakaṃ sahāyaṃ saddhiṃcaraṃ sādhuvihāridhīraṃ*
*abhibhuyya sabbāni parissayāni careyya ten' attamano satīmā.*

*no ce labhetha nipakaṃ sahāyaṃ saddhiṃcaraṃ sādhuvihāridhīraṃ*
*rājā va raṭṭhaṃ vijitaṃ pahāya eko care mātaṅg' araññe va nāgo.*

*ekassa caritaṃ seyyo natthi bāle sahāyatā*
*eko care na ca pāpāni kayirā appossukko mātaṅg' araññe va nāgo.*

[328.]

### Mature: *nipakaṃ*

One who is endowed with the wisdom of maturity.

### A wise one who leads a good life: *sādhuvihāri-dhīraṃ*

A sagacious person who lives properly.

### Dangers: *parissayāni*

Coming across such a companion who dwells in loving-kindness, let one get about with him, happy and with [ever-]present mindfulness, having overcome all dangers, both the visible dangers such as [wild beasts like] lions, tigers, and so forth, and the concealed dangers such as the terrors of lust, hate, and the like. That is the meaning.

[329.]

### Let one wander alone, like a king (who has left behind a conquered) land: *rājā va raṭṭhaṃ . . . eko care*

Like a royal sage, who has gone(16) [forth] relinquishing [his] kingdom. This is what is said: just as a king who has made a territorial conquest, thinks, "This which is called the kingdom is a source of great heedlessness. Of what use to me is ruling a kingdom?" [And he] leaves the conquered territory, enters the great woods, becomes a recluse by "going forth" in ascetic fashion, and gets about all by himself in all the modes of deportment, so let one get about all by oneself.

### Like the elephant in the Mātaṅga forest: *mātaṅg' araññe va nāgo*

Just as this great elephant, called *Mātaṅga*[17] because of his going [from the herd], having considered in this manner, roams all by itself in this forest in all the modes of deportment, [thinking,] "Now I live hedged around by she-elephants, young elephants, and baby elephants. I eat grass whose tips have been eaten [by others] and parts of branches bent down. I drink water that is muddied. As I get down [to a water course] and as I get out(18) [of it], she-elephants go brushing past me. Better that I live alone, separated from the herd." Let one get about alone in the same way. That is the meaning.

[330.]

### A life of solitude is better: *ekassa caritaṃ seyyo*

For one who has gone forth, who takes delight in singleness from the time of going forth, better is the solitary life.

## There is no companionship with the childish one: *natthi bāle sahāyatā*

The minor moral virtue, the medium moral virtue, the major moral virtue, the ten subjects of conversation, the thirteen *dhutaṅga* practices, insight-wisdom, the Four Paths, the Four Fruits, the three [kinds of] gnosis, the six kinds of] higher gnosis,[19] and the great deathless Nibbāna—this is that "companionship" impossible to obtain with the aid of a childish person. Whence [is it said]: "No companionship with the childish one."

## Let one wander alone: *eko care*

For this reason, let one get about alone in all modes of deportment.

## And do no wrongs: *na ca pāpāni kayirā*

Just as this *Mātaṅga* elephant gets about comfortably wherever it wills in this forest, with little exertion, unattached, so let one get about, becoming solitary; and let one not do even a little of unwholesome deeds. That is the meaning.

Therefore you too, if you do not obtain proper companions, should remain as solitary dwellers. Thus the Teacher, pointing out this fact, made this dhamma-proclamation to those bhikkhus.

331. When a need has arisen, friends are a blessing,
A blessing is contentment with whatever [there be],
A blessing is the wholesome deed at the end of life,
A blessing it is to relinquish all sorrow. (23.12)

332. A blessing in the world is reverence for mother,
A blessing, too, is reverence for father,
A blessing in the world is reverence for the recluse,
A blessing too the reverence for the *brāhmaṇa*. (23.13)

333. A blessing is virtue into old age,
A blessing is faith established,
A blessing is the attainment of insight-wisdom,
A blessing it is to refrain from doing wrongs. (23.14)

*atthamhi jātamhi sukhā sahāyā tuṭṭhī sukhā yā itarītarena puññaṃ sukhaṃ jīvitasaṃkhayamhi sabbassa dukkhassa sukhaṃ pahānaṃ.*

*sukhā matteyyatā loke atho petteyyatā sukhā*
*sukhā sāmaññatā loke atho brahmaññatā sukhā.*

*sukhaṃ yāya jarā sīlaṃ sukhā saddhā patiṭṭhitā*
*sukho paññaya paṭilābho pāpānaṃ akaraṇaṃ sukhaṃ.*

[331.]

## When a need has arisen: *atthamhi jātamhi*

When a need has arisen—for example, in the case of one who has gone forth, when [it is the time for] making robes or settling disputes, and so forth, and in the case of a lay person, when [it is the time for] plowing [fields], or when [confronted with] oppression by persons who associate with the powerful, and so forth —[at such times] friends, such as those who can accomplish the task or pacify the affair [in hand], are indeed a blessing.

## A blessing is contentment with whatever [there be]: *tuṭṭhī sukhā yā itarītarena*

Because lay persons undertake such acts as burglary, not content with what they have, and those gone forth [undertake] all kinds of impropriety and [yet] in this way do not find [any] satisfaction, therefore this alone is a blessing—namely, being content with what is one's own, be it whatever, small or large.

## A blessing is the wholesome deed at the end of life: *puññaṃ sukhaṃ jīvitasaṃkhayamhi*

The wholesome act done close to the time of death, on a large scale [just] as one preferred, is indeed a blessing [because of its potential good effect on the nature of one's subsequent life].[20]

## (A blessing it is to relinquish) all sorrow: *sabbassa dukkhassa* (*sukhaṃ pahānaṃ*)

And Arahantship, which is the relinquishing of all suffering of the whirl [of existence], is indeed *the* blessing in this world.[(21)]

[332.]

## Reverence for mother: *matteyyatā*

Proper conduct toward [one's] mother.

## Reverence for father: *petteyyatā*

Proper conduct toward [one's] father. Both [terms] of course refer to attending upon parents. When they [come to] know that [their] children would not look after [them], parents either bury their wealth in the ground or they bestow it upon others. Further, a bad reputation accrues to them, [to the effect that] they do not look after their parents. And also, they at their own death are born in the hell called Gūtha.[22] But those who look after [their] parents will inherit their wealth and also receive praise [for their dutiful conduct]. And after death they are born in a state of happiness. Thus it is that these two [proper conduct toward father and mother] are said to be a blessing.

## Reverence for the recluse: *sāmaññatā*

Proper conduct toward those who have gone forth.

## Reverence for the brāhmaṇa: *brahmaññatā*

Proper conduct indeed toward those by whom the unwholesome has been discarded—that is, Buddhas, Paccekabuddhas, and disciples.

By both [of these terms, that is, recluse and *brāhmaṇa*] the condition of maintaining them through the four requisites is indicated. This too is stated to be a blessing in the world.

[333.]

## Virtue: *sīlaṃ*

Adornments such as jeweled earrings, colored clothes, and so forth, are attractive only on persons of appropriate [age groups]. In this case, [what is] an adornment on the young does not become attractive in old age, and [what is] an adornment on older persons is not attractive[(23)] in youth. [Such an unsuitable adornment] creates only trouble by giving rise to scorn [as, for example, when someone says,] "I think he is a mad man." On the other hand, moral virtue such as [observance of] the five precepts[24] or the ten precepts[25] is certainly attractive at all levels of age, in the young as well as in the old. It only brings joy by giving rise to praise [expressed in such words as: ] "A blessing is virtue [practiced even] into old age!"

## Established: *patiṭṭitā*

[A blessing is] faith, both ordinary and transcendent,[(26)] unshakably established,

## A blessing is the attainment of insight-wisdom:

*sukho paññaya paṭilābho*

[And] a blessing is the attainment of insight-wisdom, both ordinary and transcendent.

## (A blessing it is to) refrain from doing wrongs:

*pāpānam akaraṇaṃ* (*sukhaṃ*)

And not to do [those] deeds [that are] unwholesome, by destroying [their] causes,(27) is a blessing in this world. That is the meaning.

# CHAPTER XXIV

## Craving
## *Taṇhā-vaggo*

334. The craving of a person who lives heedlessly
Grows like a *māluvā* creeper.
He moves from beyond to beyond,
Like a monkey, in a forest, wishing for fruit. (24.1)

335. Whomsoever in the world
This childish entangled craving overcomes,
His sorrows grow,
Like *bīraṇa* grass, well rained upon. (24.2)

336. But whosoever in the world
Overcomes this childish craving, hard to get beyond,
From him, sorrows fall away,
Like drops of water from a lotus leaf. (24.3)

337. This I say to you. Good fortune to you [all],
As many as are here assembled.
Dig out the root of craving,
As one searching for *usīra* digs out *bīraṇa* grass.
Let not Māra break you again and again,
As a river, a reed. (24.4)

*manujassa pamattacārino taṇhā vaḍḍhati māluvā viya*
*so plavati*(1) *hurāhuraṃ phalam icchaṃ va vanasmiṃ vānaro.*

*yaṃ esā sahatī jammī taṇhā loke visattikā*
*sokā tassa pavaḍḍhanti abhivaṭṭhaṃ va bīraṇaṃ.*

*yo c'etaṃ sahātī jammiṃ taṇhaṃ loke duraccayaṃ*
*sokā tamhā papatanti udabindū va pokkharā.*

*taṃ vo vadāmi bhaddaṃ vo yāvant' ettha samāgatā*
*taṇhāya mūlaṃ khaṇatha usīrattho va bīraṇaṃ*
*mā vo naḷaṃ va soto va māro bhañji punappunaṃ.*

[334.]

## (The craving of a person) who lives heedlessly (grows like a *māluvā* creeper): *(manujassa) pamatta cārino (taṇhā vaḍḍhati māluvā viya)*

Of the person who lives [a life that is] heedless—with heedlessness characterized by slackening of awareness—neither meditative-absorption, nor insight, nor Path and Fruit develop.

Just as a *māluvā* creeper, weaving [itself] over a tree, enveloping it all around, grows to [bring about] its destruction, so does craving grow [in such a person] due to its arising over and over again, depending on the six "sense-doors." That is the meaning.

## He moves from beyond to beyond: *so palavati hurāhuraṃ*

That person, being under the subjection of craving, springs up(2) or runs [about], in existence after existence. [And] like what?

## Like a monkey, in a forest, wishing for fruit: *phalam icchaṃ va vanasmiṃ vānaro*

Just as a monkey, desiring the fruits of trees, catches hold of the branch of any tree, lets it go, and catches hold of another [and, in this way,] runs around in the forest, [so does that person run around in *saṃsāra*]. [That monkey] does not get to the state where it can be said that it lies down without a branch [to grasp]. Similarly the person who is subject to craving, running from existence to existence, does not get to the state where it can be said that he comes to the noncontinuation of craving, not getting an object [to crave for].

[335.]

## Whomsoever: *yaṃ*

That person whom craving overpowers. This craving, which has six outlets, which is called *jammī*(3) because of its childish nature, which is designated as *entangled (visattikā)* because of its being [like] a poison food, because it has poison flowers and poison fruit, because of being [like] consuming a poison *(visa)*, because it is enmeshed in [visible] forms, and so forth, and because it is [something] "entwined and enmeshed."

Within such a person [who is overpowered by craving] sorrows grow, sorrows that are the roots of the whirl [of existence], just as *bīraṇa* grass grows, [when] watered by rain falling again and again in the forest. That is the meaning.

[336.]

### (But whosoever . . . overcomes . . . craving) hard to get beyond: *(yo c'etam sahatī . . . taṇhaṃ) . . . duraccayaṃ*

The person who overpowers craving, which is hard to transcend—as was said [above]—because it is hard to cross over, to give up,

### (From him, sorrows fall away): *(sokā tamhā papatanti)*

From that person sorrows, which are the roots of the whirl [of existence], fall away,

### (Like drops of water from a lotus leaf): *(udabindū va pokkharā)*

They do not stay [in that person], just as a drop of water fallen on a lotus leaf does not remain [there]. That is the meaning.

[337.]

### This I say to you: *taṃ vo vadāmi*

Because of this reason I speak to you.

### Good fortune to you [all]: *bhaddaṃ vo*

Good [luck] to you! May you not come by destruction, like this Kapila.[4] That is the meaning.

### Dig out the root of craving: *taṇhāya mūlaṃ khaṇatha*

With the gnosis of the Path of Arahantship, dig out the root of craving that has six doors, Like what?

### As one searching for *usīra . . . bīrana* grass: *usīrattho va bīraṇaṃ*

Just as a person who has need of *usīra* digs up the *bīraṇa* grass with a large hoe,[5] so dig up the root of this. That is the meaning.

### Let not Māra break you again and again as a river, a reed: *mā vo naḷaṃ va soto va māro bhañji punappunaṃ*

Let not Māra—[be it Māra] as death, as the defilements, as a divine being[6]—break you up repeatedly as the [flood] stream of a river, rushing down with great speed, [crushes] a reed that has grown up in the river waterway. That is the meaning.

338. As long as the roots are unharmed, firm,
A tree, though topped, grows yet again.
Just so, when the latent craving is not rooted out,
This suffering arises again and again. (24.5)

339. For whom the thirty-six streams,
Flowing to what is pleasing, are mighty,
That one, whose view is debased,
The currents, which are thoughts settled on passion, carry away. (24.6)

340. Streams flow everywhere;
A creeper, having burst upward, remains.
Having seen the creeper that has arisen,
Cut out with insight-wisdom its root. (24.7)

341. Moved along and soaked by craving,
Delights arise in a being.
Those who are bound to the agreeable, looking for pleasure,
Do indeed go on to birth and old age. (24.8)

342. Accompanied by craving,
Folk crawl around like a trapped hare,
Being held by fetters and bonds.
They come by suffering again and again, for long. (24.9)

343. Surrounded by craving,
Folk crawl around like a trapped hare.
Therefore, let a bhikkhu dispel craving,
Wishing for his own detachment. (24.10)

*yathā pi mūle anupaddave daḷhe chinno pi rukkho punar eva rūhati evaṃ pi taṇhānusaye anūhate nibbattatī dukkham idaṃ punappunaṃ.*

*yassa chattiṃsatī sotā manāpassavanā bhusā*
*vāhā vahanti duddiṭṭhiṃ saṃkappā rāganissitā.*

*savanti sabbadhī sotā latā ubbhijja tiṭṭhati*
*taṃ ca disvā lataṃ jātaṃ mūlaṃ paññāya chindatha.*

*saritāni sinehitāni ca somanassāni bhavanti jantuno*
*te sātasitā sukhesino te ve jātijarūpagā narā.*

*tasiṇāya purakkhatā*(7) *pajā parisappanti saso va bādhito*
*saṃyojanasaṅgasattā dukkham upenti punappunam cirāya.*

*tasiṇāya purakkhatā pajā parisappanti saso va bādhito*
*tasmā tasiṇaṃ vinodaye bhikkhu ākaṅkhī virāgam attano.*

[338.]

## Roots: *mūle*

When the five kinds of root of a tree—those that have spread straight in four ways—that is, in the four [principal] directions and [also] downward—

## Unharmed: *anupaddave*

Are not harmed by any kind of harm such as being cut, being split, or being attacked by pests [lit. living beings],

## Firm: *daḷhe*

When they are well established, due to having attained firmness,

## A tree, though topped, grows yet again: *rukkho chinno pi punar eva rūhati*

That tree grows again, even if it is cut in its upper part, in its branches and twigs.

## Just so, when the latent craving: *evam pi taṇhānusaye*

In the same way, when the latent disposition to craving,[8] with its six doors,

## Is not rooted out: *anūhate*

Is not fully hewn down by means of the gnosis of the Path of Arahantship,

This suffering arises again and again: *nibbattati dukkham idaṃ punappunaṃ*

This suffering of many kinds—such as birth, and so forth, in existence after existence—renews its life again and again.

[339.]

Of whom (the thirty-six streams,) flowing to what is pleasing, are mighty: *yassa (chattiṃsatī sotā) manāpassavanā bhusā*

That person whose craving is *mighty (bhusā)*, strong, and is "pleasant-flowing" in that it flows to, and exists in, pleasing forms—consisting of *thirty-six streams (chattiṃsatī sotā)* on account of the activations of craving—that is, eighteen activations dependent on the internal [*āyatanas*] and eighteen on the external[9]—

Whose view is debased: *duddiṭṭhiṃ*[(10)]

That person, whose view is debased because of disabled understanding,

The currents (that are thoughts settled on lust, carry away): *vāhā (vahanti . . . saṃkappā rāga-nissitā)*

Thoughts mixed with passions—and not with meditative-absorption or insight—carry [that person away], having become torrents, on accout of their greatness due to repeated arising.

[340.]

Streams flow everywhere: *savanti sabbadhi sotā*

These streams of craving are said to flow everywhere, in the sense [1] of their "flowing" into all objects such as [visible] forms, and the like, [and in the sense] [2] that all craving for forms, sounds, smells, tastes, touch, and [conceivable] concepts "flow" together throughout all existence.[(11)]

A creeper, having burst upward, remains: *latā ubbhijja tiṭṭhati*

[Craving, being] like a vine—in the sense of its encircling and entwining—remains on the six objects such as [visible] form, and so forth, having arisen through the six [sense-]doors.

Having seen the creeper that has arisen: *taṃ ca disvā lataṃ jātaṃ*

Having seen that creeper of craving, according to the place of its origination, [reflecting thus,] "Here arising, it comes to be,"

Cut out, with insight-wisdom its root: *mūlaṃ paññāya chindatha*

Cut it off at its root, with path-insight, as one cuts off with a knife a creeper that has grown in the woods. That is the meaning.

[341.]

Moved along and soaked by craving: *saritāni sinehitāni ca*

[Delights] which have "gone along" or "stretched forth" [toward diverse objects]; [delights] which are "soaked" with attachment held toward [possessions] such as robes, and so forth—that is, [delights which are] "smeared" with the "oil" of craving. That is the meaning.

Delights arise in a being: *somanassāni bhavanti jantuno*

Such delights there are for a being [who is] in the subjugation of craving.

Who are bound to the agreeable: *te sātasitā*

They, persons who are subject to craving, who, taking resort to the delightful, the pleasurable,

Looking for pleasure: *sukhesino*

Become seekers of pleasure—

Those (men) do indeed go on to birth and old age: *te ve jātijarūpagā (narā)*

Persons who are such indeed come by birth, decay, disease, and death.

[342.]

(Accompanied by craving), folk: *(tasiṇāya purakkhatā) pajā*

These beings, who are accompanied by craving *(taṇhā)*, which is called *tasiṇā* because of its frightening [*tas*-] [character],

(Crawl around like) a trapped (hare): *(parisappanti saso va) bādhito*

Crawl, are in fright, like a hare trapped by a hunter in the forest,

Being held by fetters and bonds: *saṃyojana-saṅga-sattā*

Being bound by the tenfold fetter, and by the sevenfold attachment(12)—such as attachment to lusts, and so on, being stuck there itself [in fetters and attachments]—

They come by suffering again and again, for long: *dukkham upenti punappunaṃ cirāya*

Come by suffering such as birth, and so forth, repeatedly [and] for a long stretch [of time]. That is the meaning.

[343.]

Therefore, let a bhikkhu dispel craving, wishing for his own detachment: *tasmā tasiṇaṃ vinodaye bhikkhu ākaṅkhī virāgam attano*

Because beings are surrounded and entwined by craving, therefore let the bhikkhu who is desiring, hoping for, Nibbāna—which is the exit from one's own passions, and so forth—dispel that craving by means of the Path of Arahantship; let him remove it and cast it away. That is the meaning.

344. Who is free of the underbrush, but attached to the forest,
Who, set free from the forest, runs back to the forest;
Come, see that person,
Who, released, runs back to bondage itself. (24.11)

*yo nibbanatho vanādhimutto vanamutto vanam eva dhāvati*
*taṃ puggalam etha*(13) *passatha mutto bandhanam eva dhāvati.*

The meaning of the verse is: the person who is free from "underbrush"[14] due to having "gone forth," discarding the "underbrush" that is attachment to the household life, who [on the other hand] is attached to the "penance grove" of the monastic dwelling,(15) who, having thus been freed of the forest of craving that is the bondage of lay life, runs back to that very forest of craving—that is, [to] the bondage of lay life. Come see that person! This one, freed of the bondage of lay life, runs [back] to the bondage of lay life itself!

345. That is not a strong bond, say the wise,
Which is made of iron, of wood, or of [platted] grass.
Those excessively attached to jewels and ornaments [their attachment],
And affection for sons and wives, (24.12)

346. This is a strong bond, say the wise,
Dragging down, lax [and yet] hard to loosen.
Having cut off even this, they set out,
Free of expectation, relinquishing sensual
pleasures. (24.13)

*na taṃ daḷhaṃ bandhanam āhu dhīrā yad āyasaṃ dārujaṃ babbajaṃ ca*
*sārattarattā*(16) *maṇikuṇḍalesu puttesu dāresu ca yā apekkhā.*

*etaṃ daḷhaṃ bandhanam āhu dhīrā ohārinaṃ sithilaṃ*(17) *duppamuñcaṃ*
*etam pi chetvāna paribbajanti anapekkhino kāmasukhaṃ pahāya.*

[345.]

### Which is made of iron: *yad āyasaṃ*

That which is produced out of iron—namely, an iron fetter,

### Of wood: *dārujaṃ*

And also that which is made of wood—namely, a wooden fetter,

### Or of [platted] grass: *babbajaṃ ca*

And that which is a rope fetter, produced by making a cord from *babba* grasses or from such [materials] as the fine bark [of plants], and so forth,

### (That is not a strong bond, say) the wise: *(na taṃ daḷhaṃ bandhanam āhu) dhīrā*

Sagacious persons such as Buddhas, and so forth, do not call that [sort of thing a] strong [fetter], because it is possible to cut it with [such instruments as] swords, and the like. That is the meaning.

[345.–346.]

### For jeweled ornaments: *maṇikuṇḍalesu*

With regard to jewels and ear ornaments; or, with regard to ornaments that are attractive by reason of jewels,

Excessively attached [their attachment]: *sāratta-rattā*
Becoming enamored, due to strong attachment,

(And affection for sons and wives) this is a strong (bond): *(puttesu dāresu ca yā apekkhā) etaṃ daḷhaṃ (bandhanam)*
They who are attached to [valuables like] jewels and ornaments—that attachment of theirs, and also their craving in regard to sons and wives—sagacious persons call this bondage made of defilements the [really] strong [fetter].

[346.]

Dragging down: *ohāriṇaṃ*
It takes one down, takes one downward, on account of its dragging one and causing one to fall into the four states of woe[18]—hence "dragging down."

Lax: *sithilaṃ*
It does not cut the skin or flesh at the place where [one is] bound [by it]; does not bring out blood. Without even making [one] to realize the fact [that one is] bound, it allows [one] to do[(19)] [one's] work on roads, on land, and on waterways, and so forth. Hence [it is described as] "lax."

Hard to loosen: *duppamuñcaṃ*
[And yet] it is "hard to loosen," because the bondage of defilements, once arisen owing to greed, is difficult to be loosened[(20)] from the place where it has laid [its] "teeth," as [is] a tortoise.

Having cut off even this: *etam pi chetvāna*
By means of the sword of gnosis,[(21)] [the wise] cut off even this bondage of defilement that is so firm as this and,

They set out, free of expectations, relinquishing sensual pleasures: *anapekkhino kāmasukhaṃ pahāya paribbajanti*
They leave, go forth [into the homeless state]. That is the meaning.

347. Those who are attached to passions fall back into the "stream,"
Like a spider, on a self-spun web.
Having cut off even this, the wise proceed
Free of expectation, relinquishing all suffering. (24.14)

*ye rāgarattānupatanti sotaṃ*[22] *sayaṃ kataṃ makkaṭako va jālaṃ*
*etaṃ pi chetvāna vajanti dhīrā anapekkhino sabbadukkhaṃ pahāya.*

## Like a spider on . . . a web: *makkaṭako va jālaṃ*

Just as a spider, having made a web of threads, and lying at its center, at its "umbilical circle," swiftly runs toward [any] insect or fly that has fallen at the periphery [of the web], attacks it and drinks out its [physical] essence and, returning, lies at the very same place,

## Those who are attached to passions fall back into the "stream": *ye rāga-rattānupatanti sotaṃ*

Similarly, those beings who are attached to passions, vitiated by hatred and confused by ignorance, fall into the stream of craving made by themselves—that is, they are not able to cross over it.

## Having cut off even this, the wise proceed: *etam pi chetvāna vajanti dhīrā*

But the sagacious ones break this bondage that is so hard to cross over,

## Free of expectation, relinquishing all suffering: *anapekkhino sabbadukkhaṃ pahāya*

And, being free of attachments [lit. homeless], fare on, go, relinquishing all suffering through the Path of Arahantship.

348. Let go in front, let go behind, let go in between!
Gone to the further shore of existence,
With mind released as to "everything,"
You shall not again come upon birth and old age. (24.15)

*muñca pure muñca pacchato majjhe muñca bhavassa pāragū*
*sabbattha vimuttamānaso na punaṃ jātijaraṃ upehisi.*

## Let go in front: *muñca pure*

Let go of attachment, longing, clinging, desiring, [mental] possession, obsession, grasping, craving—with reference to *khandha*s of the past—

### Let go behind: *muñca pacchato*

Let go of attachment, and so forth, with reference to the *khandha*s of the future too.

### Let go in between: *majjhe muñca*

Let go with reference to [*khandha*s *of* ] the present too.

### Gone to the further shore of existence: *bhavassa pāragū*

When this is so—having gone to the further shore of the whole threefold existence, by way of(23) higher knowledge, full understanding, relinquishment, [meditational] development and realization, living with mind liberated in regard to the "entirety" of conditioned [existence] with its divisions such as *khandha, dhātu*, and *āyatana*[24]—one does not again come by birth, decay, and death. That is the meaning.

349. For a person having thoughts disturbed,
Acute of passion, looking for the pleasurable,
Craving increases all the more.
That one, indeed, makes the bondage firm. (24.16)

350. But one who delights in allaying thoughts,
Who, ever-mindful, develops meditation on the unpleasant,
That one, indeed will make an end,
That one will cut off Māra's bond. (24.17)

*vitakkapamathitassa jantuno tibbarāgassa subhānupassino*
*bhiyyo taṇhā pavaḍḍhati esa kho daḷhaṃ karoti bandhanaṃ.*

*vitakkūpasame ca yo rato asubhaṃ bhāvayati sadā sato*
*esa kho vyantikāhiti esa cchecchati mārabandhanaṃ.*

[349.]

### Having thoughts disturbed: *vitakka-pamathitassa*

To the one who is agitated by thoughts such as thoughts of sensuality,[25]

### Acute of passion: *tibba-rāgassa*

For whom sensual attractions are acute,

Looking for the pleasurable: *subhānupassino*

Who is [given to] contemplating the desired object as pleasant, because the mind is given over [to it] by [the habit of] "seizing upon the pleasant sign," and so forth,

Craving increases: *taṇhā pavaḍḍhati*

For such a person, none of the meditative-absorptions, and the like, grows; on the contrary, craving with its six outlets indeed grows evermore.

That one, indeed, makes the bondage firm: *esa kho (daḷhaṃ karoti bandhanaṃ)*

That person indeed makes the bondage of craving firm.

[350.]

In allaying thoughts: *vitakkūpasame*

In the first meditative-absorption [in which attention is focused] on the ten unpleasant [aspects of the body][26] and which is called "the dispelling of wrong thoughts" [in regard to the body],

Ever-mindful: *sadā sato*

The one who, being ever mindful, on account of awakened heedfulness, develops that meditative-absorption on the unpleasant, being very interested therein,

That one . . . will make an end: *esa vyantikāhiti*

That bhikkhu shall put an end to the craving that leads to birth in the three [forms of] existence.

(That one will cut off) Māra's bond:
*(esa-cchecchati) māra-bandhanaṃ*

One indeed will cut off the bondage of Māra—that is to say, the three-tiered whirl [of existence].[27] That is the meaning.

351. The one who has arrived at the destination,
Free from fright, craving, and blemish,
Has broken the knives of existence.
This is the final bodily form. (24.18)

352. Without craving, free from grasping,
Skilled in terms of expression,
Who would know the combination of letters, what precedes and what follows,
He, indeed, is called one having the last physical form,
Great person of great wisdom. (24.19)

*niṭṭhaṅ gato asantāsī vītataṇho anaṅgaṇo*
*acchidda bhavasallāni antimo 'yaṃ samussayo.*

*vītataṇho anādāno niruttipaddakovido*
*akkharānaṃ sannipātaṃ jaññā pubbaparāni ca*
*sa ve antimasārīro mahāpañño mahāpuriso*(28) *ti vuccati.*

[351.]

## The one who has arrived at the destination: *niṭṭhaṃ gato*

Arahantship is the final destination of those who have gone forth in this monastic order. One who has arrived at that [state]. That is the meaning.

## Free from fright: *asantāsī*

Who is not subject to fright, on account of the absence within [him] of the fright of sensual attractions, and so forth,

## Has broken the knives of existence: *acchidda bhavasallāni*

Has broken all the "knives" that lead to [the continuation of] existence.

## This is the final bodily form: *antimo 'yaṃ samussayo*

This is that one's final existence [lit. body].

[352.]

## Free from grasping: *anādāno*

The one who is free from grasping in regard to the *khandha*s, and the like,

## Skilled in terms of expression: *nirutti-pada-kovido*

Who is skilled in the four terms [of discriminative understanding]—that is, in [the understanding of] expressions and in the other [three] terms [of discriminative understanding][29]—

## Who would know the combination of letters, what precedes and what follows: *akkharānaṃ sannipātaṃ jaññā pubbaparāni ca*

Who knows the composite structure *(piṇḍa)* of letters known as the combination of letters;(30) by the preceding letter, who knows [what will be] the succeeding letter and by the succeeding letter knows [what should have been] the preceding letter. "Knows the succeeding letter by the preceding" means: when the first part [of a word] is visible, even if the middle and final [letters] are not visible, one knows that "to those first letters,(31) the middle is this and the end is this." "Knows the preceding letter by the succeeding" means: when the end is visible and even if the beginning and middle are not, one knows that "to these final letters the middle is this and the beginning is this." And when the middle [part of the word] is visible, one indeed knows that of these middle letters, "this is the beginning and this is the end." Thus is he [a person] of great wisdom.(32)

## (He indeed . . . one having the last physical form) of great wisdom: *(sa ve antimasārīro) mahāpañño*

He is one whose body is at the end [of travels in *saṃsāra*], one greatly wise on account of being endowed with insight-wisdom that includes [the four] great modes of discriminative understanding, [namely, 1–3] the understanding of results, of conditions, and of expressions, and [4] of intuitive comprehension(33) as well as [the other aspects of understanding dhamma] such as the "group" of moral virtues, and so forth. He [for this reason] is called a great person—[and] also because of the fact of [his] liberation of mind, following the [Buddha's] statement: "I call one whose mind is liberated a great person, O Sāriputta." That is the meaning.

353. Conqueror of all, knower of all am I;
Untainted with regard to all dhammas.
Abandoning everything, released at the dissolution of craving,
Having comprehended by myself, whom shall I point out? (24.20)

*sabbābhibhū sabbavidū 'ham asmi sabbesu dhammesu anūpalitto*
*sabbañjaho taṇhakkhaye vimutto sayaṃ abhiññāya kam uddiseyyaṃ.*

## Conqueror of all: *sabbābhibhū*

One who has overcome all dhammas of the three planes [of existence],

Knower of all: *sabba-vidū*

[By whom] all dhammas of the four planes [of consciousness] have been understood,[34]

Untainted with regard to all dhammas: *sabbesu dhammesu anūpalitto*

[Who is] untainted with cravings and [wrong] views in regard to all dhammas of the three planes [of existence],

Abandoning everything: *sabbañjaho*

[Who] stands, having quit all dhammas of the three planes [of existence],

Released at the dissolution of craving: *taṇhakkhaye vimutto*

[Is] liberated by the liberation of one who has passed beyond training, [liberated] in Arahantship, which is called "the dissolution of craving" and which is brought into being at the extinction of [all] craving.

Having comprehended by myself: *sayaṃ abhiññāya*

Having understood dhammas in their divisions such as "higher knowledge," and so forth,[35] by myself,

Whom shall I point out: *kam uddiseyyaṃ*

Whom shall I point out, "This is [my] preceptor or teacher."

354. The gift of dhamma prevails over every gift,
The flavor of dhamma prevails over every flavor,
The delight in dhamma prevails over every delight,
The dissolution of craving subdues all suffering. (24.21)

*sabbadānaṃ dhammadānaṃ jināti sabbaṃ rasaṃ dhammaraso jināti sabbaṃ ratiṃ dhammaratī jināti taṇhakkhayo sabbadukkaṃ jināti.*

The gift of dhamma prevails over every gift: *sabba dānaṃ dhammadānaṃ jināti*[36]

If one were to offer robes [that are soft] as the tender leaf of the banana plant to Buddhas, Paccekabuddhas, and those influx-extinct [Arahants] who have assembled filling the entire sphere of the universe as far as the world of Brahmās, nobler [than that gift] is the benediction done at that assembly with a single four-line verse; that [material] gift is not worth a sixteenth part[37] [of the value] of that stanza, so great is [the value of] the proclamation, the recitation,[(38)] and the hearing of dhamma. Great is the good effect of that [dhamma] indeed, for one by whom it has been heard. Nobler than the gift of wholesale alms, food offered bowlful to a large gathering [of bhikkhus] of such order [as mentioned above], than the gift of medicaments offered in bowls filled with clarified butter, oil, and so forth, offered bowlful [to such a gathering], than a gift of lodgings given, by having got many hundreds of thousands of monasteries like the Mahāvihāra and mansions like the Brazen Palace[39] constructed, than the donation given by such [devotees] as Anāthapiṇḍika for the monastery—nobler than [such lavish gifts] is the gift of dhamma, of even a four-line verse made as a benediction. For what reason? Those who are doing such wholesome deeds do them only on hearing dhamma, not otherwise. If those beings were not to hear dhamma, they would not give so much as a spoonful of gruel or a ladleful of rice. For this reason, the gift of dhamma is indeed nobler than those [other] gifts.

Moreover, even such [personages] as Sāriputta, and others, who alone, other than Buddhas and Paccekabuddhas, are endowed with insight that can [even] count the [number of] rain drops [that would fall] if it rains for an entire aeon [of time]—even they were not able to attain to such [states] as the Fruit of Stream Entrance, and so forth, entirely by [the strength of] their own nature. They realized such [states] as the Fruit of Stream Entrance, and so on, after hearing dhamma proclaimed by [Arahants] like the Elder Assaji. They realized the gnosis of the perfection of discipleship [only] through the Teacher's instruction of dhamma. For this reason too, O Great King,[40] the gift of dhamma is the noblest [gift]. Hence is it said, "The gift of dhamma prevails over every gift."

## The flavor of dhamma prevails over every flavor: *sabbaṃ rasaṃ dhammaraso jināti*

All [agreeable] tastes, such as the taste of the stem [of edible plants], and so forth, and even the best [of all of them], taste of [the divine] delicacy of *sudhā*—[ultimately become] a cause for the certain experience of suffering, because they make one to fall into the whirl of *saṃsāra*. But the taste of dhamma—that is, the ninefold world-transcending dhamma[41] and the thirty-seven dhammas conducive to enlightenment—[42] this taste alone is noble. Hence is it said, "the taste of dhamma prevails over every taste."

## The delight in dhamma prevails over every delight: *sabbaṃ ratiṃ dhammaratī jināti*

The delight in sons and daughters, in wealth, in women, and the numerous [other] kinds of delight, such as that of dance, song, music, and so forth, are [ultimately] causes for suffering alone, making [one] to fall into the whirl of *saṃsāra*. But this joy that arises within one who either speaks dhamma or hears dhamma, produces a sense of elation, brings out tears and makes hairs to stand on end. It puts an end to the whirl of *saṃsara*; it is [a state] having [its] end in the Fruit of Arahantship. Hence, of all delights, this kind of delight in dhamma is the best. Hence is it said, "Delight in dhamma prevails over every delight."

### The dissolution of craving subdues all suffering: *taṇhakkhayo sabbadukkhaṃ jināti*

The extinction of craving is Arahantship, which comes into being at the end of the dissolution of craving. Because it overcomes the entirety of suffering of the whirl, it is the best [state] of all. Hence is it said, "The dissolution of craving subdues all suffering."

355. Possessions strike down one deficient in wisdom,
But not those seeking the beyond.
Through craving for possessions, one deficient in wisdom
Strikes oneself down as one would the others. (24.22)

*hananti bhogā dummedhaṃ no ve pāragavesino*
*bhogataṇhāya dummedho hanti aññe va attanaṃ.*

### Not those seeking the beyond: *no ve pāragavesino*

Possessions do not strike [down] those persons who are seekers of the further [shore].

### (Strikes) oneself (down) as . . . others: *(hanti) aññe va attanaṃ*

The person who is deficient in insight strikes [down] himself indeed, like one striking down others, due to the craving born on account of possessions.

356. For fields, grasses are the bane,
For humankind, sensual attraction is the bane.
Hence, to those free from sensual attraction
What is given yields much fruit. (24.23)

357. For fields, grasses are the bane,
For humankind, ill will is the bane.
Hence, to those free from ill will
What is given yields much fruit. (24.24)

358. For fields, grasses are the bane,
For humankind, confusion is the bane.
Hence, to those free from confusion
What is given yields much fruit. (24.25)

359. For fields, grasses are the bane,
For humankind, longing is the bane.
Hence, to those free from longing
What is given yields much fruit. (24.26)

*tiṇdosāni khettāni rāgadosā ayaṃ pajā*
*tasmā hi vītarāgesu dinnaṃ hoti mahapphalaṃ.*

*tiṇadosāni khettāni dosadosā ayaṃ pajā*
*tasmā hi vītadosesu dinnaṃ hoti mahappahalaṃ.*

*tiṇadosāni khettāni mohadosā ayaṃ pajā*
*tasmā hi vītamohesu dinnaṃ hoti mahapphalaṃ.*

*tiṇadosāni khettāni icchādosā ayaṃ pajā*
*tasmā hi vigaticchesu dinnaṃ hoti mahapphalaṃ.*

[356.]

## Grasses are the bane: *tiṇa-dosāni*

Grasses [i.e., weeds] like *sāmaka,* and the like, when they grow [among cultivated crops], spoil the fields of pulses and grains;(43) due to it [i.e. presence of weeds] they cease to give high yields.(44) [Likewise] sensual attraction within, arising in beings, vitiates them. Thereby what is given to them is of no great benefit [to the giver]. But what is given to those in whom intoxicants are extinct is of great benefit(45) [to the giver]. Hence is it said: "For fields, grasses are the bane" [st. 356]. In the other stanzas [357–59] too, the mode [of interpretation] is the same.

# CHAPTER XXV

## The Bhikkhu
## *Bhikkhu-vaggo*

360. Restraint with the eye is commendable,
Commendable is restraint with the ear.
Restraint with the nose is commendable,
Commendable is restraint with the tongue. (25.1)

361. Restraint with the body is commendable,
Commendable is restraint with speech.
Restraint with the mind is commendable,
Commendable is restraint in all [the senses].
The bhikkhu who is restrained in all [the senses],
Is freed from all suffering. (25.2)

*cakkhunā saṃvaro sādhu sādhu sotena saṃvaro*
*ghāṇena saṃvaro sādhu sādhu jivhāya saṃvaro.*

*kāyena saṃvaro sādhu sādhu vācāya saṃvaro*
*manasā saṃvaro sādhu sādhu sabbattha saṃvaro*
*sabbattha saṃvuto bhikkhu sabbadukkhā pamuccati.*

[360.]

### With the eye: *cakkhuna*

When a visible object comes within the range of a bhikkhu's eyesight [lit. eye-door] and [he is] not being attracted to the object [if it is] pleasant, not annoyed at the object [if it is] unpleasant, [and] not begetting confusion through lack of proper insight, [then] it is said that he has exercised "restraint," [or] "closure," [or] "covering," [or] "guarding" in regard to the door. Commendable is restraint with the eye of that one. The same manner [of interpretation applies] in regard to the "doors" of the ear, and so forth. Restraint or nonrestraint does not arise(1) directly [at the moment of presentation of an object] at the sense outlets such as the eye, and so forth. It occurs afterward at [what is known as] the *javana* [-instant] in the stream [of events constituting a cognitive-connative experience]. Nonrestraint, when it arises at that [*javana*-instant] in an unwholesome stream [of mental events] is fivefold [i.e., has five characteristic expressions, namely]: lack of faith, impatience, sloth, heedlessness, and ignorance. Restraint, when it arises in a wholesome stream [of mental events also] is fivefold [as]: faith, patience, energy, heedfulness, and understanding.

[361.]

## Restraint with the body: *kāyena saṃvaro*

The [basic] sensitivity of body, as well as the body as the motor organs, is appropriate in this context. Both of them indeed constitute the physical "door." Therein the restraint at the "door" of the sensitivity of body is of course [usually] mentioned. At the "door" of the motor organs too [there are such acts as] killing, stealing, and misconduct, which take place with them as their basis. That "door" becomes unrestrained on account of these [acts], arising in an unwholesome stream [of psycho-physical events], together with [the activity of] the motor organs. It becomes restrained on account of abstention from killing, and so forth, arising in a wholesome stream [of events].

## Commendable . . . with speech: *sādhu vācāya*

Here too speech really is [the element that generates] speech as a motor activity. That "door" becomes unrestrained on account of lying, and so forth, arising together with it, and restrained on account of abstinence from lying, and so on.

## Restraint with the mind: *manasā saṃvaro*

Here too there is no covetousness, and the like, with a mental act other than the mental act of *javana*. On account of covetousness, and the like, arising at the "mind-door"(2) at the instant of *javana*, that "door" becomes unrestrained, and restrained on account of abstinence from covetousness, and so forth.

## Commendable . . in all [the senses]: *sādhu sabbattha*

Good is restraint in regard to them all, such as in regard to the "door" of the eye, and so forth. With this the eight "doors" of restraint and the eight "doors" of nonrestraint have been referred to. The bhikkhu who is at those eight "doors" of nonrestraint does not become liberated from the entirety of the suffering caused by the whirl. He who is at the eight "doors" of restraint becomes liberated from the entire suffering caused by the whirl. Hence it is said: "The bhikkhu who is restrained in all [the senses] is freed from all suffering."

362. The one restrained in hand, restrained in foot,
Restrained in speech, the one of best restraint,
Having delight in introspection, composed, solitary, contented—
That one they call a bhikkhu. (25.3)

*hatthasaññato pādasaññato vācāya saññato saññatuttamo*
*ajjhattarato samāhito eko santusito tam āhu bhikkhuṃ.*

### Restrained in hand: *hattha-saññato*

One is restrained in hand on account of not resorting to frivolous gestures of the hand and beating, and so forth, of others with the hand.

### Restrained in speech: *vācāya saññato*

The same mode [of interpretation applies] in the second line too: [one is] restrained in speech on account of not resorting to lying, and so forth, through [one's] words.

### Of best restraint: *saññatuttamo*

One who is restrained in [one's whole] personality(3) by not resorting to shaking [one's] body, raising [one's] head [immoderately], gesturing with the eyebrows, and so forth. That is the meaning.

### Having delight in introspection: *ajjhatta-rato*

One who takes delight in contemplation of [appropriate] meditation topics, which constitute "that whose field [of action] is the inner [self],"

### Composed: *samāhito*

[who has one's thoughts] well maintained,

### Solitary, contented: *eko santusito*

Who is moving about in solitude [and] is well contented; whose mind is contented with what has been attained from [the time of practicing] insight[-meditation]. All those "in training" starting from the virtuous common person are said to be "contented persons," because they are contented with their attainment. The Arahant, however, is indeed "definitely contented." This [here] has been said in regard to him.

363. A bhikkhu, restrained in speech,
Who speaks in moderation, who is not haughty,
Who illustrates the meaning and the message,
Sweet is his speech. (25.4)
(The commentary understands the first part of the second line to mean, "who speaks with insight.")

*yo mukhasaññato bhikkhu mantabhāṇī*[(4)] *anuddhato*
*atthaṃ dhammaṃ ca dīpeti madhuraṃ tassa bhāsitaṃ.*

### Restrained in speech: *mukha-saññato*

"You are a slave, an outcaste," and so forth, "you are lowborn," "you are immoral"—by not saying such [words], and so forth, even to slaves and outcastes [one becomes] restrained in speech.

### Who speaks in moderation: *mantabhāṇī*

*Mantā* means insight. Hence, one who is in the habit of speaking with that [insight].

### Not haughty: *anuddhato*

One whose mind is calmed.

### Who illustrates the meaning and the message: *atthaṃ dhammaṃ ca dīpeti*

Proclaims both the interpretation that has been stated [in the tradition] and the dhamma that is the [Buddha's own] instruction.

### Sweet: *madhuraṃ*

The speech of such a bhikkhu is said to be sweet. But one who supplies only the interpretation but not the [canonical] text *(pāli)*, or one who supplies the text but not the interpretation, or one who supplies neither, that one's speech is not said to be sweet.

364. Abiding in dhamma, delighting in dhamma,
Reflecting on dhamma, remembering dhamma,
A bhikkhu, does not fall away
From dhamma true. (25.5)

*dhammārāmo dhammarato dhammaṃ anuvicintayaṃ*
*dhammaṃ anussaraṃ bhikkhu saddhammā na parihāyati.*

## Abiding in dhamma: *dhammārāmo*

[Someone is called] *dhammārāma* because the dhammas of tranquility [-meditation] and insight [-meditation] are [like] a residence *(ārāma)* to one, in the sense that one "dwells"(5) [in these meditations].

## Delighting in dhamma: *dhammarato*

One who takes delight in the same dhamma [i.e., meditation] is [called] *dhammarata.*

## Reflecting on dhamma: *dhammaṃ anuvicintayaṃ*

[Someone is described as] "reflecting on dhamma" because of [one's] thinking of that same dhamma [i.e., meditation] again and again. Giving attention to that dhamma, "giving [one's] mind" [thereto] is the meaning.

## Remembering dhamma: *dhammaṃ anussaraṃ*

Constantly mindful of that very dhamma.

## Does not fall away from dhamma true: *saddhammā na parihāyati*

Such a bhikkhu does not fall away from the dhammas that are favorable to enlightenment, which are of thirty-seven divisions, or from the ninefold dhamma that transcends the world. That is the meaning.

365. Let one not treat what one has received with scorn,
Let one not live envying others.
A bhikkhu who is envying others
Does not come to integration [of mind]. (25.6)

366. If though a bhikkhu has received but little,
He does not treat his receipt with scorn,
Him, indeed, the gods praise,
Who is living purely, unwearied. (25.7)

*salābhaṃ nātimaññeyya nāññesaṃ pihayaṃ care*
*aññesaṃ pihayaṃ bhikkhu samādhiṃ nādhigacchati.*

*appalābho pi ce bhikkhu salābhaṃ nātimaññati*
*taṃ ve devā pasaṃsanti suddhājīviṃ atanditaṃ.*

[365.]

## (Let one not treat) what one has received (with scorn): *sa lābhaṃ (nātimaññeyya)*

"The gain" that accrues to oneself. One who discards [the custom] of going for alms from house to house, and finds one's sustenance through impropriety, treats what one gets [by begging for alms] with scorn, despises it, loathes it. Hence [what is meant is]: refrain from treating it with scorn by not acting in this manner.

## (Let one) not (live) envying others: *nāññesam pihayaṃ (care)*

Do not go about desiring the gain of others. That is the meaning.

## Does not come to integration [of mind]: *samādhiṃ nādhigacchati*

A bhikkhu who is desiring the gain of others gets into [a life of] being preoccupied on account of their robes, and so forth,[(6)] and does not attain to either the concentration of absorption or the concentration of access.[7]

[366.]

## He does not treat his receipt with scorn: *salābhaṃ nātimaññati*

A bhikkhu who, even being one who receives little, walks the alms-round in due order [from house to house, be they of] families of high status or low status, is called "one who does not treat his receipt with scorn."

### Him, indeed, (the gods praise, who is living purely, unwearied): *taṃ ve (devā pasaṃsanti sudhājīviṃ atanditaṃ)*

Such a bhikkhu, who is said to be of pure livelihood because of the worthiness of his life and who is [said to be] "unwearied" because of not being lazy, because he finds his living "by the strength of his legs" [i.e., by regularly walking the alms-round]—even the gods praise [such a bhikkhu]; they eulogize him. That is the meaning.

367. For whom there is no "sense of mine"
Toward what is name-and-form, in every way,
Who does not grieve because of what is not;
He, indeed, is called a bhikkhu. (25.8)

*sabbaso nāmarūpasmiṃ yassa natthi mamāyitaṃ*
*asatā ca na socati sa ve bhikkhū ti vuccati.*

### Toward all that is name-and-form: *sabbaso nāmarūpasmiṃ*

In regard to the entire "name-and-form" [i.e., all the varied aspects constituting the human personality] occurring as the five *khandha*s—[namely] the four [groups of "mental" phenomena] beginning with "feeling" as well as the [nonmental group, that is to say] the mass of [phenomena making up] physical [personality].[8]

### For whom there is no "sense of mine": *yassa natthi mamāyitaṃ*

For whom there is no holding [of all this] as "[This] I [am]" or "[This is] mine,"

### Who does not grieve because of what is not: *asatā ca na socati*

And who does not grieve, is not tormented, when that "name-and-form" comes by decay and degeneration, thinking, "[Alas,] my name [or] form . . . [or] consciousness has decayed," but, rather, perceives [the matter thus], "What has decayed in me is what is liable to decay and degeneration,"

### He indeed is called a bhikkhu: *sa ve bhikkhū ti vuccati*

Such [a person] as this, who is free from identifying even with "name-and-form" existing in good condition, who does not grieve even by its being nonexistent, is called a bhikkhu. That is the meaning.

368. A bhikkhu dwelling in loving-kindness,
Who is pleased in the Buddha's instruction,
Would attain the state that is peace,
The pacification of the *saṅkhāra*s, bliss. (25.9)

369. O bhikkhu, bail out this boat.
Bailed out, it shall go quickly for you.
Having cut away both lust and hate,
You shall then reach Nibbāna. (25.10)

370. Let one cut away the five, relinquish the five,
And, especially, cultivate the five.
A bhikkhu who has gone beyond five attachments
Is called "One who has crossed the flood." (25.11)

371. Meditate, O bhikkhu, and be not heedless.
Let not your mind whirl in the strand of sensuality.
Do not swallow a metal ball, being heedless,
While burning, do not lament, "This is woe." (25.12)

372. There is no meditative absorption for one who lacks insight;
There is no insight for one who is not meditating.
In whom there is meditative absorption and insight,
Truly, he is in Nibbāna's presence. (25.13)

373. For a bhikkhu who has entered an empty house,
Whose mind is at peace,
Who perceives dhamma fully,
There is delight unlike that of mortals. (25.14)

374. Howsoever one thoroughly knows
The rise and demise of the *khandha*s,
One attains joy and delight
That is ambrosia for those who are discerning. (25.15)

375. Here, this is the first thing for a bhikkhu of insight:
Guarding the sense faculties, contentment,
And restraint in the *pātimokkha*.
Associate with good friends
Who are living purely, unwearied. (25.16)

376. Let one be in the habit of friendly relations,
Of competent conduct let one be.
Being of abundant joy thereby,
One shall make an end of suffering. (25.17)

*mettāvihārī yo bhikkhu pasanno buddhasāsane*
*adhigacche padaṃ santaṃ saṃkhārūpasamaṃ sukhaṃ.*

*siñca bhikkhu imaṃ nāvaṃ sittā te lahum essati*
*chetvā rāgaṃ ca dosaṃ ca tato nibbānam ehisi.*

*pañca chinde pañca jahe pañca vuttari bhāvaye*
*pañca saṅgātigo bhikkhu oghatiṇṇo ti vuccati.*

*jhāya bhikkhu mā ca pamādo mā te kāmaguṇe bhamassu*(9) *cittaṃ*
*mā lohaguḷaṃ gilī pamatto mā kandi dukkham idaṃ ti ḍayhamāno.*

*natthi jhānaṃ apaññassa paññā natthi ajjhāyato*
*yamhi jhānaṃ ca paññā ca sa ve nibbānasantike.*

*suññāgāraṃ paviṭṭhassa santacittassa bhikkhuno*
*amānusī ratī hoti sammā dhammaṃ vipassato.*

*yato yato sammasati khandhānaṃ udayabbayaṃ*
*labhatī pītipāmojjaṃ amataṃ taṃ vijānataṃ.*

*tatrāyam ādi bhavati idha paññassa bhikkhuno*
*indriyagutti santuṭṭhi pātimokkhe ca saṃvaro*
*mitte bhajassu kalyāne suddhājīve atandite.*

*paṭisanthāravutty*(10) *assa ācārakusalo siyā*
*tato pāmojjabahulo dukkhassantaṃ karissati.*

[368.]

## Dwelling in loving-kindness: *mettā-vihārī*

One who is exerting oneself in loving-kindness as an object of meditation, as well as one who has attained the triad or tetrad of meditative-absorptions by [developing] loving-kindness is called "one dwelling in loving-kindness."

## Pleased: *pasanno*

He is pleased in the instruction of the Buddha: he indeed relishes [the fact of] being pleased [in the Buddha's instruction]. That is the meaning.

## The state that is peace: *padaṃ santaṃ*

This is a term for Nibbāna. Even a bhikkhu such as this indeed attains, experiences, Nibbāna, which is the dimension of peace, which is referred to as bliss because it is the highest bliss and [also because it is] the "pacification of *saṅkhāras*" due to the fact that all *saṅkhāras* have become tranquil [when it has been attained].

[369.]

## O bhikkhu, bail out this boat: *siñca bhikkhu imaṃ nāvaṃ*

O bhikkhu,[(11)] bailing out this ship of personality of the water of wrong thoughts, throw [that water] away—bail it out [in this manner]:

## Bailed out, it shall go quickly for you: *sittā te lahum essati*

Just as a ship, on the ocean, heavy with water [that has seeped through a hole], bailed out [by the crew] and becoming light, reaches a goodly harbor fast, without getting sunk—because the crew closed up its fissures and emptied it of the water—in the same way, when with restraint you "close up" the fissures of the sense outlets such as the eye, this ship of your personality filled with the water of wrong thoughts, will go fast to Nibbāna, without sinking in the whirl of *saṃsāra,* being light because emptied of the water of wrong thoughts [that had] arisen.

## Having cut away: *chetvā*

Cut away the bondages of lust and hate. Having cut them away and [having] attained Arahantship,

## You shall then reach Nibbāna: *tato nibbānam ehisi*

Thereafter you will reach Nibbāna without substrates left. That is the meaning.

[370.]

## Let one cut away the five: *pañca chinde*

Let one cut off, with the three earlier [lit. lower] Paths the five grosser fetters[12] that lead one to the states of woe below—as a man [would cut off] with a knife a rope tied around [his] foot.

### Let one relinquish the five: *pañca jahe*

Let one abandon, relinquish, indeed, let one cut off by means of the Path of Arahantship, the five subtler fetters[13] that lead one to the *deva* worlds above—as a man [would cut off] a rope tied around [his] neck. That is the meaning.

### Let one cultivate the five: *pañca vuttari bhāvaye*

Let one cultivate especially the five faculties such as faith, and so forth,[14] in order to transcend the [five] subtler fetters.

### Who has gone beyond five attachments is called "One who has crossed the flood": *pañca saṅgātigo . . . ogha-tiṇṇo ti vuccati*

When [this is] thus [achieved], the bhikkhu is indeed said to have crossed over the floods; by stepping over the five attachments of lust, hate, confusion, self-estimation, and [wrong] views, one, indeed, is said to have crossed the four floods.[15] That is the meaning.

[371.]

### Meditate, O bhikkhu, (and be not heedless): *(mā ca pamādo) jhāya bhikkhu*

O bhikkhu, meditate, by the two [kinds of] meditative-absorptions[16] and also do not be heedless—[be heedful] by living mindfully with reference to physical deeds, and the like.

### Let not (your mind) whirl (in the strand of sensuality): *mā (te kāmaguṇa) bhamassu (cittaṃ)*

May your mind not whirl in the fivefold strand of sensuality.[17]

### Do not swallow a metal ball: *mā lohaguḷaṃ giḷi*

Those who are heedless with the heedlessness characterized by the relinquishing of [meditative] attention *(sati)*, swallow a metal ball heated in hell. Hence I tell you: Do not swallow a metal ball by being heedless. Do not [act in such a way that you will] lament, burning in the state of woe: "This is woe, this is woe!" That is the meaning.

[372.]

### There is no meditative absorption: *natthi jhānaṃ*

For one who lacks insight, which is concomitant with enterprise and which generates meditative-absorption, there is no meditative-absorption.

### There is no insight: *paññā natthi*

For one who is not meditating, there is not that insight whose characteristics are thus stated: "The bhikkhu who is integrated [of mind] understands and sees reality as it is."

### In whom there is meditative absorption and insight: *yamhi jhānaṃ ca paññā ca*

That person in whom both of these exist indeed is standing near Nibbāna. That is the meaning.

[373.]

### Who has entered an empty house: *suññāgāraṃ paviṭṭhassa*

The one who is seated, applying [the] mind to the subjects of meditation, in any solitary place whatever, without abandoning the meditative task,(18)

### Whose mind is at peace: *santa-cittassa*

Whose mind is calmed,

### Who perceives dhamma fully: *sammā dhammaṃ vipassato*

Who gains insight into dhamma by [understanding] cause and condition,

### There is delight unlike that of mortals: *amānusī ratī hoti*

There arises even [the] divine joy that is insight—namely, the eight attainments.[19]

[374.]

### Howsoever one thoroughly knows the rise and demise of the *khandhas*: *yato yato sammasato khandhānaṃ udayabbayaṃ*

One who is exerting [oneself] in regard to the thirty-eight objects [of meditation],[20] [and] contemplates the arising of the five *khandhas* by [their] twenty-five characteristics [of arising] and [their] dying away by the twenty-five characteristics [of dying away],[21] exerting [oneself] in any manner(22) on any topic of meditation agreeable to one, at any agreeable time such as the forenoon, afternoon, and so forth,

### (One attains) joy and delight: *(labhatī) pīti-pāmojjaṃ*

So contemplating the rise and fall of *khandhas*, one attains to the joy of dhamma, the delight of dhamma,

## That is ambrosia for those who are discerning: *amataṃ taṃ vijānataṃ*

The joy and delight that is born when "name-and-form" [the nature of the psycho-physical personality] appears clearly [before one's mind] together with [the nature of their] causes, and which is ambrosia itself to the discerning, the sagacious ones who understand, because it causes the attainment of the great Nibbāna that is deathless.

[375.]

## Here . . . for a bhikkhu of insight: *idha paññassa bhikkhuno*

In this monastic order, for a sagacious bhikkhu,

## This is the first thing: *tatrāyam ādi*

This is the first matter [to observe].

## Guarding the sense faculties: *indriya-gutti*

Now, indicating the first matter that was referred to by *ādi,* the [text] says "restraint of senses" *(indriyagutti),* and so forth. The first matter is the fourfold virtue leading to purity. Within that, [1] the restraint of senses is what is referred to as *indriyagutti.*

## Contentment: *santuṭṭhi*

Contentment as regards the four requisites. Thereby both [2] pure livelihood, and [3] the virtue associated with [the proper attitude toward] the requisites have been indicated.

## And (restraint) in the *pātimokkha*: *pātimokkhe ca (saṃvaro)*

By this the fulfillment of [4] that foremost virtue known as [the observance of] the *pātimokkha* is indicated.

## Associate with good friends: *mitte bhajassu kalyāṇe*

Let one discard improper companions who have given up the task [that ought to be performed] and associate with good friends,

## Unwearied: *atandite*

Who are not indolent, inasmuch as they gain their living by virtue of "the strength of their legs" [i.e., by walking the alms-round],

## Living purely: *suddhājīve*

And who are "living purely" on account of the worthiness(23) of [their] way of living.

[376.]

## Let one be in the habit of friendly relations: *paṭisanthāravutty assa*

Be one who observes "friendly relations" by [maintaining a personal] conduct of which the constituent elements are [1] a relationship of cordial sharing with regard to material things and [2] a [similar] cordial relationship with regard to dhamma [that one has understood]. That is the meaning.

## Of competent conduct let one be: *ācārakusalo siyā*

[What is referred to here as] conduct is virtue as well as [observance of due] rites and practices. Be skilful therein, [be] one who is proficient [therein].

## Being of abundant joy thereby: *tato pāmojja-bahulo*

Being "of abundant joy" on account of [your] joy born of the observance of mutual sharing and competence of conduct, you(24) will put an end to the entire suffering of the whirl. That is the meaning.

377. As the jasmine
Sheds its withered flowers,
So, O bhikkhu,
Shed sensual attachment and hatred. (25.18)

*vassikā viya pupphāni maddavāni pamuñcati*
*evaṃ rāgaṃ ca dosaṃ ca vippamuñcetha bhikkhavo.*

## Jasmine: *vassikā*

The jasmine creeper.

## Withered flowers: *maddavāni*

Withered flowers. This is what is stated: just as the jasmine creeper relieves from the stem the flowers that blossomed the previous day and that have "grown old," so you too relinquish blemishes such as sensual attachment, and so forth.

378. A bhikkhu, with body pacified, speech pacified,
Who is possessed of peace, well composed,
Who has thrown out the world's material things,
Is called the "one at peace." (25.19)

*santakāyo santavāco santavā susamāhito*
*vantalokāmiso bhikkhu upasanto ti vuccati.*

### With body pacified: *santakāyo*

One is called "with body pacified" on account of the absence of violence to life, and so on [in one's actions],

### Speech pacified: *santavāco*

[So called] because of the absence of lying, and the like [in one's speech],

### Possessed of peace: *santavā*(25)

[So called] because of the absence of craving, and the like [in one's own thoughts],

### Well composed: *susamāhito*

[So called] because of the three "doors" such as the body, and so forth, being well disciplined,

### Who has thrown out the world's material things: *vanta-lokāmiso*

[So called] because one has "thrown out the worldly things" [i.e., sensual pleasures] by means of the four Paths—

### A bhikkhu . . . is called the "one at peace": *bhikkhu upasanto ti vuccati*

[Such a] bhikkhu is said to be "pacified" because of internal sensual attachment, and so forth, has been calmed. That is the meaning.

379. You yourself reprove yourself,
You yourself set yourself in order.
As a bhikkhu who is self-guarded, aware,
You shall dwell at ease. (25.20)
(The commentary understands the second line to mean,
"You, yourself, examine yourself.")

380. Oneself, indeed is patron of oneself,
Oneself is one's own guide.
Therefore, restrain yourself,
As a merchant, a noble steed. (25.21)

*attanā coday' attānaṃ paṭimāse'ttam attanā*
*so attagutto satimā sukhaṃ bhikkhu vihāhisi.*

*attā hi attano nātho attā hi attano gati*
*tasmā saññamay' attānaṃ assaṃ bhadraṃ va vāṇijo.*

[379.]

You (yourself) reprove yourself: *(attanā) coday' attānaṃ*

You yourself criticize yourself; cause [yourself] to reflect [upon your conduct].

You (yourself) set yourself in order: *patimāse*(26) *('ttam attanā)*

You yourself examine yourself.

Who is self-guarded: *so atta-gutto*

When this is [achieved], you, O bhikkhu, being "self-guarded"—due to being guarded by your [own] self—

Aware: *satimā*

[And] being full of awareness—due to mindfulness [constantly] at hand—

You shall dwell at ease: *sukhaṃ vihāhisi*

You shall dwell at ease in all the modes of deportment. That is the meaning.

[380.]

## Patron: *nātho*

Refuge, support.

## Who else [could be] one's patron: *ko hi nātho paro*

Inasmuch as it is not possible [for one] to depend upon another [lit. another's personality *(attabhava)* ] to do wholesome deeds and become "one who is on the way to heaven," or to develop the Path and become "one who has realized the Fruits [of the Path]"—hence what other [person is there, who] may become [one's] support? That is the meaning.

## Therefore: *tasmā*

Because one is one's own guide [*gati*, lit. course], support, refuge—therefore,

## As a merchant, a noble steed: *assaṃ bhadraṃ va vāṇijo*

You too restrain yourself, guard [yourself], stopping the arising of the unwholesome that has not arisen, and discarding [the unwholesome] that has arisen on account of [any] neglect of mindfulness, just as one who expects [to obtain] a profit from a good *ājānīya*(27) horse controls it, stopping it from going to unsuitable places, and attends on it, bathing it and feeding it three times a day. When this is [achieved], you will come by higher [attainment], worldly and beyond the worldly, beginning with the first meditative-absorption. That is the meaning.

381. A bhikkhu, of abundant joy,
Pleased in the Buddha's instruction,
Would attain the state of peace,
The blissful allayment of the *saṅkhāra*s. (25.22)

*pāmojjabahulo bhikkhu pasanno buddhasāsane*
*adhigacche padaṃ santaṃ saṃkhārūpasamaṃ sukhaṃ.*

## (A bhikkhu) of abundant joy: *pāmojja-bahulo (bhikkhu)*

A bhikkhu who by nature is of abundant joy,

## Pleased in the Buddha's instruction: *pasanno buddhasāsane*

Relishes a sense of satisfaction in the instruction of the Buddha,

### Would attain the state of peace; the blissful allayment of the *saṅkhāras*: *(adhigacche) padaṃ santaṃ saṃkhārūpasamaṃ sukhaṃ*

Would attain to Nibbāna, which is called "the state of peace, the blissful allayment of the *saṃkhāras*,"

382. Truly, a young bhikkhu
Who engages in the Buddha's instruction
This world illumines,
Like the moon set free from a cloud. (25.23)

*yo ha ve daharo bhikkhu yuñjati buddhasāsane*
*so imaṃ lokaṃ pabhāseti abbhā mutto va candimā.*

### Engages in: *yuñjati*

Strives, exerts oneself.

### World illumines: *lokaṃ pabhāseti*

That bhikkhu illumines in entirety this world of *khandhas*, with the gnosis of the Path of Arahantship, as does the moon set free from clouds, and so forth. That is the meaning.

# CHAPTER XXVI

## The *Brāhmaṇa*
## *Brāhmaṇa-vaggo*

383. Having striven, cut off the stream!
Dispel sensualities, O *brāhmaṇa*,
Having known the dissolution of the *saṅkhāras*,
A knower of the Unmade are you, O *brāhmaṇa*. (26.1)

*chinda sotaṃ parakkamma*(1) *kāme panuda brāhmaṇa*
*saṅkhāranaṃ khayaṃ ñatvā akataññū' si brāhmaṇa.*

### Having striven, cut off the stream: *chinda sotaṃ parakkama*

The stream of craving cannot be "cut off" by a simple effort; therefore "cut" that stream off by striving with a mighty effort united with insight.

### Dispel lusts: *kāme panuda*

Drive away both [kinds of] sensualities.[2]

### *Brāhmaṇa*: *brāhmaṇa*

In this context this [word] is a form of addressing "those in whom the intoxicants are extinct" [Arahants].

### Having known the dissolution of the *saṅkhāras*: *saṅkhārānaṃ khayaṃ ñatvā*

Having understood the dissolution of the five *khandhas*—

### A knower of the Unmade are you: *akataññū 'si*

When this is [achieved], by having come to know Nibbāna, which is not "made" of any such thing as gold, and so forth, you are "one who knows the Unmade."

384. When, with regard to two dhammas,
A *brāhmaṇa* has reached the further shore,
Then of that knowing one
All fetters come to an end. (26.2)

*yadā dvayesu dhammesu pāragū hoti brāhmaṇo*
*atha' ssa sabbe saṃyogā atthaṃ gacchanti jānato.*

When, (with regard to two dhammas) a *brāhmaṇa* has reached the further shore: *yadā (dvayesu dhammesu) pāragū hoti brāhmaṇo*

When this one in whom the intoxicants are extinct [i.e., Arahant] has reached the "further shore" in regard to dhammas that are twofold, [i.e.] tranquility- and insight-meditations, by having gone to the furthest point of higher knowledge, and so forth,

Then all fetters of that . . . one: *atha'ssa sabbe saṃyogā*

Then all fetters such as the fetter of lusts, and so forth, which are capable of keeping one yoked to the whirl—

Of that knowing one come to an end: *atthaṃ gacchanti jānato*

All fetters such as the fetter of lusts, and so forth, come to an end for one who understands [the noble truths][3] in this manner. That is the meaning.

385. For whom the farther shore or the nearer shore
Or both does not exist,
Who is free of distress, unyoked,
That one I call a *brāhmaṇa*. (26.3)

*yassa pāraṃ apāraṃ vā pārāpāraṃ na vijjati*
*vitaddaraṃ*(4) *visaṃyuttaṃ tam ahaṃ brūmi brāhmaṇaṃ.*

The farther shore: *pāraṃ*

The six internal *āyatana*s,

The nearer shore: *apāraṃ*

The six external *āyatana*s,

(The farther shore and the nearer shore): *pārāpāraṃ*
Both of these—

For whom . . . does not exist: *yassa . . . (na vijjati)*
For whom all of this does not exist as [objects of] holding [in terms of] "I [am this]" or "[This is] mine",[5]

Free of distress: *vītaddaraṃ*
Who is "free of distress" due to the disappearance of the distress of defilements,

Unyoked: *visaṃyuttaṃ*
Who is unyoked of all defilements,

That one (I call) a *brāhmaṇa: tam ahaṃ brāhmaṇaṃ (brūmi)*
I call a *brāhmaṇa.*

386. The one meditating, free of dirt, quietly sitting,
Tasks done, free of intoxicants,
Who has obtained the goal supreme,
That one I call a *brāhmaṇa.* (26.4)

*jhāyiṃ virajam āsīnaṃ katakiccaṃ anāsavaṃ*
*uttamatthaṃ anuppattaṃ tam ahaṃ brūmi brāhmaṇaṃ.*

The one meditating: *jhāyiṃ*
One who is meditating by the twofold meditative-absorption,[6]

Free of dirt: *virajaṃ*
Free of sensual passion,

Quietly sitting: *āsīnaṃ*
Seated alone in the forest [meditating],

Tasks done: *katakiccaṃ*
Due to having accomplished the sixteen tasks by means of the Four Paths,[7]

Free of intoxicants: *anāsavaṃ*

Due to the absence of the intoxicants [in that person],

Who has attained the goal supreme: *uttamatthaṃ anuppattaṃ*

That is, Arahantship—

That one I call a *brāhmaṇa*: *tam ahaṃ brūmi brāhmaṇaṃ*

That is the meaning.

387. By day glows the sun,
At night shines the moon,
In war-array the monarch glows.
Meditating, a *brāhmaṇa* glows.
But all day and night
The Buddha glows in splendor. (26.5)

*divā tapati ādicco rattiṃ ābhāti candimā*
*sannaddho khattiyo tapati jhāyī tapati brāhmaṇo*
*atha sabbam ahorattiṃ buddho tapati tejasā.*

By day glows (the sun): *divā tapati (ādicco)*

[The sun] shines by day—but at night not even the way by which it has gone is to be seen.

(At night shines) the moon: *(rattiṃ ābhāti) candimā*

The moon, too, freed of clouds, and so forth, shines only at night, not by day.

In war-array (the monarch glows): *sannaddho (khattiyo tapati)*

A king shines [when] decked in all his regalia [lit. ornaments], resplendent with gold and jewels, and surrounded by the fourfold army;[8] [he does] not [shine] [were he to be] in [some] unknown guise.

Meditating (a *brāhmaṇa* glows): *jhāyi (tapati brāhmaṇo)*

[The Arahant], in whom the intoxicants are extinct, shines [when] meditating, having left the crowd.

(But all day and night the Buddha glows) in splendor:
*(atha sabbam ahorattiṃ buddho tapati) tejasā*

But the Fully Enlightened One shines at all times indeed with this fivefold brilliance: [1] with the power of [virtuous] conduct(9) overcoming the power of vice; [2] with the power of goodness overcoming the power of its absence; [3] with the power of [true] insight overcoming the power of [wrong] "insight"; [4] with the power of merit overcoming the power of its absence, and [5] with the power of dhamma overcoming the power of *adhamma*. That is the meaning.

388. As "one who has banished wrong" is one a *brāhmaṇa*;
Because of "living in calm" is one called a *samaṇa*.
Dispelling one's own stain
—Therefore is one called "gone forth." (26.6)

*bāhitapāpo ti brāhmaṇo samacariyā samaṇo ti vuccati*
*pabbājayaṃ attano*(10) *malaṃ tasmā pabbajito ti vuccati.*

Living in calm: *samacariyā*

By living [in virtue], having calmed all unwholesome [states of mind].

Inasmuch as [one is called] a *brāhmaṇa* due to banishing unwholesome deeds, and a recluse due to living [in virtue] having calmed all unwholesome [states of mind], so also one who lives dispelling one's stains of passions, and so forth, is called "[one who has] gone forth" due to that act of dispelling. That is the meaning.(11)

389. A *brāhmaṇa* would not attack a *brāhmaṇa*,
Or let loose [wrath] upon him.
Shame on one who strikes a *brāhmaṇa*,
And greater shame [on one] who lets loose [wrath] upon him.(12) (26.7)

390. When there is exclusion from what is pleasant to the mind;
That is no little good for the *brāhmaṇa*—
Whenever the intent to harm does cease,
Then indeed is sorrow calmed.(13) (26.8)

*na brāhmaṇassa pahareyya nāssa muñcetha brāhmaṇo*
*dhī brāhmaṇassa hantāraṃ tato dhī y'assa muñcati.*

*na brāhmaṇass' etad akiñci seyyo yadā nisedho manaso piyehi*
*yato yato hiṃsamano nivattati tato tato sammati-m-eva dukkhaṃ.*

[389.]

## Would (not) attack: *pahareyya*

He who knows "I am a *brāhmaṇa*"—that is, one whose intoxicants are extinct, would not attack another, be he one in whom the intoxicants are extinct, or [be he] any [*brāhmaṇa*] by birth[14] [only].

## Nor let loose [wrath] upon him: *nāssa muñcetha*

And he, a *brāhmaṇa* with intoxicants extinct, [if] attacked, would not let loose [any] hatred toward him who attacked him, would not show him any anger. That is the meaning.

## Shame: *dhī*

I condemn him who attacks a *brāhmaṇa*—that is, one whose intoxicants are extinct.

## And greater shame: *tato dhī*

But he who, attacking the attacker in retaliation, lets loose hatred toward him, I indeed condemn him even more.

[390.]

## (That is) no little good: *etad akiñci seyyo*

That the *brāhmaṇa* whose intoxicants are extinct does not return abuse to him who abuses and does not return attack to him who attacks is not just "any [slight] nobleness," [it is] not a noble quality of limited measure. It is indeed a greatly noble quality.[15] That is the meaning.

## When there is the exclusion from what is pleasant to the mind: *yadā nisedho manaso piyehi*

What is pleasant to the mind of a person of wrathful nature is the arousal of wrath. He exercises offense[16] even toward parents and Buddhas, and the like, by means of these [wrathful acts]. Hence his[17] holding of mind away from these [thoughts]—the banishing of the thought that arises under the sway of hate—is not just "any [slight] noble thing."(18) That is the meaning.

(Whenever) the attempt to harm (does cease):
*(yato yato) hiṃsamano (nivattati)*

The thought [that is full] of hatred. On whatever grounds his thought [full] of hatred ceases to be—going to extinction through the Path of Non-Returner—

Then indeed is sorrow calmed:
*tato tato (sammati-m-eva dukkhaṃ)*

On those very grounds the entire suffering of the whirl ceases to be. That is the meaning.

391. Of whom there is nothing ill done
With body, with speech, with mind,
Who is restrained in these three bases,
That one I call a *brāhmaṇa.* (26.9)

*yassa kāyena vācāya manasā natthi dukkaṭaṃ*
*saṃvutaṃ tīhi ṭhānehi tam ahaṃ brūmi brāhmaṇaṃ.*

Ill done: *dukkaṭaṃ*

Blameworthy action that gives suffering and leads [one] to the states of woe.

(Restrained) in these three bases: *(saṃvutaṃ) tīhi ṭhānehi*

The "door" [of whose senses] is closed in order to prevent the entry of physical misconduct, and so forth, through the three avenues [of misconduct] such as the body, and so on[19]—

I call a *brāhmaṇa: (tam ahaṃ brūmi brāhmaṇam)*

Such [a person] I call a *brāhmaṇa*. That is the meaning.

392. From whom one would learn dhamma
Taught by the Fully Enlightened One,
Let one pay homage to that one
As a *brāhmaṇa* to the sacrificial fire. (26.10)

*yamhā dhammaṃ vijāneyya sammāsambuddhadesitaṃ*
*sakkaccaṃ taṃ namasseyya aggihuttaṃ va brāhmaṇo.*

## The sacrificial fire: *aggihuttaṃ*

Just as a *brāhmaṇa* will pay homage to the sacrificial fire respectfully with proper attendance and with offerings, and so forth, so let one pay homage to that teacher from whom one could learn dhamma proclaimed by the Tathāgata.

393. Not by matted hair, or by clan,
Or by birth does one become a *brāhmaṇa*.
In whom is truth and dhamma,
He is the pure one, and he is the *brāhmaṇa*. (26.11)

*na jaṭāhi na gottena na jaccā hoti brāhmaṇo*
*yamhi saccaṃ ca dhammo ca so sucī*(20) *so ca brāhmaṇo.*

## Truth: *saccaṃ*

That person in whom there is the knowledge of truth obtained by understanding the four [noble] truths in the sixteen ways,[21] and the ninefold dhamma that transcends the world, he is both the pure one and the *brāhmaṇa*. That is the meaning.

394. What's the use of your matted hair, O you of poor insight?
What's the use of your deerskin garment?
Within you is the jungle;
The exterior you groom. (26.12)

*kiṃ te jaṭāhi dummedha kiṃ te ajinasāṭiyā*
*abbhantaraṃ te gahanaṃ bāhiraṃ parimajjasi.*

## What's the use of your (matted hair): *kiṃ te (jaṭāhi)*

O you of poor insight, what is the use of this matted hair and this cloth of *ajina* deerskin with [the deer's] hooves, worn [by you]?

## Within: *abbhantaraṃ*

For your inside is a forest of defilements, and so forth. You merely polish your exterior, smooth like the dung of elephants and horses [which from the outside does not appear ugly to an onlooker].

395. One who wears rags from a dust heap,
Lean, having veins [visibly] spread over body,
Meditating alone in the forest,
That one I call a *brāhmaṇa*. (26.13)

*paṃsukuladharaṃ jantuṃ kisaṃ dhamanisanthataṃ*
*ekaṃ vanasmiṃ jhāyantaṃ tam ahaṃ brūmi brāhmaṇaṃ.*

## Lean: *kisaṃ*

[Bhikkhus] wearing the rag robe are thin and lean [lit. of little flesh and blood] and on their bodies the veins spread out [visibly, for they are] following a [rigorous] practice that befits them. Hence [the text] says thus.

## (Meditating) alone in the forest: *ekam vanasmiṃ (jhāyantaṃ)*

[Such an austere bhikkhu] who is meditating by himself in a solitary place I call a *brāhmaṇa*. That is the meaning.

396. And I do not call one a *brāhmaṇa*
Merely by being born from a [*brāhmaṇa*] womb,
Sprung from a [*brāhmaṇa*] mother.
He is merely a "*bho*-sayer"
If he is a possessor of things.
One who has nothing and takes nothing,
That one I call a *brāhmaṇa*. (26.14)

*na cāhaṃ brāhmaṇaṃ brūmi yonijaṃ mattisambhavaṃ*(22)
*bhovādi nāma so hoti sa ce*(23) *hoti sakiñcano*
*akiñcanaṃ anādānaṃ tam ahaṃ brūmi brāhmaṇaṃ.*

## From a womb: *yonijaṃ*

One who is born of the womb,

### Sprung from a mother: *mattisambhavaṃ*

Who has sprung up in the womb of a *brāhmaṇa* mother,

### A "bho-sayer": *bhovādi*

Who goes about saying "*bho, bho*" when addressing [others] is called "one who says *bho*" [i.e., one who merely knows proper etiquette in greeting others].

### Who has nothing (and takes nothing, that one I call a *brāhmaṇa*): *akiñcanaṃ (anādānaṃ tam ahaṃ brūmi brāhmaṇaṃ)*

[But] I call one a *brāhmaṇa* who is not a possessor of anything—that is, of things such as passions, and so forth; one who "does not take" anything by the four forms of grasping.[24] That is the meaning.

397. Who does not tremble,
Having cut off every fetter,
Who has gone beyond attachments, unbound,
That one I call a *brāhmaṇa*. (26.15)

*sabbasaṃyojanaṃ chetvā yo ve na paritassati*
*saṅgātigaṃ visaṃyuttaṃ tam ahaṃ brūmi brāhmaṇaṃ.*

### Every fetter: *sabba-saṃyojanaṃ*

The tenfold fetter.[25]

### Does not tremble: *na paritassati*

[One who] does not become frightened due to craving,

### Who has gone beyond attachments: *saṅgātigaṃ*

Who has transcended attachments due to having gone beyond the passions, and so forth,[26]

### Unbound: *visaṃyuttaṃ*

Who is free from the fetters, due to [one's] not having any of the four bonds,[27] I call a *brāhmaṇa*. That is the meaning.

398. Having cut off the strap and thong,
Cord, together with the bridle,
Who has lifted the bar, awakened,
That one I call a *brāhmaṇa*. (26.16)

*chetvā nandhiṃ varattaṃ ca sandānaṃ*(28) *sahanukkamaṃ*(29)
*ukkhittapaḷighaṃ buddhaṃ tam ahaṃ brūmi brāhmaṇaṃ.*

Strap: *nandhiṃ*

Hate, which has the function of tying,

Thong: *varattaṃ*

Craving, which has the function of binding,

Cord, together with the bridle: *sandānaṃ sahanukkamaṃ*

The sixty-two [wrong] views[30] together with the bridle—namely, the latent propensities[31]—

Who has lifted the bar: *ukkhitta-paḷighaṃ*

Who has cut off all this, who, due to having removed the bar of ignorance, is called "one whose bar is lifted,"

Awakened: *buddhaṃ*

Who is awakened on account of having realized the four truths, that one I call a *brāhmaṇa*. That is the meaning.

399. Who unangered endures
Insult, assault, and binding,
Whose strength is forebearance, who has an army's strength,
That one I call a *brāhmaṇa*. (26.17)

*akkosaṃ vadhabandhaṃ ca aduṭṭho yo titikkhati*
*khantībalaṃ balāṇīkaṃ tam ahaṃ brūmi brāhmaṇaṃ.*

Assault: *adduṭṭho*

One who bears up, with mind that is unangered, [the] abuse [heaped on one] through the ten ways of abusing,[32] and assault with hands, and so forth, and [even] binding with fetters, and the like,(33)

### Whose strength is forebearance: *khantībalaṃ*

Who is strong in forebearance, due to [one's ] being endowed with the strength that is forebearance,

### Who has an army's strength: *balānīkaṃ*

Who has an army's strength, due to being endowed with the strength of forebearance that has become [one's] "army"(34) because of its springing up [in one] again and again, one [who is such] I call a *brāhmaṇa*. That is the meaning.

400. Who is free of anger, who observes the duties,
Who is virtuous, free of the flow [of craving],
Controlled, and in the final body,
That one I call a *brāhmaṇa*. (26.18)

*akkodhanaṃ vatavantaṃ sīlavantaṃ anussutaṃ*
*dantaṃ antimasārīraṃ tam ahaṃ brūmi brāhmaṇaṃ.*

### Who observes the duties: *vatavantaṃ*

Who follows [lit. is endowed with] the practice of *dhutaṅga*,[35]

### Virtuous: *sīlavantaṃ*

Who is virtuous with the fourfold virtue of purity,[36]

### Free of the flow [of craving]: *anussutaṃ*

Who is [described as] without " upflow" due to the absence [in one] of the "upflow" of craving,

### Controlled: *dantaṃ*

Who is controlled by restraint of the six senses,

### In the final body: *antima-sārīraṃ*

Who is "in the final body" because the present life is at the termination of *saṃsāra*, that one [who is such] I call a *brāhmaṇa*. That is the meaning.

401. Like water on a lotus petal,
Like a mustard seed on the point of an awl,

Who is not smeared with sensualities,
That one I call a *brāhmaṇa*. (26.19)

*vāripokkharapatte va āragge-r-iva sāsapo*
*yo na lippati kāmesu tam ahaṃ brūmi brāhmaṇaṃ.*

### Who is not smeared (with sensualities): *yo na lippati* (*kāmesu*)

In the same way one who is not "smeared" within by both kinds of sensualities,[37] and in whom[(38)] passion does not abide, I call that one [who is such] a *brāhmaṇa*.

402. Who comes to understand, even here,
The destruction of sorrow,
Who has put aside the burden, who is free of the bonds,
That one I call a *brāhmaṇa*. (26.20)

*yo dukkhassa pajānāti idh' eva khayaṃ attano*
*pannabhāraṃ visaṃyuttaṃ tam ahaṃ brūmi brāhmaṇaṃ.*

### Of sorrow: *dukkhassa*

Of the suffering that is the *khandha*s.

### Who has put aside the burden: *pannabhāraṃ*

Who has laid down the burden of the *khandha*s [that constitute suffering],

### Who is free of the bonds: *visaṃyuttaṃ*

Who is released from the four bonds,[39] or from all defilements, that one [who is such] I call a *brāhmaṇa*. That is the meaning.

403. One having profound insight, wise,
Proficient as to path and nonpath,
Who has attained the highest goal,
That one I call a *brāhmaṇa*. (26.21)

*gambhīrapaññaṃ medhāviṃ maggāmaggassa kovidaṃ*
*uttamatthaṃ anuppattaṃ tam ahaṃ brūmi brahmaṇaṃ.*

## One having profound insight: *gambhīrapaññaṃ*

Who is endowed with insight-wisdom that is effective in regard to profound [matters such as the] *khandha*s, and so forth,

## Wise: *medhāviṃ*

Wise due to [possession of] insight-wisdom that is the sap of dhamma,

## Proficient as to path and nonpath: *maggāmaggassa kovidaṃ*

Due to competence in regard to the path and what is not the path, knowing, "This is the path to the state of woe, [this] to the state of weal, [this] to Nibbāna, and this is not the path [to them],"

## Who has attained the highest goal: *uttamatthaṃ anuppattaṃ*

Who has reached the noble goal that is Arahantship, that one [who is such] I call a *brāhmaṇa*. That is the meaning.

404. One who is not gregarious
With both householders and homeless ones,
Living without an abode, desiring but little,
That one I call a *brāhmaṇa*. (26.22)

*asaṃsaṭṭhaṃ gahaṭṭehi anāgār.ehi cūbhayaṃ*
*anokasārim appicchaṃ tam ahaṃ brūmi brāhmaṇaṃ.*

## One who is not gregarious with both: *asaṃsaṭṭhaṃ . . . ubhayaṃ*

Not contaminated by lay persons or by homeless ones: that is the meaning. Getting about without attachments due to not having [the five kinds of contact, namely] seeing, hearing, conversation, enjoying(40) [improper] and [sensual] physical contact.

## Living without an abode: *anokasāriṃ*

Who is not leading a life of attachment [i.e., the household life, that one [who is such] I call a *brahmaṇa*. That is the meaning.

405. Having laid down the rod
With regard to beings, the frightful and the firm,

Who neither slays nor causes to slay—
That one I call a *brāhmaṇa*. (26.23)

*nidhāya daṇḍaṃ bhūtesu tasesu thāvaresu ca*
*yo na hanti na ghāteti tam ahaṃ brūmi brāhmaṇaṃ.*

### Having laid down: *nidhāya*

Having laid down, having lowered [weapons of offense],

### The frightful: *tasesu*

In regard to " those in fright" with the fright of craving,

### The firm: *thāvaresu*

[And] in regard to "the firm ones," [who are firm] due to the absence of craving,

### Who neither slays: *yo na hanti*

Who in this way is one who has laid down arms in regard to all beings, by virtue of hate having left [one], and who never kills any [living] thing(40) oneself or gets others to kill, that one I call a *brāhmaṇa*. That is the meaning.

406. One who is not opposing among those opposing,
Who is calmed among those who have taken weapons,
Free of grasping among those who are grasping
That one I call a *brāhmaṇa*. (26.24)

*aviruddhaṃ viruddhesu attadaṇḍesu nibbutaṃ*
*sādānesu anādānaṃ tam ahaṃ brumi brāhmaṇaṃ.*

### One who is not opposing: *aviruddhaṃ*

One who is not opposing, due to not harboring enmity toward the populace even when they are opposed [to one] because of enmity [in them],

### Who is calmed among those who have taken weapons: *attadaṇḍesu nibbutaṃ*

Who is calmed, who has "laid down the rod," toward those "who have taken weapons" because of their not desisting from striking others with sticks or weapons that come to [their] hands,(42)

## Who is free of grasping among those who are grasping: *sādānesu anādānaṃ*

Who is "free of grasping," because of being free of such grasping among people "who have grasping"—because of taking the five *khandhas* in terms of "I" and "mine"(43)—who is "free of grasping," because of being free of such grasping—that one [who is such] I call a *brāhmaṇa*. That is the meaning.

407. From whom passion and ill will,
Conceit and ingratitude, have been shed,
Like a mustard seed from the tip of an awl,
That one I call a *brāhmaṇa*. (26.25)

*yassa rāgo ca doso ca māno makkho ca pātito*
*sāsapo-r-iva āraggā tam ahaṃ brūmi brāhmaṇaṃ.*

From whom these [qualities] like passion, and so forth, and this [quality of] ingratitude, which has the characteristic of "erasing" the goodness of others, have been shed, like a mustard seed from the tip of an awl—[indeed such qualities] do not remain in [one's] mind, just as a mustard seed does not remain atop the tip of a needle—that one [who is such] I call a *brāhmaṇa*. That is the meaning.

408. Who would speak speech that is true,
That is instructive and not harsh,
By which one would anger none—
That one I call a *brāhmaṇa*. (26.26)

*akakkasaṃ viññāpaniṃ giraṃ saccaṃ udīraye*
*yāya nābhisaje*(44) *kaṃci tam ahaṃ brūmi brāhmaṇaṃ.*

## Not harsh: *akakkasaṃ*

Not rough,

## Instructive: *viññāpaniṃ*

Causing [others] to understand the wholesome,

### True: *saccaṃ*

Conforming to reality.

### By which one would anger none: *yāya nābhisaje*

By which speech one would not cause another to "get stuck" [i.e.] by causing [that other] to be angry[45]—one in whom the intoxicants are extinct would speak only this kind of speech—hence, I call that one a *brāhmaṇa*. That is the meaning.

409. Who, here in this world, does not take what is not given,
Whether long or short, small or great,
Pleasant or unpleasant,
That one I call a *brāhmaṇa*. (26.27)

*yo'dha dīghaṃ va rassaṃ vā aṇuṃ thūlaṃ subhāsubhaṃ*
*loke adinnaṃ nādiyati tam ahaṃ brūmi brāhmaṇaṃ.*

The person who in this world does not take the possessions of another—clothing, ornaments, and so forth, be it [something] long or short; pearls, jewels, and so forth, be it small or large; [things] of little or high value, pleasant or otherwise—that one I call a *brāhmaṇa*. That is the meaning.

410. In whom are not found longings
For this world and for the beyond,
Without longing, released,
That one I call a *brāhmaṇa*. (26.28)

*āsā yassa na vijjanti asmiṃ loke paramhi ca*
*nirāsayaṃ visaṃyuttaṃ tam ahaṃ brūmi brāhmaṇaṃ.*

### Longings: *āsā*

Craving.

### Without longing: *nirāsaṃ*

One who is free of craving,

## Released: *visaṃyuttaṃ*

Who is released from all defilements, that one I call a *brāhmaṇa*. That is the meaning.

411. In whom are not found attachments,
Who is without doubts due to understanding,
Who has attained the plunge into the Deathless,
That one I call a *brāhmaṇa*. (26.29)

*yassālayā na vijjanti aññāya akathaṃkathī*
*amatogadhaṃ anuppattaṃ tam ahaṃ brūmi brāhmaṇaṃ.*

## Attachments: *ālayā*

Craving.

## Who is without doubts: *akathaṅkathī*

Who, having understood the eight matters,[46] exactly as they are, is free from the eightfold skeptical doubt.

## Who has attained the plunge into the deathless: *amatogadhaṃ anuppattaṃ*

[Who] has reached the deathless Nibbāna, having plunged [into it]— that one I call a *brāhmaṇa*. That is the meaning.

412. Who, here, has moved beyond attachment,
Both the meritorious and the detrimental,
Who is free of sorrow, free of dust, pure,
That one I call a *brāhmaṇa*. (26.30)

*yo'dha puññaṃ ca pāpaṃ ca ubho saṅgaṃ upaccagā*
*asokaṃ virajaṃ suddhaṃ tam ahaṃ brūmi brāhmaṇaṃ.*

## Both: *ubho*

Having discarded the two—the wholesome and the detrimental [states of mind].[47] That is the meaning.

Who . . . has moved beyond: *upaccagā*
Has transcended,

Attachment: *saṅgaṃ*
Attachment in its [various] categories such as [sensual] passion,[48]

Free of sorrow: *asokam*
Free of sorrow that is the root of the whirl,

Free of dust: *virajaṃ*
Free of dirt due to the absence within of the dust of passions, and so forth,

Pure: *suddhaṃ*
Pure, due to the absence of [moral] impurities—that one I call a *brāhmaṇa*.

413. Who, like the moon, is spotless, pure,
Serene, unagitated,
In whom is extinct the desire for existence,
That one I call a *brāhmaṇa*. (26.31)

*candaṃ va vimalaṃ suddhaṃ vippasannaṃ anāvilaṃ*
*nandībhavaparikkhīṇaṃ tam ahaṃ brūmi brāhmaṇaṃ.*

Spotless: *vimalaṃ*
Not having "stains" such as clouds, and the like,

Pure: *suddhaṃ*
Free of [moral] impurities,

Serene: *vippasannaṃ*
Of mind serene,

Unagitated: *anāvilaṃ*
Free of defilements; in whom there is not the agitation of defilements,[(49)]

In whom is extinct the desire for existence: *nandī-bhava-parikkhīṇaṃ*
In whom the craving for the three types of existence is extinct[50]—that one I call a *brāhmaṇa*. That is the meaning.

414. Who has passed over this [muddy] path,(51) this fortress,
Delusion, which is *saṃsāra*,
Who has crossed over it, gone beyond it, a meditator,
Passionless, without doubts,
Without grasping, pacified,
That one I call a *brāhmaṇa*. (26.32)

*yo imaṃ paḷipathaṃ duggaṃ saṃsāraṃ moham accagā*
*tiṇṇo pāragato jhāyī anejo akathaṃkathī*
*anupādāya nibbuto tam ahaṃ brūmi brāhmaṇaṃ.*

The bhikkhu who has gone past this [muddy] *path (paḷipathaṃ)* of passions, and so forth, as well as the "*fortress*" *(duggaṃ)* of defilements, and the whirl of *saṃsāra*, and the delusion *(mohaṃ)* of not having realized the four truths, who, having crossed over the four "floods," has reached the "farther shore" *(paraṃ)*, who is a meditator *(jhayī)* by the twofold meditation,[52] who is *passionless (anejo)* owing to absence of craving, who is *without doubts (akathaṅkathī)* due to absence of skeptical doubt, who, not grasping, due to the absence of "clinging," is *pacified (nibbuto)* by the calming of defilements—him I call a *brāhmaṇa*. That is the meaning.

415. Who, here, having renounced lusts,
Would go forth, a homeless one,
In whom is extinct sensual lust and existence,
That one I call a *brāhmaṇa*. (26.33)

*yo'dha kāme pahatvāna anāgāro paribbaje*
*kāmābhavaparikkhīṇaṃ tam ahaṃ brūmi brāhmaṇaṃ.*

The person who in this world goes forth, discarding both [kinds of] lust,[53] and becoming *homeless (anāgāro)*,[54] that one in whom [both] sensual lust and the lust for existence are extinct[55]—I call a *brāhmaṇa*. That is the meaning.

416. Who, here, having renounced craving,
Would go forth, a homeless one,
In whom is extinct craving and existence,
That one I call a *brāhmaṇa*. (26.34)

*yo'dha taṇhaṃ pahatvāna anāgāro paribbaje*
*taṇhābhavaparikkhīṇaṃ tam ahaṃ brūmi brāhmaṇaṃ.*

Who in this world has discarded craving with its six doors, who "goes forth," seeing no worth in the household life and becoming *homeless (anāgāro),*

## In whom is extinct craving and existence: *taṇhābhavaparikkhīṇaṃ*

Due to both craving and [the desire for] existence being extinct—that one I call a *brāhmaṇa.* That is the meaning.

417. Who, having abandoned the human bond,
Has transcended the heavenly bond,
Who is released from all bonds,
That one I call a *brāhmaṇa.* (26.35)

*hitvā mānusakaṃ yogaṃ dibbaṃ yogaṃ upaccagā*
*sabbayogavisaṃyuttaṃ tam ahaṃ brūmi brāhmaṇaṃ.*

## The human bond: *mānusakaṃ yogaṃ*

The human life span(56) and the five strands of sensuality.[57]

## (Heavenly bond): *(dibbaṃ yogaṃ)*

The same mode [of explanation applies] in regard to the word "heavenly bond."

## Who . . . has transcended: *upaccagā*

Who has discarded the human bond and transcended the heavenly bond,

## Released from all bonds: *sabba-yoga-visaṃyuttaṃ*

Who is released from all four [kinds of] bonds.[58]—[such a one] I call a *brāhmaṇa.*

418. Who, having abandoned attachment and aversion,
Who has become cool, free from substrates,

A hero overcoming the entire world—
That one I call a *brahmaṇa.* (26.36)

*hitvā ratiṃ ca aratiṃ ca sītibhūtaṃ nirupadhiṃ*
*sabbalokābhibhuṃ vīraṃ tam ahaṃ brūmi brāhmaṇaṃ.*

## Attachment: *ratiṃ*

The attachment to the five strands of sensuality.

## Aversion: *aratiṃ*

The dissatisfaction with living in the forest.

## Who has become cool: *sītibhūtaṃ*

Pacified.

## Free from substrates: *nirūpadhiṃ*

Free of moral impurities.

## A hero: *vīraṃ*

Such a heroic person who has conquered the entire world of *khandha*s, I call a *brāhmaṇa.* That is the meaning.

419. Who knows in every way
The passing away and rebirth of beings,
Unattached, well gone, awakened,
That one I call a *brāhmaṇa.* (26.37)

420. Whose course
Gods, *gandhabbas*, and humans do not know,
Whose intoxicants are extinct, an Arahant,
That one I call a *brāhmaṇa.* (26.38)

*cutiṃ yo vedi sattānaṃ upapattiṃ ca sabbaso*
*asattam sugataṃ buddaṃ tam ahaṃ brūmi brāhmaṇaṃ.*

*yassa gatiṃ na jānanti devā gandhabbamānusā*
*khīṇāsavaṃ arahantaṃ tam ahaṃ brūmi brāhmaṇaṃ.*

[419.]

Who knows (in every way) the passing away (and rebirth of beings): *cutiṃ yo vedi (sattānaṃ uppatiṃ ca sabbaso)*
Who knows in every way, with clarity, the passing away and rebirth of beings,[59] that one,

Unattached: *asattaṃ*
Due to not being stuck,

Well gone: *sugataṃ*
Because of having fared forth well,

Awakened: *buddhaṃ*
Due to understanding the four truths, I call a *brāhmaṇa*. That is the meaning.

[420.]

Whose (course gods . . . do not know): *yassa (gatiṃ na jānanti)*
Whose course these gods, and the like, do not know,

Whose intoxicants are extinct: *khīṇāsavaṃ*
Due to extinction of defilements,

An Arahant: *arahantaṃ*
Due to being far away from defilements,[(60)] I call a *brāhmaṇa*. That is the meaning.

421. For whom there is nothing
In front, behind, and in between,
The one, without anything, ungrasping,
That one I call a *brāhmaṇa*. (26.39)

*yassa pure ca pacchā ca majjhe ca natthi kiñcanaṃ*
*akiñcanaṃ anādānaṃ tam ahaṃ brūmi brāhmaṇaṃ.*

For whom there is nothing: *yassa . . . natthi kiñcanaṃ*
In whom the thing called "grasping through craving" does not exist in regard to three aspects,

In front: *pure*

In regard to *khandha*s past;

Behind: *pacchā*

In regard to *khandha*s of the future;

In between: *majjhe*

In regard to *khandha*s of the present,

Without anything: *akiñcanaṃ*

That one who has nothing whatever such as "the thing [called] passion," and so forth,

Ungrasping: *anādānaṃ*

Due to absence of any "seizing"—I call a *brāhmaṇa*. That is the meaning.

422. A bull, splendid, heroic,
A great sage, a victor,
Passionless, who has bathed, awakened,
That one I call a *brāhmaṇa*. (26.40)

*usabhaṃ pavaraṃ vīraṃ mahesiṃ vijitāvinaṃ*
*anejaṃ nahātakaṃ buddhaṃ tam ahaṃ brūmi brāhmaṇaṃ.*

A bull: *usabhaṃ*

One having strength [lit. a bull], due to comparability with a bull on account of not being perturbed,

Splendid: *pavaraṃ*

In the sense of being noble,

Heroic: *vīraṃ*

Due to being endowed with enterprise,

A great sage: *mahesiṃ*

Because of having quested(61) for the "mass" of virtues, and so forth,

A victor: *vijitavinaṃ*
Due to having overpowered the three Māras,

Who has bathed: *nahātakaṃ*
Because of having washed away the defilements,

Awakened: *buddhaṃ*
Because of having understood the four truths—a person such as that I call a *brāhmaṇa*. That is the meaning.

423. One who knows [one's] former lives,
And sees the heavens and the states of woe,
And who has reached the extinction of births,
Who has perfected higher knowledge,
Sage, who has fulfilled the final perfection,
That one I call a *brāhmaṇa*. (26.41)

*pubbenivāsaṃ yo vedi saggāpāyaṃ ca passati*
*atho jātikkhayaṃ patto abhiññāvosito muni*
*sabbavositavosānaṃ tam ahaṃ brūmi brāhmaṇaṃ.*

One who knows [one's] former lives: *pubbenivāsaṃ yo vedi*
One who clearly knows [one's] previous lives,

And sees the heavens and the states of woe: *saggāpāyaṃ ca passati*
Who sees with "the divine eye" the heavens such as the twenty-six *deva* worlds, and so forth,[62] as well as the fourfold states of woe,

Who has reached the extinction of births: *atho jātikkhayaṃ patto*
Who has reached Arahantship, which is called the extinction of [the process of] birth,

Who has perfected higher knowledge: *abhiññā-vosito*
Who having deeply understood dhamma that is to be deeply understood, having fully understood what is to be fully understood, having discarded

what is to be discarded, having realized what is to be realized—and [having accomplished all this]—has arrived at the "final end" or has reached the state of having fulfilled final perfection,[63]

## Sage: *muni*

Who is a silent sage due to having reached the state of silence by insight of the extinction of intoxicants,

## Who has fulfilled the final perfection: *sabba-vosita-vosānaṃ*

Who has fulfilled the final perfection by having lived the religious life, which is the gnosis of the Path of Arahantship and the ending of all defilements—such a one I call a *brāhmaṇa*. That is the meaning.

# NOTES

## Abbreviations

A *Aṅguttara-nikāya* (PTS edition).

APB *Dhammapadaṭṭhakathā,* edited by Ambalangoda P. Buddhadatta Thera.

BL *Buddhist Legends: Translated from the original Pali text of the Dhammapada Commentary,* by Eugene Watson Burlingame.

Cl. Skt. Classical Sanskrit

D *Dīgha-nikāya* (PTS edition).

*Dad Dharmmārtthadīpanī nam vū dharmapadārttha vyākhyāva,* by Ratgama Śrī Prañājśekhara.

Dag *Dhampiyā-aṭuvā-gāṭapadaya,* edited by Professor D. E. Hettiaratchi.

*Dp Dharmapada pradīpaya,* by V. Dharmakīrti Śrī Śrīnivāsa.

*Dhp The Dhamma (-Dharma)pada.* Unless otherwise noted, reference is to the Pali text of the *Dhamapada* and to the PTS edition.

*DhpA Dhammapadaṭṭhakathā*—the commentary on the *Dhammapada.* Several editions have been consulted. Unless otherwise noted, reference is to the PTS edition.

*Dps Dhammapada pūrāna sannaya (granthipada vivaraṇa sahita).* "The Old Commentary of the *Dhammapada* (with Glossary)," edited by Kamburupiṭiyē Dhammaratana Sthavira.

*Dv Dhammapada vivaraṇaya,* by Morogallē Siri Ñānobhāsatissa.

*Gdhp The Gāndhārī Dharmapada, Edited with an Introduction and Commentary,* by John Brough. The *Gāndhārī Dharmapada* text is found in this work on pp. 119–75.

*GdhpC The Commentary on the Gāndhārī Dharmapada* by John Brough in *The Gāndhārī Dharmapada, Edited with an Introduction and Commentary* by John Brough. The Commentary *(GdhpC.)* is found in this work on pp. 177–282.

*Jā The Jātaka: Together with Its Commentary* (PTS edition).

M *Majjhima-nikāya* (PTS edition).

*PDhp* "Text of the Patna Dharmapada," edited by Gustav Roth, *Die Sprache der ältesten buddhistischen Überlieferung: The Language of the Earliest Buddhist Tradition,* herausgegeben von Heinz Bechert, pp. 97–135.

*PDhpN* Gustav Roth, "Supplement: 1. Notes on the Patna Dharmapada", *Die Sprache der ältesten buddhistischen Überlieferung: The Language of the*

*Earliest Buddhist Tradition,* herausgegeben von Heinz Bechert, pp. 93–97.
PTS The Pali Text Society
PTSD *The Pali Text Society's Pali-English Dictionary.*
*SdhRv Saddharma Ratnāvaliya,* edited by Sir D. B. Jayatilaka.
*Sdk Saddharmakaumudī nam bhāvārtthavivaraṇasahita dhammapadapāḷiya* ("The *Dhammapada* with a Sinhalese Translation, Commentary, and Annotation Entitled Saddharmakaumudī"), by Morontuduvē Śrī Ñāneśvara Dharmananda.
Sds Ambalangoda Dhammakusala, *Saddharmasāgara nam vū dharmapadavarṇanā.*
SHB *Dhammapadaṭṭha-kathā,* edited by Kahavē Siri Ratanasāra Thera, Parts I-II (Simon Hewavitarne Bequest).
Skt Sanskrit
*Sn Sutta-nipāta* (PTS edition).
*Ssd Sanna sahita dhammapada,* edited by Heyiyantuduvē Śrī Dharmakīrti Devamitrā.
St Stanza
"Thai edition" The Thai edition of the *Dhammapadaṭṭhakathā,* edited by *Vajirañāṇa Mahāsamaṇa Ādo Sodhitā.*
*Uv Udānavarga,* herausgegeben von Franz Bernhard.
*Vin The Vinaya Piṭakaṃ* (PTS edition).
*Vl* Variant reading
V.,vv Verse, Verses

## Introduction

Notes following an asterisked note number have to do with technical problems in the Pali text of *Dhammapada* stanzas or commentary.

1. On the basis of the commentary on *Dhammapada,* st. 1–2, neither Buddhagosa nor Dhammapala can be regarded as the author of the existing commentary. See also M. Palihawadana, "Dhammapada 1 and 2 and their Commentaries." in *Buddhist Studies in Honour of Hamalava Saddhatissa* (Nugegoda, Sri Lanka, 1984), pp. 189–202.
2. See, for example, our textual notes on *Dhp.*, st. 34, 41, 43, 44, 52, 70, 83, 135, 141, 154, 162, 168, 179, 207, 371.
3. An inadequate appreciation of this genre can lead to misunderstanding. See M. Palihawadana, "Dhammapada And Commentary And Brough's Comments On Them," *Vidyodaya Journal of Arts, Science and Letters,* Silver Jubilee Volume (February 1984), pp. 260–71.
4. In the commentary, words of the original text are not usually explained as in a lexicon. Often they are woven into a long sentence in

which a given word may be explained by synonyms standing in apposition to it, by analysis into component units if it is a compound, by effecting a pause in the sentence and embarking on a long disquisition meant to clarify the meaning of the word. Or in such an explicatory sentence, a given word may not be commented upon at all, but be quoted just for the sake of weaving the other commented words into the sentence. The comment on stanza 371 of the *Dhammapada* is an example of this kind of comment. On the other hand, in st. 193, the whole of line 3 serves as a "headline," but only its last word, *dhīro,* is commented upon; and the whole of line 4 serves as the headline, but only the last two words, *sukham edhati,* are commented upon. The reason for the inclusion of the uncommented words in the headlines was to unify the two comments in a single sentence.

This procedure, however, is not always followed. A case in point is st. 58. The four comments on this stanza are syntactically unrelated to one another.

Sometimes a sentence unifying the several words commented upon is not found, but the idea they express in combination is wrapped up in a concluding sentence. Stanza 185 provides an example of such a procedure. A peculiar difficulty in translating an isolated comment of this kind is that in the Pali commentary each word is explained by an expression that fits the syntactical function of the original word. The comment on the locative form *ayoge* in st. 209 is an example of this. In order to make the translation of this commment intelligible we had to expand the headline by adding the word *yuñjaṃ* within parentheses.

Sometimes a comment takes the form of a discussion of problems or implications of the headline. The comments on *have* and *jitaṃ* in st. 104 are examples. These comments are really untranslatable as they are. In order to get over the difficulty we had to combine the two comments into one and use the entire first line as the headline. This has been indicated by putting all words of the line except *have* and *jitaṃ* within parentheses.

Sometimes the commentator uses the headline merely to introduce the comments. Such cases are *akkodhenā, asādhuṃ, kadariyaṃ* and *alikavādi* of st. 223. Under each of these terms, the commentator gives a paraphrase of the line that contains the term. To give an intelligible English version of the commentary we had to use the entire line as the headline, indicating the liberty exercised by appropriate use of parentheses.

Sometimes the commentary quotes, without any comment, a part of the verse or the final line, simply for the purpose of "rounding off' the comments that preceded. Thus in the series of stanzas 188–192, the commentator wraps up the entire comment by quoting the first line of st. 192: *etaṃ kho saraṇaṃ*: "this, indeed, is a refuge secure." The use of *tam ahaṃ brūmi brāhamaṇaṃ* at the end of the comments on stanzas 400ff. is another example of this procedure.

In some instances, the translation of the commentary read more smoothly, the sequence of comments was altered. An example of this is st. 205, where the comment on *upasamassa* follows that on *pītvā* in the original, whereas in the translation it appears before it.

5. Compare the discussion on history as process by Wilfred Cantwell Smith, *Towards A World Theology: Faith and the Comparative History of Religion* (Philadelphia: Westminster, 1981), pp. 154–57.

## Prologue

1. " 'To the state of blessed Dhamma come,' *(sampatta-saddhammapada)* means 'attained the support of saddhamma.' 'The support of saddhamma' is *saddhammapada*. He who is come *(sampatta-)* to the saddhamma is *sampatta-saddhammapada* [i.e., this is how the Pali compound is to be analyzed]. The ninefold world-transcending dhamma is called *saddhammapada* because it is the support that prevents beings from falling into states of woe and into *saṃsāra*. Because he has attained that, the Teacher is said to have attained the support of saddhamma.

"Or else, *saddhamma* is teaching. The knowledge of the teaching and knowledge of omniscience that is the source *(karuṇu)* of that [*saddhamma*] is called *pada;* [as it is said,] 'One is the Teacher in the sense that one instructs and advises people who are to be trained by [any one of] the three vehicles [i.e., Buddhas, Paccekabuddhas, and Arahants].' "

"*Dhammapada* [is in classical Sinhala] *Dampiyā*. The word 'dhamma' means the literary corpus of canonical teaching *(pāḷi)* in such passages as, 'Now, O monks, one masters dhamma [comprised of] discourses, sections of mixed prose and verse, etc.' The word '*pada*' means support *(pihiṭa)* in such places as 'support of peace' *(santipadaṃ)*. It could even mean 'portion' *(koṭas)* in such places as 'thus for him are recited portions of dhamma' *(dhammapadā)*. [The compound] *dhammapada* means [in the canonical language (Pali)] that which is dhamma and at the same time *pada*; [or in Sinhala] dhamma *(dham)* and at the same time the canonical text *(peḷa)*, dhamma and at the same time support *(pihiṭa);* dhamma and at the same time portion *(koṭas)*.

"In the sense that it [dhamma that is *pada*] does not allow the one who has accepted it to fall into a state of woe and into *saṃsāra*, it has the meaning 'support.' In the sense of components in the canonical teaching *(peḷadhamhi)* it [*pāda*] has the meaning 'portion.'

"Even though [for example] the color of red is in other flowers also, when *ratmal* ['red flower'] is mentioned [in Sinhala] only one particular flower is understood, so even though the term [*dhamma-pada*] is applicable in all these meanings, here the four hundred and twenty-two [*sic*] verses that were taught in relation to three hundred stories is alone meant by the term *dhammapada*" (*Dag.*, 3.25–4.12).

## Chapter I

1.* *GDhp.*, 201, has *maṇo-java,* and *Uv.*, xxxi, 23, has *manojavāḥ*. (*PDhp.* has *manojavā* in st. 1, but *manodbhavā* in st. 2.) "This reading obviously reflects the *kṣaṇika* nature of the dharmas, while the Pali *manomayā* seems almost to imply a Vijñanavāda view" (*GDhpC.*, p. 243). The Pali commentary naturally does not see any such implication. Following the Abhidhamma, it sees here a reference to the primacy and overall importance of cognitive consciousness *(citta)* to all other psychological experiences *(cetasikā)*, in no way denying the reality of nonmental phenomena.

2.* *GDhpC.*, p. 243, says that *vahato* is the genitive singular of an obsolescent *vahatu,* draught ox, rather than of the present participle of the root *vah*—as the Pali commentary takes; but *Uv.*, xxxi, 23, has *vahataḥ*, and *PDhp.*, 1, *vahato*, both of which support the Pali commentary.

3. "With the utilization of the phrase 'such as' *(ādi)* in this passage [in the text], one should understand all other mental activities yielding wholesome consequences. Therefore it is said, 'consciousness in all the four levels [of manifestation]'" (*Dag.*, 15.11–13).

4. On this particular physician and related incidents, see BL, I, 146–58, esp. p. 158.

5.* The usual reference is *nissatta-nijjīva-dhammā*. The detailed explanation (*DhpA.*, PTS, I, 22) also includes both *nissatta* and *nijjīva*. We have therefore preferred APB, p. 13, and SHB, p. 11, to the PTS, I, 22, which lacks *nijjīva*.

6. "'There are dhammas' *(dhammā honti)*. They become only dhammas because they are empty of the character of a self *(ātma)* or what pertains to a self *(ātmīya)*" (*Dag.*, 16.1–2).

7.* PTS, I, 22, reads: *etehi manopubbaṅgamā. Etesaṃ ti manopubbaṅgamā nāma*. The instrumental form *etehi*, as well as the punctuation, needs amendment, as in APB, p. 13: *ete hi "mano pubbaṅgamo etesaṃ" ti manopubbaṅgamā nāma*.

8. "The esteemed commentator says 'How is . . . ?' expecting [the following objection]: 'Is it not the case that consciousness precedes? If consciousness precedes, then it would be desirable [to understand the passage as meaning] that mental states (dhammas, [i.e., feelings, etc.,]) succeed [it]. In other words, is not [the reference here] relevant to phenomena occurring at a different moment [from the cognitive moment], rather than to those [that are] simultaneous [with it]?' . . . [The commentator] says that [strictly speaking] no preceding-succeeding relationship is appropriate in regard to [indivisibly] associated phenomena. Although this sense is [certainly] implied by the statement 'arise . . . at one instant,' he says 'without [the one] preceding or following [the other] . . . since he wishes to indicate [specifically] the character of [indivisible] association [of consciousness and the other mental states. . . . [The commentator] has not stated [that they] 'cease together' because [in this context] he is speaking of [only] the moment of arising" (*Dag.*, 16.5ff.).

9.* The word *mano*, which should appear immediately after *uppajjamāno*, does not occur in the PTS, I, 22.21. The MS probably "syncopated" *-māno mano* to *-māno*. We have followed APB, p. 13 (= SHB, p. 12).

10. "'Verbal misconduct' *(vacīduccaritaṃ)*: this is the same as speech-intimation *(vākvijñapti)*. It [fundamentally] refers to the connative thinking *(cetanā)* which establishes that [speech]. When one speaks of mental processes, is it not improper to say 'he speaks'? It would be correct because it refers to the causal basis *(hetubhāva)* for speaking" (*Dag.*, 18.2ff.).

The fourfold verbal misconduct is: (1) speaking falsely, lying *(musāvāda)*; (2) malicious speech, slander *(pisuṇā vācā)*; (3) rude, harsh speech *(pharusā vācā)*; (4) frivolous talk or chatter *(samphappalāpa)*, as noted in *Dps.*, p. 1; *Dad.*, p. 2; *Dp.*, p. 3; and *Sds.*, I, 25.

11. "'Threefold physical misconduct' *(kāyaduccaritaṃ)*: here, too [one] should take body-intimation [*kāyavijñapti*] as connative thinking" (*Dag.*, 18.5). The threefold physical misconduct is: (1) killing *(pāṇātipāta* or *pāṇavadha)*; (2) stealing, taking that which is not given *(adinnādāna)*; (3) sexual misconduct *(kamesu micchācāra)*. *Dps.*, p. 1; *Dad.*, p. 2; *Dp.*, p. 3; *Sds.*, I, 25.

Speech-intimation *(vacīviññatti:* Skt., *vākvijñapti)* in the Abhidhamma is a technical term for a stage between thought *(cetanā)* and its full-fledged expression in words. It is a physical state and, when one is in it, it becomes "known" by an outsider that one is about to speak. Hence it is called "intimation." Body-intimation *(kāyaviññatti)* is the technical term for a similar physical state between *cetanā* and its expression in the form of a deed. See *Sdk.*, pp. 125–27.

12. The threefold mental misconduct is: (1) covetousness *(abhijjhā)*; (2)

malevolence *(vyāpāda)*; (3) wrong view *(micchādiṭṭhi)*. *Dag.*, 18.6; *Dps.*, p. 1; *Dad.*, p. 2; *Dp.*, p. 3.

13. Relating to speech *(vacī)*, body *(kāya)*, and mind *(manas)*.
14. "'State of darkness'—being miserable, being born as dwarfs, small ants, etc., not having the capacity to see" (*Dag.* 18.7).
15. Transient existence in (1) one of the hells *(niraya)*; (2) as an animal *(tiracchānayoni)*; (3) as a *peta* [lit. "a departed being"]; (4) as an *asura*-deity. *Dv.*, p. 87. With regard to prospects among human beings, *Dp.*, pp. 3–4, notes: "Again, once he gets the status of a human being, having become poor, subject to suffering, with body smeared with dirt, with mind filled with grief, with tear-filled eyes, with an unattractive body, he will have to endure manifold misery connected with the body and the mind."
16. As in the case of Maṭṭhakundali, who, without performing customary *puñña*-acts, attained the heaven of the thirty-three gods *(tāvatiṃsa-devaloka)*, having made his mind calmly and joyfully tranquil with regard to the Buddha. See BL, I, 159–65.
17. "'Exalted offerings' means great offerings, offerings in the form of alms food, the sound of drums and musical instruments, incense and flowers, flags and banners, etc." (*Dag.*, 25.12).
18. The ten paths of wholesome conduct, frequently mentioned throughout Pali literature, are the opposite of the ten paths of unwholesome conduct, previously alluded to in the *DhpA.*, and listed above, notes 10–12. Of the ten paths of wholesome conduct, three are primarily physical: avoiding (1) killing, (2) taking what is not given, (3) misconduct regarding sensuality; four are primarily verbal: avoidance of (4) lying, (5) slander, (6) harsh speech, (7) frivolous talk; and three are primarily mental: (8) absence of covetousness, (9) absence of malevolence, and (10) the discernment of right view.
19. The three levels are "the sphere pertaining to sensuality, the fine material sphere, and the formless sphere" (*Sdk.*, p. 3).
20. "'Physically based'—having the faculty of the body as its basis; 'based otherwise'—having thought as [its] support; 'free from any basis'—ease that arises without basis." *Dag.*, 25.16ff.

"When there occurs a soft touch that brings pleasure to the body, 'ease that is physically based' is the feeling of ease itself in the thought based on body-consciousness that arises having that [soft touch] as an object [of reflection], and also in the mental activity [*javana*] [the twelfth stage] of a cognitive process *(cittavīthi)* which has the body as its 'door.'

"'Ease that is based otherwise' is the feeling of ease itself arising in the mental activity *(javana)* of the congnitive process as pertaining to such 'doors' as the eye, etc., when there is contact with objects such as pleasant forms, etc., by the remaining [sense faculties] such as eyes, etc.

"It is only in the eleven realms of sensuality *(kāmabhava)*, namely, the six *deva*-worlds, the world of men, and the four *apāya*s [states of woe], that one gets in entirety the six bases such as the eyes, etc. Therefore, only there does one get in entirety ease that is both physically based and also based otherwise. There is no 'ease free from any basis' in the realm of sensuality, because the elements of material form *(rūpadhamma*s) are found in their entirety [there].

"In the fine-material-*brahma*-worlds, the three bases, nose, tongue, and body, are not found, because the *brahmas* of the fine material realms do not become attached to the fields of smell, taste, and touch due to their cultivation of dispassion with regard to sensuality. The two—eye and ear—and the heart-element are found there [in the fine-material-*brahma*-worlds] for such things as seeing the Buddha, listening to Dhamma, etc. Therefore, it is ease associated with the three bases of eye, ear, and "heart" that one finds in the fine-material-*brahma*-worlds.

"In the formless-*brahma*-worlds there is not even a single basis such as eye, etc., because one does not find form by any means at all there, due to the power of the cultivation of dispassion with regard to form on the part of those brahmas. There, the continuity of consciousness is also without the basis of the heart. Therefore, the ease in meditative-absorption *(dhyāna)* that they receive is called 'ease free from any basis'" (*Sdk.*, p. 3). See also *Dp.*, pp. 5–6; *Sds.*, I, 36–37.

21.* "Someone of something": following APB, p. 27, and SHB, p. 13, *kassa ci pasayha,* in preference to PTS, I, 44, *kassaci te pasayha.*

22. " 'This,' namely that enmity is quelled by the absence of enmity, 'is an ancient truth'; it is a virtuous mode of life *(guṇa-dhamma)* that was habitually practiced by Buddhas, Paccekabuddhas, and Great Arahants. Or, 'this ancient truth' . . . is a path trodden by those Buddhas, Paccekabuddhas, and Great Arahants" (*Dps.*, p. 4).

23. Here the commentary proceeds as though it were quoting the words of the Buddha explaining the verse to members of the Saṅgha. Hence the use of the first and second person pronouns.

24. Here the commentary slips back into the third person when referring to the members of the Saṅgha.

25. See the previous note.

26. "'Unrestrained in senses'—this is said with regard to the eye-sense, ear-sense, tongue-sense, body-sense, and mind-sense" (*Dps.*, p.5).

27. "'Righteous' *(dhammika)* because it arises with the practice of wandering for alms. 'Not righteous' *(adhammika)* because it arises due to hypocrisy, etc." (*Dag.*, 35.9).

28. The four modes of deportment are: (1) walking, (2) standing, (3) sitting, and (4) lying down. *Dps.*, p. 5, elaborates the commentative gloss: "'inferior of enterprise'—devoid of enterprise with regard to the four modes of deportment; not endowed with physical enterprise that fulfills religious observances, that makes pure one's mode of living, and also the mental enterprise that increases wholesome qualities and withers away the defilements."
29. "'Māra'—Māra himself in the form of weakened defilements that arise in his thought process" (*Dps.* p. 7). "'Māra' means the defilements themselves, such as passion, hatred, etc., because they kill *(maraṇa)* virtuous qualities" (*Sdk.*, p. 6; so also *Dp.*, p. 12). *Sds.*, I, 86, adds a note: "Māra is met in the texts as five personages; [1] the aggregates that comprise an individual *(khandhas)*, [2] defilements *(kilesas)*, [3] tendencies conducive to a saṃsāric continuum *(abhisaṅkhāra)*, [4] death *(maccu)*, and [5] a potentate of superhuman power *(devaputta-māra)*."
30. "Felling": following SHB, p. 37, *palāsādi-sādanaṃ*, in preference to PTS, I, 76.1, *palāsādīnaṃ* (*-sādanaṃ* obviously is from *sādeti*, causative verb from the root *sad* found earlier in the comment).
31. The commentary here presents a classification of monastic offenses in an order of increasing gravity. Implied are numerous offenses in undecorous conduct. The *nissaggiya* offenses require abandonment of the improper item (bowl, robe, mat, or other possessions) and confession of the transgression to one's monastic peers. The *saṅghādisesa* are offenses that require a formal monastic conclave to adjudicate the appropriate punishment or revocation. These thirteen offenses pertain to sexual misconduct, construction of dwellings, falsely accusing another of committing an offense, divisive behavior in the monastic order, and unadmirable behavior in relationships with lay families. The *pārājikā* offenses, such as sexual intercourse, theft, murder, and exaggerating one's psychic prowess, require that the transgressor be permanently removed from the monastic order.
32. The ten disagreeable or loathesome forms are ways of contemplating a dead body: (1) as swollen, (2) discolored, (3) festering, (4) decomposing, (5) being gnawed, (6) dismembered, (7) killed and quartered, (8) bloody, (9) worm-infested, (10) reduced to a skeleton. See *Sds.*, p. 88. See below, note 22, chapter 20.
33. See above, note 26.
34. "One who is guarding methodically the six doors such as the eye, etc., because the six doorways are well closed by the door-panel of mindfulness, i.e., without occupying oneself with signs when there is an object of desire, such as 'She is a pleasing figure,' and without occupying oneself with the minor marks, such as 'Her hands are

beautiful, feet are beautiful, face is beautiful,' etc." (*Dps.*, p. 6).

35. *Dps.*, p. 6, provides the same gloss, using "three gems" *(ratanatraya)* for "three objects" *(tīsu vatthūsu)*. So also *Dv.*, p. 10; *Sds.*, I, 93; *Dps.*, p. 6.

36. "'Resolute in enterprise'—having increased enterprise with regard to the four modes of deportment, i.e., endowed with physical enterprise that fulfills religious observances and makes pure one's mode of living, and also mental enterprise that increases the wholesome qualities and withers away the defilements" (*Dps.*, pp. 6–7).

37.* Where the Pali has *apeto dama-saccena*, *Uv.*, xxix, 7, has *apeta-dama-sauratyaḥ* (i.e., as one compound word). *GDhp.*, 192, *avedu dama-soraca*, agrees with the Pali in the way the words are compounded, and with *Uv.* in having *soraca* where Pali has *saccena*. *GDhpC.*, p. 241, surmises *soraccā* the more likely original form, as against *saccena*, "obviously a replacement." *PDhp.*, 94, has the same reading as the Pali.

38. "'That pertains to the sphere of truth absolute' *(paramatthasacca-pakkhikena)* in the sense that it pertains to the sphere of Nibbāna *(nivan koṭasiyen)*" (*Dag.*, 36.7ff.). "The mental process *(cetasika)* of right speech arising so as to prevent false speech is regarded as 'truth of speech.' This is on the side of truth absolute" (*Sds.*, I, 124).

39. "Ejecting defilements"—allaying the latent traces of the defilements by means of the Four Fruit-consciousnesses *(phala-citta)*, having totally uprooted the defilements by the four world-transcending wholesome consciousnesses of Stream Entrance, Once-Returning, Non-Returning, and Arahantship, which arise having Nibbāna as objective" (*Sdk.*, p.7). So also *Sds.*, I, 125–26. The Four Paths *(maggas)* are ascending phases of a single soteriological process. They are the Path (1) of Stream Entrance or Attainment, (2) of a Once-Returner (to the human realm), (3) of a Non-Returner (to the human realm), and (4) of a perfected one, Arahant. Each Path has an upliftment of awareness as its concomitant Fruit *(phala)*.

40. The four kinds of virtue leading to purity *(caturpārisuddhisīla)* are (1) restraint in following the *pātimokkha* (a set of binding, and hence forming, precepts established for the monastic order); (2) restraint with regard to the senses; (3) purity in mode of living; (4) the utilization of robes, food, dwelling places, and medicines, provided by others, as necessary aids or supportive requisites *(paccaya)* and not as luxuries. See *Sdk.*, p. 7; *Dv.*, p. 18; *Dp.*, p. 14; *Sds.*, I, 128; *Dad.*, p. 12.

41. The commentary is referring to the gloss on st. 9, "restraint of senses and truthfulness of word that pertains to the sphere of truth absolute." *Dag.*, 36.7, glossing the *DhpA.* on st. 9, takes this as "pertaining to the sphere of Nibbāna" (see above, note 38). On st. 10, *Dag.* provides no

further gloss. *Dps.*, p. 7, not following the lead of *DhpA.* and *Dag.*, interprets "truth" in st. 10 as "the four noble truths; namely, suffering, its origin, its cessation, and the path." The more recent sources tend to interpret "endowed with truth" in st. 10 as "speaking the truth," "not lying," in contrast with "devoid of truth," in st. 9, as "not speaking the truth," "lying." See *Sdk.*, p. 7; *Dad.*, p. 11; *Dv.*, pp. 17–18; *Dp.*, pp. 13–14, and *Sds.*, I, 124–25, 128.

42. "'The wrong view of ten bases' *(dasavatthukā micchādiṭṭhi)* is the following: 'there is nothing [no fruit] in what was given, what was sacrificed, what was offerred in sacrificial oblation, no fruit or consequence of well done and poorly done deeds, there is no "this world," no world beyond, no mother, no father, no beings of spontaneous birth, and in this world there are no persons striving for inward calm and brahmins who have gone correctly, who follow along the practice completely'" (*Dag.*, 45.16ff).

*Sdk.*, p. 8, follows *Dag.*, but provides an elaboration on some of these views consistent with the Theravāda tradition—i.e., there are no beneficial effects of gifts, offerings, offerings given to the invited; one who is in another world will not come to this world and *vice versa*; there are no effects of right or wrong behavior toward one's father or mother.

On the other hand, *Dps.*, pp. 7–8, takes "the nonessential" *(asare)* as "the eight, beginning with wrong view, wrong intention, etc., together with wrong knowledge and mistaken notion of release." *Sdk.*, p.8, and *Dv.*, p. 21, follow the *Dag.*; but *Dad.*, p. 13, *Dp.*, p. 15, and *Sds.*, I, 151, follow the *Dps.* The complete list, following the *Dps.*, is: (1) wrong view, (2) wrong intention, (3) wrong speech, (4) wrong action, (5) wrong form of livelihood, (6) wrong effort, (7) wrong mindfulness, (8) wrong concentration, (9) wrong knowledge, and (10) mistaken notion of release.

According to *Dag.*, 45.20, "'The right view of ten bases' *(dasavatthukā sammādiṭṭhi)* is 'there is this world, etc.'" According to the other interpretation, "the right view of ten bases" would be "right view, right intention," etc. The *Ssd.*, p. 7, fn., notes the alternative interpretation of *Dag.*

43. "'Wrongdoer' *(pāpakārī)*—the person who is inclined to do numerous bad deeds, such as taking life, etc." (*Dps.*, p. 9; so also *Sdk.*, pp. 11–12). "Bad deeds are the five wrongs and the ten unwholesome acts" (*Dv.*, p. 27).

The five wrongs are the threefold physical misconduct (see above, note 11) together with lying and the consuming of intoxicants. One of the basic assumptions of being a Buddhist formally is that one voluntarily agrees to abstain from these five wrongs.

The ten unwholesome acts are (1) killing, (2) stealing, (3) misconduct with regard to sensuality (these comprise the threefold physical misconduct—see above, note 11), (4) speaking falsely, lying, (5) malicious speech, slander, (6) rude, harsh speech, (7) frivolous talk or chatter (numbers 4–7 represent the fourfold verbal misconduct—see above, note 10), (8) covetousness, (9) malevolence, and (10) wrong view (these three represent the threefold mental misconduct—see above, note 12). These ten unwholesome acts are noted in *Dv.*, p. 27, in this context, and are discussed fully at *Sds.*, I, 170–82.

44. This is the grief that such a person will experience as "the misery of existence in a state of woe *(apāya)*." So *Dps.*, p. 9; *Sdk.*, p. 12; *Dad.*, p. 18; *Dv.*, p. 27; *Dp.*, p. 18, and *Sds.*, I, 167.

45. Reference is to the background story given earlier in the commentary. See BL, I, 225–28.

46. "'He who has done wholesome deeds' is the person . . . who has done numerous wholesome *(puñña)* deeds such as giving, observing precepts, etc." (*Dps.*, p. 9; so also *Sdk.*, p. 12).

"The person who uses the three 'doors' [of body, speech, and mind] for the benefit of himself and for others is the faithful one who has done wholesome deeds. Wholesome deeds are the things done having subdued greed, anger, and delusion. They are of three categories, namely giving *(dāna)*, observing moral precepts *(sīla)*, and cultivation of meditation *(bhāvanā)*. They are also of ten kinds" (*Dv.*, p. 29). The ten are: (1) giving, (2) observing moral precepts, (3) cultivation of meditation, (4) honoring, (5) rendering service, (6) transferring to others that which has been attained *(pattidāna)*, (7) reflecting delightfully on the attainment of merit, (8) hearing dhamma, (9) preaching dhamma, and (10) setting one's views straight. So *Sds.*, I, 187ff. See also note 18, above.

47. In the *deva*-realms or in the human realm. So *Dps.*, p. 10. *Sdk.*, p. 12 and *Dad.*, p. 19, put the stress on the *deva*-realms. See also *Dv.*, p. 29, and *Sds.*, I, 189.

48. Reference is to the background story given earlier in the commentary. See BL, I, 228–30.

49. Reference is to the background story given earlier in the commentary. See BL, I, 242–44, regarding the woman Sumanā, long established in the Path of a Once-Returner who, having passed away, attained the Tusita heaven.

50. "'Text' *(sahitaṃ)*—i.e., the words of the Buddha. It is called 'arranged' *(sahita)* because of its consistent *(saṅgata)* meaning" (*Dag.*, 58.18–19). The tradition consistently takes the term *sahita* to refer to the words of the Buddha: "the words of the Buddha in the form of the

three *piṭakas*" (*Dps.*, p. 11; *Dad.*, p. 23; *Dv.*, p. 35; *Dp.*, p. 22); "advice of the Buddha" (*Sdk.*, p. 13).

"This refers to the 84,000 categories of dhamma that are included in the three *piṭakas*." *Dv.*, p. 35. "The words of the Buddha are called '*sahitaṃ*'. The force of the word is taken to mean 'with benefit' (*sa-hita*) in the sense that under all circumstances, whether in its ordinary or transcendent meaning, it brings benefit for all persons in the world together with (*sahita*) that of the gods" (*Sds.*, I, 221).

51.* "By this person": following SHB, p. 80, and APB, p. 98, *tathā tena*, in preference to PTS, I, 158.2, *Tathāgatena*. Obviously *tathā* here is the complement of *yathā* (two lines earlier; PTS, I, 157, last line of text)—hence the PTS punctuation also needs amendment.

52. "'Following what conforms' is following dhamma that conforms to the world-transcending dhamma" (*Dag.*, 59.3). "'He is one who follows dhamma that is in accord with dhamma' being in the secondary dhamma that is considered the practice of the first part, which is divided into the four kinds of virtue leading to purity [see above, note 40], the thirteen *dhutaṅgas* [see below, note 6 in chapter 2], and the practice of meditating on the loathesome, which are in accord with the ninefold world-transcending dharma, i.e., the four Paths, four Fruits, and Nibbāna" (*Dps.*, p. 12). "'Dhamma [in the primary sense] means the ninefold world-transcending dhamma and also the three *piṭakas* in which is told the practice for attaining that [ninefold dhamma]" (*Sdk.*, p.14). *Sds.*, I, 234, follows *Sdk.* closely.

The ninefold world-transcending dhamma (*navavidhalokuttara-dhamma*) is comprised of (1) the Path of Stream Entrance or Attainment, (2) the Fruit of Stream Entrance, (3) the Path of a Once-Returner, (4) the Fruit of the state of Once-Returning, (5) the Path of a Non-Returner, (6) the Fruit of the state of Non-Returning, (7) the Path of Arahantship, (8) the Fruit of the state of Arahantship, and (9) Nibbāna.

53. "'Knowing full well'—one who knows well the dharmas that are to be known thoroughly. Or, [one who knows well] that the whirl, that is reckoned as the aggregates of grasping, that has three levels, namely the level of sensuality, the fine material level, and the formless level, is the truth of *duḥkha* in the sense that it is contemptible; that craving (*tṛṣṇā*), itself, which has 108 subdivisions such as craving for sensuality, etc., is the truth of arising because it is the cause for the arising of *duḥkha*; the Nirvāṇa, which is the ultimate objective of the Paths and Fruits, and also which has the characteristic of peace, is called the truth of cessation because it causes the cessation of *duḥkha*, or else because it [Nirvāṇa] is the mark [of this cessation]; that the eightfold path, which is world-transcending because it goes beyond

the world considered as the aggregates of grasping, is the truth of the path because it proceeds, killing *(maraṇaya)* the defilements and also because it is to be sought after *(mārgaṇaya)* by those having Nirvāṇa as goal. Such a person [well knowing—*sammappajāno*] is one who knows very well that the truth of *duḥkha* is that which is to be completely understood; the truth of arising is that which has to be abandoned; the truth of cessation is that which has to be realized, and the truth of the path is that which is to be cultivated" (*Dps.*, p.12).

54. *Sdk.*, p. 15, elaborates the fivefold liberation: "If one were to take the agent-sense or the causal-sense as predominant, one has to take wholesome consciousness that pertains to the sphere of sensuality as 'liberation through developing the opposite of defilements,' and the wholesome consciousness that pertains to the fine material sphere and formless sphere as 'liberation through suppression of defilements,' and Path consciousness as 'liberation through the cutting off of defilements,' and the resultant Fruit *(phala)* consciousness as 'liberation through the calming down of defilements,' and Nirvāṇa as 'liberation by wholly transcending the defilements.'" See also *Sds.*, I, 245–46.

55. The four modes of grasping are: (1) grasping sensuality, (2) clinging to opinion, (3) clinging to precepts and rites, and (4) attachment to a substantialist position (*attavāda*: i.e., that there is a persistent soul, etc.).

*Sdk.*, p. 15, elaborates: "'sensuality' *(kāma)*—although sensuality is twofold, as bases of sensuality and defilements of sensuality, what is to be understood here are not form, sound, smell, taste, and touch, which are bases of sensuality because they are the object for sensuality and passion, but the defilements of sensuality which arise in the mind having these [form, etc.,] as the object. It is clinging for the sphere of the bases of sensuality or else defilements that are the cause for clinging. 'Opinion' *(diṭṭhi)*—these are the sixty-two views such as the world and self *(ātman)* are eternal, i.e., that they always exist without destruction. 'Precepts and rites' *(sīlabbata)*—the thinking that accepts such [forms of ascetic penance] as goat-precepts, cow-precepts, goat-ascetic-practices, cow-ascetic-practices, bat-ascetic-practices, etc., that holds the belief 'there is purity through precepts,' 'there is purity through ascetic practices.' 'Substantialist position' *(attavāda)*—the wrong view that there is a constant self *(ātman)* that goes through each birth pertaining to the five aggregates *(skandhas)*. That there is a constant self within the five aggregates, which are definitely impermanent, is a causeless, empty belief that does not conform to any logic or reason."

56. "'Group of five qualities of one who has passed beyond training' *(pañca asekha-dhamma-khandha)* . . . are virtue *(sīla)*, concentration *(samādhi)*, insight-wisdom *(paññā)*, release *(vimutti)*, and the experience of the gnosis of release *(vimuttiñāṇadassana)*" (*Dag.*, 59.22).

## Chapter II

1. "'Whatever wholesome mental states' (dhammas) means whatever wholesome mental states that pertain to the plane of sensuality *(kāmāvacara)*" (*Dag.*, 78.4).
2. "'They are all awareness-based'—based on that awareness which exists in the form of bringing to mind the ease experienced by those who have acquired the religious practices, by those who observe the advice that it is worthwhile to give alms, worthwhile to observe the precepts, worthwhile to cultivate concentration and wisdom, etc." (*Dag.*, 78.5).
3. "Awareness, which is 'not being bereft of mindfulness,' with regard to the sphere of qualities of good conduct, is the fundamental cause for all wholesome dharmas and for the benefit of oneself and the benefit of others, pertaining to this world and the next" (*Dps.*, p. 13).
4.* The PTS edition (I, 228) of the *DhpA.* has *padam ti iminā ti padaṃ*. APB, p. 142, has *padanti* [from the root *pad*] *iminā ti padaṃ*. The Thai edition of the *DhpA.* (II, 63) and SHB, p. 114, have *pajjanti* [also from the root *pad*] *iminā ti padaṃ*. From APB, SHB, and the Thai edition, it would appear that the commentary is explaining *padam* by way of its etymological derivation. The Pali words for "path" and "travel" are sufficiently alike to allow one to explain "path" as a derivative of "travel." This derivation totally loses its force when translated into English.
5. "It is a means for the attainment of Nirvāṇa which is called Deathless because it itself is free from old age and death and because it destroys old age and death for the noble ones who have attained it" (*Dps.*, p. 13).
6. The thirteen *dhutaṅga* practices: "[1] wearing rags acquired from dust heaps, [2] wearing the prescribed three robes, [3] resorting to begging for alms, [4] going alms-begging from house to house [in the order of houses—i.e., without making choices], [5] eating the meal 'at one sitting,' [6] eating from one vessel only, [7] refusing food offered at an inappropriate time, [8] living in forests, [9] sitting at the base of trees, [10] living in the open air, [11] frequenting a cemetery, [12] accepting whatever seat is offered, [13] remaining [even while sleeping] in a seated posture" (*Dag.*, 129.6ff., commenting on *DhpA.*, II.24 [PTS

edition]). See, further, chapter 2 of the *Visuddhimagga*, translated as *The Path of Purification* by Bhikku Nyāṇamoli (Colombo: M. D. Gunasena & Co. Ltd., 2nd edition, 1964), pp. 59–83.

7.* "Not different": following APB, p. 143, *ninnānākaraṇā* (*nir + nānākaraṇa?*) in preference to PTS, *nānākaraṇā,* I, 229. (SHB, p. 114, has *kiṃ nānākaraṇa.*)

8. "The qualities contributing to enlightenment *(bodhipakkhika-dhammas)*—here Bodhi means either the one engaged in disciplined meditation *(yogāvacarayā)* because he realizes the four noble truths, or it means the arising of Path consciousness. The fourteen qualities, such as mindfulness, enterprise, etc., are called qualities contributing to [lit. on the side of] enlightenment either [1] because they are contributive to understanding the four truths, by that person in disciplined meditation, who is called Bodhi, or [2] because they are qualities of mind linked with Path consciousness, by being suitable for the activity of realizing *(bodhana)* Path consciousness that is called enlightenment *(bodhi)*.

"The fourteen [qualities] are [1] awareness, [2] enterprise, [3] volition *(chanda)*, [4] intention *(citta)*, [5] insight, [6] faith, [7] one-pointedness of mind, [8] joy, [9] serenity, [10] equanimity, [11] delimiting-thinking, and the three abstinences: [12] right speech, [13] right action, and [14] right mode of living.

"Of these fourteen qualities, *mindfulness* is eightfold, since it has eight functions at the moment of Path consciousness, namely [1–4] the four foundations of mindfulness, [5] the faculty of mindfulness, [6] the force of mindfulness, [7] the constituent of enlightenment that is mindfulness, and [8] right mindfulness. *Enterprise* is ninefold: [1–4] the four right exertions (not grasping bad, unwholesome qualities that have not yet arisen; abandoning those that have; causing wholesome qualities to arise; continuing in those qualities), [5] the mental base of enterprise, (6] the faculty of enterprise, [7] the force of enterprise, [8] the constituent of enlightenment that is enterprise, and [9] right enterprise [or effort]. *Wisdom* is fivefold, since it has five functions, namely, [1] the mental base of delimiting-thinking, [2] the faculty of wisdom, [3] the force of wisdom, [4] the constituent of enlightenment that is reflecting on the qualities (dharmas), and [5] right view. *Faith* is twofold, since it has two functions, namely, [1] the faculty of faith, and [2] the force of faith. *One-pointedness of mind* is fourfold, since it has four functions, namely, [1] the faculty of concentration, [2] the force of concentration, [3] the constituent of enlightenment that is concentration, and [4] right concentration. *Volition, intention, joy, tranquility, equanimity, delimiting-thinking,* and the *three abstinences* are each onefold, since each has only one function, namely, the mental base of volition, the mental base of intention, the constituent of enlightenment that is joy, the constituent of enlightenment that is tranquility, the constituent of enlightenment that is equanimity, right intention *(sammāsaṅkappa)*, and the three abstinences: right speech, right action, and right mode of livelihood.

"Divisible in this way, there are thirty-seven qualities conducive to enlightenment: the four foundations of mindfulness, the four right exertions, the four bases of psychic power, the five faculties, the five forces, the seven constituents of enlightenment, and the noble eightfold path" (*Sdk.*, pp. 30–31). Virtually the same at *Dag.*, 100.13.

9. The ninefold dhamma that transcends the world: see above, note 52 in chapter 1.

10. *Sds.*, II, 315–23, elucidating "the noble ones," lists 108 categories of "disciples" *(sāvakas)*, those who have attained one or another of the Paths or Fruits, based on the *Suttanipāta* commentary *Paramatthajotikā)*. *Sds.* also refers to a different presentation found in the commentary on the *Aṅguttaranikāya (Manorathapūraṇī)*.

11. The eight attainments are: (1–4) the four stages of meditative-absorption *jhāna)*, and (5) the stage of infinity of space, (6) of infinity of conciousness, (7) the state of no-thing-ness, and (8) the stage of neither consciousness nor nonconsciousness.

12.* (With firm endeavor) "maintained constantly": APB, p. 144, *nicca-ppavattitena*, seems preferable to PTS, I, 230, *niccaṃ pavattena*, and SHB, p. 115, *niccappavattena*.

13. "'Four bonds' *(cattāro yogā)*—the four defilements that yoke a person in *saṃsāra*, namely, the bond of sensuality *(kāma)*, the bond of [craving for] existence *(bhava)*, the bond of speculative opinions *(diṭṭhi)*, and the bond of ignorance *(avijjā)*" (*Dag.*, 79.26). So also *Sdk.*, p. 17; *Dv.*, p. 43; *Dp.*, p. 27; *Sds.*, II, 342.

14.* "Giving . . . careful consideration": following APB, p. 149, and SHB, p. 119, *upadhāretvā*, in preference to PTS, I, 239.1, *upadhānetvā*.

15.* *Nābhikīrati*: for *abhikīrati*, *PDhp.* has *adhipūrati* ("fill over"?) and *Uv.*, iv, 5, *abhimardati* ("crush"?).

16.* *Dag.*, 85.26, lists the four floods. They are the same as the four bonds; see above, note 13. So also *Sdk.*, p. 19; *Dad.*, p. 30; *Dv.*, p. 47; *Dp.*, p. 30; *Sds.*, II, 368.

17.* *GDhp.*, 117, has *dhaṇa śeṭhi va rakṣadi*, with which *Uv.*, iv, 10, agrees (*śreṣṭhī va*). This yields a much better sense for line 4: "As a merchant guards [his] wealth."

18. "The seven-treasure wealth" is gold, silver, pearls, gems, lapis lazuli, conch, and the *śilā*-gem. *Dag.*, 86.12.

19.* "I will obtain": following APB, p. 160, and SHB, p. 128, *paṭilabhissāmi . . . pāpunissāmi . . . sampādessāmi,* in preference to PTS, I, 258, *paṭilabhati . . . pāpuṇāti . . . sampādeti.*

20. "'The three forms of knowledge': [1] recollection of former existences, [2] possessing the divine eye, [3] knowledge of the destruction of intoxicants. 'The six forms of higher knowledge' are [1] possessing the divine eye, [2] the divine ear, [3] the kinds of psychic power, [4] knowledge of other's thoughts, [5] recollection of former existences, and [6] knowledge of the destruction of intoxicants" (*Dag.*, 129.10, commenting on *DhpA.*, II, 24 [PTS edition, on v. 61]). These two categories are also listed at *Dag.*, 96.5–7. See also *Sdk.*, pp 20, 23–24.

21. "In the phrase 'namely, the clear divine eye *(dibbacakkhu)*' one should add the word knowledge, i.e., the clear divine-eye-knowledge" (*Dag.*, 86.18)."'. . . the palace that is called wisdom' consisting of consciousness of higher knowledge called the divine eye" (*Dps.*, p. 17). "The knowledge of the passing away and rebirth of beings is the divine-eye-knowledge" (*Sdk.*, p. 20).

22. "'Sleeping in all the modes of deportment'—among those fallen asleep in the sleep of the defilements in the four modes of deportment, due to the lack of the wakefulness of mindfulness" (*Dps.*, p. 17). So also *Sdk.*, p. 21, and *Sds.*, II, 389.

23. On the topics of meditation *(kammaṭṭhāna)*, see *The Path of Purification*, translated by Ñyāṇamoli, pp. 84–121.

24. The reference is to the background story given earlier in the commentary. See BL, II, 313–24, esp., p. 315.

25. "'Of every distinction ordinary as well as transcendent' *(lokiyalokuttarānaṃ visesānaṃ)*—ordinary distinction such as the prosperity of Sakra, etc., and transcendent distinction such as the Paths, Fruits, and Nibbāna." *Dag.*, 93.9.

26.* [*Bhaya-*]*dassivā*: *Uv.*, iv. 32, has *-darśakaḥ* in place of this form; *PDhp.*, 23, *-daṃsino*; *GDhp.*, 74, *-daśima.* It is interesting to note that *PDhp.*, 169*c* has [*bhaya-*]*damsāvi* where the Pali has [*bhaya-*]*dassino* (*Dhp.* 317a). All these forms are derivatives of the root *dṛś* with different suffixes.

27. "By the phrase 'large and small fetters' is meant the ten defilements, namely, [1] holding to the opinion of enduring substantiality *(sakkayadiṭṭhi)*, [2] [skeptical] doubt *(vicikicchā)*, [3] clinging to precept and practices (*sīlabbataparāmāsa*), [4] passion for sensual desires, (*kāmarāga*), [5] ill-will (*vyāpāda*), [6] passion for the fine-material [realm] *(rūparāga)*, [7] passion for the formless [realm] *(arūparāga)*, [8] self-estimation *(māna)*, [9] agitation *(uddhaccaṃ)*, and [10] ignorance *(avijjā)*. They are of two modes: [1] pertaining to the upper

part and [2] pertaining to the lower part. They are called fetters because they bind beings in *saṃsāra* in the sense that they cause rebirth again and again there. The five, beginning with 'holding to the opinion of enduring substantiality,' etc., are called those pertaining to the lower part because they are the cause for birth in the eleven realms of sensuality that are called 'lower' [realms], and five, beginning with 'passion for the fine-material [realm],' etc., are called those pertaining to the upper part because they are the cause for birth in the fine-material realm and the formless realm, which are called 'upper.' There is no liberation from *saṃsāra* for beings until these bonds of *saṃsāra*, which are of these two modes, are rooted out" (*Sdk.*, p. 22). See also *Sds.*, II, 406. The distinction "upper part, lower part" is also in *Dps.*, p. 18.

28. "The peaceful dhamma that becomes the objective for the Path of Arahantship for the complete rooting out of defilements is the '*parinibbāna* of the defilements.' This is also called Nirvāṇa with residue because the *khandhas*, though devoid of defilements, still remain. The same peaceful dhamma, after the death of the noble Arahant, is also called '*parinibbāna* without grasping,' because, after that event, there is no rebirth caused by grasping strongly to *saṅkhāras* in the form of craving, etc. This is also called '*parinibbāna* without residue' because it has no remainder of the *khandhas*" (*Sdk.*, p. 22).

# Chapter III

1.* For *okam-okata ubbhato* of st. 34, *Uv.*, xxxi, 2, has *okād oghāt samuddhṛtaḥ*, and *PDhp.*, 344, *okamokatta ubbhato*. It is noteworthy that for *okam okam* of *Dhp.*, v. 91, *PDhp.*, 231, and *Uv.*, xviii, 1, has *okam ogham*. Thus at both places for *oka* of *Dhp.* and *PDhp.*, the *Uv.* has (1) *oka-* (Cl. Skt., *okas*: home) and (2) *ogha-* (Skt. for flood, stream, and by implication, water), through two different derivations. The commentary knows the two distinct meanings when it says *okam-okato ti udaka-saṃkhātā ālayā*. It supports the meaning of "water" by quoting a passage from the Vinaya, *oka-puṇṇehi cīvarehi* (*Vin.*, I, 253)—i.e., this meaning was rare enough to warrant a quotation. It is interesting that Buddhaghosa in his commentary on this passage cites a variant reading, *ogha-puṇṇehi* (see *Vin.*, I, 387). We may understand this variant reading as the result of a baffled copyist substituting for the old reading *oka-puṇṇehi* the easier-to-comprehend form *ogha-puṇṇehi* (contrast the PTSD, under *oka-*).

In st. 34 it is also rather baffling to see the commentary explaining *pahātave* by the potential participial form *pahātabbam*. The

*Uv.* equivalent is *prahātavai (PDhp., prahātaye); pahātave/prahātaye/prahātavai* are all old dative infinitives. We have rendered the commentative interpretation into English by translating the line as "[fit] to discard [is] Māra's realm"—i.e., getting the potential participial sense into the line by adding the word "fit." One may well question this procedure. The alternative would be to take the stanza as meaning: "The mind is used to remain under the sway of Māra. It reels like a fish out of water in the process of trying to get away from this grip." To get this sense too we have to add "in the process of trying"—which may be challenged even more. The case needs further investigation.

2.* Pali *citta* means both "mind" and "varied" (adj.).

3. " 'Varied by way of plane, base, field [or object], and [related] action, and so forth'—plane *(bhūmi)*, in the sense of the sphere of sensuality *(kāma)*, etc.; base *(vatthu)* in the sense of eye, ear, etc.; field [or object] *(ārammaṇa)*, in the sense of form, sound, etc.; [related] action *(kiriya)* in the sense of standing, sitting, etc." *Dag.*, 95.13ff. See *Sdk.*, p. 23 *Sds.*, II, 415–55, gives a detailed enumeration of over 75 categories of *citta*, making quite clear the notion of "varied."

4. " 'Single wholesome object *(ekasmiṃ sappāya ārammaṇe)*'—one beneficial object, such as contemplating on the loathesome" (*Dag.*, 95.18ff.).

5. " 'The dissimilar object *(visabhāga ārammaṇa)*'—a dissimilar object, such as a woman [for a man] and a man [for a woman] *(itthipurisa)*" (*Dag.*, 95.19–20).

6. " 'With the oil of faith *(saddhasinehena)*'—with 'oil' *(senehen)*—that is to say, a liquid *(dravaya)* [because *seneha* means both 'oil' and 'affection']—in the form of faith in the Buddha who preached religious practice and knowledge" (*Dag.*, 95.28–96.1).

7. " 'He contemplates the *saṅkhāras*'—having contemplated the *saṅkhāras* pertaining to the three realms [of saṃsāric existence: *traibhūmakasaṃskāra*], as impermanent, etc. [awry, without substantiality]" (*Dps.*, p. 20). See also *Sdk.*, p. 23. " . . . having contemplated the *saṃskāras* connected with the sensuous, fine material, and formless realms as impermanent, etc." (*Sds.*, II, 456).

8. See above, note 20 in chapter 2.

9. See above, note 20 in chapter 2.

10. The five strands of sensuality *(kāmaguṇa)*: i.e., the strands of sensuality related to the five senses. See below, note 7, in chapter 4.

11. " 'The whirl of the three realms *(traibhūmaka)*' is called 'the sway of Māra' *(māradheyyaṃ)* because it is subject to Māra" (*Dps.*, p. 20).

12. "The three whirls are [1] the whirl of [one's] actions, [2] the whirl of defilements, and [3] the whirl of the consequences of [one's] actions.

The whirl of actions is connative thought reckoned as existence *(bhava)*, which constitutes the condition for rebirth in a future existence and mentioned in the dependent origination *(paṭiccasamuppāda)* formula as 'depending on clinging there is existence *(bhava)*,' as well as connative thought reckoned as the *saṅkhāras* connected with the previous existence, which are the cause for rebirth in this present existence, connative thought that is both wholesome and unwholesome, noted in the passage 'depending on ignorance there are the *saṅkhāras*.' The defilements, of ignorance, craving, and clinging, are the whirl of defilements. The existence which occurs in the future, namely, consciousness, name-and-form, the six spheres of senses, touch, feeling, birth, old age, and death are the whirl of the consequences of actions. Here, what is shown as the whirls of action, of defilements, and of the consequences of actions are the twelve factors of dependent origination *(paṭiccasamuppāda)*" (*Sdk.*, p. 24). See also *Sds.*, II, 457; *Dp.*, p. 38.

13.* "Proper and improper"—following APB, p. 186, and SHB, p. 148, *-yuttāyuttaṭṭhānesu* in preference to PTS, I, 300.4–5, *-yuttaṭṭhānesu*. The words echo those of the comment on *Dhp.* v. 35 (PTS, I, 295.16), *yuttaṭhanaṃ vā ayuttaṭṭhanaṃ vā*.

14. " 'Cave' here means the cave [of the body that is made up] of the four great physical elements. The four great physical elements themselves are called a cave because it [this cave] is comparable to the heart in which the mind resides" (*Dag.*, 99.9).

"Mind exists in the cave that is called this body, which exists because of the four great physical elements, also it [mind] exists dependent on the heart element [*hṛdayarūpu* = Pali *hadayarupa*]" (*Dps.*, p. 22).

The "heart element": "The existence of the mind is in association with the heart element. That [heart element] is located inside the body between the two breasts and has a color similar to the color of the outside of the red lotus petal. In its appearance, it is like a lotus bud placed upside down, having its outside petals removed. It is smooth on the outside. Inside, it is like the inside of a *vätakolu* fruit. Of those with wisdom it is slightly open. Of those without wisdom, it is closed indeed. Inside that, there is a depression about the size of a *domba* seed. There is here about half a cup of blood. The existence of the mind is in association with that blood. Because of this, it was said that 'mind is lying in a cave' " (*Sdk.*, pp. 25–26).

*Sds.*, II, 475, provides further elaboration: "In the heart of persons of passionate character, that blood is red in color; of those whose character is marked by hatred, it is of a dark color; of those whose character is marked by delusion, it is the color of water that has been used to wash meat; of those whose character is marked by argumentation, it is the color of water that has been used to boil horse gram; of those whose character is marked by faith, it is the color of the [bright red] *kinihiri* flower; and of those whose character is marked by wisdom, it is very clear. Thus does mind function in association with blood of various colors in accordance with the character of the respective persons. Therefore, the mind is said to be 'lying in a cave.'"

*Sds.*, III, 536, in another context, provides a related discussion about the heart element: "The place in which reside the mind element *(manodhātu)* and the mind-consciousness element *(manoviññāna-dhātu)* is called the fine material element that is the heart basis *(hadayavatthurūpa)*. It is called 'heart' because it is instrumental for the benefit or misfortune of beings; it is called 'basis' (site) because it is a place for the dwelling of consciousness and mental processes. The heart itself is called 'heart basis' because it is a basis for the mind element, etc., by being the support [for them]. It exists in association with about half a cup of blood inside the cavity of the heart. The Tathāgata has not preached about a material element that is the heart basis in the section about fine material elements *(rūpa)* in the *Dhammasaṅganī*. But the presence of a fine material that is the heart basis is in accord with the texts and with logic. The following passage occurring in the *Paṭṭhāna* makes this clear: 'That element [of form: *rūpa*] in association with which the mind element and mind-consciousness element exist, that element is the cause by way of support for the mind element and the mind-consciousness element.'"

15. The "threefold whirl" *(tebhūmaka vaṭṭa)* known as the bond of Māra is coeval to the three realms of sentient existence within the saṃsāric process: (1) the realm of sensuality, (2) the fine material realm (or the realm of form), and (3) the nonmaterial realm (or the formless realm). Transcending all of this is a fourth, the transcendent *(lokuttara)* realm over which Māra has no sway. A more specific interpretation of the "threefold whirl" here is (1) the whirl of [one's] actions *(kamma)*, (2) the whirl of defilements *(kilesa)*, and (3) the whirl of the consequences *(vipāka)* of one's own actions. See above, notes 11 and 12, and on this interpretation of the commentative remark, *Dad.*, p. 43; *Dp.*, p. 42.

16.* "Be he a disciple of the Buddha," *kadā ci buddhasāvako hoti,* is not found in the PTS edition, though noted (I, 309, note 6) as an alternate reading (in a Burmese manuscript). We are here following APB, p. 191, and SHB, p. 152. *Sds.*, II, 479, also follows this reading *(buddhaśrāvakayek vē da)*. The Thai edition of *DhpA.* has *sevako,* "a servant," also noted as an alternate reading in the PTS edition.

17. *Acelako ājīviko nigaṇṭho tāpaso*—an *acelaka* is one who has discarded clothes, an *ājīvika* is external . . . [text incomplete] . . . a *nigaṇṭha* is

one without clothes, and a *tāpasa* is one who wears a garment made of bark" (*Dag.*, 100.11).

18. "The thirty-seven qualities contributing to enlightenment are 'the four foundations of mindfulness, the four right exertions, the four bases of psychic power, the five faculties, the five powers (or forces), the seven constituents of enlightenment, and the noble eightfold path' " (*Dag.*, 100.13). See above, note 8 in chapter 2.

19.* In order to clarify *ananvāhatacetaso,* the commentary first deals with an instance of the use of its opposite, *āhatacitta.*

20. "Who has relinquished the wholesome and unwholesome *(kuśalākuśala)* by means of the Path of Arahantship" (*Dps.*, p. 23). "Who has destroyed by the Path of Arahantship all the wholesome and the detrimental *(pinpav)* deeds that are a cause for rebirth in a future existence" (*Sdk.*, p. 26). " . . . that destroys the wholesome and the detrimental *(pin pavu)*, that puts at a distance all the wholesome and unwholesome *(kusal-akusal)* that are a cause for continual rebirth in *saṃsāra*" (*Dv.*, p. 75).

21. " 'Such as faith, etc. *(saddhādīdhi)*'—one should take "etc." *(ādi)* in this phrase to include enterprise *(viriya)*, mindfulness *(sati)*, concentration *(samādhi)*, and wisdom *(paṇṇā)*" (*Dag.*, 100.20–21).

22.* "Remain"—following APB, p. 196, *acchanti,* in preference to PTS, I, 317.8, and SHB, p. 156, *gacchanti.* The parallel, *accheyya,* is found a few lines later (PTS, I, 318.6; SHB, p. 156.36).

23. "The defilements such as passion, etc." *Sdk.*, p. 27. "The mass of defilements such as passion, etc., are Māra in the form of defilements." *Sds.*, II, 496. See also above, note 29, in chapter 1.

24.* "Rising"—following APB, p. 196, and SHB, p. 156, *vuṭṭhāya,* in preference to PTS, I, 317.17, *paṭṭhāya.* The parallel, *vuṭṭhāya,* is found a few lines later (PTS, I, 318.9).

25.* In lines 2 and 3 (of st. 41), where the Pali has *adhi, sessati, chuddho,* and *apeta, Gdhp.*, 153, has *vari, śa'iṣidi tuchu,* and *avakada,* of which the Pali equivalents should be *upari, sayissati, tuccho,* and *apagata.* It is an extraordinary fact, as *GDhpC.*, p. 226, points out, that these very words occur in the *DhpA.* On this stanza: " . . . *na cirass'eva ayaṃ kāyo . . . paṭhaviyā upari sayissati . . . apagata-viññāṇatāya tuccho hutvā sessati.*" *GdhpC.*, p. 226, observes: "either the Prakrit represents the older verse, which has been metrically smoothed in the Pali, while the older words have survived fossilized in the traditional commentary . . . or . . . the Pali verse is older, and the Prakrit has been refashioned by using the traditional commentary." *PDhp.*, 350*bc* has *abhiśehiti, chūṭho,* and *apeta* answering to *adhisessati, chuddho,* and *apeta* of the Pali verse, thus proving the latter's ancientness.

26.* To get the sense it proposes for this verse, the commentary adds *disvā* after *disaṃ* and takes *yaṃ/taṃ* as a double accusative. *Dag.*, 103.12, does the same when it says: "Take *taṃ* as having the sense of *tassa*." The double accusative with the root *kar-* is an ancient usage (cf. *Rg Veda,* 5.30.9: *kiṃ mā karann abalā asya senāḥ,* "what will his feeble armies do to me?" [see Delbrück, *Altindische Syntax,* p. 180]).

We would get essentially the same meaning if *yaṃ/disaṃ* were the double accusative—i.e., *diso disaṃ yaṃ kayirā,* "what a foe may do to a foe," rather than the commentary's *disaṁ (disvā) diso yaṃ taṃ kayirā,* "what a thief, seeing a thief, may do to him." Alternately, we may take *taṃ* as forming a unit with *yaṃ*—i.e., *yaṃ taṃ:* "that which" rather than "what . . . to him." Still, *taṃ* seems redundant; without it the line reads more smoothly and makes better sense.

The parallel *Uv.*, xxxi, 9, has no word corresponding to *taṃ*. It also makes a more modern construction by dropping the double accusative and using a (dative-)genitive *dveṣiṇaḥ* where Pali has the accusative *disaṃ*.

As elsewhere (e.g., *Dhp.*, vv. 53, 61, 64, 65, 117, etc.), *kayirā* here is pronounced as two syllables, *-ayi-* being treated as a diphthong rather than as two vowels and a consonant. But it is possible that there were instances where *kayirā*, or a Prakritic form of it, had a trisyllabic pronounciation (as if it were *ka-yi-rā* rather than *kay*[i]*-rā*). In that case *diso disaṃ yaṃ kayirā* without the syntactically redundant *taṃ* would have also conformed to the metrically regular eight-syllable pattern. But when the disyllabic pronounciation of *kayirā* became standard, the line would have sounded metrically deficient (seven syllables) and *taṃ,* which so easily forms a unit with *yaṃ* in Pali, would have been added to restore the meter.

27. On the ten paths of unwholesome deeds, see note 43 in chapter 1, above.

28. "In many hundreds and thousands of lives" (*Dps.*, p. 24; *Sdk.*, p. 29).

29.* The singular verb is to be taken separately each time with *mātā* and *pitā*. The plural subject *ñātakā* is no doubt meant to go with a plural verb from the same root and in the same mood.

30. On this important woman and the accounts about her in the *DhpA.*, see BL, II, 59–84, 300, 328–30.

## Chapter IV

1.* *Vicessati: Uv.*, xviii, 1, has *vijeṣyate* and MS evidence admits of the parallel Pali reading *vijessati*. The commentary, however, favors *vicessati*. Apparently there was uncertainty from early times as to whether the word was from $\sqrt{ci}$: to note, discern, etc., or from $\sqrt{ji}$: to conquer. (Bernhard, *Uv.*, p. 238, has noted one *Uv.* fragment with the reading *viceṣyate*, $\sqrt{c\bar{\imath}}$. But *PDhp.*, 131, *vijehiti* definitely favors the reading *vijessati* from the $\sqrt{ji}$.

2. On *apāya*, see above, note 15 in Chapter 1.
3. "'*Dhammapadaṃ*'—a part of dhamma *(dham koṭas)*" (*Dag.*, 104.27). "'*Dhammapadaṃ*' is the part of dhamma *(dharmakoṭṭhāsaya)* reckoned as the thirty-seven factors conducive to enlightenment" (*Dps.*, p. 25).

   A discussion on the thirty-seven qualities or factors in *Sdk.*, pp. 30–31, occurring originally in this context, has been placed above (note 8 in chapter 2) where these qualities or factors were first met in the *DhpA.* text. See also *Dad.*, p. 52; *Dv.*, p. 87; *Dp.*, pp. 49–50; and *Sds.*, III, 612.
4. The person who has attained (1) the Path of Stream Entrance, (2) the Fruit of Stream Entrance, (3) the Path of Once-Returning, (4) the Fruit of Once-Returning, (5) the Path of Non-Returning, (6) the Fruit of Non-Returning, (7) the Path of Arahantship. These represent the seven kinds of "learner" *(sekha)*.
5. "Primarily, 'higher virtue' *(adhiśīlaya)* is virtue occurring in the consciousness of the Paths and Fruits or the threefold mental abstinence: right speech, right action, right mode of living. 'Higher consciousness' *(adhicitta)* is integration *(samādhi)* occurring in the consciousnesses of the Paths and Fruits or else the three namely, right enterprise, right mindfulness, right concentration, i.e., the mental qualities such as enterprise, mindfulness, and one-pointedness, since these are contributive to concentration, which is indicated under the rubric of 'consciousness.' 'Higher insight' *(adhiprajñā)* is insight occurring in the consciousnesses of the Paths and Fruits or else the two, namely, right view and right intention, i.e., the two, mental processes of insight and the mental process of investigation, which are contributive to that [higher insight].

   "Secondarily, the five virtues are called virtue *(sīla)*. The eight-factor virtue is higher than that, and the ten virtues are higher than that, and the ordinary four kinds of virtue leading to purity [see above, note 40 in chapter 1] are higher, and the world-transcending virtues, higher than that. Such is 'higher virtue' *(adhśīla)*.

   "The consciousness pertaining to the sphere of sensuality is called consciousness *(citta)*. And the consciousness pertaining to the fine material sphere is higher than that, and the consciousness pertaining to the formless sphere is higher than that, and the world-transcending consciousness is higher than that. Such is 'higher consciousness' *(adhicitta)*.

   "The insight pertaining to the sphere of sensuality is called insight *(prajñā)*. The insight that pertains to the fine material sphere is higher than that, and the insight that pertains to the formless sphere is higher than that, and the world-transcending insight is higher than that. Such is 'higher insight' *(adhiprajñā)*" (*Sdk*., pp. 31–32).

6.* *Papuppakāni*: *Uv*., xviii 18, has *puṣpakāni* without the equivalent of prefix *pa*. But *PDhp*., 134, has *prapuṣpakāni* and *GDhp*., 300, has *papavuṣe'aṇa,* proving the ancientness of the reading of the prefix. It is interesting that the ancient Sinhala commentary, however, had disregarded the prefix (see next note).

7. "'Flowers' *(papupphaka)* means the whirl [of *saṃsāra*]. That whirl is called 'flowers' because it is multiple as actions *(kam)*, defilements *(keles)*, and consequences *(vivaha)*."

"In the *Heḷaṭuvā*, the venerable author took the text as 'cutting off the flowers of Māra' *(cetvāna mārassa pupphakāni)*, leaving aside the letter '*pa*.' There, he said 'the flowers of Māra' *(mārassa pupphakāni)* means 'all that is unwholesome *(akusala)*'; i.e., by the word 'flower' *(pupphaka)* is meant what is unwholesome. The venerable author [in the *Heḷaṭuvā*] said by the word 'flower' indeed the categories of the five strands of sensuality *(pañcakāmaguṇa)* are [usually] meant. So, 'cutting off the flower of Māra *(mārassa puppham chinditvā)*' means 'cutting off craving for the categories of the five strands of sensuality'" (*Dag*., 105.15 ff.).

The literary corpus known as the *Heḷaṭuvā* is also noted by its Pali title in the Pali commentative literature as *Sīhaḷaṭṭhakathā*. This corpus is considered by tradition to have been a Sinhala translation of commentaries brought by Mahinda to Sri Lanka. The corpus seems to have been in existence untill approximately the thirteenth century.

About the five strands of sensuality, the *Sdk*., p. 32, says: "The five bases for sensuality, namely, form, sound, smell, taste, and touch are called the strands of sensuality either because they are the objects of passion for sensuality or because they bind the minds of ordinary persons, or the persons themselves, to *saṃsāra*."

The *Dps*., p. 26, follows the lead of the *Dag*. in combining the two strands of one basic understanding held separately in the *DhpA*., "the whirls of the three levels of existence," and in the nonextant Sinhala commentaries *(Heḷaṭuvā)*—i.e., the five strands of sensuality that bring about all that is unwholesome. "'Of Māra'—that which belongs to Māra in the form of defilements *(kleśamārayā)*; 'flowers'—the five strands of sensuality or the dharma of suffering of the three levels of existence, namely, the whirl of actions, the whirl of defilements, and the whirl of consequences [of actions]."

8. "'Going to Nirvāna' *(nivan yāma)* means not being born, not undergoing rebirth in any place after death by the pacification of the

five *skandha*s due to the uncompounded element becoming objectively experienced in Path-and-Fruit consciousness—the uncompounded element which is so called because it has not sprung up by the force of any causative factor such as ignorance, craving, action *(karma)*, nutriment, and condition of material environment" (*Sdk.*, p. 32). See also above, note 28 in chapter 2.

9.* "Turns his mind" following APB, p. 221; SHB, p. 176, *manaṃ peseti*, in preference to PTS, I, 361, *manaṃ na peseti*.

10. The five strands of sensuality: see above, note 7.

11.* "Not wanting [any] other": following APB, p. 221; SHB, p. 176, *aññam apatthento*, in preference to PTS, I, 362, *aññaṃ patthento*.

12. "'Be they connected with oneself [i.e., internal]' refers to strands of sensuality such as among women and men, etc., in bathing and massaging, etc. 'Be they connected with material objects' refers to strands of sensuality such as gold and silver, wherewithal for beds and chairs, etc." (*Dag.*, 113.7).

13. "'The End-Maker'—Māra himself" (*Dps.*, p. 27).

14.* Parallel to *pupphaṃ*, *GDhp.*, 292, has *puṣpa*; *Uv.*, xviii, 8, *puṣpād*. *GDhpC.*, p. 267, points out that we may have here an instance of a double accusative with *ādāya* (cf. *vṛkṣam avacinoti phalāni*, etc., of commentators on Pāṇini I, 4.51, as Brough notes). In that case the commentative construing of *pupphaṃ* with *aheṭhayaṃ* must be questioned. The meaning would better be: "as a bee flies off, taking away the nectar from a flower." *PDhp.*, 127, has *puṣpā*, which agrees with the *GDhp.* and *Uv.* readings.

15. "The topics of meditation pertaining to oneself, such as head-hair, etc." (*Dag.*, 115.11).

16. "'In the immediate experience of ease'—any one of the experiences of ease of *deva*s and *brahma*s" (*Dag.*, 115.12).

17. On the *dhutaṅga* practice, see above, note 6 in chapter 2.

18.* *Sakubbato*: for this world *PDhp.*, 126, has *kurvvato*; *GDhp.*, v. 291, *kuvadu*; and *Uv.*, xviii, 7, *kurvataḥ*. The *sa-* before the present participle in the Pali verse is questionable. The meter too becomes more regular without this *sa-*. It would seem that the Pali tradition at some stage added this *sa-*, probably to make 52*d* similar to 51*d* *(sakubbato/akubbato)*.

19.* *Pāribhaddaka*: APB, p. 234; SHB, p. 186. PTS, I, 383, has *pālibhaddaka*.

20.* "Word of the Buddha": PTS, I, 383, and SHB, p. 186, have *vaṇṇasaṇṭhānasampanna-agandha-puppha-sadisaṃ* after *Buddha-vacanaṃ*. APB drops this (p. 234). Our translation follows APB.

21.* "Kinds of garland": following APB, p. 256, and SHB, p. 203, *mālāvikatiyo*, for PTS, I, 419, *mālā-nikatiyo*.

22. "Such as giving *(dāna)*, observing moral precepts *(sīla)*, etc." (*Dps.*, p. 30).
23. Reference is to the background story given earlier in the commentary. See BL, II, 59–84.
24.* For *pavāti*, PTS, I, 422, notes the *v.l. pavāyati* (Burmese and Cambodian MSS). The old *Uv.* MS (called Ph MS in Franz Bernhard's ed.) has *pravāyate. GDhpC.*, p. 268, recommends that *pavāyati* should be "restored to the Pali text." The reading *pavāti*, however, is supported by *Dps.*, p. 30, and by the parallel *pravāti* of *Uv.*, vi, 16, favored by Bernhard, although the *Gdhp.*, 295, *pad'idi* (probably "an accidental corruption for *prava'idi*"*: GDhpC.*, p. 268) may be taken as supporting the reading *pavāyati. PDhp.*, 121, has *pravāti*, which supports the existing Pali reading.
25.* *Mallikā*, often translated "jasmine" or a kind of jasmine, is really not a jasmine, but a flower resembling a jasmine in color and shape. It is called *idda/sīnidda/bōlidda* in Sinhala.
26.* "Everywhere": following APB, p. 262, and SHB, p. 207, *sabbattham-eva*, in preference to PTS, I, 430, *sabbatthakam-eva.*
27. Reference is to the background story given earlier in the commentary. See BL, II, 90–91.
28. "'Release through elimination' means the meditative-absorption *(jhan* [*jhāna*]*)* of the fine material and formless spheres; 'release through cultivating the opposite' means meditation *(bhavun* [*bhāvanā*]*)* with regard to the sphere of sensuality [or of those of the sphere of sensuality]; 'release through cutting off' [defilements] means the Paths; 'release through subsidence' [of defilements] means the Fruits; and 'release through moving away' is Nibbāna" (*Dag.*, 125.22 ff.). See also above, note 55 in chapter 1.
29.* *Saṃkārabhūtesu . . . puthujjane:* the Pali commentary cites *puthujjane* (i.e., locative singular, as in the verse) and first explains it as a singular form. Later it cites *puthujjanesu* (in the plural) as qualified by *saṃkārabhūtesu*. This is obviously problematic.

Where Pali has *saṃkārabhūtesu, GDhp.*, 304, has *saghasa-dhama'u* whose Pali equivalent would be *saṃkhāta-dhammā* (a word found in *Sn.*, v. 1038, *saṃkhātadhammāse . . . sekhā*: see *GDhpC.*, p. 269). If an original *saṃkhātadhammāse* was in line 1 of the text, lines 3 and 4 would have been in the plural, as indeed *Uv.*, xviii, 13, *vyatirocante śrāvakāḥ*, suggests. (And st. 59 would then read: "Similarly the disciples of the Buddha who have realized the dhamma . . . shine forth by reason of their wisdom, whereas common mortals are blind" [*GDhpC.*, p. 269]). On the other hand, *Uv.* has *saṃkārabhūte'sminn* in line 1, which may be an attempt to regularize the grammar after the problematic *-bhūtesu* found its way into the text. *(PDhp.*, 136*ab*, has *saṃkārabhutesu . . . puthujjane*, as in the Pali, and also the plural *atirocanti . . . sāvakā* in lines *c* and *d*.)

30.* "Worthy of being placed": APB, p. 270, and SHB, p. 214, *patiṭṭhāraham*, seems preferable to PTS, I, 446, *patiṭṭhitāraṃ*.

31.* "Fulfills" and "surpassing": following APB, p. 270, and SHB, p. 214, *ārādhetvā . . . atirocati*, in preference to PTS, I, 446, *ārādhetvā . . . atirocetvā*.

## Chapter V

1.* "Coming": following APB, p. 278, and SHB, p. 220, *āgacchantaṃ*, in preference to PTS, II, 13, *āgacchante*, in view of *aparampi* occurring twice in the sequel.

2.* "Everyone who is asked": following APB, p. 278, and SHB, p. 220, *pucchitapucchitā . . . vadanti*, in preference to PTS, II, 13, *pucchitapucchitakāle . . . vadati*.

3. On the thirty-seven qualities or factors contributing to enlightenment, see above, note 8 in chapter 2.

4. The Pali phrase, "This *saṃsāra*, O bhikkhus, is of unknown beginning, its prior end does not appear [to one's vision]" is a quotation from the *Saṃyutta-nikāya* (PTS edition), II, 178.

5.* "If one does . . . come across": following APB, p. 285, *labheyya ce*, in preference to PTS, II, 24, and SHB, p. 226, *labheyya c' eva*.

6. "'Minor virtue'—the special characteristics of the three terms, minor virtue, etc., should be understood as in the *Brahmajāla-sutta* [of the *Dīgha-nikāya*]" (*Dag.*, 129.2ff.).

"'Minor virtue' is, in this context, abstinence from taking life, stealing, misconduct with regard to sensuality, lying, slander, harsh speech, gossip, enterprises dealing with seeds and plants, eating at the wrong time, seeing dances, hearing songs, instrumental music, comedies, using high beds and big beds, accepting gold and silver, accepting raw grain, raw meat, women and girls, maid and men servants, goats and sheep, cocks and pigs, elephants, horses, and mares, fields and sites, engaging in travel as messenger, buying and selling, fraud in weighing, fraud in coins, fraud in measuring, crookedness, cheating, deception, torturing, and imprisoning."

"'Intermediate virtue' is abstaining from hoarding seven [kinds of thing], seeing the twenty-seven comic shows, the twenty-one forms of heedlessness in gambling, the eighteen kinds of high seat, the twenty forms of adornment, the thirty-two forms of base talk, talk leading to divisiveness, the six ways of going about as messenger, the fivefold deceit, and flattery for gain."

"'Major virtue' is abstaining from the thirteenfold art of foretelling on the basis of physical characteristics, the twenty-fivefold talk about characteristics of jewels, the twenty-fourfold talk about the aspects of lunar eclipse, the twelvefold talk about the military movements of the king, the thirteenfold talk about rain, the nineteen ways of matchmaking, the twenty-fourfold subjects of surgery," (*Sds.*, IV, 776–77).

7. "'The ten topics of discussion' *(dasakathāvatthūni)* are [1] unpretentious discussion, [2] discussion yielding contentment, [3] discussion on austere penance *(sallekha)*, [4] discussion about solitude, [5] discussion about engendering resolution, [6] discussion about virtue, [7] discussion about concentration, [8] discussion about wisdom, [9] discussion about release, [10] discussion about the vision of gnosis [of release]" (*Dag.*, 129.4ff.). For a very detailed discussion of this, see *Sds.*, IV, 777ff.
8. PTS, II, 24, reads *vipassanāguṇaṃ*, whereas the Thai ed., III, 120, APB, 285, and SHB, 226, read *vipassanāguṇā*. The *Dag.* provides no gloss. We are here following the variant reading *vipassanāñāṇaṃ* noted in PTS, II, 24, n. 24, as Fausbøll's preferred reading.

   "'Insight' is the wisdom that sees the *saṃskāra*-dhammas as impermanent because they are in a process of arising and passing away; they are sorrowful because they oppress you again and again; they are without self because they are not within one's control" (*Sds.*, IV, 782).
9. On the four Paths and four Fruits, see above, notes 39 and 52 in chapter 1.
10. *Dag.*, 129.6ff., provides once again a complete listing of the thirteen *dhutaṅga* practices, the three forms of knowledge, and the six forms of higher knowledge. On these, see above, notes 6 and 20 in chapter 2.
11. That is, the three considerations regarding the sons, as noted in the text, plus three parallel considerations regarding riches: "They are lost." "They are diminishing." "They will be lost." Hence one is anxious in this context in six ways.
12. Reference is to the background story given earlier in the commentary. This person was reborn, deformed, in a low caste *(caṇḍāla)*, and was, while begging, smitten by his grandsons. See BL II, 115–16.
13.* "Very childish": following APB, p. 228, and SHB, p. 229, *andhabālo*, in preference to PTS, II, 30, *attatobālo*.
14. "'An advocate of the *dhuta (dhutavādo)*'—one who proclaims the virtues of the *dhutaṅga* practices" (*Dag.*, 130.8). For these thirteen practices, see note 6 in chapter 2.
15. Reference is to the background story given earlier in the commentary. See BL, II, 117.
16.* "One who is childish": following APB, p. 289, SHB, p. 229, *bālo nām' esa*, in preference to PTS, II, 31, *bālo nām' esā*.

17.* "This is [right] conduct," etc.: following APB, p. 289, SHB, p. 229, *āyam cāro ayaṃ vihāro ayaṃ ācāro ayaṃ gocaro*, in preference to PTS, II, 31, *ayaṃ cāro vihāro ācāro gocaro.* Cf. the pronoun stated eight times in the sequel: *idaṃ sāvajjaṃ idaṃ anavajjaṃ*, etc.

18. " 'Pasture' *(gocara)* is the 'family that is endowed with faith' "—i.e., devotees who can be depended on for subsistence (*Dag.*, 130.16).

19. " 'This is worthy of practicing; this is not worthy of practicing': thoughts *(vitak)* of renunciation, etc., are what is meant by 'this is worthy of practicing.' Thoughts of sensuality are what is meant by 'this is not worthy of practicing.' 'This is what has to be penetratively seen' means the Paths and Fruits should be penetratively seen. 'This is what should be realized' means Nibbāna *(nivan)* should be realized. 'Dhamma to be practiced' refers to the religious practice. 'Dhamma to be penetratively realized' means the Paths, Fruits, and Nibbāna are to be penetratively realized" (*Dag.*, 130.19ff.).

20.* "Know . . . discriminatingly": following APB, p. 289, SHB, p. 230, *vijānati*, in preference to PTS, II, 32, *jānati. Vijānāti* is the word from the verse. The usage is the parallel of *rasaṃ vijānāti . . . lokuttaradhammam pi vijānāti* of the comment on *Dhp.*, 65 (PTS, II, 33).

21.* For Pali *madhuvā, GDhp.*, v. 283, has *mahoru-*, which raises the possibility that *madhuvā* is a change from an original *madhuraṃ*. See *GDhpC.*, pp. 262–63.

22.* "[As he is] being made to undergo various vicissitudes": following APB, p. 300, *vividhā'kamma-karaṇā kāriyamānassa* (but analyzing the words in this way, rather than as *vividhākamma-karaṇā-kāriyamānassa)*, in preference to PTS, II, 50, *vividhā kammakaraṇā kayiramānassa,* and SHB, p. 238, *vividhā kammakaraṇa karīya-mānassa*. The case of *akammakaraṇā* is probably neuter accusative plural.

23.* *Saṅkhata-dhammānaṃ*. Cf. with this *Uv.*, xxiv, 20E, *svākhyāta-dharmasya; Mahāvastu* III, 435, *svākhyāta-dharmāṇāṃ*; and *PDhp.*, 390, *sākkhāta-dhaṃmāṇāṃ*. The meaning underlying this reading is "of those who have well proclaimed [i.e., taught] dhamma." *GDhp.*, 313, however, has *saghasa-dhameṣu,* which *GDhpC.*, p. 269, says goes back to *saṃghāda*, the equivalent of *saṅkhāta* on which the Pali form is based. We have here, therefore, evidence of two textual traditions, or two ways in the tradition of handling the text—so far as this stanza is concerned.

24.* "Beyond the pale of qualities like virtue, etc.": following SHB, p. 244, *sīlādiguṇā paribāhiro*, in preference to APB, 307, *sīlādi-guṇā 'pari-bhāvito*; PTS, II, 63, *sīlādiguṇaparibāhiro. Dps.*, pp. 36ff., *śīlādi-guṇayen paribāhira vū*, supports the SHB reading.

25.* "Discourse concerning . . . individuals": following *APB*, p. 307, SHB, p. 244, *puggalādhiṭṭhānā desanā*, in preference to PTS, II, 63, *puggalādhiṭṭhānā*. The comment in PTS is unpunctuated and suggests that the editor did not fully comprehend its import.

26.* "One . . . who refrains from eating": following APB, p. 307, *abhuñjantassa*, in preference to PTS, II, 63, and SHB, p. 244, *abhuñjantānam*. The word is clearly the parallel of *abhuñjantassa* in the background story (PTS II, 62, lines 22–23).

27.* "That intention": following APB, p. 307, and SHB, p. 244, *tassā . . . (cetanāya)*, in preference to PTS, II, 63, *tassa . . . (cetanāya)*.

28.* "Coagulate like freshly extracted milk" *(sajju-khīraṃ va muccati)*: the translation follows the commentative interpretation and the traditional Pali text *(sajjukhīraṃ* as a compounded word). *PDhp.*, 107, however, has *sajjaṃ chīraṃ* (uncompounded), paralleling *Uv.*, ix, 17, *sadyaḥ kṣīram*. This suggests the reading: "coagulate . . . swiftly as does milk." Incidentally, *PDhp.*, like the Pali, has *muccati* for Skt. *mūrcchati*, which would normally be represented as *mucchati*.

29.* *Sukkaṃsaṃ* agrees with *Uv.*, xiii, 2, *śuklāṃśaṃ*. *PDhp.*, 177, however, has *śukraṃś taṃ*. The commentative interpretation of *sukkaṃsaṃ* is not altogether convincing and one wonders whether a different meaning was originally intended.

30.* "Renowned": the commentary takes *ñattam* (from the root *ñā*, "to know") as "the fact of knowing" as well as "the fact of being known"—i.e., in both active and passive senses.

31.* "That . . . of his": following APB, p. 314, and SHB, p. 250, *tassa hi taṃ*, in preference to PTS, II, 73, *tassa hitaṃ*.

32.* *Pūjā*: one would have expected to find an accusative form here. In fact *PDhp.*, 178, and *Uv.*, xiii, 3, have the accusative, *pūjāṃ*. Obviously *pūjā* here represents an original accusative for some reason or other altered to this form.

33.* *Kiccākiccesu kismi ci:* this is an unusual juxtaposition. The first word is plural, although the second (which goes with it) is singular. *PDph.*, 179, however, has the regular *kiccākiccesu kesu ci*, as does *Uv.*, xiii, 4, *kṛtyākṛtyeṣu keṣu cit*.

34.* In both *PDhp.*, 180, and *Uv.*, xiii, 5, these two lines, represented as one in our Pali text, combine with the equivalent of *Dhp.*, v.75*ab*, to form an independent verse.

35.* "*Niddesa*": Cf. *Dag.*, 138.18, *pāpicchatā padayaṭa kaḷa nideshi*—"in the exposition on the term *pāpicchatā*."

36.* "Soiled": following APB, p. 316, SHB, p. 252 (and supported by *Dag.*, 138.22) *uklāpa-senāsanāni*, in preference to PTS, II, 77, *lāmakāni*. It is not improbable that *Dag.* "*uklāpāni*" was the original reading.

37. On the four kinds of requisites *(paccaya)*, see the fourth category mentioned above in note 40 in chapter 1.

38.* "What must be obtained": following SHB, p. 252, *laddhabbāni honti*, in preference to PTS, II, 78, and APB, p. 316, *laddhabbāni hontu.*

39. " 'The ninefold self-estimation *(māna)*' is the ninefold self-estimation that arises such as 'I am better than the superior, etc.' " (*Dps.*, p. 39). According to *Dv.*, p. 191 (note on *Dhp.*, v. 94), the nine are: "[1] I am better than my superior, [2] I am the same as my superior, [3] I am worse than my superior, [4] I am better than my equals, [5] I am the same as my equals, [6] I am worse than my equals, [7] I am better than my inferior, [8] I am the same as my inferior, [9] I am worse than my inferior."

40.* " 'Good fortune of having the substrates'—the good fortune of [having this] existence *(atbävu sapuva)*" (*Dag.*, 142.3). The PTS, II, 102, reads *upasampadā*, "the higher ordination," while noting five sources with our chosen reading. We are taking *upadhisampadā* on the basis of *Dag.*, 142.3, reference and following APB, p. 331, SHB, p. 264, as well as the Thai ed., III, 189.

41. *Sāvaka* is from the root *su:* to hear or listen to.

42. " 'Counsel and instruction': to point out a fault that has already appeared is called counsel; to discipline one about faults before they appear is called instruction" (*Dag.*, 142.8). Cf. *Dhp.*, 77, and the commentative gloss on this verse.

43. *Buddha* is from the root *budh:* to understand.

44.* "Compounded dhammas": following PTS, II, 103, *saṃkhata-dhammānaṃ*. APB, p. 332, and SHB, p. 264, have *saṃkhatāsaṃkhata-dhammānaṃ*, which arguably gives the better sense.

45. " 'As are discordant with dhamma'—that have been acquired improperly *(adhämin upanu)*" (*Dag.*, 142.10).

## Chapter VI

1.* The equivalent *GDhp.*, 231, has *nisedara pravatara* (*niṣeddhāraṃ pravaktāraṃ* found in Uv., xxviii, 7) in line 1, for which *GDhpC.*, p. 246, suggests: "one who prohibits and exhorts." *GDhpC.* says that the Pali commentary is strained and that the Prakrit has "the feel of authenticity." However, *PDhp.*, 206, *nidhino va pravattāraṃ*, is very close to the Pali reading and seems clearly to support the commentative interpretation.

2. M, III, 118. The English quoted in the text is the translation by I. B. Horner, *Middle Length Sayings*, III, 162.

3.* For *hi so piyo*, *PDhp.*, 207, has *hetaṃ priyaṃ*. *Appiyo* in line *d* is also *apriyaṃ* in *PDhp*. This seems to suggest the sense: "For the good this is pleasant, but to the bad it is unpleasant."

4.* "Counselling one indeed instructs": following APB, p. 336, and SHB, p. 268, *ovadanto yeva anusāsati*, in preference to PTS, II, 110, *avadanto eva anusāsati*.

5. See above, note 42 in chapter 5.

6. "Housebreaking and highway robbery, etc.," according to *Dps.*, p. 41; so also *Sdk.*, p. 46; *Dad.*, p. 85; "housebreaking, highway robbery, causing pain, cutting, chopping, killing . . . " (*Dv.*, p. 159). See also *Dp.*, p. 82. The sources noted relate this form of conduct to inferior persons among the laity.

7. "'The twenty-one kinds of wrongdoing *(anesana)*'—in twenty-one categories such as 'giving bamboo, giving flowers, etc.'" (*Dag.*, 143.22–23). *Dps.*, p. 41, notes that the wrongdoing in this context pertains to the conduct of bhikkhus.

*Sds.*, IV, 900, lists the twenty-one kinds of wrongdoing *(anesana)*, expedients that ill-behaved bhikkhus might utilize in order to win over the laity: (1) giving (to the laity) bamboo sticks that belong to the Saṅgha community, (2) giving palm leaves, betel, etc., (3) giving flowers, (4) fruit, (5) fibrous sticks (to brush the teeth), (6) giving water for washing the face, (7) water for bathing, (8) giving ungents, powders, etc., (9) clay (for various purposes such as bodily cleanliness), (10) words of flattery, (11) speech that is only partially true (12) comforting children in various ways, (13) acting as a messenger to lay persons, (14) acting as a physician, (15) as an emissary, (16) going on errands about lay persons' lands, etc., (17) exchanging possessions with lay persons, (18) giving bribes, (19) determining building sites, (20) advising on auspicious moments, (21) sooth-saying by bodily characteristics.

8. "Contacting with body" is often used when referring to realization of dhamma. The meaning is "perceiving directly." Some Sinhala editions, however, have *nāmakāyena phusanto:* "contacting with mind." So APB, P. 345; SHB, p. 274.

9. "In the phrase, 'contacting with body [or mind; i.e., perceiving directly] ([*nāma*] *kayena phusanto*),' the Paths and Fruits should be understood. In the phrase 'realizing as object,' wisdom should be understood. By the use of the term 'etc.' *(ādi)*, occurring in the phrase 'comprehension, etc.,' through full knowledge [of the fact of *dukkha*], one should understand also full knowledge through elimination [of its origin], full knowledge through cultivation [of the path], and full knowledge through realization [of its cessation]. The exact knowledge of suffering (*duk*), its arising and elimination, and the cultivation of the path that brings about the realization of its cessation is what is

intended. By the use of the term 'etc.' *(ādi)*, occurring in the phrase 'suffering, etc.,' one should understand its arising and the path leading to its cessation. 'The noble truths' are the truths that bring about a state of nobleness" (*Dag.*, 145.23–29). See also above, note 53 in chapter 1.

10.* "Living with tranquil mind": following APB, p. 345, and SHB, p. 275, *cetasā viharanto*, in preference to PTS, II, 127, line 7, *cetasā ti viharanto*.

11.* "Although": following APB, p. 357, and SHB, p. 285, *kiñcāpi*, in preference to PTS, II, 148, *kiñcipi*.

12. " 'They are not shaken,' because there is no satisfaction, opposition, elation, or dejection with regard to the eight aspects of ordinary life such as gain, loss, shame, fame, blame, praise, comfort, and suffering" (*Dps.*, p. 43. So also *Sdk.*, p. 48; *Dad.*, p. 88; *Dv.*, note, p. 165. *Dp.*, p. 85, adds, "People without [proper] knowledge with regard to the eight aspects of ordinary life become elated with joy, become penitent with suffering."

" 'Aspects of ordinary life *(lokadhammā)*' means the nature of ordinary life *(lokasvabhāvaya)*. There is no one in the world who does not come under the sway of these aspects. Even Buddhas are subject to them. These are the aspects of the world of beings that cannot be brought under one's control. The world goes on according to these. These aspects will last as long as the world lasts" (*Sds.*, IV, 927).

13.* *GDhp.*, v.225, has *emu dhamu ṣuṇitvaṇa*, where Pali has *evaṃ dhammāni sutvāna*. The original version of the Pali too could have been *evaṃ dhammaṃ suṇitvāna*, giving the present text by transposition of *-ni-*, as *GDhpC.*, p. 245, points out. *Uv.*, xvii, 11, *evaṃ śrutvā hi saddharmaṃ*, looks like a conscious emendation. Although *dhammāni* in the neuter plural certainly seems unusual, *PDhp.*, 276, *dhaṃmāṇi śottāna* decisively supports the Pali reading.

14.* "Agitated": following SHB, p. 287, *khubbhati*, in preference to PTS, II, 152 (and APB, p. 359), *khambhati*.

15.* *GDhpC.*, p. 245, says that *cajanti* should be rejected in favor of *v. l. vajanti*, which agrees with a restored *Uv.* reading, *vrajanti* (JRAS, 1912, p. 371); underlying both *vrajanti* and *vajanti* there might have been a reading *vayanti*, itself a mistake for *viyanti*. The *GDhp.*, 226, reading for this word, *vivedi*, "would then represent a replacement of the verb *vi-i* by the rather stronger form *vi-apa-i (vyapenti)*." On this basis *GDhpC.* translates the line thus: "With respect to everything religious men stand aside—are indifferent." In line *a*, both *PDhp.*, 80, and *Uv.*, xxx, 52, have *bhavanti* as the verb, but *Uv.*, has *sāpatrapaḥ* for *sabbattha*. In line *c, PDhp.* has *muṭṭhā uttavā* for the Pali *phuṭṭhā atha vā*. The latter, however, is supported in toto by *GDhp.*, 226, *phuṭha adhava*, and partially by *Uv. spṛṣṭā hi*. All this goes to show how poorly the text of this verse has been transmitted and how risky it is to make any conjectures regarding its original form.

16.* The commentary interprets *lapayanti* as both a causative and a simple verb. It takes *kāmakāmā* as an ablative of cause (cf. *Uv.*, xxx, 52*b*, *kāmahetoḥ*). In form *lapayanti* is causative (cf. *GDhp.*, 226*b*, *lavayadi*; *Uv.* xxx, 52*b*, *lapayanti*). The causative interpretation ("nor do they get others to prattle") seems to suggest an earlier meaning, which the tradition has lost (due to some kind of corruption of the text?).

17. "All phenomena (dhammas)" such as the five *khandhas*, the bases of interplay of consciousness, senses, and sense objects *(dhātu)*, and the spheres of interaction of senses and sense objects *(āyatana)*, etc. So *Dps.*, p. 43.

18. See above, note 12.

19.* *Viveke yattha dūramaṃ*: the construction (is passive, as can be seen from the *DhpA.* comment on v. 88a—*yasmiṃ viveke imehi sattehi durabhiramam:* "in disengagement, [relishing] wherein is to be relished with difficulty by these beings." Incidentally, this clarifies *duppabbajjaṃ* of *Dhp.*, v. 302, on which see the note below.

20. " '*Okā*' means 'from the household [life of a layman],' i.e., 'from the home of the five strands of sensuality.' '*Anokaṃ*' means the state of one who has gone forth [into monastic life], which is not the home of the five strands of sensuality. Or '*okā*' means 'from *saṃsāra*' or 'from the home of the defilements.' '*Anokaṃ*' means Nibbāna, which is not the home of defilements. '*Āgamma*,' 'having come,' means 'having gone forth from the household and come to the state of one who has gone forth [into monastic life]. Or, *āgamma* would mean 'for the sake of' Nibbāna *(nivan)*, which is to be attained, 'having gone forth' from *saṃsāra*" (*Dag.*, 151.14ff.).

21. "'One who has nothing *(akiñcana)*,' i.e., who is without obstacles such as sensual attachment *(rāga)*, etc., or without obstacles such as children [lit. sons], wives, female and male servants, cows and buffalos, wealth and grains, etc." (*Dps.*, p. 46).

22. " 'The five hindrances': desire for sensuality, ill will, sloth and torpor, agitation and remorse, and [skeptical] doubt" . . . called hindrances because they deflect virtuous qualities such as meditation, release, Paths and Fruits, etc." (*Sdk.*, p. 51).

23. " 'In the factors conducive to enlightenment'—in the seven factors conducive to enlightenment" (*Dag.*, 151.23). *Dps.*, p. 46, broadens the number of categories: " . . . in the seven factors conducive to enlightenment or in the thirty-seven qualities contributing to enlightenment."

" 'The seven factors conducive to enlightenment' are the seven mental processes: mindfulness, insight-wisdom, enterprise, joy, tranquility, one-pointedness-of-mind, equanimity, which arise simultaneously in world-transcending consciousnesses having Nibbāna as object, and in ordinary consciousnesses at different moments having various objects" (*Sdk.*, p. 52). See also note 8 in chapter 2, above.

24. "'The four kinds of clinging *(upādāna)*'—sensuality, speculative opinion, precepts, and rites, and maintaining the notion of self." *Dag.*, 152.1–2. " 'Without clinging'—without taking as 'me' or 'mine' any among the four bases of clinging" (*Dps.*, p. 46). See also above, note 55 in chapter 1.

25. "'A state of undefinability *(apaṇṇattika bhāvaṃ)*'—that is to say, there is not even living existence *(divana/jīvati)* of self *(tumā/atta)* in the case of an Arahant who has attained *parinibbāna (pirinivī rāt)*. The definability that is current, such as Sariputta and Moggalana, etc., exists with reference to the existence of the *khandha*s, which are there so long as there is no *parinibbāna*. That which will continue to exist [will be] definable. It is said 'he went to an undefinable state,' since nothing [remained of him] immediately after [*parinibbāna*]" (*Dag.*, 152.4ff.).

"Those who have attained *parinirvāna* in this twofold way [i.e., with substrata remaining and without substrata remaining]—they will reach a state of undefinability like a lamp that has no more fuel" (*Dps.*, p. 46). *Sdk.*, p. 52, adds, "the state where there is no definition such as a living being, a person, etc."

## Chapter VII

1. "'The four bonds'—the accumulation of covetousness ... of ill will ... of clinging to precept and rituals ... of a bias [to say] this [alone] is truth [all else is falsehood]" (*Dag.*, 152.22). Cf. note 13 in chapter 2, above.
2. Reference is to the background story given earlier in the commentary. See BL, II, 197–98.
3. "Because he is king with regard to dhamma that is taught" (*Dag.*, 152.24).
4.* "Every attachment": following SHB, p. 295, *ālayālayaṃ*, in preference to PTS, II, 170 (and APB, p. 369), *ālayaṃ*.
5.* The *Uv.* parallel, xvii, 1, *okam oghaṃ jahante te*, conveys this sense quite explicitly: They leave (their) home which is the "flood" (i.e., *saṃsāra* with its bonds and attachments, "flood" being a common metaphor for worldly existence). See above, note 1 in chapter 3, on *Dhp.*, v. 34.

6. "'The three states of existence'—[1] sensual, [2] form or fine material, and [3] formless. 'The four ways of birth'—[1] egg-born, [2] water-born, [3] born through union [of male and female], and [4] spontaneous are the four ways of birth. 'The five "courses" [after death]'—[1] the hells, [2] the sphere of crawling existence, [3] departed beings, [4] devas, and [5] men are the five 'courses.' 'The seven stations of consciousness'—[1] diverse bodies and diverse perceptions, [2] one body and diverse perceptions, [3] diverse bodies and one perception, [4] one body and one perception, [5] the sphere of perception of space, [6] the sphere of perception of consciousness, and [7] the sphere of perception of no-thing are the seven stations of consciousness. 'The nine abodes of beings'—the previous seven and [8] beings without perception and [9] beings with neither perception nor nonperception are the nine abodes of beings" (*Dag.*, 153.29ff.).

7. "'Influxes'—the four influxes such as the influx of sensuality, etc." (*Dps.*, p.48). "These are [1] desire for sensuality, [2] desire for existence, [3] wrong views, and [4] ignorance" (*Sdk.*, p.55). See also above, note 13 in chapter 2.

"[They] are called influxes [or intoxicants] because they flow through the six doors such as the eyes, etc., and because they flow out up to the end of the universe in terms of space, and up to 'change of lineage' *(gotrabhu)*, consciousness in terms of dharmas, and because they are fermenting in consciousnesses for an unlimited time in *saṃsāra* without beginning and end" (*Sdk.*, p. 55).

"One should understand that the influx of sensuality is sensual attraction that arises when an agreeable form, etc., is met as an object of the six doors such as the eyes, etc.; and the influx for existence is clinging that arises with regard to existence; and the influx of views is wrong views that exist upon considering form, etc., as permanent, beautiful, pleasant, having a soul *(ātmaya)*; and the influx of ignorance is delusion that veils the actual situation *(yathārthaya)* of the inherent nature of impermanence, suffering, and absence of soul with regard to form, etc." (*Sdk.*, p. 56).

8. On the ninefold self-estimation *(māna)*, see above, note 39 in chapter 5. And see also *Sdk.*, p. 57, for a full listing.

9.* "Indeed": following APB, p. 375, and SHB, p. 300, *eva ca*, in preference to PTS, II, 181, *evaṃ ca*.

10. On the five kinds of release, see above, the commentative gloss on st. 19, note 54 in chapter 1; note 28 in chapter 4.

11. "'Who has no faith'—not for one is there faith by the words of another because one knows, having realized for oneself, ordinary and world-transcending virtuous qualities such as meditative-absorption, insight, Path and Fruits, etc., which have been penetrated to by one. Or,

there is no faith in any teacher other than the Buddha" (*Dps.*, p. 51).

12. This is a pun; *akataññu* also means "ungrateful."
13. This is a pun; *sandhicchedo* also means "burglar" i.e., one who enters a house by breaking through the joints or weak points.
14.* "The person of this kind": following APB, p. 379, and SHB, p. 303, *so evarūpo naro*, in preference to PTS, II, 188, *so evarūpo naro sa ve.*

## Chapter VIII

1.* For *api ce* of *Dhp.*, 100, and *PDhp.*, 377, *Uv.*, xxiv, 1, has *yac ca*; *GDhp.*, 306, has *bi ya* ( = *'pi ca*). In such instances *ca* seems to be the equivalent of *ce* (see note 13 below and PTSD, under *ca*, 3, conditional use). In strict accordance with the commentary we would have had to translate "suppose [there were] even a thousand statements . . . better [than they is] one single word."
2.* "They are": following APB, p. 390, *tā ca*, in preference to PTS, II, 208, *tāva*.
3. On the three knowledges, see above, note 20 in chapter 2 (*Dag.*, 129.10).
4. The five aggregates (*khandhas*: factors in the analysis of individuality) are (1) material form, or body (*rūpa*), (2) feeling (*vedanā*), (3) sensation (*saññā*), (4) *saṅkhāras*, and (5) consciousness (*viññāṇa*). So *Dv.*, p. 705 (on *Dhp.*, v. 374). See also *Dp.*, p. 193 (on *Dhp.*, v. 202). See also below, note 20 in this chapter.
5. The eighteen *dhātus* (bases of interplay of consciousness, sense, and sense objects) are represented by the interplay of consciousness with the internal *āyatanas*, or six senses, and external *āyatanas*, or corresponding sense objects, yielding the resultant six sense-consciousnesses. On the internal and external *āyatanas*, see the immediately following note (*Sdk.*, p. 186 [on *Dhp.*, 385]). The six consciousnesses formed in this analysis of 18 *dhātus*, resulting from the interplay of (1–6) the six senses and (7–12) the six sense objects, are (13) eye-consciousness, (14) ear-consciousness, (15) nose-consciousness, (16) tongue-consciousness, (17) body-consciousness, and (18) mind(*manas*)-consciousness.
6. The *āyatanas* (spheres of interaction of senses and sense objects) are (1) the eyes, (2) ears, (3) nose, (4) tongue, (5) body, and (6) the mind-organ (*manas*), together with (1) material form, (2) sound, (3) odor or smell, (4) taste, (5) tangibles, and (6) dhammas. So *Sdk.*, p. 186 (on *Dhp.*, v. 385).
7. Although the complete traditional list of the *indriyas*, faculties, characteristic aptitudes, is twenty-two in number (see under *indriya* in

PTSD), our sources mention frequently a common sixfold division: (1) the sense faculty of the eye, (2) ear, (3) nose, (4) tongue, (5) body, (6) mind (*manas*). So *DhpA.*, I, 76 (on *Dhp.* 7–8); *Dp.*, p. 12; *Sds.*, IX, 2477 (on *Dhp.*, 375). But *Sdk.*, p. 6, and *Sds.*, I, 78–81, 89–92, commenting on *Dhp.* 7–8, indicate the larger list by adding to these six "the faculty of femininity, the faculty of masculinity, etc." *Sdk.*, p. 181, commenting on *Dhp.* 370, mentions the faculties of faith, enterprise, mindfulness, concentration, and wisdom, which form a part of the complete list of twenty-two. These five also represent the fivefold category of *bala*s—i.e., strength or powers.

8. The five strengths or powers (*bala*s) are (1) faith, (2) enterprise, (3) mindfulness, (4) concentration, and (5) wisdom. On the interrelatedness of the *bala*s with the *indriya*s, see the immediately preceding note and note 8 in chapter 2.
9. The seven constituents of enlightenment (*bojjhaṅga*s) are mentioned above, note 23 in chapter 6.
10. The four foundations of mindfulness are with regard to (1) the body, (2) the sensations, (3) the mind, and (4) dhammas. See above, note 8 in chapter 2.
11.* That is, the regular form is *jito*, not *jitam*. *Uv.*, xxiii, 4, *jitaḥ* and *PDhp.*, 320, *dānto*, correspond to the masculine form *jito* rather than *jitaṃ* found in our text.
12. "No *gandharva* such as Timbarū, Nārada, etc., is able to make it a nonvictory" (*Dps.*, p. 54).
13.* *PDhp.*, 380, has *yac cha* where Pali has *yaṃ ce*.
14.* "Gone into a forest": following APB, p. 403, and SHB, p. 322, *vanaṃ pavisitvā*, in preference to PTS, II, 233, *vanaṃ pavisitvā pi*.
15.* "Offerings given to invited guests": following APB, p. 404, SHB, p. 323, and *Dag.*, 165.5, *pāhunadānaṃ*, in preference to PTS, II, 234, *pahutadānaṃ*.
16.* "And": following APB, p. 406, and SHB, p. 325, *c'assa*, in preference to PTS, II, 239, *v'assa*.
17. "'Of one who is a meditator'—one who is given to meditational-absorption on an object or on a characteristic—i.e., the *bhikkhu* engaged in the meditation of tranquility and insight" (*Dps.*, p. 56). See also *Dag.*, 168.4.
18. "'Thoughts (*vitakka*) directed to sensuality' is thinking of satisfying the senses, such as eye, ear, etc., through the five strands of sensuality, such as form, sound, etc., which are pleasing to the mind. 'Thoughts characterized by ill will' is thinking of harming another, 'let him be killed, let him be destroyed.' 'Thoughts characterized by harming' is thinking of harassing, oppressing another" (*Sdk.*, p. 63).

19. "Meditation on the characteristics and meditation on the object" (*Dag.*, 169.2–3).

20. "Not seeing the rise and demise of the five *khandhas* by means of the twenty-five characteristics"—

"The coming into being of the five aggregates is [their] rise, their dissolution is [their] demise. To consider the coming into being of form *(rūpa)* on account of ignorance, craving, action *(kamma)*, and food, and also to see the mere characteristic of its instantaneous coming into being, without looking for its causative aspect; thus one should consider the rise of form in five ways. Likewise, to consider the rise of the [other] four aggregates of feeling *(vedanā)* . . . cognition *(saññā)* . . . *saṅkhāras* . . . and consciousness *(viññāṇa)* each as coming into being by ignorance, craving, action, and contact, and also to see the mere characteristic of each of them instantaneously coming into being; thus should the rise of the [other] four aggregates be viewed, each in five ways. Thus the rise of the five aggregates . . . is seen in twenty-five ways. To see that the rise of the aggregates is stopped by abolishing [the foregoing] causes [such as] ignorance, craving, action, and food [or contact], and also to see the mere cessation [of each of the aggregates]—[in this way, their] cessation [also] should be seen in twenty-five ways" (*Dp.*, p. 117). The same appears at *Dag.*, 170.3ff. in its characteristically terse style.

# Chapter IX

1. Reference is to the background story given earlier in the commentary. See BL, II, 262–64. On wholesome deeds, see above, note 46 in chapter 1, for the standard list of ten, and for the standard list of ten unwholesome deeds, see above, note 43 in chapter 1. See also *Dv.*, p. 241, note, for a list of both in a discussion of this stanza (*Dhp.*, v. 116).

2.* "Let him do it": PTS, III, 9, APB, p. 431, and SHB, p. 347, all have *karoth' eva,* which seems questionable. PTS records the *v. l. karot' eva* (no doubt *karotu +eva,* imperative, 3rd person, singular), which perhaps explains the sense of *kayirātha* (optative, 3rd person, singular) acceptably. (*Dps.,* pp. 59, 60, explains *kayirātha* of *Dhp.,* 117*b,* 118*b,* with *karannē yi,* which answers to Pali imperative/optative, 3rd person singular.)

3.* "It": following APB, p. 440, *etam,* in preference to PTS, III, 20, and SHB, p. 352, *evam.*

4. Reference is to the background story given earlier in the commentary. See BL, II, 274–76.
5. Allusion is made to the background story given earlier in the commentary. See BL, II, 276–81, esp. p. 279.

## Chapter X

1.* This translation follows the commentary. The meaning of this verse is far from clear. Its equivalent in both *PDhp.* and *Uv.* is preceded by another line that begins, "If you move yourself, like a metal [?] that has been struck. . . ." In the second line both *Uv.*, xxvi, 5, and *PDhp.*, 200, seem to speak of a *kaṃsi/kaṃsa* that is *not* struck, whereas the Pali commentary speaks of one that has been struck and "flattened out."

2.* "Harass": following APB, p. 462, and SHB, p. 373, *hanato,* for PTS, III, 58, *paharantassa.*

3.* *Pāceti: PDhp.*, 201, has the regular form *pājeti* (from *pra* + $\sqrt{aj}$. See Wilhelm Geiger, *Pāli Literature and Language*, translated by B. Ghosh, 2nd ed. (University of Calcutta, 1956), Part II, para. 39.3, p. 85. *Uv.*, i, 17, has *prāpayati.* Cf. also *GDhp.*, 148, *payedi.*

4.* "Suffers": following APB, p. 466, and SHB, p. 377, *tappati,* in preference to PTS, III, 64, *paccati.*

5.* "In one eye": APB, p. 470, and SHB, p. 380, *ekacakkhuka,* seems preferable to PTS, III, 70, *ekacakkhula.*

6.* For the problematic *rajo va jallaṃ*, *PDhp.*, 196, seems to read *rajo celaṃ* (MS evidence is not decisive). *Uv.*, xxxiii, 1, has *rajo malaṃ.* The *PDhp. rajo celaṃ* may mean "dusty cloth," which fits the context well.

7. " 'Eightfold doubt'—doubt arising with reference to eight bases: doubt about [1] the Buddha, [2] Dhamma, [3] the Sangha, [4] the beginning [of things], [5] the end [of things], [6] the past and future, [7] the causal relation of [all] this, and [8] dhammas that have conditionally arisen" (*Dag.*, 182.31ff.).

8.* *Bhavātha:* following APB, p. 479, and SHB, p. 387, in preference to PTS, III, 86, *hotha.* For this word the parallel text of *PDhp.*, 330, has *carāṇo* and that of *Uv.*, xix, 1, has *careta.* Lines *e* and *f* of the Pali verse do not tally with the corresponding texts of *PDhp.* and *Uv.*, which are themselves divergent on this point.

9. "Faith is a wholesome mental process that causes calm joy in the mind and mental processes with regard to the object that occurs with it in the thought procedures themselves. That faith itself is twofold, such as customary and world-transcending. Of the two, the mental process of faith that occurs in thoughts pertaining to Paths and Fruits is called

world-transcending faith because it causes calm joy in the thought with regard to the object of *Nirvāṇa*, and that [mental process of faith] itself, when it has to do with customary wholesome thoughts is called customary faith because it causes calm joy in thoughts with regard to the qualities, etc., of the three gems" (*Sdk.*, p. 76).

10. On the fourfold virtue leading to purity, see above, note 40 in chapter 1.
11. "With the integration considered as the eight attainments pertaining to the realm of form and the formless realm *(rūpārūpa)*" (*Dps.*, p. 71). See also above, note 11 in chapter 2.
12. On the three forms of understanding, or knowledge, see above, note 20 in chapter 2. See also *Dag.*, 184.31–185.1.
13. The eight forms of understanding, or knowledge, are (1) knowledge by insight *(vipasanāñāṇa)*, (2) knowledge of psychic power constituted by the mind *(manomayiddhi)*, (3) knowledge of the divisions of psychic powers *(iddhippabheda)*, (4) the heavenly ear, (5) knowledge of the thoughts of others, (6) knowledge of future abodes, (7) knowledge of the divine eye, (8) gnosis of the destruction of the influxes. So *Sdk.*, p. 77. See also *Dag.*, 185.2, and notes 20 and 21 in chapter 2.
14. " 'The fifteen modes [or forms] of conduct' are the fifteen dhammas of conduct: [1] restraint with regard to precepts, [2] guarding the 'doors' with regard to the senses, [3] knowing the proper measure with regard to food, [4] striving vigilantly *(jāgariyanuyoga)*, [5] faith, [6] a sense of shame, [7] a sense of fear, [8] learning, [9] enterprise, [10] mindfulness, [11] wisdom, and the four [12–15] meditative-absorptions pertaining to the fine material realm" (*Dag.*, 185.3).

## Chapter XI

1.* For Pali *hāso*, *GDhp.*, v. 143, has *harṣo*; *Uv.*, i. 4, has *harṣaḥ*. It would seem that *hāso* represents a form of the root *harṣ-* rather than the root *hās-*, "due to a misunderstanding of *hasso* (< *harṣo*) as if equivalent to *hāsyo* which would readily be 'corrected' to *hāso*" (*GDhpC.*, p. 217). If so, the "correction" must be very ancient: *PDhp.*, 233, also has *hāso*.
2. "These are said to be the 'eleven fires': [1] passion, [2] hatred, [3] delusion, [4] illness, [5] old age, [6] death, [7] sorrow, [8] lamentation, [9] physical suffering, [10] depression, and [11] excessive effort" (*Sdk.*, pp. 80–81).
3. The darkness of the eightfold ignorance, listed in *Dag.*, 187.12–15, refers to the same eight as met previously as the "eightfold doubt." See above, note 7 in chapter 10.
4.* Whereas *bhijjati* is in the present tense, *GDhp.*, 142, *bhetsidi*, and *Uv.*,

i, 34, *bhetsyate* are future forms. So is *PDhp.*, 260, *bhijjīhiti*. The commentative explanation, using a specific future verb, suggests that the future tense would have been more apt, although the text in use already had the present verb. "Since, however, futures such as *bhecchati* are sufficiently rare in Pali to invite alteration, it seems probable that the future may be the original form in this verse" (*GDhpC.*, p. 217).

5. This is an allusion to the background story given earlier in the commentary. See BL, II, 334.

6.* "Because it is . . . putrid": following APB, p. 493, and SHB, p. 399, *pūtitāya*, in preference to PTS, III, 111, *pūtikāyaṃ*.

7.* "Of yours": following APB, p. 493, and SHB, p. 399, *tava deho*, in preference to PTS, III, 111, *tad eva deho*.

8.* PTS, APB, etc., have the form *alāpūn-eva*. *GDhp.*, 154, has *ala'uṇi ba*. A comparable verse of the *Divyāvadāna* (v. 561) has *alābur iva*. "The spelling with *-p-* is probably a late pedantry . . . and *-b-* is cited from the Burmese manuscripts (*DhpA.*, [PTS edition] iii, 112). Moreover, inasmuch as the commentary has *viya* . . . the verse should be restored to *alābūni va*" (*GDhpC.*, p. 226). The evidence of the *GDhp.* and the *Divyāvadāna* makes it clear that the Pali stanza 149 has telescoped two original stanzas (*GDhp.*, 154, 155), as *GDhpC.* points out. *PDhp.* has no parallel verse.

9. Allusion is made to the background story given earlier in the commentary. See BL, II, 335.

10.* For lines 1 and 3 of stanza 150, *GDhp.*, 284, has *nakara aṭhi-pakara . . . yatra rako ya doṣo ya*, agreeing with *Uv.* (Chakravarty edition, xvi, 23), *nagaraṃ asthi-prākāraṃ . . . yatra rāgaś ca deṣaś ca* (*Uv.*, Bernhard edition, has a *hy—hi*—after *nagaram* and *deṣaś ca* in the sanskritized form of *dveṣaś ca*). ". . . it would seem that *rāgo* and *doso* have been replaced in the Pali . . . in order to make the stanza fit better into its chapter on old age" (*GDhpC.*, p. 263). *PDhp.* has no parallel stanza.

11.* "Early and late food, etc.": following SHB, p. 402, *pubbanna-parannādīnaṃ*, and PTS, III, 118, *pubbaṇṇa-paraṇṇādīnaṃ*, in preference to APB, p. 498, *pubbannādīnaṃ*. The PTS reading is substantiated by *Dag.*, 190. *Dag.* understands by *pubbaṇṇa* such pulses as black and green gram and by *aparaṇṇa* such grains as rice. The senses are reversed in the source quoted by PTSD (under *anna*). The PTSD explanation of *sūpeyya* as "boiled or prepared" is not exact enough to enlighten us in this context. The distinction probably was that some kinds of grain formed the first dish, whereas others were "to serve as curry" *( = sūpeyya)*—i.e., they were "later" dishes (the words literally mean "earlier food," "later food"). The reference here is to a "silo" for storing these two kinds of food grains, after harvesting.

12.* "Good health": following APB, p. 498, *aroga-*, in preference to PTS, III, 118, and SHB, p. 402, *āroga-*.

13.* "Done": following APB, p. 498, *-karaṇa-*, in preference to PTS, III, 118, and SHB, p. 402, *-karaṇa-*.

14.* *GDhpC.*, pp. 227–28, says that the commentative interpretation fails to convey the contrast that was probably intended in the stanza. "For the whole point is that, unlike the king's chariot, the doctrine does not wear out, 'because good men teach it to other good men', their disciples and successors." *GDhpC.* also says that the reason for this is the failure to see the potential dative sense of forms like *sabbhi*, which is of course rare: "The usage existed, nevertheless, and was noted by Bloch from the Aśokan inscriptions." *Uv.*, i, 28, *santo hi taṃ satsu nivedayanti*, perhaps confirms the sense proposed by *GDhpC. PDhp.* has no parallel stanza.

15. "This one" refers to Lāḷudāyi Thera mentioned in the background story given earlier in the commentary. See BL, II, 343–45.

16. On the ninefold self-estimation, see above, note 39 in chapter 5.

17. On the six sense-doors, see above, note 26 in chapter 1.

18.* *Visaṃkhitaṃ:* so in all printed editions consulted and in *Dps. Uv.*, xxi, 7*d*, has *visaṃskṛtam*, for which the more common Pali form would be *visaṃkhataṃ*, which PTS, IV, 128, footnote 1, notes as a *v.l.* (Burmese MSS).

19.* "Wisdom of enlightenment": following APB, p. 503, and SHB, p. 407, supported by *Dag.*, 191: *yena ñāṇena sakkā taṃ daṭṭhuṃ*, in preference to PTS, III, 128, *yena kāraṇena sakkā so daṭṭhuṃ.*

20.* "Mixed up as it is": following APB, p. 503, *missattāya*, in preference to PTS, III, 128, *missitāya.*

21.* "I have attained": the commentary explains *ajjhagā* with *adhigato 'smi*, thus seeing in it a first person singular. This is how *Dps.* also explains the word (p. 75). However, *Uv.*, xxxi, 7, has *adhyagāḥ*, second person singular. The last two lines according to *Uv.* should mean: "The mind having attained freedom from *saṃskāra*s, here itself you have come to dissolution," "you" obviously being the "housebuilder." However, it seems preferable to take *ajjhagā* as a third person singular *( = adhyagāt)* and connect the last line with the subject of the sixth line: "The mind has attained freedom from *saṃkhāra*s. It has come to the end of cravings."

22.* *Atikhīṇā:* so in PTS, III, 132, *Dps.*, p. 76, and *Dag.*, 192. APB, p. 506, and SHB, p. 409, have *atikhittā* (*Uv.*, xvii, 4, has *atikīrṇā*). The commentative exegesis does not seem to do justice to the prefix *ati-*. If the reading were *atikhittā*, it might have meant "overshot" (?).

23.* For *anutthunaṃ*, GDhp., 139*b*, has *anuṣvaru*, agreeing with *Uv.*, xvii,

4 (Chakravarty edition), *anusmaran:* so *GDhp.*, p. 217. *PDhp.*, 230, has *anutthanaṃ*, which is obviously cognate with Pali *anutthunaṃ*. See PTSD, under *anutthunāti*.

24. Reference is to the background story given earlier in the commentary. See BL, II, 346–48.

25.* "No . . . getting away": following APB, 506, and SHB, p. 409, *gamanābhāvo*, in preference to PTS, III, 132, *gamanabhāvo*.

## Chapter XII

1. "'Master of dhamma' because he has mastery with regard to the teaching of dhamma. The same is stated by the phrase 'by virtue of his skill in discourse'" (*Dag.*, 193.17–18). See also above, note 3 in chapter 7.

2. "'Practicing the conduct of the "noble family"' is being content with whatever robes [one has], etc., and taking delight in meditation" (*Dag.*, 194.2–4).

3. Our translation follows the commentary. The interpretation of this verse is uncertain, due to the fact that the crucial second line is divergently handed down in the four available textual traditions (*Dhp.*, *PDhp.*, *GDhp.*, and *Uv.*).

4. On the tenfold path of the unwholesome, see above, note 43 in chapter 1.

5.* "Definitely unvirtuous": following APB, p. 519, and SHB, p. 420, *accaṇtadussīlo*, in preference to PTS, III, 153.7, *accantadussīlyo*.

6.* "Life" or "personality": following APB, p. 519, and SHB, p. 420, *attabhāvaṃ otatam*, in preference to PTS, III, 153.16, *otatam*.

7.* "Spreading over": PTS, III, 153.14, has *otarantī*. APB, p. 519, and SHB, p. 420, have *ottharanti*. *Dag.*, 196.13, has *otatantī*. Our translation answers to either *ottharantī* or *otatantī*. The PTS reading of *otarantī* probably represents a miscopying of *otatantī* in the MS.

8. We have preserved the structure of the commentative sentence without simplifying it, so that the reader will get a sense of the stylistic complexity of the original comment.

9.* For *kaṭṭhakasseva*, *GDhp.*, 258*e*, has *kaḍakaseva*. The Prakrit *kaḍaka* is the equivalent of Sanskrit *kaṇṭaka*: bamboo. "There is a strong suspicion that the anomalous *kaṭṭhaka* in the Pali tradition is merely a miscopying for *kaṇṭaka* probably through the intermediate stage of *kaṇṭhaka*" (*GDhpC.*, p. 255). This is confirmed by *PDhp.*, 316 *c*, which reads *palāni kaṇṭakass' eva*.

10.* It is interesting that the Sanskrit version of this verse in the Pali

*DhpA.* is found in *Uv.*, xiii, 1. See the *Uv.* edition by Bernhard, i, 200, citing parallel texts.

11. On the four states of woe, see above, note 15 in chapter 1.

12.* "And to Nibbāna": the word used here is *agati. Dag.*, 197.12, explains *agati* as Nibbāna. Literally *agati* means "[that which has] no movement."

13.* *SdhRv.*, p. 656, and the later Sinhala Buddhist exegetical tradition, e.g., *Sdk.*, p. 91, and *Dad.*, p. 170, interpret this differently. They take the commentative text (i.e., *DhpA.*), at this point as *upajjhāyādivattāni pi hāpetvā vā* (cf. APB, p. 523): "even to the neglect of duties in respect of the preceptor, etc." However, the old Sinhala *sannaya* (*Dps.*, p. 80, *c* [13th or 14th century]) gives the above interpretation (*upādhyāya vat ādiya no pirihelā da*: "and not neglecting the duties regarding [one's] preceptor, etc."). It would seem that it took *bhāvetvā ca* as the commentative text, as does the PTS edition. The commentative text, as well as its interpretation, deserve further study.

The text of the relevant comment in the *SdhRv.* is as follows: "Lay persons should not neglect the benefit accruing to oneself be it ever so small, in preference to great benefits accruing to others. . . . Here, moreover, the matter has been stated in the course of [giving instructions on] a meditation-topic. Hence, by way of attending to one's purpose, one should not neglect the duties in respect of fellow bhikkhus, the shrines of the temple, or one's preceptors. Only those who perform [such] customary duties are able to attain to Path and Fruit. So all that is also 'one's own purpose.' But if one, having developed enterprise, is on the point of achieving realization within a few days, one would accomplish that—even to the neglect of duties in respect of the preceptor, etc. Since customary duty is also performed with a view to achieving realization itself, there is no harm in relaxing it, if that contributes to realization" (*Saddharma Ratnāvaliya*, edited by Sir D. B. Jayatilaka, Part V [Colombo: Anula Press, 1934], p. 656).

## Chapter XIII

1. On the five strands of sensuality (*pañcakāmaguṇa*), see note 10 in chapter 3 and note 7 in chapter 4, above.

2.* Following PTS, III, 163, and APB, p. 525, *paṭisevitabbo*. However, SHB, p. 425, *na paṭisevitabbo*, gives a much better sense in the context: "It is the lowly quality that should not be resorted to, even by camels and bullocks."

3. "Improper views are the childish views that are [fundamentally]

twofold—i.e., eternalist and annihilationist, which have been censured by the wise. They [the improper views] themselves are sixty-two" (*Sdk.*, pp. 91–92).

4.* *Dag.*, 198.17ff., understands "world" *(loka)* here to be *saṃsāra*, the cycle of births (so also *Dps.*, p. 81; *Sdk.*, p. 92). This seems legitimate because one who has transcended the cycle of births is commonly regarded as "beyond the worldly" *(lokuttara)* and one caught up in it as "worldly" *(lokiya)*. That it is prudent not to prolong the continuance in *saṃsāra* is a common idea in Theravāda thought. That is probably why the commentator says that the one who resorts to lowly qualities is an augmenter of the world, without elaborating on it. The comment at *GDhpC.*, p. 213, "Such a frank confession of ignorance by a commentator as to the meaning of a word is so rare that it seems almost ungracious for a modern successor to add his own conjectures" is unwarranted.

5.* Although the Pali commentary treats *uttiṭṭhe* as a noun in the locative case, *Uv.*, iv, 35, has *uttiṣṭhet*, and *PDhp.*, 27, has *uṭṭheyā*, as a hortative verb (comparable to the other verb in the stanza, *pamajjeyya*). Translators have usually treated it as a hortative verb, thus following another old interpretation in preference to that of the Pali commentary.

6. On the four modes of deportment see above, note 28 in chapter 1.

7. Reference is to Prince Abhaya, who figures in the background story given earlier in the commentary. See BL, III, 4–5.

8. "These, namely, craving, views, self-estimation, anger, ignorance, defilements, misconduct, are the sevenfold attachments *(saṅgayō)*. Some say [they are] the seven latent dispositions *(anusaya)*, i.e., passion, hatred, self-estimation, views, [speculative] doubt, passion for existence, and ignorance. The activity of clinging with regard to the *saṃskāra*s, having taken the five *skandha*s as a sentient being, a person, etc., is in the mode of either craving, views, etc., or passion, hatred, etc. Hence they are called attachments" (*Sdk.*, p. 94).

9. Allusion is made to the background story given earlier in the commentary. See BL, III, 18.

10. *Dag.*, 200. 5–6, notes these as four: (1) will *(chanda)*, (2) thought *(citta)*, (3) enterprise *(viriya)*, and (4) investigation *(vimaṃsa)*.

*Ṛddhi* [psychic power] is so called because it leads one to attain prosperity *(samṛddhiya)* or because it brings about accomplishment *(siddha)*.

That *ṛddhi* itself is tenfold; [1] *ṛddhi* of determination, [2] of miraculous transformation, [3] mind-made, [4] of the pervasion of knowledge, [5] of the pervasion of concentration, [6] noble, [7] brought about by consequences of action, [8] brought about by merit, [9] made of [esoteric] learning, and [10] *ṛddhi* of right exertion. One should know the details of this after consulting the *Visuddhimagga* or after inquiring from someone who knows.

"These [four], will, thought, enterprise, investigation, are called 'bases of psychic power' *(ṛddhipāda)* because they are the means *(upāya)* for attaining *ṛddhi*" (*Sdk.*, pp. 95–96).

11.* Following APB, p. 534, SHB, p. 433, and *Dps.*, p. 84, *savāhiniṃ*, in preference to PTS, III, 177, *savāhanaṃ*.

12. *Dps.*, p. 84, mentions a well-known initial phrase indicating the verses describing Māra's armies, "'Your first army is sensual lust, aversion is called the second,' etc." *Sdk.*, p. 96, quotes two full Pali verses that enumerate the forces of Māra:

Your first army is sensual lust; aversion is called the second.
Your third is hunger and thirst; craving is proclaimed the fourth.
Sloth and torpor are your fifth; fear is proclaimed the sixth.
Doubt is your seventh; hypocrisy and obstinacy are the eighth.

Whatever gain, veneration, honor, and fame wrongly acquired,
And whoever praises oneself and despises others,
These, O Namuci, are your army, the fighting force of the Dark One.
One incompetent does not conquer them; but having cut them away,
One achieves bliss.

13. "The twenty-six kinds of heaven: There are six heavens of the sphere of sensuality, such as the Cātumahārājika, etc., sixteen brahma-worlds, such as the *Brahmapārisajja*, of the fine material sphere, and four brahma-worlds, such as the realm of infinite space, of the formless [or nonmaterial] sphere" (*Sdk.*, p. 97). Cf. also the terse comment in *Dag.*, 201.9–10. For a brief description of one of these brahma-worlds, see below, note 4 in chapter 15.

14. *Nāga*s are a kind of semidivine being frequently mentioned in Indian literature. They are represented as living in regions below the earth, whence they often come via rivers, etc. Their physiognomy is represented as partially resembling a cobra, whence their name *nāga* (cobra).

*Supaṇṇa*s (Skt., *suparṇa*: "beautiful of wing") also figure in Indian literature, Buddist as well as Hindu. They too are superhuman beings, winged like birds.

*Vemānika-peta*s (from *vimāna*: the palatial vehicle of a divine being) are departed spirits who alternatively enjoy heavenly bliss and suffer the agony of ghosts. Their abodes resemble the *vimānas*. See *Sdk.*, p. 97.

15.* Following SHB, p. 441, and APB, p. 543, *na ekasmiṃ*, in preference to PTS, III, 192, *ekasmiṃ*.

## Chapter XIV

1.* The commentary, as well as the Sinhala tradition (cf. *Dag.*, 202), breaks up *noyāti* thus. Evidently they took it to be a phrase joined by *sandhi*, in which case the present reading is a simplification of *noyyāti*. *Uv.*, xxix, 52, *anveti na*, does not help us to envisage the Pali development. (*Dps.*, p. 82, follows the commentative exegesis, but simply quotes the extant reading without breaking it up as *na uyyāti.*) *PDhp.*, 277, has *na upeti*, which seems to support *no yati* (=*na u yāti*?).

2. Allusion is made to the background story given earlier in the commentary. See BL, III, 31–35.

3.* Following *Dag.*, 202, reading *saṃsibbita-parisibbita-pariyonaddha(na)ṭṭhena* in preference to PTS, III, 198, *saṃsibbita-pariyonaddhaṭṭhena*. SHB, p. 443, and APB, p. 547, have *saṃsibbita-parisaṃsibbita-pariyonaddhaṭṭhena*, which is very close to *Dag*. The *-na-* of *Dag. pariyonaddhana* is, however, questionable.

4. "Craving is like a net because it intertwines and envelopes" (*Dps.*, p. 86).

5. PTS, III, 198, has also *visattamanatāya*, a word of uncertain meaning and not found in the Sinhala sources.

6. On the five hindrances, see note 22 in chapter 6, above.

7. The third category of awakened ones, mentioned in the text, represents the Pali word *anubuddhā*, meaning those who have attained enlightenment, but who have done so having followed the instruction of a Buddha. The term is glossed at *Sdk.*, p. 102, by "preeminent disciples *(agraśrāvaka)*"; so also *Sdk.*, pp. 98–99; and in *Dv.*, p. 386, by "Arahant" *(rahat)*.

8. Allusion is made to the background story given earlier in the commentary. See BL, III, 61–62.

9.* Our translation accords more closely with *nāhosi* of SHB, p. 464, and APB, p. 572, than with *natthi* of PTS, III, 240.

10.* Cf. *Dag.*, 214, *dukkhakkhandha äyi sutanhi*, "in such *suttas* as the *Dukkhakkhandha*." See the PTS edition of the *Majjhima-nikāya*, I, 83–90 *(Mahādukkhakkhandasutta)*, and I, 91–95 *(Cūḷadukkhakkhandhasutta)*.

11. A *devatā* tried to tempt Venerable Samiddhi, but he remained

steadfast in his determination to pursue the religious life. See *Saṃyutta-nikāya*, I, 8ff. (PTS edition).

12.* Our translation is closer to *savaṇena* of APB, p. 573, and SHB, p. 465, than to PTS, III, 241, *savanante*.

13.* The commentator says the apparent accusative singular form is misleading; it stands for the nominative plural form *bahū*. *PDhp.*, 216, has *bahū; Uv.*, xxvii, 3, *bahavaḥ* (both nominative plural). Obviously *bahuṃ* is by "attraction" of the word *saraṇaṃ* coming almost next. It is interesting that *Dag.* has not failed to comment on the point. See *Dag.*, 215.16ff.

14.* *Dag.*, 215.18ff., notes *pabbate* has been used by the commentator to indicate that there is "transference of gender" in the word *pabbatāni* of the stanza. Most interesting to note is that *PDhp.*, 216, has *parvvate* where the Pali has *pabbatāni*.

15. "'Obtain sons, and so forth—with the term 'and so forth' one should include acquisition of wealth, acquisition of territory, and so forth" (*Dag.*, 215.20).

16. This formula can be found in the *Visuddhimagga*, PTS edition, I, 198–221. Cf. also D, II, 93–94, III, 5; M, I, 37; A, III, 285–86.

The complete formula reads:

"He is the Blessed One, the Worthy Being, the Fully Enlightened One, endowed with knowledge and noble conduct, the well-gone, knower of the worlds, incomparable trainer of human beings who are amenable to be trained, teacher of men and gods, the Blessed Awakened One.

"Well proclaimed by the Blessed One is Dhamma that is visible, timeless, characterized by [the imperatives] 'Come! Look!', leading on, to be known personally by the wise.

"Well set out [on the Path] is the community of the Blessed One's disciples, directly set out is the community of the Blessed One's disciples, properly set out is the community of the Blessed One's disciples, fully set out is the community of the Blessed One's disciples—that is to say, the four pairs of persons, the eight persons [i.e., those who have attained the four Paths and the four Fruits]. This community of the Blessed One's disciples is to be given offerings, is to be welcomed, is to be given gifts, is to be honored, is an incomparable field of merit for the world."

17. "In the phrase 'worshiping other *titthiyas* [monks of other religious orders], and so on,' by the term 'and so on' one should include devoting oneself to another dhamma, to another sangha, and so forth" (*Dag.*, 215.27–29).

18. "'Who has gone for refuge to these'—that is, the world-transcending

going for refuge because doubt and wrong knowledge with regard to the objects such as the Buddha, etc., are put aside by the knowledge accompanying the Paths. The person endowed with these Paths is one who has gone for refuge by way of this knowledge" (*Dag.*, 215.30–34).

19. This "middle country" refers to ancient middle India, or *dambadiva* (Pali: *jambudīpa*) according to *Dad.*, p. 190, *Dv.*, p. 398, and *Dp.*, p. 186.
20. *GDhpC.*, p. 234, cites approvingly a translation for this line, appearing in the verse and commentary, proposed by Paul Thieme: "that family is radiant in happiness."
21.* Following APB, p. 579, SHB, 469, *sakkā*, for PTS, III, 250, *sukham*. (*Dps.*, p. 91, translates "inasmuch as it is possible.")
22. On the *dhutaṅga* practices, see above, note 6 in chapter 2.
23. This passage can be found in the PTS edition of *Aṅgutāra-nikāya*, IV, 164.
24. The four requisites are robes, alms bowls, dwellings, and medicaments.
25.* Following APB, p. 581, and SHB, p. 470, *samatikkanta-taṇha-diṭṭhi-māna-papañca*, in preference to *samatikkante taṇhā-diṭṭhi-māna-papañca* of PTS, III, 252.
26.* One would have expected this comment to read (1) *tiṇṇo ti atikkanto; tiṇṇa-soka-pariddave ti atikkanta-soka-pariddave* or (2) *tiṇṇo ti atikkanto; tiṇṇa-soka-pariddave ti ime dve atikkante*. However, APB, p. 580, has *tiṇṇo ti atikkanto; tiṇṇa-soka-pariddave ti atikkanta-soka-pariddave; ime dve atikkante ti attho*. PTS, III, 252, has all this except for the second *atikkanta-*. SHB, p. 470, has all of it except for the initial *tiṇṇo ti atikkanto*.
27. Reference is to the *brahmā* Ghaṭīkāra, mentioned in the background story given earlier in the commentary. See BL, III, 68–69.
28.* Our tentative (and no doubt strained) translation bypasses considerable textual difficulties in the commentary and the verse, such as (1) the form *nānaṃ* (APB, p. 580, which seems preferable to PTS, III, 252, and SHB, p. 470, *dānam*); (2) the absence of (i) *nibbute*, which one would logically expect after *kilesa-parinibbāna-nimittena*, and of (ii) a word suggesting the sense "only" along with the expression "distinctions are applicable" *(bhedā yujjanti)*; (3) the plural *bhedā*, which looks questionable; (4) *imettam iti* of the verse (which *Dps.*, p. 92, strangely breaks up as *imam ettam iti*), which too is problematic. (As for the comment on this, we have followed APB, p. 580: *imettam iti kena cīti: imaṃ ettakaṃ imaṃ ettakaṃ ti kena cīti: api saddo idha sambandhetabbo*, which is different from the reading in PTS, III, 252, in that *-attho* found in line 14 of the latter is missing here.) *Dhp.*, 195, 196 (which incidentally have no parallels in *PDhp.*, *Uv.*, or *GDhp.*), as well

as the commentary on them, require much further study.

29.* See the PTS edition of *Vimānavatthu,* p. 44.

## Chapter XV

1.* Following SHB, p. 472, *ye mayaṃ*, in preference to PTS, III, 257, line 6, *yaṃ*.

2. "'The five kinds of hate'—the fivefold animosities such as taking life, etc." (*Dps.*, p. 92; so also *Sdk.*, p. 111, *Dad.*, p. 193).

*Sds.*, VIII, 1895, provides a complete list: (1) killing, (2) taking what is not given, (3) sexual misconduct, (4) false speaking, (5) drinking intoxicating spirits. This source notes that the word used here for hate *(vera)* has also the meaning of "wrongdoing" *(pāpa)*.

3. The five strands of sensuality are (1) form, (2) sound, (3) odor, smell, (4) taste, (5)tangibles. So *Sds.*, VIII, 1897.

4. "The brahma-world into which persons who have attained the second meditative absorption, and who have died without falling from that state, are born is called Ābhassara. There, from the bodies of those brahmās, having continuity of skandhas, which has arisen as a result of the enjoyment of the meditative absorption characterized by joy, radiance issues forth like streaks of lightning going out from layers of clouds. Therefore, they themselves and the brahma-world in which they live are called Ābhassara ('Resplendent')" (*Sdk.*, p. 112). See also above, note 13 in chapter 13.

5.* *GDhpC.*, 238–39, discusses the grammatical problem involved in *jayaṃ*. If, as a noun, it is the subject of the sentence, we should expect the masculine nominative singular *jayo*. The commentator takes it as a present participle meaning "(one who is) conquering." The Sinhala interpretations, such as *Sdk.*, on this verse, *anun dinā gannā pudgala temē* ("the person who gains victory over others"), and *SdhRv.*, p. 848, *jaya labannāhu* ("he who gains triumph"), as usual follow the commentary.

6.* Following PTS, III, 263, *añño rogo, tikicchito, vinassati,* in preference to APB, p. 587, and SHB, p. 476, *aññe rogā, tikicchitā, vinassanti*. The PTS readings are supported by *Dag.*, 220.

7.* Following APB, p. 587, and SHB, p. 476, *tadaṅgavasena*, in preference to PTS, III, 263, *vayena*. *Dag.*, 220.15, also has *tadaṅgavasena*.

8. On the five *khandhas*, see above, note 4 in chapter 8.

9. On the ninefold dhamma that transcends the world, see above, notes 39 and 52 in chapter 1.

10.* For *dhīro ca sukkha-saṃvāso*, *Gdhp.*, 176, has [*dhi*] *ra du suha-savasa*, whose equivalent, *PDhp.*, 70, *dhīrāt tu sukha-saṃvāso* seems to be. The latter admits of a straightforward rendering: "From the wise one [there is] pleasant company." The Pali commentator's analysis, *sukho saṃvāso etenā ti sukhasaṃvāso*, seems to be, as *GDhpC.*, p. 236, points out, "merely a grammarian's ingenuity" and the sense given by it is "awkward" and "dictated by context." *Uv.*, xxx, 26, *dhīrais tu sukha-saṃvāso*, agrees with *GDhp.* and *PDhp.* in not taking the first word as a nominative.

11.* In *PDhp.*, 71, we find the introductory *tasmā hi* and the first line "syncopated" into the single line *tassā hi dhīraṃ ca bahuśśutañ ca.*

12.* *GDhpC.*, p. 236f., questions the commentative explanation, which "derives" *dhorayha* from *dhura* + √*vah-*. It says that *dhorayha* in fact is an "eccentricity" in spelling, with which may be contrasted the more appropriate spelling in *Milindapañha*, p. 288: *dhoreyya*, comparable with Sanskrit *dhaureya* (*Uv.*, xxv, 25) and Prakrit *dhoreya/dhoriya*. *PDhp.*, 71, has *dhoreya* where the Pali has *dhorayha.*

13.* Following APB, p. 592, and SHB, p. 479, *tesaṃ vattapaṭivattaṃ kātuṃ labhanabhāvo*, in preference to PTS, III, 271, which omits *kātuṃ*. (Cf. *Dps.*, p. 96, *vatāvat koṭā gänma.*)

14. Cf. *Dag.*, 222.13–14: "[Textual] learning *(āgama)* means the word of the Buddha; [spiritual] attainments *(adhigama)* means the world-transcending dhamma."

## Chapter XVI

1.* *Attānuyoginaṃ*: *PDhp.*, 173, *Uv.*, v, 9, and *GDhp.*, 266, have *artha-* where the Pali has *atta.*

2.* Whereas PTS, III, 275, has *vesiyāgocara* (with which cf. PTSD, under *vesiyāgocara*), APB, p. 594, SHB, p. 481, *Dag.*, 222, and *Dps.*, p. 97, all have *vesiya-gocara.*

3. "Engaging oneself in 'thinking that is not well grounded': resorting to the sixfold impropriety—the habitat of prostitutes, etc.; and not engaging oneself in 'thinking that is well grounded': thinking about the *saṃskāra*s as impermanent, etc." (*Sdk.*, p. 117).

The sixfold impropriety: "By the phrase 'not befitting' *(ayoga)* is indicated the places with which one should not engage oneself—[1] of prostitutes, [2] of women whose husbands are either deceased or are abroad, [3] of women who have not entered marriage and have grown old in the house, [4] of eunuchs who have defilements excited and agitated, [5] of nuns, and [6] liquor shops frequented by drunkards.

. . . these places are reckoned within 'thinking that is not well grounded'"(*Sds.*, VIII, 1933).

4. "'Higher virtue *(adhisīla)*, etc.'—by 'etc.' one should include training in higher consciousness *(adhicitta)* and higher insight or wisdom *(adhipaññā)*" (*Dag.*, 223.3). See also above, note 5 in chapter 4.
5. On the five strands of sensuality, see above, note 3 in chapter 15.
6.* Cf. *Dps.*, p. 98: "*saṃskāras* such as gold, silver, jewels, pearls, etc."
7.* PTS, III, 287–88, has *saccavādinaṃ* for both text and commentary. APB, p. 602, SHB, p. 488, and *Dps.*, p. 100, all have *saccavedinam*. *Dag.* has no comment on this. *Uv.*, v, 24*b*, and *PDhp.*, 295 have *satyavādinam*. (*GDhp.*, 322*b*, has no comparable word.) The Thai edition consulted, VI, 152, also has *saccavādinam* in the verse.
8. On the four virtues leading to purity, see above, note 40 in chapter 1.
9. "Knowing the four noble truths because of realizing them in sixteen ways, such as understanding, abandoning, etc." (*Dps.*, p. 101).

   "With respect to each and every Path, such as Stream Entrance, etc., penetrative knowledge connected with the four truths—suffering, arising, cessation, path—is fourfold, i.e., understanding, abandoning, realization, and [meditative] cultivation. The penetrative knowledge of the four noble truths in regard to the four Paths [thus] becomes sixteenfold" (*Sdk.*, p. 120). See also above, note 9 in chapter 6.
10. "'The three kinds of training' are the three trainings of higher virtue, higher consciousness, and higher insight" (*Dag.*, 255.11–12). See above, note 4.
11.* *Uv.* ii, 9, has *avasrāvī* where Pali has *anakkhāte*, and *anāvilo* where Pali has *phuṭo*. The verse seems to have suffered considerable modification in transmission. Inasmuch as *phuṭa* ( = Sanskrit *sphuṭa*) also has the meaning "open, clear," and *Uv.* has *anāvila*, "undisturbed," it seems preferable to deviate from the commentative interpretation (which is also followed in *Dag.*, 225, and *Dps.*, p. 101) and translate *manasā phuṭa* as "clear of mind" rather than "filled with thoughts." (There is no parallel verse in *PDhp.* and *GDhp.*)
12. The Paths of Stream Entrance, Once-Returning, and Non-Returning, with their corresponding Fruits. So *Sdk.*, p. 120; *Sds.*, VIII, 1956.
13. "Having attained the Fruit of Non-Returner, having arisen in the brahma-world called Aviha, and going from that place by means of the rebirth process up to the brahma-world of Akaniṭā, he is called 'one whose stream is upward bound.' He, having become an Arahant there, attains *parinirvāna*" (*Sdk.*, p. 120).
14. The verse is addressed to bhikkhus who mourned the death of their preceptor, according to the background story given earlier in the commentary. See BL, II, 91–92.

# Chapter XVII

1. On the ninefold self-estimation, see above, note 39 in chapter 5.
2. On the ten fetters, see above, note 27 in chapter 2.
3.* If we assume *sati* after *appasmiṃ pi*, the Pali will give the meaning "when there is even a little." However, all the other versions have the ablative here—i.e., "even from a little." (*PDhp.*, 293, *appā pi*; *GDhp.*, 281, *apadhu*; *Uv.*, xx, 16, *alpād api*.)
4. "'Sage *(muni)*' means one who knows this world and the other world, one's own benefit and also the benefit of others. Sages are numerous, such as the sage who lives the household life, the sage who has renounced the household life, the sage who is a learner, the sage who has gone beyond learning, the solitary sage, the sage of sages. Among these, the layperson himself who has thoroughly understood Dharma, having reached the Paths and Fruits, is called the sage who lives the household life. And the one who has 'gone forth' [into the monastic life], who is exactly like that [in the understanding of Dharma, having reached the Paths and Fruits], is called the sage who has renounced the household life. And the seven persons who are learners, beginning with the one standing in the path of Stream-Entrance up to the one standing in the Path of Arahantship, represent the sage who is a learner. And the Arahant who has destroyed all intoxicants, having reached the Fruit of Arhantship, is called the sage who has gone beyond learning. And the venerable Pratyekabuddha is called the solitary sage. And the Fully Enlightened One is called the sage of sages" (*Sdk.*, p. 123).
5. The three doors are (1) body, (2) mind, and (3) speech. So *Sds.*, VIII, 1974. *Sdk.*, pp. 125–28, discusses them at length.
6. "'Unshakeable,' which is not changing" (*Dag.*, 230.15). "'Unshakeable,' from which there is no departure [into another saṃsāric existence]. 'The abode,' i.e., the Deathless Great Nirvāṇa" (*Dps.*, p. 104).
7. The three trainings are training in virtue *(sīla)*, integration *(saṃādhi)*, and insight *(paññā)*. So *Dp.*, p. 214; *Sds.*, VIII, 1998. *Dv.*, p. 461, speaks of training in higher virtue *(adhisīla)*, higher thought or consciousness *(adhicitta)*, and higher insight *(adhipaññā)*. On the three trainings, see above, note 5 in chapter 4.
8. "'Upon Nibbāna intent'—for the ones practicing meditativeness *(yoga)*, who are intent on the cessation of the defilements" (*Dps.*, p. 104). See also *Sdk.*, p. 124; *Dad.*, p. 210; *Dv.*, p. 461.
9.* *GDhp.*, 241, has *aṇu'ija* where Pali has *anuvicca*. After examining

alternative suggestions, *GdhpC.*, pp. 250–51, favors deriving the word from *anu-vid* ("to know thoroughly"), i.e., that it is a "hyper-Palism" for *anuvijja (anu-vidya)*, like *manta* for *manda*. This is doubtful, for *PDhp.* has the word exactly as in the Pali. (See also below, note 4 in chapter 25).

10.* Both *Uv.*, xxix, 47, and *GDhp.*, 241, differ from *Dhp.*, 229, in regard to the word *suve-suve*, which is a temporal adverb. *Uv.* has *śubhāśubham* ("good and bad") and *GDhp.*, *śuhaśuhu* (no doubt meaning the same). The *Uv.* version also differs from *Dhp.*, 229, in having an entirely different pair of lines in *c/d* carrying the meaning: "That praise of the wise ones is well-proclaimed. Not so (praised?) is he who is praised by the ignorant"—*praśaṃsá sā samākhyātā/na tu ajñair yaḥ praśaṃsitah. PDhp.*, 287*b*, however, has exactly the same wording as *Dhp.*, 229*b* (and the rest of the *PDhp.* verse is also basically similar).

If the stanza begins, as in *GDhp.*, by saying that the wise discern both "the good and the bad" aspects of a person, would it immediately thereafter go on to call that person "one of unblemished character" also? The *GDhp.* version, having *achidravuti* in line *c*, would make one think that that is exactly what the stanza does.

Inasmuch as the *Dhp.* and the *Uv.* both differ from the *GDhp.*—the *Dhp.* by changing "good and bad" to "day-after-day," and the *Uv.* by not having the reference "unblemished conduct"—one wonders whether these two represent attempts at excluding a seeming discrepancy or anomaly. It is worth noting that *DhpA.* contains an echo of the sense of the *Uv.* lines—i.e., the words, "The blame or praise of the childish ones is not a [true] measure." Is this another instance of "fluctuation of material between commentary and text" (*GDhpC.*, p. 256)?

11.* PTS, III, 329, shows the commentary as explaining this word as (1) *acchiddāyā vā sikkhāya vattamānam* or as (2) *acchiddāya vā jīvitavuttiyā samannāgatattā*. APB, p. 625, and SHB, p. 506, drop *vattamānam* and make both *sikkhāya* and *jīvitavuttiyā* to go with *samannāgatattā*. This of course gives a more symmetrical version to the comment. However, at *Dps.*, p. 105, the explanation (1) *acchidra vū śikṣāyehi pavatnā vū nohot* (2) *acchidra vū jīvita-vṛtti ättā vū* gives support to the PTS reading of the first part of the comment, but makes one wonder whether in the second part the original word may have been *samannāgataṃ*.

12. Reference is to Atula who, in the background story given earlier in the commentary, seeking to hear Dhamma, found fault with Revata for remaining silent, found fault in Sāriputta for speaking at length on Abhidhamma, which Atula failed to grasp, and found fault in Ānanda

for preaching in brief. See BL, III, 111–13. (*GDhp*., 237, has *adura*, and *PDhp*., 284, *ādhora*, instead of *atula*.)

13.* Although PTS, APB, and SHB all have *taṭaṭatāyati*, *Dag*., 231, proceeds as if the text had *kaṭakaṭāyati* (i.e., makes a *kaṭa-kaṭa* sound). *Dps*., p. 105, *karakarayā doḍā*, also suggests a reading with *-k-* rather than *-t-*.

14.* Following APB, p. 624, and SHB, p. 506, *imassa kathāya*, in preference to PTS, III, 328, *imissā kathāya*. *Dps*., p. 102, translates the phrase as *mugē kathā* ("this one's talk").

15. On the four virtues leading to purity, see above, note 40 in chapter 1.

16. That is, "against the fourfold misconduct of speech such as lying, etc." (*Dps*., p. 106). *Sds*., VIII, 2007, notes this fourfold misconduct as (1) lying, (2) malicious speech, slander, (3) rude, harsh speech, and (4) frivolous talk, chatter. See note 10 in chapter 1, above.

17. That is, "against the threefold misconduct of mind such as covetousness, etc." (*Dps*., p. 106). *Sds*., VIII, 2007, lists this threefold misconduct as (1) covetousness, (2) malevolence, ill will, and (3) wrong view. See also note 13 in chapter 1, above.

18. (1) Taking life, (2) taking what is not given, (3) sexual misconduct. So *Dps*., p. 106; *Sds*., VIII, 2006. See also above, note 11 in chapter 1.

19.* Following APB, p. 625, and SHB, p. 507, *gāthā-dvaye pi*, in preference to PTS, III, 331, *gāthāya pi*.

## Chapter XVIII

1. Or, following the commentary, "Make an island for yourself."

2. "The fivefold pure abodes such as Avihā, etc." (*Dag*., 232.19). "'The fivefold pure abodes' such as Avihā, Atappā, Sudassa, Sudassī, Akaniṭṭha, are the heavenly places of the pure ones. They are called 'pure abodes' because they are the abodes for pure beings only, i.e., Non-Returners and Arahants. . . . as it is said [in the Pāli texts ] 'Only persons who are Non-Returners are born in the pure abodes.' They attain Nirvāna there, having reached the Fruit of Arahantship" (*Sdk*., p. 128). See also note 13 in chapter 16, above.

3. Or, following the commentary, "Make an island for yourself."

4.* *GDhpC*., p. 209–11, discusses the use of *dīpa* ( = Skt. *dvīpa*, "island" and *dipa*, "lamp") in Middle Indian, on occasion with a double sense. Thus *dīpa* in st. 238 can be taken as a "light" or as an "island." But in *Dhp*., vv. 235–38, where the Chinese has translated in terms of "light," ". . . the context makes it certain that this was the sense primarily intended. . . . The literal sense is the common metaphor of a journey and a translation with 'island' reads rather quaintly: 'You have started on your journey to Yama's presence . . . there is no inn where you can pass the night and you have laid in no provisions for the journey; therefore be sensible, get yourself an island and press on rapidly.' If forced to continue walking through the night, a sensible man will find a lamp more serviceable." *GDhpC.* does not, however, reject the commentative reference to the shipwrecked traveler. See *GDhpC.*, p. 211. *Uv.*, xvi, 36, has *dvīpam* ("island").

5. The three ages of life: youth, middle age, and old age. So *Sds.*, VIII, 2014.

6.* For PTS, III, 344: *dhonā vuccati cattāro paccaye idam atthitāya alam etenā ti*, and SHB, p. 513, *dhonā vuccanti cattāro paccayā idam attham ete ti*, APB, p. 632, has *dhonā vuccati cattāro paccaye idam attham ete ti*. The *Dps.*, p. 109, explanation of *atidhonacārinaṃ* as *satara pasaya pasvikā paribhoga karana prajñāyen ikmuṇuhu* is close to the Pali *cattāro paccaye paccavekkhitvā paribhuñjana (ka) paññam . . . atikkamitvā carantam*, which can be construed as the essence of the commentative explanation. *Dag.*, 233, has; (i) *idam attham paccavekkhitvā yi yojanu*, (ii) *ete: paccaye*, which suggests that the PTS readings (*idam*) *atthitāya* and *etena* are both erroneous.

In place of *atidhonacārinaṃ* in this verse, *Uv.*, ix, 19, has *aniśamya cārinam*, which would corroborate the "*paccavekkhitvā . . . carantam*" sense attributable to *dhonacārinaṃ* on the basis of the Pali commentary. All of this makes one think that the Pali tradition as well as the old Sinhala exegetes took (i) *dhonā̆* as "circumspection" or "insightfulness" (as can be seen in the *Niddesa* too; see PTSD, under *dhona*) and (ii) *atidhonacārin-* in this context as "not being within the limits of circumspection in regard to the utilization of the four requisites." The *Uv.* reading, however, suggests that the Skt. tradition was not very comfortable with the word *dhonā̆*. The second meaning attributed to the word in PTSD (namely, the four requisites) thus rests on a questionable interpretation of the commentative explanation. We have basically followed the sense adopted in *Dps.*, to which the APB text seems to be closest. *PDhp.*, 160, *vidhūna (-cariyaṃ)* shows that *atidhona* is an ancient authentic reading, but is not helpful in elucidating the meaning of it.

7. "'The four requisites'—robes, alms bowl, dwellings, medicaments" (*Dv.*, p. 482). See also *Sdk.*, p. 130, and above, note 40 in chapter 1.

"The bhikkhu who lives in the habit of seeing the fear of *saṃsāra*, who takes even the smallest mistake as great . . . thinks . . . 'I wear robes in order to dispel cold and heat, to do away with inconveniences such as wasps and mosquitoes, sun and wind, cobras and vipers, etc., and in order to cover those places that are shameful. I do not take food for the sake of pleasure and enjoyment, to increase desire for sensual gratification, to become fat, round out thin places, nor for the sake of adornment; but I take food in order merely to support the body, to dispel suffering of hunger and thirst . . . for observing celibacy, in order that no suffering and pain arises. I resort to dwelling places in order to make one-pointed the mind, having destroyed cold and heat. . . . I take medicinal requisites . . . in order to be healthy" (*Sds.*, VIII, 2021–22).

8.* Following APB, p. 632, and SHB, p. 513: *yāni kammāni . . . tāni*, in preference to PTS, III, 344, *sāni kammāni . . . tāni.*

9. "'You have become the charcoal'—you have come to destroy the family like the charcoal cinder that burns the hands" (*Dag.*, 233.28).

10.* Following APB, p. 635, and SHB, p. 515, *daṭṭhuṃ pihema,* in preference to PTS, III, 350, *daṭṭhabbā*. *Dps.*, p. 110, has *daknāt no kämäti va* ("not even wishing to see").

11. Originally the *salāka* was a "marked piece of wood" used as a ballot in taking the vote in ecclesiastic proceedings in the Saṅgha. "*Salāka* alms," however, are the meals that each family of a community supporting a monastery provided for the bhikkhus, at a given interval (e.g., once a year, once every three months, etc.).

12.* Taking *aṭṭhavatthukaṃ* for PTS, III, 350, *atthavatthukaṃ*.

13. "'Eight-faceted [ignorance]'—it is called 'eight-faceted' in the sense that it arises in four ways, i.e, with regard to suffering, etc., and with four bases, i.e., with regard to the beginning, etc." (*Dag.*, 234.1). "'Ignorance'—ignorance, which is the ignorance that exists regarding eight basic points, such as suffering, etc." (*Dps.*, p. 110). "That [eight-faceted ignorance] is not knowing the eight basic points: [1] the truth of suffering, [2] the truth of its arising, [3] the truth of its cessation, [4] the truth of the path, [5] not knowing the beginning of *saṃsāra*, [in a personalistic religious sense], [6] the end of *saṃsāra*, [7] both the beginning and the end of *saṃsāra*, and [8] not knowing dependent origination [of phenomena]" (*Dp.*, p. 224). Compare the eightfold doubt detailed in note 7 in chapter 10.

*Sds.*, VIII, 2029–30, treats "ignorance" here more generally, i.e., as ignorance of the nature of the *skandha*s, *āyatana*s, *dhātu*s, the senses, the four truths, etc.

14.* Does the word *dhaṃsi* mean "audacious," "importunate," (Skt. *dharṣin-*), as suggested by Anderson, rather than as derived from the root *dhaṃs-*, "to destroy" (Skt. *dhvaṃs-*), as understood by the commentary? See *GDhpC.*, p. 244. *PDhp.*, 164, has *dhansinā*; *GDhp.*, 221, *dhakṣiṇa*; *Uv.*, xxvii, 3, *dhvāṅkṣiṇā*.

15.* Following APB, p. 636, and SHB, p. 516, *amātādayo va*, in preference to PTS, III, 352, *amātaram eva*.

16. "'Impropriety of the twenty-one kinds'—resorting to the twenty-fivefold [*sic*] impropriety, such as giving flowers, giving fruits, etc." (*Dag.*, 234.5). See above, note 7 in chapter 6.
17. According to *SdhRv.*, p. 764ff., thinking that people would have suspicions about him.
18. "'As if tying up the knot'—like tying up the loop-knot of the robe (*gäṭavaṭu*)" (*Dag.*, 234.11).
19.* Following APB, p. 637, and SHB, p. 517, *paresaṃ gunadhaṃsanatāya*, in preference to PTS, III, 353, *paresaṃ guṇaṃ dhaṃsanatāya.*
20. This represents the etymological meaning of the word. *SdhRv.*, p. 766, takes this to mean "By one who has crafty devices."
21. "'Physical impudence,' i.e., impudence of body, speech, and mind. All actions done with the body are called physical impudence. One should understand the other [modes of] impudence in this manner" (*Dag.*, 234.26).
22.* APB, p. 638, and SHB, p. 517, have *anallīnena*, where PTS, III, 354, has *anu alīnena. Dag.*, 235, has *anallikena*. The PTS reading is difficult to make sense of.
23.* Following APB, p. 638, *passatā*, in preference to PTS, III, 355, and SHB, p. 517, *passato.*
24. The six means such as [1] with one's hands, [2] through another, [3] with a sharp weapon, [4] with a cudgel, [5] with charms, and [6] with psychic powers" (*Dag.*, 235.5–7).
25. *Dag.*, 235.8, mentions that there are twenty-five means of improper appropriation, but notes only "theft, etc." *Sds.*, I, 170, lists five means of improper appropriation, i.e., taking what is not given (1) by theft, (2) by using force, (3) through deceit, (4) by the use of strategems, and (5) through the casting of lots.

    The twenty-five are: (1) five of improper appropriation of many kinds of property, (2) five of one (i.e., sentient) kind of property, (3) five with one's own hands, (4) five through "prior preparation," and (5) five through theft, etc. (*Saṅkhya-dhamma-dīpikā*, pp. 267ff.).
26.* Following SHB, p. 518, and *Dag.*, 235.9, *-bhaccesu*, in preference to PTS, III, 356, APB, p. 639, and the Thai edition, VII, 21, *-bhaṇḍesu.*
27.* Following PTS, III, 356, and *Dag.*, 235, *avapetvā*, in preference to APB, p. 639, and SHB, p. 518, *aṭṭhapetvā. Dag.* further explains *avapetvā* as a contraction of *avāpetvā*. Perhaps from *vāpeti*: "to cause to sow." *Dps.*, p. 111, explains "without employing in a befitting [venture] like trade or industry."
28.* Following APB, p. 639, and SHB, p. 518, *akusalamūlaṃ*, in preference to PTS, III, 356, *akusalamūlaṭṭhena.*
29.* Following APB, p. 640, and SHB, p. 519, *dadāti*, in preference to PTS, III, 359, *dadanti. PDhp.*, 328, has *dadanti . . . janā.*

30.* *Uv.*, x, 12*b*, has *yathāvibhavato* ("according to their wealth"). But *PDhp.*, 328, has *yathā prasadaṃ*, which agrees with the Pali. There is no *GDhp.* parallel.

31.* *Uv.*, x, 13*b* has *tālamastakavaddhatāḥ*. *PDhp.*, 329*b*, *mūlogghaccaṃ*. The reading *mūlagacchaṃ* agrees with the Pali, *mūlagacchaṃ*, which is attested to in *Dag.*, 235. There is no *GDhp.* parallel.

32.* "'Integration of mind *(samādhi)*' means one-pointedness of the wholesome mind. (That is, the wholesome mind that is well established on a faultless object.) It is threefold, i.e., instantaneous, access, and absorption. Here, [1] one-pointedness that comes into being in the mind just for a moment is called instantaneous integration *(kṣanikasamādhi)*. [2] The state of one-pointedness that comes into being in the mind of the sphere of sensuality by the suppression (subduing) of the five hindrances, (namely, desire for sensuality, ill will, sloth and torpor, agitation and remorse, and [skeptical] doubt) [cf. note 22 in chapter 6, above] is called access-integration *(upacārasamādhi)* because it moves in the vicinity of absorption-integration *(arpaṇāsamādhi)*. These two [modes of] integration are mundane, pertaining to the sphere of sensuality. [3] Absorption-integration is twofold: mundane and world-transcending. Of these two, the very strong state of one-pointedness of the mind that has reached the state of the fine material sphere and the formless sphere by the manifestation of the constituents of meditative-absorption *(dhyāna)* such as fixed thinking, etc., is called mundane absorption-integration. The state of one-pointedness that is associated with Path and Fruit consciousness, that arises having Nirvāṇa as object, is called world-transcending absorption-integration" (*Sdk.*, p. 9, regarding *DhpA.* [PTS, I, 114] on *Dhp.*, 11).

33. "'Path-integration *(mārga-samādhi)*' is the state of one-pointedness that comes into being in the mind, having Nirvāṇa as object at the instant of Path consciousness *(mārgacitta)*. 'Fruit-integration *(phala-samādhi)*' is the one-pointedness that comes into being in the mind when one lives having caused to arise Fruit consciousness *(phala-citta)* with regard to the object, which is Nirvāṇa. Path consciousness such as Stream-Entrance, etc., after it arises once, destroying the defilements that should be destroyed by it, and after it passes away, does not arise again, because there is no point in it [Path consciousness] arising several times. Because Path consciousness is thus instantaneous, Path integration is also instantaneous. But Fruit consciousness that arises subsequent to the Path moment could be caused to arise again by entering into the Fruit attainment *(phalasamavat/phalasamāpatti)*. This is the dwelling at ease in this visible life on the part of noble persons" (*Sdk.*, p. 134).

34.* For *ūnā va* of PTS, III, 363, and SHB, p. 522, APB, p. 653 has *ūnatā va*, which makes better sense. It may, however, be an emendation, for this very reason.

35. Or, following the commentary, "As a hunter of birds [covers] his body with twigs."

36.* *GDhp.*, 272, has *upuṇadi* where Pali has *opuṇāti*. *GDhpC.*, p. 259, says that this indicates that the word is derived from *utpunāti* (not *avapunāti*). The *GDhpC.* suggestion regarding the derivation (from *utpa-* to *uppu-* to *ūpu-* to *opu*) is strikingly proved correct by the *PDhp.*, 166, reading *uppunāti*.

37.* Although *kali* ("the throw that brings defeat") and *kitavā* ("gambler") are well attested from as far back as *Rg Veda*, x, 34 (and were used with those meanings in Pali—see PTSD, under both terms), the commentary here gives other meanings for these two words, as well as for the common *saṭha* ("deceitful," but here taken as a "hunter of birds"). The interpretation of *kali* as "body" (as the instrument of evil actions?) may be taken as an extension of its other (possibly derivative) meaning, "the evil one." But the explanation of *kitavā* as "a covering of sticks" is surprising. One wonders whether the common meaning was disregarded because the word appears here as *kitavā*, whereas one would have expected *kitavo* if the common meaning was really applicable in this context. *GDhp.*, 272, *kali va kiḍava śaḍha*, answers closely to the Pali line and does not throw any light as to the derivation of *kitavā*. But *Uv.*, xvii, 1, *kṛtvā* (for *kṛtavā*?), may suggest a connection with *kṛta*: "the winning throw," i.e.,* *kṛtavant*: "successful gambler," giving rise to *kitavant-*. This possibility is now further strengthened by the parallel word in *PDhp.*, 166, which is surmised to be *kṛtavāṃ*. (The *PDhp.* editor puts a question mark on the word.)

38.* Where *Dph.*, v. 253*b* has *ujjhāna*, *Uv*, xvii, 2*b* has *avadhyāna*, and *PDhp.*, 269, *ojjhāya* (both from *ava* +√*dhyā-*). The *Dag.*, 238, explanation of *ujjhāna* as *avañana-saññayen*: "with the notion of deprecation," also reflects a form related in meaning to *ava* +√*dhyā*, "to regard slightingly."

39.* APB, p. 661, SHB, p. 529, and *Dps.*, p. 114, read so, whereas PTS, III, 378, has *bāhiro*.

## Chapter XIX

1.* Tentatively following APB, p. 662, *dhammaṭṭho ti: rājā hi attano*, etc., in preference to PTS, III, 381, *dhammaṭṭho rājūhi attanā*, etc., and SHB, p.530, *dhammaṭṭho rājā hi attanā*, etc., as this seems to be the only available reading capable of yielding sense. However, *Dps.*, p. 115, *rajun visin viniścaya dharmayehi pihiṭuvana laddē da* ("even though one has been appointed by kings"), probably reflects that the *v. l. rājūhi* (rejected by both APB and SHB) was present even at the time of that work. The reason why we cannot follow *Dps.* here is that all editions have *ṭhito* where the *Dps.* interpretation leads us to expect *ṭhapito.*

2.* Following APB, p. 662, and SHB, p. 530, *kassa cid eva issara jātikassa,* in preference to PTS, III, 382, *devaissarajātikassa.*

3.* APB, p. 663, has *pāpeti,* where PTS, III, 382, has *phandayati,* and SHB, p. 530, *phandāpeti.* The forms preferred by PTS and SHB literally mean "causes to throb." The APB *pāpeti* ("causes to move") represents a more direct paraphrase of *nayati* of the *Dhp.* verse.

4. "The person who has security because he is free from danger, who is without enmity because there is no enmity of the five modes of bad conduct such as taking life, etc., who is without fear because there is no fear of him among the populace and he himself is not afraid, he is called a sagacious one" (*Sdk.*, p. 137).

"'The five hostilities'—the five hostile mental processes involved in taking life, etc." (*Dag.*, 239.2). See note 2 in chapter 15, above.

5.* Where Pali has *passati, Uv.*, iv, 21, has *spṛśet* and *GDhp.*, v. 114, has *phasa'i* (= *sparśayet,* causative optative), whose exact parallel, *phassaye,* is found in *PDhp.*, 32. *GDhpC.*, pp. 211–12, noting comparable usage in Pali, as e.g., in *Jā.*, V. 251, *dhammaṃ kāyena phassayam,* says, "The reading *passati* . . . is certainly an error, probably as old as the commentary."

6.* Following APB, p. 666, and SHB, p. 533, *parijiṇṇo vuddhabhāvappatto,* in preference to PTS, III, 388, *parijiṇṇa-vuddhi-bhāvappatto.*

7. See above, note 9 in chapter 16 and note 53 in chapter 1.

8.* PTS, III, 388, has *ahiṁsābhāvena. Dag.*, 239, has *ahiṃsana bhāvena.* SHB, p. 533, and APB, p. 666, have *ahiṃsanabhāvo.* We have followed PTS and *Dag.*

9. "Loving-kindness, compassion, sympathetic joy, and equanimity" (*Dag.*, p. 116).

"The 'limitless' are loving-kindness, compassion, sympathetic joy, and equanimity. Here, loving-kindness is wishing benefit and welfare for all beings in the manner, 'May all beings by happy.' Compassion is the desire to free beings who have fallen into suffering. Sympathetic joy is the tender contentment that arises in the mind when one sees beings who have attained comfort. Equanimity is being even-minded [not partial] in regard to all beings. These are called 'limitless' because they have limitless numbers of beings as object" (*Sdk.*, p. 138). See below, notes 19 and 20 in chapter 21.

10.* *Dag.*, 240, APB, p. 667, and SHB, p. 533, *issā-manako,* seems preferable to PTS, III, 389, *issa mānako.*

11. " 'The five kinds of avarice' are avarice that is fivefold, namely, avarice with regard to [1] abode, [2] family, [3] gain, [4] physical attractiveness (*vaṇṇa*), and [5] dhamma" (*Dag.*, 240.5).

" 'Avarice with regard to abodes' is the miserly attitude regarding dwelling places and institutions, night lodgings and day lodgings, etc. The bhikṣu himself who is possessed of avarice with regard to abodes does not like the coming of another bhikṣu to the dwelling places, etc., where he is living. Even the one who has arrived, he desires to send away immediately. 'Avarice with regard to family' is the miserly attitude regarding the family supporting him or the family of relatives. The monk possessed of that does not like another monk going to the families which he [usually] visits. 'Avarice with regard to gain' is the miserly attitude regarding the four requisites such as robes, etc. The monk possessed of that is not pleased upon seeing something gained by another bhikṣu even though he be virtuous. 'Avarice with regard to dhamma' is the miserly attitude with regard to the dharma that he has learned. The monk possessed of that does not like to expound to others the dharma that he has learned. 'Avarice with regard to physical attractiveness [lit. complexion]' is the miserly attitude with regard to physical beauty and beauty of character. The monk possessed of that does not like to hear of the physical characteristics of others or to hear comments about their virtuousness, etc." (*Sdk.*, p. 139).

12. On the thirteen *dhutaṅga* practices, see above, note 6 in chapter 2. "They are called 'constituents of ascetic practice' (*dhutaṅga*) because each destroys defilements that are opposed to each of them. The description of this should be known having consulted the section on *dhutaṅga* in the *Visuddhimagga*" (*Sdk.*, p. 140).

13.* PTS, III, 391, has *appamattesu (ārammaṇesu icchāya) pavattesu (ca lobhena)*. SHB, p. 534, and APB, p. 668, have *asampattesu . . . pattesu. Dps.*, p. 118, explains the words with *asamprāpta . . . samprāpta. Dag.*, 240, also has *no pat (vat . . .).* Obviously the text should be either as in SHB and APB, or *appattesu . . . pattesu,* as in the Thai edition, VII, 52.

14.* For Pali *vissaṃ dhammaṃ, GDhp.*, v. 67, has *veśma dharma. GDhpC.*, pp. 191–92, regards the Pali commentary explanation of *vissa* as *visama* as reflecting an old interpretation, for *Mahāvastu* III, 422, also has *viṣamāṃ dharmāṃ.* It also mentions that a part of this verse preserved in a bilingual Agnean fragment reads *veṣma-dharmām,* and surmises that a reading with *-m-* must have been current at a very early date. Pali *vissa,* then, though also derivable from *viśva,* is really from *veśma,* "house," through *vesma/visma* (hence leaving room for a play upon words), and the actual sense of the phrase was "a dharma no better than that of living in a house," i.e., "concerned . . . with obtaining enough food to eat." The reading adopted in Bernhard's *Uv.*, xxxii, 18, is *veśmāṃ dharmaṃ*, agreeing with the above interpretation.

PTS, III, 393, *vissagandham* (compound form) yields better sense. However, APB, p. 665, and SHB, p. 535, *vissaṃ gandhaṃ* (uncompounded) is attested by *Dag.*, 240.

15.* SHB, p. 535, and APB, p. 668, have *opuṇāpetvā* ("having winnowed away"), where PTS, III, 393, has *panuditvā* ("having set aside"). *Dps.*, p. 118, *duru koṭa* ("having distanced" or "banished") seems to favor PTS. *Dag.* provides no clue.

16.* Following PTS, III, 395, *hoti*, in preference to APB, p. 669, and SHB, p. 536, *na hoti*.

17. " 'Liberation'—the Fruit of Arahantship. 'Vision of the understanding of liberation'—knowledge of the five suppressions [of defilements]" (*Dag.*, 240.24). On the fivefold suppressions, see above, note 54 in chapter 1, and note 28 in chapter 4.

18.* Following PTS, III, 396, *kasmā*, in preference to APB, p. 670, and SHB, p. 537, *tasmā*.

19.* The commentary suggests that *ahiṃsā*, is an old instrumental, i.e., an archaic form whose more modern form would be *ahiṃsāya*.

20.* For *vivicca, PDhp.*, 272, has *vivitta, Uv.*, xxxii, 31, *vivikta*, and *GDhp.*, 65, *vevita*. The Pali tradition also has preserved a reading *vivitta*: see *DhpA.*, III, p. 399. APB, p. 671, opts for *vivitta*, but *Dps.*, p. 120, has *vivicca. See GDhpC.*, p. 191.

21.* Of the exegetes, *Dps.* alone (p. 120) interprets the line as standing for *vissāsam mā āpādi* with a distinctly prohibitive sense, "Do you not come to contentedness in existence" *(bhavayehi viśvāsayaṭa nahamak pämiṇa); āpādi*, then, would be aorist second singular. In so explaining, *Dps.* leaves the *na* of v. 271*a* out of consideration. The commentary, however, explains *māpādi* as a third person verb ( = *na āpajjeyya:* Let one not get into . . . ) with no overtly prohibitive sense.

Perhaps, in *Dhp.* vv. 271–72, *na sīlabbata mattena . . . vissāsa mā 'pādi* is, as is sometimes the case in old Pali verses, a not very erudite expression meaning "do not be content, not by mere ritual observance." In that case, *vissāsa mā* may be regarded as a contraction of *vissāsaṃ mā*.

Confusion on the part of the textual tradition on this is perhaps reflected in the way *bhikkhu nāma* is handled. PTS, III, 400, has this phrase before *vissāsaṃ na āpajjeyya*, while having the vocative *bhikkhu* immediately after *idaṃ vuttaṃ hoti*. APB, pp. 671–72, and SHB, p. 538, apparently being uncomfortable with this vocative form, drop it altogether and put *bhikkhu nāma* in its place, and not immediately before *vissāsaṃ na āpajjeyya*. But the *Dhp.* verse clearly has the vocative form, as can be seen even from the commentary (*aññataraṃ ālapanto*).

What *Uv.* has done is evidently a case of "straightening out" the difficulty by avoiding the archaic usage with *mā* and substituting the optative exhortative expression *na śīlavrata-mātreṇa . . . bhikṣur viśvāsam āpadyet*, thus altering the vocative in the second verse to a nominative (*Uv.*, xxxii, 31*a* and 32*a*). But *GDhp.*, v. 66*c*, *bhikhu viśpaśa mavadi*, seems to be a faithful echo of *Dhp.* v. 272*c*, as is *bhikkhū viśśasa māpādi* of *PDhp.*, 273. (On *bhikkhū*, nom. or voc., see *PDhpN.*, p. 96. The division of the words in *PDhp.*, 273, is questionable.)

22. "The four fine material attainments [of meditative-absorption], namely, the first, second, third, and fourth, and the four formless attainments, i.e., the sphere of space, the sphere of consciousness, the sphere of no-thing-ness, and the sphere of neither-perception-nor-nonperception"(*Sdk.*, p. 142). See also the latter part of note 6 in chapter 7, above).
23. Reference is to the background story given earlier in the commentary. See BL, III, 147–48.

## Chapter XX

1.* APB, p. 672, *Dv.*, p. 537, etc., read *salla-satthanam*. PTS, III, 402, note 7, and SHB, p. 538, note 1, record the *v. l. salla-kantanam*, with which cf. *Uv.*, xii. 9*b*, *śalya-kṛntanaḥ* (the root *krt:* to cut) and *PDhp.*, 360*b*, *śalla-sraṃsano* (the root *sraṃs:* to fall?). We have translated *santhanaṃ* as "extrication," following the commentary (contrast PTSD: "appeasement"). But as in many other instances of textual variance, the meaning is uncertain.
2. *Dag.*, 241.13, has the reading *micchādiṭṭhigatamaggā*, "the paths traversed by wrong views." All other Sinhala sources consulted agree with the PTS, III, 402, *dvāsaṭṭhidiṭṭhigatamaggā*, "the paths traversed by the sixty-two [wrong] views." These sixty-two views are mentioned in the *Brahmajāla Sutta* of the *Dīgha-nikāya* (PTS ed., vol. I, 1–46). For an English translation of this discourse, see T. W. Rhys Davids, translator, *Dialogues of the Buddha*, Part I (London: Luzac & Co, Ltd., 1956 [first published, 1899]), pp. 1–55.
3. "The world-transcending middle way comprised of eight constituents, namely, right view, right intention, right speech, right action, right livelihood, right effort, right mindfulness, right concentration" (*Sdk.*, p. 143).

4. "By 'and so on' *(ādi)* one should understand abandonment [of the cause], realization [of the cessation], and cultivation [of the path]" (*Dag.*, 241.17–19).
5.* *Dag.*, 241.21, explains *sacco brāhmaṇo* as the Brāhmana Sacca.
6.* SHB, p. 539, has *pahātabbaṭṭhena,* "in the sense that [suffering?] is to be eliminated [by their means?]" after *sacchikātabbaṭṭhena.*
7. *Dag.*, 241.25, explains this as "in the sense that it should be penetrated into by Path insight alone" *(eka maga-ñaṇin piḷivijiya yutu aṭin).*
8. " 'With the five [kinds of] eye'—the [natural] eye of flesh, the divine eye, the eye of wisdom, the all-seeing eye, and the Buddha-eye" (*Dag.*, 241.30).

"'The eye of flesh' is the [ideal] natural eye with the five hues, which can see through even a crystal stone that is a *yojana* in thickness even in the fourfold darkness [at midnight, in the dark part of the month, under thick rain clouds, in a dense jungle—cf. *Sdk.*, p. 156]. The 'divine eye' is the knowledge by which . . . one sees beings who are in the process of passing away and arising. The 'eye of wisdom' is the knowledge that sees all dharmas pertaining to the three times [past, present, and future]. The 'Buddha-eye' is the knowledge that sees beings such as those having little dust [obtuseness] in their eyes, etc., that is, the knowledge of inclinations and dispositions *(āśayānuśaya)* [of beings]. The 'all-seeing eye' is omniscience; there is nothing that does not come within its sphere" (*Sdk.*, p. 144).
9. "Tricking Māra away": following PTS, III, 403–4, *mārass eva vañcanaṃ.* However, SHB, p. 539, has *mārabandhanam,* "the binding of Māra," and APB, p. 673, has *māra-phandanam,* "the shaking up of Māra."

"'Tricking Māra away'—destroying the army of defilements" (*Dag.*, 242.3). "He tricks away the armies of Māra that are the defilements, which are shown as, namely, 'Your first army is sensual lust, aversion is called the second,' etc., together with Devaputra Māra [Māra as a superhuman potentate]" (*Dps.*, p. 121). See above, note 12 in chapter 13.
10. " 'Two [kinds of] meditation—the meditation that arises on the object and the meditation that arises on the characteristics" (*Dag.*, 242.9).
11.* For *dukkhe* (locative), *PDhp.*, 374, has *dukkhā; GDhp.*, 106, *dukha;* and *Uv.*, xii, 5, *duḥkhāt* (ablative).
12.* Following PTS, III, 405, *nirujjhantā.* SHB, p. 547, and APB, p. 674, have *nirujjhanato:* by virtue of the fact that they cease to be.
13.* Following APB, p. 674, SHB, p. 547, and *Dag.*, 242, *nibbinno,* in preference to PTS, III, 405, *nibbindato.*
14. "Because the dharmas that are the *saṅkhāra*s are being oppressed by arising and ceasing to be" (*Dps.*, p. 123; so also *Sdk.*, p. 146).

15.* Following PTS, III, 407, *anattā suññā*. SHB, p. 540, and APB, p. 675, have *attasuññā*, "devoid of self."

16.* *Alasiyam:* on this, see *GDhpC.*, p. 80.

17. "'Three kinds of wrong thought'—such as thoughts of lust *(kāma)*, etc." (*Dps.*, p. 124). "The three kinds of wrong thought are those of lust, ill will, and harm *(vihiṃsā)*" (*Sdk.*, p. 147; so also *Dad.*, p. 241, *Dv.*, p. 544). See also note 18 in chapter 8, above.

18.* For *visodhaye* (opt. verb), *PDhp.*, 279, has *viśodhiya* (absolutive), and *Uv.*, vii, 12, *viśodhayan* (pres. participle).

19. On the four forms of verbal misconduct, see above, note 10 in chapter 1.

20. "By 'and so forth' one should understand ill will and wrong views" (*Dag.*, 243. 22).

21. "'[Such as the Buddhas] who are seekers of the mass of [factors that constitute] moral virtue, etc.'—i.e., seeking the mass of moral virtue *(sīla)*, concentration or integration *(samādhi)*, and insight-wisdom *(paññā)*" (*Dag.*, 243.23). ". . . . those who have sought the five groups of dharmas such as moral vitrue, etc." (*Dps.*, p. 124). *Sdk.*, p. 148, elaborates: "The Buddhas, Pratyekabuddhas, and Great Arahants are called 'sages' *(ṛṣi)* because they have practiced the seeking of the five groups of dharmas, namely, moral virtue, concentration or integration, insight-wisdom, liberation, and vision of the gnosis of liberation" (*Sdk.*, p. 148).

22. "'Thirty-eight objects'—the thirty-eight objects, taken in this context, are the fire *kasiṇa* . . . " (*Dag.*, 244.17ff.).

The thirty-eight objects are "the thirty-eight topics of meditation *(kamaṭahan)*: [1–8] the eightfold *kasiṇa*, namely, earth-*kasiṇa*, water-*kasiṇa*, fire-*kasiṇa*, air-*kasiṇa*, blue-*kasiṇa*, yellow-*kasiṇa*, blood-red-*kasiṇa*, clear-*kasiṇa*, and [9–18] the ten loathesome objects, namely, a swollen corpse, a bluish one, one that is festering, one having holes, one eaten [by animals], one scattered, one severed and scattered about, one smeared with blood, one infested with worms, one which is just bones, and [19–25] the seven recollections, namely, recollection of the Buddha, of Dhamma, of the Sangha, of moral virtues, of generosity, of deities, of pacification, and [26–28] the threefold mindfulness, namely, mindfulness of the body, of death, of breathing, and [29–32] the four brahma-abodes, namely, loving-kindness, compassion, sympathetic joy, equanimity, and [33–36] the four formless [meditative-absorptions], namely, the sphere of space, the sphere of consciousness, the sphere of no-thing-ness, the sphere of neither-perception-nor-nonperception, and [37–38] these two determinants of perception, i.e., of the unattractiveness of food and of the four physical elements [earth, fire, water, air]" (*Sdk.*, p. 148).

23.* For *nārisu* ("women"), *PDhp.*, 362, has *ñātisu*, and *Uv.*, xviii, 3, *bandhuṣu* ("relatives").

24. The allusion is to the background story given earlier in the commentary. See BL, III, 159–61.

25.* Following SHB, p. 548, and APB, p. 683, *jāti-ādi-bhayam*, in preference to PTS, III, 424, *jāti-ādi-bhayam pi*.

26.* The use of √*vas*- (in *vassaṃ vasissāmi*) is found only in the Pali. All others have √*kṛ*-: *PDhp.*, 365 *vaśśā kariṣyāmi; GDhp.*, 333, *vaṣa kariṣamu; Uv.*, i, 38, *varṣaṃ kariṣyāmi*.

27.* Brough (*GDhpC.*, p. 276) treats this as a questionable reading, and says "it would seem that there is a very strong prima facie case for *sampannaṃ* as the correct word." (*Sampannam* is the form occuring at *Mahābhārata*, xii, 169, 13, 17, whose first two lines are a parallel of *Dhp.*, v. 287*a*/*b*, as noted at *GdhpC.*, p. 267.) Brough is suspicious of the reading *sammattaṃ*, "inebriated," partly because it looks like a repetition of the idea already expressed by *byāsatta*, "entangled." Not only *PDhp.*, 366, and *Uv.*, i, 40—works that Brough apparently did not consult—but also two very old Sinhala works, *Dag.*, and *Dps.*, substantiate the reading *sammattaṃ* (see the note immediately following).

Another of Brough's views is that the commentary refers to a cow as the man's possession; scarcely a reason for inebriation. One of the same Sinhala sources has "oxen" here (see below, note 29 in this chapter); the other word, *gāvī*, can be either singular or plural; in fact, *Dps.*, p. 127, clearly treats it as a plural (*denu*, "cows"). Even otherwise, Buddhists of old would not have regarded it as impossible for one to get "intoxicated" by a trifling possession. It is also hard to reconcile Brough's idea that the reading "arouses . . . suspicion" because it introduces a tautology (which it may not in fact do), with the amazing comments he makes elsewhere on the poetic talents of the composer of these verses (see, e.g., his comments on *Dhp.*, v. 285 at *GDhpC.*, p. 269: "incompetent poet . . . filling a hole in his verse" and "incapable of perceiving the destructive effect on his verse of using 'autumnal' to stop another gap," etc.).

28.* Following APB, p. 688, *Dag.*, 246, and PTS, III, 433, *sammattaṃ*, in preference to SHB, p. 552, *sampannaṃ*. *Dps.*, p. 127, *itā matvä*, "very intoxicated," substantiates *sammattaṃ*.

29.* Following SHB, p. 552, and APB, p. 688, *goṇā abhirūpā, arogā . . . bhāravahā*, in preference to PTS, III, 433, *goṇo . . . abhirūpo, arogo . . . bhāravaho*. *Dps.*, p. 127, translates *gonhu*, etc. (plural), clearly substantiating *goṇā*, etc.

30.* PTS, III, 433, *sattamānasaṃ*. SHB, p. 552, and APB, p. 688, *āsattamānasaṃ*.

31.* PTS, III, 433, has *patthanatāya*. APB, p. 688, and SHB, p. 552, have *patthanāya*. *Dps.*, p. 127, *pätīm vaśayen*, "by way of desiring," seems to favor the PTS reading more.
32.* PTS, III, 433, *sattamānasaṃ*. SHB, p. 552, and APB, p. 688, *vyāsattamānasaṃ*.
33. On the four requisites, see above, note 7 in chapter 18.
34.* The commentary explains *adhipannassa*, "for one seized," with *abhibhūtassa*, "for one subject." The equivalent of the latter is in fact the word found in *PDhp.*, p. 367, and *Uv.*, i, 40—a further example of "fluctuation of material between the traditional commentary and the text" (*GDhpC.*, p. 256), noted elsewhere "on a more extensive scale" (see above, note 25 in chapter 3).
35.* Following PTS, III, 434, and APB, p. 689, *putte ca pitaro ca*, in preference to SHB, p. 552, *putte ca dhītaro ca*.
36. On the four virtues leading to purity, see above, note 40 in chapter 1.

## Chapter XXI

1.* The fifteenth-century Sinhala author and poet Srī Rahula, in his work *Pañcikā Pradīpa*, refers to this verse and says that *mattā* here is in the feminine gender (see W. Srī Subhūti, *Nāmamālā*, Maradana, Sri Lanka: Mangala Press, 1876/1965, p. xxxvii). *PDhp.*, 77, and *Uv.*, xxx, 30, have the word in its Sanskrit form, *mātrā*.
2. It is noteworthy that *Dag.*, 250, says that what is meant here is indeed the *uposatha* and *dāna* that serve as a foundation to "the dissolution of the whirl" of *saṃsāra: vivaṭṭaka pādaka pehekam . . . dan ev*.
3.* Brough (*GDhp.*, p. 147) records *pamuccati* as the verb here (*Dhp.*, 291*d*), whereas other editions have *parimuccati*, which is supported not only by *Uv.*, xxx, 2, but also by *GDhp.* itself (cf. *parimucadi*, *GDhp.*, v. 179).
4. On the *dhutaṅga* practice, see above, note 6 in chapter 2, and note 12 in chapter 19.
5.* This "etymology" (*ut* + *nala*) reflects the meaning given to the word traditionally. For *unnaḷānaṃ* (at *Dhp.*, 292), *PDhp.*, 267, has *unnattā* (?) *nāṃ*. See the long discussion on this word in *GDhpC.*, p. 179ff. Our translation follows the commentary and is tentative.
6. On the four intoxicants or influxes, see above, note 7 in chapter 7.
7.* *Khattiya* is the Pali form of *kṣatriya*, the name of the ruling caste in ancient India.
8. The six internal *āyatana*s are (1) the eyes, (2) ears, (3) nose, (4) tongue, (5) body, and (6) mind *(manas)*; the six external *āyatana*s are (7) form,

(8) sound, (9) smell, (10) taste, (11) tangibles, and (12) dharmas. See *Sdk.*, p. 153.

9. A form of homiletical punning on the "etymology": intoxicant or influx/sword—*āsava/asi*.
10. The learned in ancient India were the *brāhmaṇa*s, because their caste duties made it incumbent upon them to learn the Vedas and ancillary subjects of study.
11. On the five hindrances, see note 22 in chapter 6, above.
12. The entire formula is: "He is the Blessed One, the Worthy Being, the Fully Enlightened One, endowed with knowledge and noble conduct, the well-gone, knower of the worlds, incomparable trainer of human beings who are amenable to be trained, teacher of men and gods, the Blessed Awakened One." See *Sds.*, VIII, 2262–73.
13. "Well proclaimed by the Blessed One is Dhamma that is visible, timeless, characterized by [the imperatives] 'Come! Look!,' leading on, to be known personally by the wise." See *Sds.*, VIII, 2274–80.
14. "Well set out [on the Path] is the community of the Blessed One's disciples, directly set out is the community of the Blessed One's disciples, properly set out is the community of the Blessed One's disciples, fully set out is the community of the Blessed One's disciples, that is to say the four pairs of persons, the eight persons [i.e., those who have attained the four Paths and the four Fruits]. This community of the Blessed One's disciples is to be given offerings, is to be welcomed, is to be given gifts, is to be honored, is an incomparable field of merit for the world" (*Sds.*, VIII, 2280–83).
15. "This is said with regard to well-grounded thought on the loathesome pertaining to the thirty-two parts of the body such as hair of the head, hair of the body, etc." (*Dag.*, 252.5). *Dv.*, p. 578, lists the thirty-two parts as follows: (1) hair of the head, (2) hair of the body, (3) nails, (4) teeth, (5) skin, (6) flesh, (7) sinews, (8) bones, (9) bone marrow, (10) kidneys, (11) heart, (12) liver, (13) pleura, (14) spleen, (15) lungs, (16) intestine, (17) bowels, (18) abdominal content, (19) excreta, (20) bile, (21) phlegm, (22) pus, (23) blood, (24) sweat, (25) fat, (26) tears, (27) fatty tissue, (28) saliva, (29) nasal mucous, (30) fluid that lubricates the joints, (31) urine, (32) the brain.
16. *Dag.*, 252.7ff., quoting Pali phrases, enumerates the nine "cemetery [contemplations]": (1) as if one would see a body, swollen, discarded in a cemetery, (2) a body . . . broken up and eaten by crows, (3) a heap of bones without flesh but smeared with blood, (4) a heap of bones completely devoid of flesh and blood, (5) bones scattered in all directions, (6) white bones, (7) bones over a year old, (8) bones stacked in a heap, (9) bones decayed and turned to powder. See also note 32 in chapter 1, above.

17. The four elements of the body, according to *Dag.*, 252.14: earth/mass, water/moisture, fire/heat, and air.
18. On the *kasiṇa*s and related meditative practices, see the section on *kasiṇa*s in the *Visuddhimagga,* and note 22 in chapter 20, above.
19. "Harmlessness *(ahiṃsā)* is compassion that arises in the heart *(lehi)*, having seen beings experiencing suffering. Being engaged in the meditative cultivation of compassion in this manner, 'he lives having permeated one direction with a mind endowed with compassion,' seeing beings experiencing many sufferings, he constantly thinks, 'May these beings be free from suffering!' " (*Dp.*, p. 263). See above, note 9 in chapter 19.
20. "Meditative cultivation of loving-kindness is bringing to mind again and again such thoughts as 'May all beings be free from suffering' in such manner as 'May all beings be free of hatred, free of ill will', etc. 'May they be free of disease. May they be happy.' Especially, it is wishing well for others in one's own mind, with genuineness. By developing loving-kindness, hatred disappears, one promptly reaches concentration *(samādhi)*; on one's face is an agreeable hue and radiance. And one is dear to all people, and is lovingly protected by the gods" (*Dp.*, p. 263). See above, note 9 in chapter 19.
21.* The text of the commentary here seems to be very faulty. The readings are as follows:
    1) PTS, III, 459; SHB, p. 564; ADB, p. 702: *kiñcāpi hi heṭṭhā karuṇā bhāvanāya vuttattā.*
    2) PTS/APB: *idha sabbā pi avasesa-bhāvanā;* SHB: *idha sabbā pi avasesā bhāvanā nāma.*
    3) PTS: *idha pana mettābhāvanā ca adhippetā;* SHB: *idha pana mettābhāvanā va adhippetā;* APB: *mettābhāvanā ca adhippetā.*

    Our translation can be justified only if the original text read:
    1) *kiñcāpi hi heṭṭhā karuṇābhāvanāya vuttattā*
    2) *idha sabbā pi avasesā bhāvanā (vattabbā)*
    3) *idha pana mettābhāvanā va adhippetā.*

    This does not agree with any one of the three major editions consulted. *Dag.* and *Dps.* do not contain any clues to clarifying the issue. Our translation thus has to be treated as only a hesitant attempt to capture what might have been in the mind of the commentator.
22.* *GDhpC.*, pp. 256–57, has a long note on *Dhp.*, 302. Brough's comments there seem to be unduly harsh and it is difficult to agree with him that "there is little chance of reaching certainty" about the meaning. The Pali commentary evidently sees here a "contracted sentence" with the subject left to be understood. Obviously that subject is a neuter *pabbajjaṃ* (in place of the more common feminine *pabbajjā*). In the sentence *pabbajjaṃ nāma duppabbajjaṃ,* "hard to be

gone forth is the going forth," the last word answers to a Sanskrit *ṇyat kṛdanta: duṣpravrājyam.* (In fact, the parallel, *Uv.*, xi, 8*a*, has *duṣpravrajyam.*) The sentence closely resembles the next sentence of the verse: *durāvāsā gharā,* "hard to be lived in are homes." Cf. also *Dhp.*, 245, *hirīmatā dujjīvaṃ,* which stands for *hirīmatā jīvitaṃ dujjīvaṃ.* Cf. also *Dhp.*, 87, *viveke . . . dūramaṃ,* discussed above, note 19 in chapter 6.

23.* Where Pali has *bhajati, GDhp.*, 323, has *vayadi,* and *Uv.*, x, 8, has *vrajate. GDhpC.*, pp. 272–73, draws attention to the comparable *Sn.* 1143 line, *yaṃ yaṃ disaṃ vajati bhūripañño.* Probably *bhajati* is an adaptation from an earlier version that had *vajati*—i.e., line 3 might have meant, "Wherever he goes. . . ."

24. "Here, faith means both ordinary faith and transcendent faith. Both of them have the characteristic of being faith in the qualities of the three gems [Buddha, Dhamma, Sangha] and in *karma* and its consequences" (*Sdk.*, p. 156).

25.* Following *Dag.*, 253, SHB, p. 566, APB, p. 705, *anāthapiṇḍikādīnam,* in preference to PTS, III, 464, *anāthapiṇḍikādīhi.*

26. "The sevenfold noble wealth which is [1] the wealth of faith, [2] of moral virtue, [3–4] of a sense of shame and of fear, [5] of learning, [6] of generosity, and [7] insight-wisdom" (*Dag.*, 253.25–29). So also *Sdk.*, p. 156.

27. " 'In the fourfold darkness', i.e., [1] in the dark fortnight of the month, [2] in the middle of the night, [3] in a thickly covered forest, [4] with the sky covered with a layer of rain clouds" (*Dag.*, 255.10). So also *Sdk.*, p. 156.

28.* Following SHB, p. 569, and APB, p. 708, *tathārūpā,* in preference to PTS, III, 470, *tathārūpa-.*

29.* For *damayaṃ,* from √*dam-* (to control), all other versions have a word from √*ram-* (to delight): *PDhp.*, 314, *ramayaṃ; GDhp.*, p. 259, *ramahi; Uv.*, xxiii, 2, *ramayet.* In the next line only *PDhp.* has a word corresponding to *ramito* (i.e., *ramitā*); the other two versions have *vasa* (*GDhp.*) and *vaset* (*Uv.*).

30. "Like the Brazen Palace" *(lohapāsāda-sadise)*. The site of the Brazen Palace, dating from the second century B.C., and ruins representing various stages of reconstruction, can be seen today in the ancient city of Anurādhapura, Sri Lanka.

31.* Following SHB, p. 570, and APB, p. 709, *catuririyā pathesu,* in preference to PTS, III, 472, *sabbiriyāpathesu. Dps.*, p.134, has *satara iriyavuvehi ma,* "in the four postures." *Dps.* consistently echoes the wording of the commentary.

32.* Following SHB, p. 570, and APB, 709, *pavivitte vanante,* in preference to PTS, III, 472, *pavivitto vanante. Dps.*, p. 134, has *strī-*

*puruṣa-śabdādiyen vivikta vū . . . valhi,* "in the woods that are secluded from sounds of men and women, etc."

# Chapter XXII

1.* *GDhpC.*, p. 258, discusses at length the present tense verb in *Dhp.*, 306*b*: "Although the precise form can only be guessed, there need be no doubt that the verse started its career with a verb in the past tense. . . . Most probable would be an aorist, *na karam ti āha*; or perhaps . . . *n'akaraṃ*. . . . After the aorist has come to be felt archaic, *karomi*, first as an explanation, and then as a replacement, leads directly to the Pali readings"—i.e., *na karomi ti cāha, na karomiccāha,* and *na karomi cāha,* none of which can therefore "seriously claim to be original." However, the ancientness of the present tense form is proved by *PDhp.*, 114, which too has *na karomīti āha,* and the old MSS of *Uv.* (viii, 1), which have *na karomīti prāha* and *na karoti āha* (see Bernhard, *Uv.*, I, p. 161). Obviously, what prompts *GDhpC.* to suspect the reading and suggest complex alternatives to it is the idea that the present tense does not make good sense here. This is an assumption that can be questioned. Perhaps the composer of the verse had in mind the offender who defensively says that he "does not do" (present tense) that kind of thing?

2.* What follows this statement in the commentary is, after PTS III, 477, *nihīnakammā manujā, paratthā ti padassa pana purato pecca-padena sambandho;* according to APB, p. 711, and SHB, p. 572, *nihīnakammā manujā paratthā ti. tassa padassa pana purato pecca-padassa sambandho.* Both of these present difficulties in translating, which suggests that the text in either case is questionable. If the phrase *paratthā ti* had occurred twice after the word *manujā,* sense can be made out. This is the procedure followed in our translation.

3\. *Sds.*, I, 207, commenting on *Dhp.*, v. 17, generally describes the *peta*s as being oppressed by hunger and thirst, having emaciated bodies, feeding on "saliva, nasal discharge, mucous from the throat, excreta, urine, placentas, and dead bodies." They are frightening to behold. "They have a very small mouth like the eye of a needle. They have protruding eyes like the eyes of a crab." They strike each other with red-hot weapons and drink the blood. "In this way, one is not able to explain fully the suffering experienced by the *preta*s. With regard to this, only the Buddha has the ability [to explain fully]."

4.* Following APB, p. 713, and SHB, p. 574, *tato,* in preference to PTS, III, 481, *tatto.*

5.* The word *uppathacārī*, at PTS, III, 482, is not found in APB, p. 714, or SHB, p. 574. However, *Dag.*, 256, quotes it.

6.* SHB, p. 576, has *kayirā*, so also APB, p. 715, supported by *Dag.*, 137. PTS, III, 485, has *kayiram*, obviously the equivalent of Skt. *kāryam*.

7. On the practice of resorting to impropriety, see above, note 3 in chapter 16.

8.* SHB, p. 576, and APB, p. 715, *thirakatam*, is supported by *Dps.*, p. 137 *(tara koṭa mä)*. PTS, III, 485, *thirataram*, is, however, not very different in meaning.

9.* Following APB, p. 715, *anivattasamādano hutvā*, in preference to PTS, III, 485, and SHB, p. 576, *avattasamādāno hutvā*. *Dps.*, p. 137, paraphrases *avasthita vū samādāna äti vä*, which supports APB. PTS, III, 485, notes *v.l. anivattita*, which suits the context very well.

10.* Following APB, p. 717, *dvār' aṭṭāla-uddāpa-parikhā 'dīni*, in preference to PTS, III, 488, *aṭṭāla-uddāma-parikhādīni*, and SHB, p.577, *dvār-'aṭṭāla-uddāma-parikhādīni*. The APB reading is supported by *Dps.*, p.138, paraphrase, *doraṭu-aṭalu-padanam-agala*, and *Dag.*, 257, *uddāpa-parikhādīni*. *Dag.* explains *uddāpa* (not *uddāma*) as "foundations of outer wall" *(bihi pavurehi pavaru piḷu)*, with which *Dps. padanam* agrees.

11. External bases/internal bases ( = *āyatanas*). See notes 5 and 6 in chapter 8, above.

12. "The state of unimpairment of the senses such as the eye, etc." (*Sdk.*, p. 160).

13.* The commentary explains these with *alajjitabbe, lajjitabbe*. So too *Dps.*, p. 139, *lajjā kaṭa yutu tanhi, lajjā nokaṭa yutu tanhi*. *PDhp.*, 169, *alajjitabbe; Uv.*, xvi, 6, *alajjitavye;* and *GDhp.*, 273, *alajidavi*, support this. PTS, III, 490, *alajjitā ye* and *lajjitā ye* should therefore be changed to *alajjitāye, lajjitāye*. See Geiger, *Pali Literature and Language*, sec. 203, p. 223.

14. Reference is to the background story, regarding an episode with naked Jain ascetics, given earlier in the commentary. See BL, III, 196.

15.* The editions of *DhpA.* seem to be all unsure as to the significance of this word. *Dps.*, with help from *Uv.* and *GDhp.*, shows us that the word is a development of the potential participle *lajjitabbe* (see above, note 13, in this chapter). PTS, III, 490, seems to be right for the first sentence of the comment, *appaṭicchannena hirikopīnangena lajjitabbaṃ*, and APB, p. 718, on the next sentence, *te pana taṃ appaṭicchādetvā vicarantā alajjitāye na lajjanti nāma*. In this second sentence, APB rightly preserves the headline clause *alajjitāye na lajjanti nāma*. SHB, pp. 578f., seems to be most confused as to the handling of *(a)lajjitāye*. Our translation follows the PTS wording for the first sentence and the APB wording for the second.

16. "Acceptance of what is not real *(näti artha)* is called holding to what is empty. Acceptance of what is distorted as real is called holding to what is wrong" (*Dag.*, 258.16–18).

17. " 'In regard to the tenfold right view'—the tenfold right view such as 'there is [fruit in] what is given, there is [fruit in] what is offered,' etc. 'And to the dhamma that has served as its foundation,' to the textual dhamma *(peḷa dam)* that is the basis for right view" (*Dag.*, 258.24ff.).

*Sdk.*, p. 162, says: "that which is without error *(niravadya)* is [1] the tenfold right view which is the absence of the ten unwholesome acts such as taking life, etc. [see note 18 in chapter 1, above] or [the tenfold right view] namely, 'there is fruit-consequence with regard to what is given,' etc., and [2] the instruction in dharma (*damdesum*) that is conducive to the arising of that right view."

18. " 'In the tenfold wrongview'—such as 'there is nothing [in what is] given, etc.' " (*Dag.*, p. 259.1). According to *Sdk.*, p. 162, "The erroneous *(sāvadya)* means [1] wrong view, wrong intention, wrong speech, wrong actions, wrong livelihood, wrong effort, wrong mindfulness, wrong concentration, wrong knowledge, wrong release, or the tenfold wrong view, such as 'there is nothing [in what is] given, there is nothing [in what is] offered,' and [2] the instruction of a dharma that conduces to the arising of that wrong view."

## Chapter XXIII

1.* *Cāpāto patitaṃ*: *GDhpC.*, pp. 273–74, discusses this "grammatically and metrically" "awkward phrase," whose equivalent in *GDhp.*, 329, is *cavadhivadida*. Brough is inclined to see behind these forms a *samāsa*—i.e., *cāpātipatita*. The soundness of this conjecture is now strikingly proved by *PDhp.*, 215, which has *cāpātipatite śare*. Brough also thinks it "well nigh essential to assume that the original verse had a causative participle *-pātita*," rather than the extant *-patita*.

2. "By the eight [kinds of] ignoble behavior such as professing to have seen what has not been seen, etc." (*Dag.*, 259.10).

The complete formula runs: (1) professing to have seen what has not been seen, (2) to have heard what has not been heard, (3) to have remembered what has not been remembered, (4) to have known what has not been known, (5) professing not to have seen what was seen, (6) not to have heard what was heard, (7) not to have remembered what was remembered, (8) and not to have known what was known.

3.* Following APB, p. 721, and SHB, p. 581, *mama bhāro,* in preference to PTS, IV, 3, *bhāro*. The commentary here reechoes a statement from the background story: *dussīlehi kathitakathānaṃ sahanaṃ nāma mayhaṃ bhāro.*

4.* Following PTS, IV, 4, *rājā pi,* in preference to SHB, p. 581, and APB, p. 721, *rājā. Dps.*, p. 140, *raja da,* "the king too," substantiates the PTS reading.

5.* Following *Dag.*, 259.13–14, *nibbisevana, keles popi näti,* "Not having the disturbance of the defilements."

6.* Following SHB, p. 581, and APB, p. 722, *catūhi ariya-maggehi,* in preference to PTS, IV, 4, *catumaggasaṅkhātena.*

7. The commentative gloss on this verse (*Dhp.*, 324) has been translated by Burlingame, under the heading "Native gloss," in BL, III, 205.

8.* *Dag.*, 260.20 reads *tutta-tomare* and explains the former as having two spikes and the latter as having a single spike. APB, p. 726, adopts this reading.

9.* PTS, IV, 14, reads *hatthisālaṃ pavesitamattaṃ,* as does the Thai edition, VII, 150, which, occurring in the accusative case, is problematic. Our translation follows the *v. l.* (noted at PTS, IV, 14, n. 15) *tam atthaṃ (sandhāya),* as appears in APB, p. 726.

10.* Following APB, p. 726, and SHB, p. 585, *nāga-vanam,* in preference to PTS, IV, 14, *nāga-bhavanam.*

11.* Following APB, p. 726, and SHB, p. 585, *(mātā pana) me,* in preference to PTS, IV, 14, *(mātā pan') assa.*

12.* Following APB, p. 727, and SHB, p. 585, *vane,* in preference to PTS, IV, 15, *bhavane.*

13.* *Dag.*, 260, where these terms are explained, uses *āhara-hatthaka.* So *Dps.*, p. 142, and APB, p. 726. But SHB, p. 586, and PTS, IV, 16, have *āhārahatthaka.* The former is preferable.

14. Reference is to the background story given earlier in the commentary. See BL, III, 211.

15.* The commentary and *Dps.*, p. 144, take *Mātaṅga* as the name of an elephant—i.e., *mātaṅgaraññe va nāgo* seems to be taken as *mātaṅgo araññe iva nāgo.* Reducing *mātaṅgo* and *araññe* into *mātaṅgaraññe* by *sandhi* in such circumstances seems unusual. It would be more natural to take *mātaṅgaraññe* as a *samāsa,* but in that case M. would be the name of a forest. The commentary also tries to derive Mātaṅga from the √*gam-*, though in a rather unclear way.

Elsewhere in the Pali tradition, M. is the name of the well-known outcaste who humbled the pride of *Brāhmaṇas,* and, in at least two references, also of a forest with which he was connected (see G. P. Malalasekera, *Dictionary of Pali Proper Names,* under *Mātaṅga* and *Mātaṅgārañña*).

The parallel verses in *PDhp.* (10/11) have *mātaṃgāranne va nāgo,* and one version of *Uv.*, xiv, 16 (the parallel of *Dhp.*, 330), has *mātaṅgāraṇye nāgavat.* The wording in all three versions (*Dhp.*, *PDhp.*, and *Uv.*) is such that we can translate the phrase as "like the elephant in the *Mātaṅga* forest"—which would not preclude its being called the *Mātaṅga* elephant, as does the commentary. Taken thus the awkward *sandhi* combination does not arise.

16.* PTS, IV, 29, *rajjato rājisi viya* seems problematic. APB, p. 724, and SHB, p. 591, have . . .*gato mahājanaka-rājā viya*, "like the king Mahājanaka who went forth. . . ." That this was a *DhpA.* reading even in the fourteenth century is suggested by *Dps.*, p. 144, *raṭa hārā piyā . . . pravrajyāvaṭa elambi mahā janaka rajahu men*, "like king Mahājanaka who left the country and set forth." PTS, *rājisi*, "royal sage," may, however, represent a still earlier reading, which may have been superseded by the reading *mahājanaka-rājā*. But *rajjato* seems best rejected in favor of *gato.*

17. The background story (see BL, III, 211–13) relates the activities of the elephant named Pārileyyaka.

18.* The readings at this point are confused. PTS, IV, 30, has *ogāhantassa ca me tiṇṇassa ca.* APB, p. 724, has *ogāhantassa ca me otiṇṇassa ca,* SHB, p. 592, has *ogāhā c'assa me uttiṇṇassa* ("as I get out from my bath"?).

19. *Dag.*, 262.11ff., comments: "'The minor [moral virtue],' the medium moral virtue, and the major moral virtue are mentioned in the *Brahmajāla Sutta* [see above, note 6 in chapter 5 and note 2 in chapter 20], 'the ten subjects of discussion or conversation'—such as unpretentious talk, etc. [see above, note 7 in chapter 5], 'the thirteen *dhutaṅga* practices'—such as wearing rags gathered from a dust heap, etc. [see above, note 6 in chapter 2], [the Four Paths and Four Fruits: see above, notes 39 and 52 in chapter 1],' 'the three [kinds of] gnosis'—such as of former abodes, etc. [see above, note 20 in chapter 2], 'the six [kinds of] higher gnosis'—such as forms of psychic powers *(iddhi)*, etc. [see above, note 20 in chapter 2]."

20. "The merit that one acquires at the time of one's death is a comfort. This merit is a comfort because it is a support for those who live in this world, and for those who have lived here and who pass away and go to the next world, and for those who have reached the next world" (*Sds.*, IX, 2362).

21.* PTS, IV, 34, has *imasmiṃ loke,* which APB, p. 736, and SHB, p. 593, lack.

22. "'They are born in the hell of Gūtha [excrement],' they are born in the hell of excreta, as befits the action of not caring for mother and father" (*Dag.*, 263.15–16).

23.* APB, p. 737, and SHB, p. 594, have sobhati. PTS, IV, 35, has *sobhanti*.

24. The five precepts are: (1) I undertake the precept to refrain from taking life, (2) to refrain from taking what is not given, (3) to refrain from sexual misconduct, (4) to refrain from lying, (5) to refrain from taking spirituous drinks, malt liquor, wines—foundations for heedlessness.

25. The ten precepts: the five listed above and (6) to refrain from taking food at an improper time, (7) to refrain from dancing, singing, music, and unseemly shows, (8) to refrain from using garlands, perfumes, and unguents, things that beautify and adorn, (9) refrain from using high and luxurious seats, (10) and to refrain from accepting gold and silver.

26.* SHB, p. 594, and APB, p. 737, have *lokiya-lokuttarato duvidhā;* PTS, IV, 35, has *lokiya-lokuttarā duvidhā.*

27.* This is explained in *Dag.*, 263, as "by way of destroying the cause *(pasa nasana visin)*." Thus *setu* is given the same meaning as *hetu.* Inasmuch as *setu* normally means "bridge," has it been used to indicate "unwholesome deed" as the "bridge" to the continuity of the whirl of *saṃsāra* and so as its cause? *Dps.*, p. 146, says the following: "Not doing unwholesome deeds because [they have been] eradicated by the Path is a blessing." Here again the suggested meaning is the cause, which is eradicated.

## Chapter XXIV

1.* This is the reading in *Dps.*, p. 146, APB, p. 741, and SHB, p. 579. PTS, IV, 44, has *palavati. Uv.*, iii, 4, has *sa hi saṃsarate punaḥ punaḥ* for *so plavati hurāhuraṃ* of *Dhp. PDhp.*, 137, has *sā prāplāvate hurāhuraṃ* (*tahnā* of line *b* being the subject).

2.* *Uplavati* (doubtless from *ut* plus the root *plu-*) in SHB, p. 597, and APB, p. 741. *Uppalavati* is the reading in PTS, IV, 44.

3.* *Uv.*, iii, 9*a*, has *grāmyām* ("rustic," "unrefined") in place of this word. The meaning given by Sinhala commentators ("childish"—*Dps.*, p.146; *Dag.*, 264) is much the same.

4. Reference is to Kapila, in the background story given earlier in the commentary, who became intoxicated by misappropriating his great learning, became desirous of personal gain, in the habit of harsh speech, and, although in former times, just after the *parinibbāna* of Kassapa, a former Buddha, he was a member of the monastic order, he lived such an obnoxious life that he was born into Avīci hell, to be

reborn as a fish during the era of the Blessed One, to return again to Avīci hell. See BL, III, 215–18.

5. *Usīra,* which has medicinal properties, is said to be the root of *bīraṇa* grass.
6. Māra: see note 29 in chapter 1, and note 12 in chapter 13.
7.* For *purakkhata, PDhp.*, 149, has *purekkhaṭa*—obviously another form of the same word. *Uv.*, iii, 6, has *upaskṛtāh* ("equipped with"?). The Pali commentary explains the word as meaning "accompanied by" *(parivārita)*. Our translation, which is tentative, follows the commentary.
8. "The latent dispositions *(anuśayas)* are the defilements that are as if sleeping in the continuum of the mind *(citta santānaya)*, having reached a subtle nature that is conducive to birth [i.e., to surfacing] or acquiring a causal condition for arising . . . like the poison of a rat [that can remain dormant in a bitten body to flare up in a serious illness at any time]. They are sevenfold: desire for [existence at] the sensual level, desire for [other] existence, anger, self-estimation, [wrong] views, [speculative] doubt, and ignorance [see note 8 in chapter 13]. In this context, what is spoken of as "propensity of craving" are the sensual passion and passion for existence" (*Sdk.*, p. 168, following *Dps.*, pp. 147–48).
9. "'The eighteen activations [of craving] dependent on the internal *(āyatana)*'—craving itself arising in one's stream of consciousness with regard to the six objects, pertaining to the past, future, and present, is called the 'eighteen activations of craving.' 'The eighteen activations [of craving] dependent on the external *(āyatana)*—this should be taken in the same manner as the previous comment" (*Dag.*, 265.13ff.).

   "'Thirty-six streams' . . . namely, the eighteen activations of craving that exist having the internal *āyatana*s, such as eyes, etc., as their sphere, and the eighteen activations of craving that exist having the external *āyatana*s, such as form, etc., as their sphere" (*Dps.*, p. 148).

   "Here, the thirty-sixfold craving exists in three dimensions, i.e., craving for sensuality, craving for existence, craving for the cessation of existence, having as its shpere the six internal *āyatanas* [i.e., $3 \times 6 = 18$], namely, eyes, ears, nose, tongue, body, mind, and the six external *āyatanas* [i.e., $3 \times 6 = 18$], namely, form, sound, smell, taste, touch, dharmas, is called the [$18 + 18$] thirty-six streams" (*Sdk.*, p. 169). See above, notes 5 and 6 in chapter 8.
10.* Following *Dps.*, p. 148, APB, p. 743, and SHB, p. 599, in preference to PTS, IV, 48, *duddiṭṭhaṃ*.
11.* Following APB, p. 743, and SHB, p. 599, *sabbabhavehi*, in preference to PTS, IV, 49.

12.* On the tenfold fetter, see above, note 27 in chapter 2. On the sevenfold attachment, see above, note 8 in chapter 13.Our translation follows APB, p. 743, and SHB, p. 600, which have *dasavidhena saṃyojana-saṅgena, sattvidhena rāgasaṅgādinā ca. Dps.* paraphrase, p. 149, also follows this. PTS, IV, 50, however, has *dasavidhena saṃyojanena saṅgena c'eva sattavidhena rāgādinā ca.*

13.* In the *Dhp.* verse, *Dps.*, p. 150, and PTS, IV, 53, have *eva* ("indeed") in line *c*. But APB, p. 745, and SHB, p. 601, have *etha* ("come"). However, *Dps.* and PTS have in the body of the commentary *evaṃ* ("thus"). *PDhp.*, 151, also has *etha,* but *Uv.*, xxvii, 29*c* does not have the word. The text of the comparable *GDhp.*, 92*c*, is incomplete.

14. See also the commentative discussion translated in the text, above, on *Dhp.* vv. 283–84.

15.* Following PTS, IV, 53, and APB, p. 746, *vihārasaṅkhāte (Dps.*, p. 150, *vihāraya yi kiyana lada)*. SHB, p. 601, has *dibbavihārasaṅkhate.*

16.* *Sāratta-rattā: PDhp.*, 143, also has this form, but *GDhp.*, 169, has *sarata-cita* and *Uv.*, ii, 5, *saṃraktacittasya.* The word *saṃrakta* is used by *Dps.*, p. 150, too, in glossing *Dhp.*, 345*c*—and this may reflect a continuing paraphrase of *sāratta* by *saṃrakta.* What, then, is the final *-ratta*? Brough says, " . . . *sāratta-rattā* is awkward to explain and may perhaps be due simply to *rāga-rattā* two stanzas later" (*GDhpC.*, p. 230.) It is interesting to note that *Dps.*, being perhaps aware of the difficulties involved, proposes also an alternate interpretation, which takes *sāratta* as *sāratva* ("value"): "attached *(ratta-)* to jewels and ornaments on account of their value." This ingenious explanation, however, does not get us out of the other difficulty the word creates, that of relating it to the rest of the sentence. For want of any other alternative, we have treated *sāratta-rattā* as generally meaning "excessively attached" (as the commentary explains), but as constituting an incomplete or elliptical clause, which merges with the next sentence by a word that is left to be "understood." This is obviously not satisfactory.

17.* *Sithilaṃ* ("lax"): in its place, *PDhp.*, 144, has *sukhumaṃ* ("fine/subtle") and *Uv.*, ii, 6*b*, *susthiram* ("very firm").*GDhp.*, 170*b*, has *śiśila.* The question is discussed in *GDhpC.*, p. 231. We have again simply followed the commentary in our translation.

18. On the four states of woe, see above, note 15 in chapter 1.

19.* PTS, IV, 56, has *kātuṃ na deti,* "does not allow one to do." Contrast *Dps.*, p. 150: *siyalu karmāntayanṭa avasara dena heyin,* "because it allows occasion for every activity." APB, p. 748, and SHB, p. 603, have *kātuṃ deti,* "allows one to do."

20.* APB, p. 748, and SHB, p. 603, have *dummociyaṃ.* PTS, IV, 56, has *dommocayaṃ.*

21.* PTS, IV, 56, *ñāṇa-maggena,* "by the path of gnosis." SHB, p. 603, and APB, p. 748, have *ñāṇakhaggena,* which is supported by *Dps.*, p. 150, *jñāna-khaḍgayen,* "by the sword of gnosis."

22.* *Dhp.*, 347: a parallel verse is found in *GDhp.*, 171, but not in *Uv.* or *PDhp.* The question of the aptness of the metaphors of this verse is discussed in *GDhpC.*, pp. 232–33. In this discussion, Brough severely criticizes the commentator's handling of the pronoun *ye,* "those who." Brough's comment can be summed up as follows: when the commentator explained *dhīrā vajanti* as he necessarily had to do, he was "left with *ye anupatanti* hanging loose" and was "forced to supply a correlative for which the verse gives no warrant: *te taṃ samatikkamituṃ na sakkonti*" ("they are not able to cross over it"). "It is, however, possible that *ye,* as nom. plural, is a misunderstanding . . . and that the original author intended the word as neuter singular. . . . This would give a very much better-knit syntactical structure to the verse . . . *yat sroto rāgaraktā anupatanti, etac chittvā dhīrā vrajanti.*" (The wise go "cutting off" that stream in which those enamored of pleasure fall.)

However, does the commentator really offer *te taṃ samatikkamituṃ na sakkonti* as a correlative to *ye*? The commentary, if summarized, would read as follows: *yathā nāma makkaṭako sayaṃ kataṃ jālaṃ* [*punapunaṃ anupatati*], *evaṃ ye rāgarattā* [*te*] *sayaṃ kataṃ taṇhāsotaṃ anupatanti.* [=*te taṃ samatikkamituṃ na sakkonti*]. *dhīrā* [*evaṃ duratikkamaṃ*] *etaṃ* [*bandhanam*] *pi chinditvā. . . . anapekkhino gacchanti.* According to this, which closely follows the wording of the commentary, *te tam,* etc., is given only as an elaboration of *taṇhāsotam anupatanti.* If so, Brough's critique of the commentary would have been misplaced, although his conjecture regarding the original syntactical structure may (or may not) be valid regardless of this critique.

23.* Following APB, p. 752, *-vasena pāragato,* in preference to SHB, p. 607, *-vasena pāragu pāragato,* and PTS, IV, 63, *-pāragu-vasena pāragato.*

24. On the *khandha*s, see above, note 4 in chapter 8; on the *dhātu*s, see above, note 5 in chapter 8; on the *āyatana*s, see above, notes 5 and 6 in chapter 8.

25. "One pressed down by the threefold thoughts such as thoughts of sensuality, ill will, aggressiveness" (*Dps.*, p. 152).

26. On the ten unpleasant (aspects of the body), the ten loathesome objects, see above, note 22 in chapter 20.

27. On the three-tiered whirl of existence, see above, note 11 in chapter 3.

28.* The parallel *PDhp.*, 147*d*, does not have the word *mahāpuriso.* Inasmuch as this regularizes the meter for the fourth line, we may regard *mahāpuriso* as an intrusion into the MSS, probably a scribal gloss for *mahāpañño*.

29. "Fourfold.... discriminative understanding *(paṭisambhidā):* the understanding that is diversified as [1] the understanding of the result of causes *(artha),* [2] the understanding of causes or conditions *(dharma),* [3] the understanding of the language of Magadha ([*dharma-*]*nirutti),* and [4] the modes of intuitive comprehension *(paṭibhāna)*" (*Sdk.*, p. 173). See also *Sds.*, IX, 2416ff. In this context *nirutti* (from *nir* +$\sqrt{vac\text{-}}$) means "word" or "expression," and the Theravāda tradition takes it as (words of) the Pali language (called traditionally the language of Magadha), in which the school's canonical texts are composed. See also *Dhp.*, 363, where the commentator equates dhamma with "[canonical] text" and *attha* with "[commentative] interpretation."

30.* Following APB, p. 757, and SHB, p. 611, *akkharānaṃ sannipātasaṅkhātaṃ,* in preference to PTS, IV, 90, *akkharānaṃ sannipātaṃ. Dps.*, p. 154, *akṣarayangē sannipātaya yi kiyana lada,* is the Sinhala equivalent of the APB and SHB reading.

31.* APB, p. 757, and SHB, p. 611, have *imesaṃ ādi-akkharānaṃ idaṃ majjhaṃ.* PTS, IV, 71, has *imesaṃ ādi-akkharānaṃ sannipātaṃ idaṃ majjham.*

32.* Following APB, p. 757, and SHB, p. 611, *evaṃ mahāpañño.* However, the occurrence of this here does not seem to be appropriate, because this comment on the word *mahāpañño* comes in this paragraph. PTS, IV, 71, breaks up *evaṃ* and *mahāpañño* by the punctuation, and the Thai edition has *eva* for *evaṃ.* The wording here needs further study.

33.* APB, p. 757, SHB, p. 611, and PTS, IV, 71, all read *attha-dhamma nirutti paṭisambhidānaṃ,* thus leaving out *paṭibhāna* from the traditional *paṭisambhidā* list. One would expect *-paṭibhānānaṃ,* which in fact is the reading of the Burmese MS referred to in PTS, IV, 71, note 7. We have followed that clue, corroborated by the Thai edition consulted, VIII, 36, in our translation.

34.* ". . . all dharmas of the four planes, i.e., the sphere of sensuality, the fine material sphere, the formless sphere, and the world-transcending sphere" (*Sdk.*, p. 173). So also *Sds.*, IX, 2425. See also note 19 in chapter 1, above.

35. "... having realized the four noble truths in the categories such as 'that which should be fully understood, etc.'" (*Dps.*, p. 154). "... having penetratively understood the dharma of the four truths" (*Sdk.*, p. 173). On these categories of understanding, see above, notes 53 in chapter 1, 9 in chapter 6, and 9 in chapter 16.

36. An English translation of the commentative gloss of this verse (*Dhp.*,

v. 354), entitled "Native gloss," can be found in BL, III, 237–39.

37. Sixteenth part: Belangoda Ānanda Maitreya, in his *Dhammapada Pāḷiya hā Siṇhala Dharmapadaya* (Nugegoda, Sri Lanka: Modern Book Co., 1979), p. 176, explains "sixteenth part" as meaning $1/16^{16}$ and not 1/16.

38.* Following *Dag.*, 269, SHB, p. 613, and APB, p. 760, *vācanaṃ,* in preference to PTS, IV, 74, *vacanaṃ.*

39. The site of the Mahāvihāra and the Brazen Palace can be seen today in the ancient city of Anurādhapura in Sri Lanka.

40. Reference is to the background story, given earlier in the commentary, in which Sakka, king of the gods, was addressed with this verse by the Buddha, who thereby provided answers to four corresponding questions that neither all the deities of the ten thousand world systems nor Sakka himself could answer. See BL, III, 236–37.

41. On the ninefold world-transcending dhamma, see above, note 52 in chapter 1.

42. On the thirty-seven dhammas contributing to enlightenment, see above, note 8 in chapter 2.

43.* "Pulses and grains": see note 11 in chapter 11.

44.* PTS, IV, 81 and SHB, p. 617, have *bahuphalāni.* But APB, p. 764, has *bahusassāni,* and the most ancient source available, *Dag.*, 270, has *bahuṭṭhānā;* cf. *bahuṭṭhānāni,* a *v. l.* recorded in PTS and SHB.

45.* Following PTS, IV, 82, *khīnāsavesu dinnaṃ pana mahapphalaṃ hoti,* not found in APB, and SHB.

## Chapter XXV

1.* Following APB, p. 766, *n'uppajjati,* in preference to PTS, IV, 85, and SHB, p. 619, *uppajjati.* The sense given by *n'uppajjati* is in keeping with the Abhidhamma theory of apperception, to which allusion is again made under the term *javana.*

2.* *At the mind-door:* editions of the commentary read *manodvāre,* but *Dps.*, p. 158, translates *manodvārayen.* So also *Sdk.*, p. 206. This suggests that the reading should be *manodvārena*—in which case we should translate, "through [or along with] the mind-door."

3.* *Dps.*, p. 159, explains this thus: "who is restrained in body, because of the absence of physical excesses such as shaking the head, knitting the eyebrows, etc."

4.* For *manta-bhāṇī, GDhp.* (vv. 24*e*, 25*b*, 54*b*) has *maṇa-bhaṇi;* the *Uv.* (viii, 10; xxviii, 8) has *manda-bhāṣī.* At *Gdhp.*, 237, too, *maṇa-bhaṇi* occurs; the parallel *Uv.*, xxix, 45, has *alpa-bhāṇim,* but the Tibetan translation of this shows, according to *GdhpC.*, pp. 248–49, that it has been made from a version that has *manda-* as the first member of the compound. It would thus seem that *maṇa-* of the *GDhp. maṇa-bhaṇi* is the equivalent of Sanskrit *manda. GDhpC.* surmises that the Pali *manta-bhāṇī* also stands for an original *manda-bhāṇī.* It is a "redactor's creation," a "hyper-Palism" made through a desire "to produce a more literary appearance" in the text. This *manta-bhāṇī,* as well as *maṇa-bhaṇi* of *GDhp.*, 54, should, then, mean "speaking in moderation." In fact, in the *Dhp.*, 227, corresponding to *GDhp.*, 237, the Pali parallel of *maṇa-bhaṇi* is *mitabhāṇī,* which indisputably means "speaking in moderation."

Then why does the Pali commentary explain *manta* as "insight"? *GDhpC.* takes it that the commentary thought that *manta* here is the same word whose meaning is explained in a stock phrase, *mantā vuccati paññā,* "*mantā* means insight." ("Although this *mantā* was later taken as a fem. sg., there is little doubt that the phrase originally meant it as a nom. pl.: [so the stock phrase really must have meant] 'the term "mantras" is . . . a synonym for *prajñā*'"—an understandable development from the Vedic tradition where *mantras* were sacred texts of wisdom.)

However, *PDhp.*, 54, the equivalent of *Dhp.*, 363, has *mantābhāṣī,* and this obviously gives rise to fresh questions. First of all, it seems remarkable that *PDhp.* also has the same "fossilized" nom. pl. form *mantā* known to the Pali exegetes. On the other hand, if *mantă-* is a "redactor's creation," the fact that both *Dhp.* and *PDhp.* have it can be quite significant. Do they both stem from similar textual traditions that differed from the precursors of *GDhp.* and *Uv.* in having this "redactor's creation"?

Though it seems possible to agree with the substance of Brough's textual criticism *(GDhpC.),* it must be said that the effect of taking *manta-* as a development from *manda-* is to introduce to the "original verse" the very tautology on whose grounds he questions the validity of *sammattaṃ* in *Dhp.*, 287. See also above, note 27 in chapter 20.

5.* PTS, IV, 95, APB, p. 771, and SHB, p. 623, have *tattha nivāsana-ṭṭhānaṭṭhena,* which compares with *Dps.*, p. 160, *vāsasthānaya koṭa äti.*

6.* PTS, IV, 95, *tesaṃ cīvarādi kāraṇena,* in preference to APB, p. 773, and SHB, p. 625, *tesaṃ cīvarādi karaṇena.*

7. On the integration of mind that pertains to access and absorption, see above, note 32 in chapter 18.

8. "'In regard to name-and-form'—i.e., name and form, being the five factors constituting individuality, namely, the physical *(rūpa)* [and the

following four, falling into the category of 'name', *nāma*] feeling, sensation, *saṅkhāras*, and consciousness" (*Dps.*, p. 161).

9.* From at least the time of *Dps.* (12th century) the Pali tradition of Sri Lanka has taken *Dhp.*, 371*b*, *mā te kāmaguṇe bhamassu cittaṃ,* as meaning "Do not cause your mind to whirl in the five areas of sensuality": *tāgē sita pas kam kotaṣhi nahamak bamavayi* (*Dps.*, p. 162). (Cf. *SdhRv.*, p. 1058, *topagē situt paskam guṇayehi no pavatvava:* "And do not exercise your mind in the fivefold strand of sensuality.") The Sinhala verb *bamavayi,* which *Dps.* gives as the equivalent of *bhamassu,* is a second person singular causative form answering to Sanskrit *bhrām̆ayasva.* The latter could have come to Pali as *bhamassu* through an intermediate form * *bhamessu,* in which *bhame-* would represent the causative base *bhramaya-*.

The Pali commentary also understands the line in exactly the same way. Its position is summed up in its comment *bhamassū ti: pañcavidhe ca te kāmaguṇe cittaṃ mā bhamatu.* On this comment *GDhpC.*, p. 194, says, "This is full of difficulties. The second person imperative is recklessly interpreted as third person. By its position *te* should be acc. pl. of the pronoun *tat;* but to make any sense of the sentence, it must be gen. sg. of *tvaṃ.*" This is a clear case of not understanding the technique of the Pali commentaries. The exact significance of the commentator's statement is: "In saying 'do you not let your mind whirl in the fivefold strand of sensuality,' what the verse means is: 'may not your mind whirl.'" The use of a third person verb to explain a sentence with a second person verb is not reckless. The commentator does not mean *bhamatu* to be understood as the grammatical equivalent of *bhamassu.* He is merely explaining the general idea. The position of *te* in the commentative sentence is also irrelevant; at this point the commentator leaves the word *te* unexplained (because its meaning is obvious), and so cites *te kāmaguṇe* exactly as it is in the verse, without altering its position to suit the prose syntax.

The question of the development of the form *bhamassu* is much more vexed. If we had only the Pali evidence to go by, we could have taken the commentary and the Sinhala works based on it as providing a credible explanation. Even *GDhp.*, 75, *bhametsu* taken by itself can be squared with this explanation (i.e., *bhametsu* as a variant of * *bhamessu* with a dissimulating-*ts*-for-*ss*-). However, *PDhp.*, 37, *mā vo kāmaguṇā bhrameṃsu cittaṃ,* alters the situation completely. Obviously *bhrameṃsu* here is aorist third person plural from a causative base of the root *bhram-*, and *kāmaguṇā* is the subject of the sentence. Senart's conjecture on the original meaning of the line ("Let not the *kāmaguṇas* cause your mind to stray"—*GDhpC.*, p. 195 is, then, absolutely on the right track (and most of Brough's long comment, *GDhpC.*, pp. 194–96, is rendered ineffective by the new evidence, especially his idea that *bhamassu* "was imported into the Pali editions" in place of a supposed earlier reading *bhavassu*). It would now seem that *bhramemsu,* or rather the form on which *bhramemsu* itself is based, assumed the form *bhamassu* (via * *bhamessu*?) in the Pali tradition and then came to be regarded (probably due to the final-*ssu*) as an imperative second sing. form. Because the nom. pl. *kāmaguṇā* would then be inexplicable, it probably got altered to the loc. sing. *kāmaguṇe*. The tradition, however, succeeded in eliciting a credible sense out of the new reading and that is probably what mattered most in its own reckoning.

10.* See *GDhpC.*, pp. 189–90, on *GDhp.*, vv. 59, 60. The meaning given to Buddhist Hybrid Sanskrit *pratisaṃstāra,* "distribution severally (of gifts)," as well as the Tibetan commentary, would validate the commentative interpretation that explains the Pali *paṭisanthāra* as *dhamma*-and *āmisa-paṭisanthāra:* ". . . the word describes the situation where the layman makes his gift to the begging monk, while the latter gives in return his 'gift of the doctrine'" (*GDhpC.*, p. 190), or as we would say, "gift of dhamma" in return for "gift of material things" *(āmisa)*.

11.* SHB, p. 631, has the word "bhikkhu" at this place in the commentary. APB, p. 779, and PTS, IV, 108, do not have it.

12. "The five fetters, such as opinions about enduring individuality, [skeptical] doubt, clinging to precept and rituals, passion for sensuality, and ill will, which lead one downward, he cuts off by the three Paths mentioned above, namely Stream-Attainment, etc., like a person who cuts with a knife a cord tied around the foot" (*Dps.*, p. 162).

13. "He gets rid of the five fetters, such as passion for form, passion for the formless, self-estimation, agitation, and ignorance—which are termed belonging to the upper part because they bring about the fine material *(rūpa)* and formless *(arūpa)* realms called the upper region—having severed them by the Path of Arahantship like a person who cuts with a knife a cord tied around the neck" (*Dps.*, p. 162).

14. The five (spiritual) faculties are faith, enterprise, mindfulness, concentration, and insight-wisdom. *Sdk.*, p. 181.

15. "The floods of sensuality, etc." (*Dps.*, p. 162). See also above, notes 13 and 16 in chapter 2.

16. "Twofold in the sense of meditative-absorption that arises depending on an object and meditative-absorption that arises depending on characteristics" (*Dps.*, p. 162).

17. On the fivefold strand of sensuality, see above, note 3 in chapter 15.

18.* Following, tentatively, APB, p. 780, and SHB, 631, *kammaṭṭhānam avijahitvā*. PTS, IV, 110, has *kāyaṭṭhānaṃ vijahitvā*. *Dag*. and *Dps*. offer no clues.
19. On the eight attainments, see above, note 11 in chapter 2.
20. On the thirty-eight objects (of meditation), see above, note 22 in chapter 20.
21. On the arising and passing away of the *khandhas* in terms of twenty-five characteristics, see above, note 20 in chapter 8.
22.* Following APB, p. 780, and SHB, p. 631, *yena yenākārena purebhatta-pacchābhattādisu kālesu* . . . , in preference to PTS, IV, 110, *yena tenākārena purebhattādisu vā kālesu*. *Dps*., p. 163, has *peravaru pasvaru ādi yam kisi kalekhi*, which seems to support APB and SHB readings rather than the PTS.
23.* Following PTS, IV, 111. APB, p. 781, has *sārajīvitāya;* SHB, p. 532, has *sādhujīvitāya*.
24.* Following the *v. l. tvaṃ*, noted in the PTS, IV, 111, n. 12, adopted by APB, p. 781, and the Thai ed., VIII, 78.
25.* Following APB, p. 783. PTS, IV, 114, has *santamano;* however, it reads *santavā* in the verse (*Dhp*., v. 378).
26.* Taking *paṭimāse* as imperative, second person singular ( = *paṭi-māsaya*). The meaning given by the commentary is repeated at *Dps*., p. 165, *parīkṣa kara* (imperative, second person singular).
27.* PTS, IV, 117, adds *taṃ* after *ājānīyam*. This is not found in APB or SHB.

## Chapter XXVI

1.* Whereas PTS, IV, 139, has *parakkama* (which would be imperative second singular), APB, p. 796, SHB, p. 646, and *Dps*., p. 167, have the absolutive *parakkamma,* comparable with *PDhp*., 34, *parākrāmma,* and *Uv*., xxxiii, 60, *parākramya*. (Incidentally, for *sotaṃ* of this line, *PDhp*. alone has a form not derived from *srotas*, i.e., *sūtraṃ*).
2. "Drive away from the continuum of mind lust for objects and lust for passions [defilements] in order to sever the stream of craving" (*Dps*., p. 167).
3. "The one who knows well the four noble truths in the sense of knowledge of the truths and knowledge of what should be done, etc., namely, penetrative understanding of the fact *(satya)* of suffering, abandoning of the fact of its origin, etc." (*Dps*., p. 167).
4.* For *Dhp*., 385, *vīta-ddara* ("free of distress"), *PDhp*., 40, has *vīta-jjara; GDhp*., 35, has *vikada-dvara;* and *Uv*., xxxiii, 27, has *vīta-rāga*.

Such variation is usually an indication of uncertainty as to the correct form of the term in question. Brough tends to regard *vikada-dvara* as a derivative of *vigata-jvara* ("free of the fever"). *PDhp. vīta-jjara* could also stem from an original with *-jvara* (i.e., *vīta-jvara,* which has been conjectured as the form behind Pali *vītaddara*—see *GDhpC.*, pp. 185–86).

5. "The eyes, ears, nose, tongue, body, and mind are the six internal *āyatana*s, and form, sound, smell, taste, tangibles, and dharmas are the six external *āyatana*s. [See also notes 5 and 6 in chapter 8.] They are called *āyatana*s in the sense that they are the locations where mental processes that arise, having form, etc., as objects are born (arising places) and where they collect together (assembly places), and because they prolong the suffering of *saṃsāra,* through defilements issuing from [the internal *āyatana*s] such as the eye, having [the external *āyatana*s] such as form as their objects" (*Sdk.*, p. 186).
6. Twofold meditative-absorption: "Meditation fixed on objects and meditation regarding characteristics" (*Dps.*, p. 168). The first is "the eight attainments . . . to be obtained by training the mind in concentrating on one of the thirty-eight objects such as 'earth, *kasiṇa,* etc." And the second means "insight wisdom, path, and fruit . . . to be obtained by reflecting on the three characteristics" (*Sdk.*, p. 19). On "attainments," see note 11 in chapter 2, above; on *kasiṇa,* note 22 in chapter 20; on insight/characteristics, note 8 in chapter 5.
7. On the "sixteen tasks by means of the Four Paths," see above, note 9 in chapter 16.
8. The fourfold army is comprised of elephants, cavalry, chariots, and infantry.

9.* Following PTS, IV, 144, *caraṇa-tejena,* in preference to APB, p. 799, and SHB, p. 648, *sīla-tejena. Dps.*, p. 169, *caraṇa-tejasa,* and *Dag.*, 277, *saraṇa-dham tejin,* support the PTS reading.

10.* PTS, IV, 145, SHB, p. 649, APB, p. 800, and *Dps.*, p. 169, all have *pabbājay' attano.* What we would expect on the basis of the commentary here is a present participle—i.e., *pabbājayam attano*—which is how it is quoted at *GDhp.*, p. 121 (probably based on a Burmese *v. l.* referred to in PTS, IV, 145, n. 6). For *pabbājaya(ṃ), GDhp.* 16, has *parvahi'a,* and *Uv.*, xi, 15, *pravāhiya* (older MS) and *pravrājayitvā* (the revised, more sanskritized version). *GDhpC.*, p. 183, surmises that in *GDhp. parvahi'a* and the older *Uv. pravāhiya* we can see an old "pseudo etymology," which tried to explain *pravrajita* ( = Pali *pabbajita; GDhp. parva'ida*) from the causative base of the root *vah-* (so that *pravrajita* can be explained as *pravāhita-mala:* "he whose stains have been carried away"?). On the other hand, the Pali *pabbājayam* and the later *Uv. pravrājayitva* seem to be attempts "to tidy up the matter by connecting the word at least with the correct verb"—namely, the root *vraj-*.

11.* The commentary utilizes etymological punning for a homiletical purpose: *brāhmaṇa/bāhita; samaṇa/sametvā; pabbajita/pabbājana.*

12.* *GDhpC.*, pp. 179–80, suggests that it would be better to take *brāhmaṇa* as the subject of both clauses in lines *a/b* and also to take the same person as "the object of both acts" referred to in *c/d*. Accordingly, *GDhpC.* suggests that we may translate the verse thus: "A (true) Brahman should not strike a Brahman nor revile him." "Shame on the person who strikes a Brahman and even more shame on one who would show him anger."

On this difficult stanza Gustav Roth has devoted considerable attention in "Particular Features of the Language of the Ārya-Mahāsāṃghika-Lokottaravādins and their Importance for Early Buddhist Tradition" *(Die Sprache der ältesten buddhistischen Überlieferung: The Language of the Earliest Buddhist Tradition,* Heinz Bechert, ed. [Göttingen: Vandenhoeck & Ruprecht, 1980]), pp. 88–89. In this he brings to light not only the text of the Patna Dharmapada containing, inter alia, its version of this stanza, but also a version found in *Abhisamācārikā Dharmā,* a Vinaya text of the Mahāsāṅghika-Lokottaravāda school, which quotes this stanza as a *dharma-pada* recited by the Buddha in the course of a story he is said to have told. (In the story the leader of a gang of thieves, identified with a certain Brahman, desists from attacking a merchant's son, identified with the Arahant Sāriputra).

Thus we have now five versions of this stanza. In these five versions the crucial fourth line is represented thus:

a. Pali *Dhp./GDhp.*:
*Dhp.*, 389:*tato dhī y'assa muñcati*
*GDhp.*, 11:*tada vi dhi yo ṇa mujadi*

b. *Abhisamācārika/Uv.*
*Abhis.*:*taṃ pi dhik yo'sya muñcati*
*Uv.*, xxxiii, 63:*dhik taṃ yaś ca pramuñcati*

c. *PDhp.*, 46:*yassa vāsuna mu[ṃ]ccati*
*(vāsuna* = either *va* + *asuna* or *ca* + *asuna)*

Roth, with the help from the narrative context in which it is set in the *Abhisamācārikā,* translates lines *c/d* of the stanza appearing in that text as follows: "Shame on the slayer of a Brahman, and (on the Brahman), who deprives him (he who is admonished not to kill a Brahman) of his life." As for *PDhp.* version, he says that *asuna* there is a Prakrit acc. pl. (=Skt. *asūn*) used with the root *muc-* with the same significance as

Skt. *prāṇān muñcati* "deprives (one) of (one's) life." Thus *yo ca assa asuna muṃccati* of *PDhp.* = "And (shame on the Brahman) who deprives him of his life."

The Pali wording, however, does not have the equivalent of *asuna* to go with the root *muc-*, and therefore does not admit of a translation like the above. When one translates the words as they are in the Pali version, one gets neither an adequate sense, nor even anything really like the traditional explanation that the commentary gives ("The one who retaliates against an attacker on oneself is even more to be condemned than the one who attacks an Arahant"). The stanza obviously needs further study.

13.* The translation follows the commentative interpretation, which is also reflected in *Dps.*, p. 170. The extremely intricate textual problems of the stanza are discussed in detail in *GDhpC.*, pp. 180–83; " . . . corruption on the grand scale of the present verse is a rarity"(*GDhpC.*, p. 180). *GDhpC.* observes that most of the errors were already fossilized in this form at the time of the compilation of the commentary, "and there is therefore no direct evidence that the Pali text was ever any better." "It is thus possible, indeed probable, that the traditional text of the verse as it appears in the editions is to be accepted as the genuine Pali text. On this view, an editor of the Pali verse should not attempt to emend it, though he may wish to mark it as corrupt, and will, if he is wise, refrain from attempting to translate the untranslatable" (*GDhpC.*, p. 180).

14.* Whereas PTS, IV, 147, has *aññassa vā brāhmaṇassa,* APB, p. 802, and SHB, p. 650, have *aññatarassa vā jāti-brāhmaṇassa,* of which *Dps.*, 169, *ektarā jāti-brāhmaṇayaku,* is a direct Sinhala translation. We have preferred this to the PTS reading.

15.* *Adhimattam eva seyyo:* PTS, IV, 148, and APB, p. 802 (cf. *Dps.*, p. 170, *mahat vū ma śreyaseki*). SHB, which lacks this phrase here, has it later on (i.e., at the end of the second comment, p. 426, after "not just any slight or noble thing").

16.* *Esa . . . aparajjhati:* PTS, IV, 148. APB, p. 802, and SHB, p. 650, have *manussā aparajjhanti.*

17.* *Assa:* PTS, IV, 148. SHB, p. 650, and APB, p. 802, have *avassaṃ.*

18.* *Na kiñci seyyo:* PTS, IV, 148. *Na akiñci seyyo:* SHB, p. 650, and APB, p. 802.

19. The three avenues are body, speech, and mind. So *Dps.*, p. 170; *Sdk.*, p. 188; *Dv.*, p. 739.

20.* Following *Dps.*, p. 171, APB, p. 804, and SHB, p. 652, in preference to *so sukhī* of PTS, IV, 152. Cf. also *Uv.*, xxxiii, 7*d*: *sa śucir brāhmaṇaḥ sa ca.*

21. On the sixteen ways of considering the four noble truths, see above, note 9 in chapter 16.

22.* *Yonijaṃ matti-sambhavaṃ* (cf. *GDhp.*, 17, *yoneka-matra-sabhamu*): *GDhpC.*, p. 183, observes that these two words seem awkward and forced, that they probably represent an older phrase such as *yoniya-matta-sambhavaṃ* or *yoniyaṃ matta-sambhavaṃ*, which has yielded the present forms by a process of "false correction." *GDhpC.* has not shown how that phrase should be translated, although *yoniya* is explained as a derivative of *yoni* ( = *yonya*?) and *matta* is explained as the equivalent of Sanskrit *mātra*. "Whose [Brahman] extraction is merely uterine"?
23.* Following *Dps.*, p. 172, SHB, p. 655, and APB, p. 807. PTS, IV, 158, has *save*. Cf. *Uv.* xxxiii, 15*d*, *saced bhavati*, etc. *GDhp.*, v. 17, has *sayi bhodi*. However, the commentary seems to fit the reading *sa ve*.
24. "By the four forms of grasping, i.e., lust, [wrong] views, clinging to precepts and rituals, holding a substantialist position *(attavāda)*" (*Dag.*, 297.8). See also above, note 24 in chapter 6.
25. "From among the tenfold fetters, three fetters, i.e., the view of enduring substantiality, [skeptical] doubt, clinging to precepts and rituals, and the power *(śaktiya)* of all the fetters that lead to states of woe are got rid of by the Path of Stream-Entrance; and the gross aspects pertaining to two, namely, passion for sensuality and ill will [are got rid of] by the Path of a Non-Returner; and these two (are abandoned) completely by the Path of a Non-Returner. And five [more] fetters, namely, passion for the fine material [realm], passion for the formless, self-estimation, agitation, and ignorance [are got rid of] by the Path of Arahantship" (*Sdk.*, p. 190). See above, note 27 in chapter 2.
26. These attachments are seven according to *Sdk.*, p. 190. On these seven, see above, note 8 in chapter 13.
27. On the four bonds, see above, note 13 in chapter 2.
28.* *Sandānaṃ*: PTS, IV, 161. *Dps.*, p. 173, APB, p. 809, and SHB, p. 656, read *sandāmaṃ*.
29.* There is uncertainty as regards the form *sahanukkamaṃ*. *GDhp.*, 42, reads *samadikrammi* (absolutive from *sam-ati-kram*) and *Uv.*, xxxii, 58, *duratikramaṃ* (from *dur-ati-kram*).
30. On the sixty-two wrong views, see above, note 2 in chapter 20.
31. On the latent dispositions *(anusaya*s*)*, see above, note 8 in chapter 24.
32. "The ten ways of abusing such as 'You are a thief! You are a child! etc." (*Dag.*, 280.6–7). *Sdk.*, p. 191, gives the following statements as "the ten ways of abusing": "[1] You are a cheat, [2] just a kid, [3] an imbecile, [4] a slovenly camel, [5] a stupid ox, [6] an ass, [7] vile, [8] a beast, [9] for you there is no hope of weal, [10] you should be happy in your hell of woe!"
33.* Following *Dag.*, 280, *Dps.*, p. 174, SHB, p. 657, and APB, p. 810,

*andubandhanādīhi*. PTS, IV, 164, has *anubandhanādīhi*.

34.* This phrase differs in the various editions: *anīkabalena* is the reading in *Dag.*, 280, PTS, IV, 164, and APB, p. 810; *khantibalena* occurs in APB, p. 810, and SHB, p. 658 (PTS, IV, 164, has *khantibalānīkena* instead).

35. On the *dhutaṅga* practices, see above, note 6 in chapter 2.

36. On the fourfold virtue of purity, see above, note 40 in chapter 1.

37. "Lust for objects and lust for defilements" (*Sdk.*, p. 191).

38.* *Yasmiṃ*, following SHB, p. 659, and APB, p. 812. PTS, IV, 167, has *tasmiṃ*.

39. On the four bonds, see above, note 13 in chapter 2.

40.* Following APB, p. 816, and SHB, p. 662, *paribhoga*, as against *paribhogatā*, PTS, IV, 172. *Dps.*, p. 175, has *paribhoga (-saṁsargaya)*.

41.* PTS, IV, 176, and APB, p. 817, *kiñci*. SHB, *kañci*.

42.* Following APB, p. 819, and SHB, p. 665, *hatthagatehi daṇḍehi vā satthehi vā*, in preference to PTS, IV, 180, *hatthagate daṇḍe vā satthe vā virujjhamāne pi*.

43.* Following SHB, p. 665, and APB, 819, *mamaṃ*, in preference to PTS, IV, 180, *manaṃ*.

44.* *Na abhisaje* should clearly be optative third singular from the normal present stem of the root *saj-*. To explain this the commentary uses *laggāpeyya* ("would cause to get stuck"), which is optative third singular from the causative stem of the synonymous root *lag-*. It then adds *kujjhāpana-vasena:* "by way of causing anger"—which looks like an attempt to justify the causative form of the main explanatory word.

The verb in the comparable *PDhp.*, 43, is *abhiṣape*, which must be from the root *śap-*, to curse or revile, making line *c* to mean: "by which he may revile no one," quite an apt sense in this context. *Uv.*, xxxiii, 17, *yayā nābhiṣajet kaś cid*, agrees with the Pali so far as *abhisaje* is concerned but deviates from it in using the nominative *kaścit*. (But one MS has the *v. l. kiṃcid-*. See Bernhard, *Uv.*, p. 466). It is noteworthy that the Tibetan translation of this line of the *Uv.* ("who has not generated *kleśas*"), quoted in *GDhpC.*, p. 184, does not agree with the extant *Uv.* reading. The parallel *GDhp.*, 22, with *na viṣa'i*, would not disagree with the Pali reading. Inasmuch as *abhi-saj-* has the alternate meaning "revile" in Sanskrit, it is possible to reconcile *abhisaje* and *abhiṣape* and translate the Pali line also as "by which he may revile no one."

45. "Such as would not make anyone's mind stuck in anger" (*Dps.*, p. 177).

46. "Such as the Buddha, Dhamma, etc." (*Dag.*, 222.24). "The eight matters are the Buddha, Dhamma, the Saṅgha, precepts, a former end (the *skandha*s of the past), a future end (the *skandha*s of the future), a

former and a future end (the *skandhas* of the past and the *skandhas* of the future), causality, and dharmas that have arisen conditionally (causes and things that have sprung up from causes). Persons of deficient insight have doubts [in their minds] about these eight matters" (*Sdk.*, p. 194).

47. "'The meritorious' *(puñña)*, 'the wholesome' *(kusala)*, 'the detrimental' *(pāpa)*, what is unwholesome *(akusala)*; 'both,' these two; 'who has gone beyond,' who has set aside, or, in other words, one has destroyed both these sides—the wholesome, because the wholesome acts which are devoid of association with defilements are incapable of producing consequences *(vipāka)*, and the unwholesome acts, because all defilements have been abandoned by the Path of Arahantship" (*Dps.*, p. 178).

"Even Arahants perform meritorious acts *(pinkam)* such as giving *(dāna)*, etc. Yet, the thoughts that arise when those venerable ones, who have destroyed the defilements such as ignorance, craving, etc., perform meritorious acts are not wholesome thoughts *(kusalsit)*. Because they are mere actions without consequences *(vipāka)*, they are action-thoughts *(kriyā sit)*. [So also *Sds.*, IX, 2572.] Therefore there is no merit for Arahants. What more can be said about the fact of there being no detrimental acts for the venerable ones who have destroyed all that is unwholesome by the Path of Arahantship?" (*Sdk.*, p. 195). So also *Dv.*, p. 776. See also above, note 20 in chapter 3.

48. On attachments, see above, note 8 in chapter 13.

49.* APB, p. 826, and SHB, p. 671, have *kilesāvilatta-rahitam.* PTS, IV, 192, has *kilesāvilantarahitaṃ.*

50. Sensual existence *(kāmabhava)*, fine material existence *(rūpabhava)*, and formless existence *(arūpabhava)*; *Sds.*, IX, 2576. Other sources do not comment, because the meaning is clear in the context of the commentary and because *lokuttara,* "beyond the worldly" experience, would not involve craving.

51.* [Muddy] path: following the Sinhala translations of *palipatha*: *Dv.*, p. 779, *Sdk.*, p. 227, etc. *Dag.*, 283, simply says *(rā)magu:* "the path (of passions)." The meaning is uncertain.

52. See above, note 6.

53. "Lust for objects, lust for defilements," according to *Dps.*, p. 180.

54. "'Homeless'—one who has 'gone forth' [into the monastic order]" (*Dps.*, p. 179).

55. "Lust for objects, lust for defilements, and lust for sensual existence, for fine material existence, and for formless existence are destroyed" (*Dps.*, p. 179). Burlingame, BL, III, 312, has missed the point of the commentary. Unfortunately, this has led him to write, "As an illustration of the glossographer's stupid handling of difficult words,

the short gloss on stanza 415 . . . has been translated" (BL, I, 28).

56.* Following APB, p. 846, and SHB, p. 688, *mānusaka-āyuṃ,* in preference to PTS, IV, 225, *mānusa-kāyaṃ. Dps.,* p. 180, has *manuṣya . . . āyuṣaya.*

57. On the five strands of sensuality, see above, note 3 in chapter 15.

58. On the four bonds, see above, note 13 in chapter 2.

59. "Because it is not possible to see with the divine eye the mind *(cittaya)* of passing away and the mind of rebirth, the two—passing away and arising again—are mentioned, having taken [into consideration] the proximate position of the mind at passing away and the proximate position of the [mind of] rebirth" (*Dps.*, p. 181). So also *Sdk.*, p. 197.

60.* The commentary makes use of etymological punning: *arahant/āraka.*

61.* The commentary makes use of etymological punning: *mahesi/esita.*

62. With the twenty-six *deva* worlds are to be taken the world of human beings and the *brahmā* worlds. So *Dv.*, p. 792.

63. "One who has arrived at the 'final end,' having known through superlative knowledge, is one who has done what should be done by means of the Four Paths, in this manner: having known especially dharmas of knowledge and liberation *(vidyā-vimukti)* (Paths and Fruits) which should be known by superlative knowledge, [1] having thoroughly understood the fact *(satya)* of suffering (the five *skandha*s) that should be thoroughly understood, [2] having abandoned (destroyed) the fact of the origin (of suffering), i.e., craving which should be abandoned (destroyed), [3] having realized the fact of cessation that should be realized (i.e., having penetratively known Nirvāna that should be penetratively known), [4] having cultivated the fact of the path that should be cultivated (developing the noble eightfold path that should be developed in the mind)" (*Sdk.*, p. 199).

# BIBLIOGRAPHY

*The Aṅguttara-nikāya.* Part I, edited by the Rev. Richard Morris, 2nd ed., revised by A. K. Warder; Part II, edited by the Rev. Richard Morris; Parts III-V, edited by E. Hardy. London: Published for the Pali Text Society by Luzac & Co., Ltd., Part I, 1961; Part II, 1955; Parts III–V, 1958.

Brough, John. *The Gāndhārī Dharmapada: Edited with an Introduction and Commentary.* London Oriental Series, volume 7. London: Oxford University Press, 1962.

Burlingame, Eugene Watson. *Buddhist Legends: Translated from the original Pali text of the Dhammapada Commentary,* Parts I–III. London: Published for the Pali Text Society by Luzac & Co., Ltd., 1960 (first published as volumes 28–30 of Harvard Oriental Series, Cambridge, Mass.: Harvard University Press, 1921).

*The Commentary on the Dhammapada.* Edited by H. C. Norman, Vols. I–IV. London: Published for the Pali Text Society by Luzac & Co., Ltd., 1970 (first published, 1906).

Dhammakusala, Ambalangoda. *Saddhammasāgara nam vū dharmapadavarṇanā,* 9 vols. Colombo: Anula mudranālaya, 1965–1970.

*Dhammapada pūrāṇa sannaya (granthipada vivaraṇa sahita),* "The Old Commentary of the Dhammapada (with a Glossary)." Edited by Kamburupiṭiyē Dhammaratana Sthavira. Colombo: Maha Bodhi Press, 1926.

*Dhammapadaṭṭhakathā.* Edited by Ambalangoda P. Buddhadatta Thera. Colombo: M. D. Gunasena & Co., 1956.

*Dhammapadaṭṭha-kathā.* Edited by Kahavē Siri Ratanasāra Thera, revised by Mahagoda Siri Nanissara Thera, Parts I–II. Published by the Trustees of the Simon Hewavitarne Bequest. Colombo: The Tripitaka Publication Press, 1919.

*Dhammapadaṭṭhakäthāva.* Edited (in Thai script) by Vajirañāṇa Mahāsamaṇa Ādo Sodhitā, Vols. I–VIII. Bangkok: Mahāmakuṭarājavidyālaya, 1966–1975.

*Dhampiyā-aṭuvā-gäṭapadaya.* Edited by Professor D. E. Hettiaratchi. Published by the Press Board of the Sri Lanka University at the University Press, 1974.

Dharmānanda, Morontuduvē Śrī Ñāneśvara. *Saddharmakaumudī nam bhāvārtthavivaraṇasahita dhammapadapāḷiya* ("The Dhammapada with a Sinhalese Translation, Commentary, and Annotation Entitled Saddharmakaumudi"). Finally revised and approved by Kahāvē Śrī

Sumaṅgala Ratanasāra, 3rd edition. Colombo: Śrī Bhāratī Press, 1946 (first published, 1927).

*The Digha Nikāya*. Vols. I and II edited by T. W. Rhys Davids and J. Estlin Carpenter; Vol. III edited by J. Estlin Carpenter. London: Vols. I and III Published for the Pali Text Society by Luzac & Co., 1949, 1960; Vol. II, Geoffrey Cumberlege, Oxford University Press, 1947.

Geiger, Wilhelm. *Pali Literature and Language*. Authorized English translation by Batakrishna Ghosh, 2nd edition. Calcutta: University of Calcutta, 1956.

*The Jātaka: Together with its Commentary,* Vols. I–VI. Edited by V. Fausbøll. London: Published for the Pali Text Society by Messrs. Luzac & Co., 1962–1964.

*Majjhima-nikāya*. Vol. I edited by V. Trenckner; Vols. II–III edited by Robert Chalmers. London: Published for the Pali Text Society by Luzac & Co., Ltd.: vol. I, 1964; vols. II–III, 1960.

Ñāṇobhāsatissa, Morogallē Siri. *Dhammapada vivaraṇaya*. Colombo: M. D. Gunasena, 1962.

*The Pali Text Society's Pali-English Dictionary*. Edited by T. W. Rhys Davids and William Stede. London: Luzac & Co., Ltd., 1966 (first published 1921–1925).

Prajñāśekhara, Ratgama Śrī. *Dharmmārtthadīpanī nam vū dharmmapadārttha vyākhyāva*. Revised by Dehigaspē Paññāsāra. Mudrapita, Sri Lanka: Lawco Press, 2497/1953.

Roth, Gustav. "Particular Features of the Language of the Ārya-Mahāsāṃghika-Lokottaravādins and their Importance for Early Buddhist Tradition," *Die Sprache der ältesten buddhistischen Überlieferung: The Language of the Earliest Buddhist Tradition* (Symposien zur Buddhismusforschung, II). Herausgegeben von Heinz Bechert. Abhandlungen der Akademie der Wissenschaften in Göttingen. Göttingen: Vandenhoeck & Ruprecht, 1980, pp. 78–135.

*Saddharma Ratnāvaliya*. Edited by Sir D. B. Jayatilaka. Colombo: Anula Press, 1934.

*Sanna sahita dhammapadaya*. Edited by Heyiyantuduvē Śrī Dharmakīrti Devamitrā (3rd impression). Colombo: Laṅkabhinava viśrāta yantrālayehi, 1911.

Śrīnivāsa, V. Dharmakīrti Śrī. *Dharmapada pradīpaya*. Colombo: M. D. Gunasena, 1966.

*Sutta-Nipāta*. New edition by Dines Andersen and Helmer Smith. London: Published for the Pali Text Society by Geoffrey Cumberlege, Oxford University Press, 1948.

*Udānavarga*. Herausgegeben von Franz Bernhard, Band I. Abhandlungen der Akademie der Wissenschaften in Göttingen Philologisch-Historische Klasse. Göttingen: Vandenhoeck & Ruprecht, 1965.

*The Vinaya Piṭakaṃ*, Vols. I–IV. Edited by Hermann Oldenberg. London: Published for the Pali Text Society by Luzac & Co., Ltd., 1964.

# INDEX

The index is designed as an aid for the English reader and is not intended to be inclusive of every significant term or concept occurring in the text.